Palgrave Insights into Apocalypse Economics

Series Editor

Richard Westra, Poland and Center for Macau Studies, University of Macau, Macau, China;
Institute of Political Science, University of Opole, Opole, Poland

This series is set to become the lodestone for critical Marxist and related Left scholarship on the raft of apocalyptic tendencies enveloping the global economy and society. Its working premise is that neoliberal policies from the 1980s not only failed to rejuvenate capitalist prosperity lost with the demise of the post-Second World War 'golden age' economy but in fact have generated a widening spectrum of pathologies that threaten humanity itself. At the most fundamental level the series cultivates state of the art critical political economic analysis of the crises, recessionary, deflationary and austerity conditions that have beset the world economy since the global meltdown of 2008–2009. However, though centered on work that critically explores global propensities for devastating financial convulsions, ever-widening inequalities and economic marginalisation due to information technologies, robotised production and low wage outsourcing, it seeks to draw on exacerbating factors such as climate change and global environmental despoliation, corrupted food systems and land-grabbing, rampant militarism, cyber crime and terrorism, all together which defy mainstream economics and conventional political policy solutions.

For critical Marxist and related Left scholars the series offers a non-sectarian outlet for academic work that is hard-hitting, inter/trans-disciplinary and multiperspectival. Its readership draws in academics, researchers, students, progressive governmental and non-governmental actors and the academically-informed public.

More information about this series at
https://link.springer.com/bookseries/15867

Jesús Muñoz-Bandala

Keynes's Evolutionary Spirit

A Philosophical Journey through His Work

palgrave
macmillan

Jesús Muñoz-Bandala
Independent Researcher
Mexico City, Mexico

ISSN 2523-8108 ISSN 2523-8116 (electronic)
Palgrave Insights into Apocalypse Economics
ISBN 978-3-030-90149-3 ISBN 978-3-030-90150-9 (eBook)
https://doi.org/10.1007/978-3-030-90150-9

JEL Classification Code: B, B1, B10, B19, B2, B20, B22, B3, B30, B31, B4, B40, B41, B59, E, E00, E10, E12, E19, Y, Y8, Z, Z00, Z10

Cover illustration: Dina Belenko/Alamy Stock Photo

This Palgrave Macmillan imprint is published by the registered company Springer Nature Switzerland AG
The registered company address is: Gewerbestrasse 11, 6330 Cham, Switzerland

I dedicate this book to three persons whom I certainly love the most and who made it possible. Love is understanding. The first one is my wife Gabriela, certainly an example of encouragement. The second one is my father Jesús, who is my inspiration due to his inquisitive and focused method of study. Last but not least is my mother Elsa, who is the hero of my life for her devotion to our family. What is more, she taught me to write with passion. I thank them for their guidance in the search for a response to my favorite themes, which are liberty, individualism, equality among human beings, and the effects of geography on life.

Mexico City, September, 2021.

Foreword

Jesús Muñoz Bandala has written a remarkable work of scholarship. He takes us through Maynard Keynes's contributions from his earliest writings to his last, putting them within a novel structure of philosophical reconstruction in an evolutionary setting. The author relates his arguments and provides the evidence for them in later sections of the chapters and in appendixes to the chapters. The overall result is a challenging re-reading of Keynes himself and the relevance of this for the application of his fundamental contributions to the great issues that face the economics profession today.

G. C. Harcourt
Emeritus Reader in the history of economic theory, Cambridge
Emeritus Fellow Jesus College Cambridge
Professor Emeritus Adelaide
Currently Honorary Professor School of Economics, UNSW, Sydney

Preface

The objectives of the author must be clear as a deep Swiss lake. This is a work of philosophical reconstruction, not exempt of economic perspicacy. But how valid is writing about another's philosophy? Are we projecting ourselves? This book attempts to avoid this projection by resorting to many types of sources and writing techniques such as investigations, analyses, citations, comparisons, and dialogues. Indeed, it should be called *Why One Should Read Keynes*. What is this all about? Firstly, this writing proves that an exceptional talent may modify social issues, unlike in the abstract way Hegel preaches their solutions. Second it provides a contribution to the topic related to the continuity-discontinuity question on Keynes's economics and philosophy (see O'Donnell, 2021) by regarding them as interrelated and dynamic and hence as evolutionary.

About the purpose of this book, why write another text on Keynes's *oeuvre* and life? Just like an evolution from the *Treatise on Money* (1930) to the *General Theory of Employment, Interest and Money* (1930), which is a common exercise for historians of economic thought and monetary theorists, Keynes's life may be analyzed from an evolutionary perspective. His dynamic development is not straightforwardly visible for most of us but for the writer it is a pleasure highlighting his finest hours. For example, the magic of Keynes's juvenilia papers, or his practice of observing his oeuvre from a distinct vantage point (like King Philip IV of Spain stared at *El Escorial* at the distance) in the last Chapter of *GT*. This book also describes why he is considered as a true European, devoid of illusions, but still proposing great plans. These and similar questions are intended to be answered in this cultural voyage, conducted through the analysis of his works and activities, including his ethical stance. This exercise is practical and hence modern, contributing lessons for our concerns of today, for example, uncertainty as a guide for scrutinizing the future, even for the case of the financial crises occurred in 2008.

Regarding rationale and novelty, evolution has a dynamic (multilateral and interrelated) continuity that only becomes visible after tracing influences throughout time. The evolutionary perspective associated to the gist of Keynes is hereby glimpsed by explaining how he passes from one stage to another, a practice that—if it is conducted in a clever manner—always yields success. Paying prices is the formula. Indeed, a winding path exists throughout his economic and philosophical life. This book is thus an outline of Keynes's stages: in his youth, as a young adult, as a young old human being, as a mature man, and as an experienced adult. Therefore, this is a portrait of a man who would provide formulae for alleviating poverty in the form of unemployment; who illuminated cultural deficiencies but also offered solutions for them but based on duty.

About product differentiation, let's meditate on what is the focus of this book? This is not a biography like the legendary document penned by his student Harrod or the one magnificently sculptured by Skidelsky. This is not even an economic biography like that penciled by Moggridge. This is not a speculative treatise or a transcription of an old course on macroeconomics. The present book attempts to conduct a philosophical analysis of Keynes's evolutionary accomplishments in a double sense. It provides an outline of his core concepts and their uses, simultaneously sketching a philosophy of life taken into social practice. This outline of non-conventional insights on Keynes's philosophy is undertaken by means of the synchronized consideration of five branches of philosophy, namely ontology, epistemology, ethics, political philosophy, and esthetics. Remarkably enough, the emphasis is placed upon ethics. But the book also uses a philosophy of science assessment, specifically a Lakatosian perspective on Keynes's scientific progress for identifying his core to capture his evolutionary path. This scientific account does not exclude narratives about Keynes's philosophical episodes while considering remarks on the opinions of leading authorities on Keynes. The purpose is corroborating Keynes's timelessness.

What is the added value of this book? It is about the integrity of Keynes's *oeuvre* and is circular which means all chapters are multi-directionally related but self-contained. The apparent heterogeneity of its chapters unassumingly reflects the diversity of Keynes's life. Some may be more interesting than others, depending on the personality of the reader. Its epicenter may be Chapter 2 which indicates Keynes's directions after—or in relation to—the breakthrough *oeuvre GT*. Another departure point could be Chapter 11 dealing with the analysis of 'MEB' attesting to Keynes's harmonious contributions to ethics. Due to these characteristics of the book, it is complementary to other specialized texts. The book proposes a new evolutionary perspective about Keynes's overall bequeath. An evolutionary perspective brings about wholistic progress while the interpreter is on the road, filling gaps in the path while detecting progress.

A final word is about its international appeal. This book intends to unify Keynes's thinking strands. In this vein, perhaps Keynes's universal message is that no natural harmony exists, and this ontic argument means no *deux es machina* imposes order to human activity explaining why uncertainty prevails. Otherwise, Keynes's universal message is about the possibility of amelioration of our individual and social conditions. These insights attest both to his Britishness and to his European legacy but provide a global meaning to his work, which can be grasped by departing from distinct techniques. Comparisons with foreign intellectuals are offered, for example, Burke and Nietzsche as well as a fictional dialogue with Friedman. Finally, the book is written from a non-European and non-Anglo-Saxon perspective, corroborating the reach of Keynes's work.

Mexico City, Mexico
September 1921

Jesús Muñoz-Bandala

Acknowledgments

I have been working with passion on Keynes for 30 years, whom I met by serendipity. In the meantime I have been drawing inspiration from academic sources. I have given conferences related to Keynes's themes in Lancaster University (UK), UMKC (US), the Levy Economics Institute (US), Georgetown University (US), UAM (Mexico), and UNAM (Mexico). In these events I share with others the spirit of research in the form of wise and varied advice. I have visited libraries in many places as well as archives in Cambridge, England. My editor Julie McMurtry in Washington DC provided a superb English-language perspective to my writings. I was also inspired by the Australian economist G. C. Harcourt who has been a beacon on the theme of Keynes's economics for a long time. I am also grateful to two anonymous referees for their meaningful comments. None of them is responsible for the defects in what follows. I also want to acknowledge those publishers who gave me permission to publish in this book a previously published chapter from a book on Keynes. I am grateful to those publishers who accepted my manuscript, as they perceived its potential to contribute something to any kind of reader. I only ask from my readers to open up their spirits to this reading.

Mexico City
September 2021

Contents

Abbreviations

EB	*Essays in Biography*
ECC	'The Economic Consequences of Mr. Churchill'
ECP	*The Economic Consequences of the Peace*
EP	*Essays in Persuasion*
EPG	'Economics Possibilities for our Grandchildren'
GT	*The General Theory of Employment, Interest and Money*
ICU	International Clearing Union
JMK	John Maynard Keynes
QTM	Quantity Theory of Money
RT	*A Revision of the Treaty*
TGE	'The general theory of employment'
TM	*A Treatise on Money*
TMR	*A Tract on Monetary Reform*
TP	*A Treatise on Probability*

List of Tables

CHAPTER 1

Overview and Introduction

This is a book in the fields of history of economic thought and philosophy about Keynes's *oeuvre*, a fascinating subject which can be narrated by episodes. There are developments throughout his evolution: Bloomsbury, Versailles, *GT*, the Galton Conference, Broadcasting, CEMA. Evolution is a natural situation in which transitions do not apparently follow a sequence, or perhaps a situation emerging when a person is conducting activities beyond expectations with no seeming change of *leitmotiv*. There may be, nonetheless, apparent thematic shifts, and the interesting issue is detecting how new tendencies emerge—taking into account the durations of sequences and their heterogeneous impacts.

1.1 Objectives and Means

Scholarship on Keynes's economics has increasingly captured worldwide attention both inside and outside academia since the world financial crisis occurred in 2007, but the fascination with Keynes's work, especially in philosophy, re-emerged during the 1990s. What are the magic and essence of Keynes's philosophy? Keynes's work will hereby be outlined for the purpose of analyzing the nature of his holistic and philosophical

J. Muñoz-Bandala, *Keynes's Evolutionary Spirit*,
Palgrave Insights into Apocalypse Economics,
https://doi.org/10.1007/978-3-030-90150-9_1

thought. Some Keynes scholars state that Keynes's philosophy is continuous[1] (Braithwaite 1975, Carabelli 1998; O'Donnell 1989), whereas others argue that it is discontinuous (Bateman 1996; Davis 1994), according to Donnini Maccio (2013).

Keynes's purpose was always the amelioration of humankind which could be attained by means of an ethical evolution achieved after economic stabilization. He reached this conclusion after examining his life experience, especially after he writes *The General Theory of Employment, Interest and Money* or *GT* in 1936 (Chapters 2 and 9). In this background, this author contends that Keynes's philosophy is evolutionary rather than continuous or discontinuous. To prove this contention is the objective of the book. The argument is that Keynes's evolution is neither uniform nor linear but straightforward (with some setbacks) in the long period. The pertinence is that the evolutionary character of Keynes's overall work is what makes it alive and hence appealing. The means is the identification of the validity of his philosophy by the assessment of its sources, reception, scientific legitimacy, critique, and legacy. This connecting thread is followed throughout the chapters in this book by outlining both the validity and progress of Keynes's Scientific Research Program (SRP) in the light of economic, social, and philosophical problems, examining the form of his theoretical and empirical progressiveness.

This book contains Chapters useful for the specification of the aims, methods, and terminology in Keynes's *oeuvre*, with the goal of drawing theoretical and practical inferences about both the nature and worth of his legacy. The use of specific fields of philosophy falsifies (that is, provisionally might prove, as opposed to verifies which supposedly proves forever) the evolutionary argument of this author. The chronicle and description of influences on Keynes are centered upon dominant personalities and events as reflected in his work and activities. The book is written for the economist, the philosopher, the social scientist, and the occasional professional interested in Keynes's legacy and epoch. Chapters vary in terms of intensity (in the eyes of the readers), intentionality (Keynes was multifaceted), and objectives (he was required for different tasks during distinct epochs), but all Chapters are connected. The assembly among them is a task undertaken here but also left to the reader.

1.2 A Brief Initial Description of This Book

No single book can encompass the wealth of Keynes's message. This book deals only with its foundations and applications. The claim of evolution in Keynes's roots will be assessed by analyzing his insights under the framework of his Scientific Research Program (SRP). A *SRP* is a Lakatosian concept comprised of a core, a positive heuristic, and a protective belt. The examination of his core will offer conclusions about his legacy from the viewpoint of the philosophy of science. The aim is to investigate its strength and conditions for progress after falsifying them against reality in terms of fulfillment, predictions, or comparisons with other *SRPs* (see ensuing paragraphs). This is so because the strength of the core provides a theory with a dynamic and falsifiable character.

The second qualitative means used to test whether Keynes's message is evolutionary is the inspection of its deepness, amplitude, and applicability in his publications and activities. Keynes's armor is examined in terms of its essence, a relevant approach consistent with Keynes's epistemology. Initial evidence for this task of inspection is found in studying the massive literature on Keynes's work in recent times. In other words, furthering the study of assumptions, foundations, and methods in Keynes—and hence the gist of his search for the truth—may constitute additional evidence for identifying the patterns of his intellectual and spiritual evolution, for example in his work, *The Economic Consequences of the Peace* or *ECP (1919)*.

At the risk of being pre-emptive this author states that the analysis of Keynes's grounding is comprised of the examination of the following philosophical elements: historical time; organicism; uncertainty; lack of a self-regulating system; non-ergodicity; and both heterogeneity and asymmetry in nature, within and among objects. These interrelated and evolutionary foundations are also comprised of the inductive method; the nature's fallacy—organicism; irrationality; intuition and convention; a rejection of reliance on both quantitative methods and dogmatism; and a disbelief in human logic.

In other words, it is hereby assessed whether and how Keynes casts doubts on the existence of a Cartesian-Kantian atomic, self-regulating, certain, and rational social universe, or whether and why Keynes proposes alternative basic insights which advocate for neither eternal nor ubiquitous truths. Thus, his core is analyzed in terms of the background of the following philosophical branches throughout his *oeuvre*: ontology, epistemology, ethics, political and social philosophy, highlighting their links with economics. Chapter 2 about *GT* focuses on epistemology. The question is what determines the level of output in a monetary economy, but the background and the implications create a philosophical tenet for the assessment of his entire *oeuvre*. Chapters 3 and 4 about Keynes's connections make use of the five philosophical fields mentioned. Chapter 5 on *ECP* in the aftermath of World War I focuses on economics and political philosophy. Chapter 6 about probability concentrates on the logical and epistemological dimensions. Chapter 7 is about evolutionary treatises in economics. Chapter 8 deals with ethics, political philosophy, and futurism of Capitalism. Chapter 9 is on the political and social philosophy of *GT*, appropriately placed in Keynes's evolutionary path. Chapter 10 deals with the economic, political philosophy and epistemological scopes of post-*GT* Keynesianism, before 1990. Chapter 11 is about the ethics in the literary jewel 'MEB'. Chapter 12 deals with Keynes's economics, political philosophy, and epistemology in the aftermath of World War II. These variations are as pronounced as was Keynes's life which was in constant flux. But Chapter 13 unifies all themes as amalgamation is the mission of philosophy for the sake of capturing reality, especially Appendix 13.1 which deals with the use of Keynes's insights in a postcrisis modern world.

The titles and contents of the Chapters are formally outlined in A Synopsis of the Chapters. The book is circular since the reader can start at any point but also in the sense that its philosophical themes are dealt with in a chronological form in terms of Keynes's life, but their array does not preclude the reader from moving back or on to the discernments exposed in the previous or subsequent chapters. All chapters are strengthened by appendices, to grasp the reach and interdisciplinary character of Keynes's work. The exercise yields surprising results in terms of Keynes's generosity, which is detailed in the conclusions.

1.3 Characteristics and Aims of the Book

This book is about Keynes's overall philosophical bequeath but providing a lively and dynamic account of his intellectual character, not only focused in biography or in economics but also in his way of life. Keynes anticipated problems and lived them. The hypothesis is thus that Keynes offered an instinctive, dynamic, and holistic explanation of social phenomena which originated in his ethics coupled with his life lessons and scientific imagination. He pleaded for an evolutionary transformation of society, wherein his evolutionary thinking survives by conveying a meaning for future generations (see Appendix 13.1). Keynes's vision of the future was undertaken for the goal of human amelioration. Keynes throws new light on method, theory, concerns, policy goals, and human behavior, especially after creating macroeconomics in 1936. Hence Keynes's foundations are outlined for reopening and extending his insights to such topics as his critiques of Victorian and Edwardian values, classical notions of probability, and classical economics.

Another aim is to answer whether Keynes's vision on human progress is universal. For that purpose, his view on the progression and the impact of Capitalism in humankind is assessed, to explain why Keynes is a cultural figure. The foundations of his thinking made him sustain beliefs about organicism (the whole is more than the sum of its parts), pluralist methods, uncertainty, and irrational expectations. Keynes's *oeuvre* is also investigated with the goal to find out how his work was incorporated under orthodoxy or even betrayed, ignored, misinterpreted, neglected, or considered as unnecessarily controversial. A parallel task is to investigate the nature of Keynes's innovations. This book will also analyze Keynes's work in relation to the influence of other groups, such as the 'Apostles' or the Bloomsbury Group; the insights contributed by his collaborators, for example, Richard Kahn; and the works of other great thinkers such as G. E. Moore (his mentor). In the event the reader is acquainted with all these insights, then this book may function as a synthesizer of articles and books on Keynes's main topics, one of which is his modernity.

1.4 Keynes the Social Scientist

This book is a complement, a challenge to received viewpoints, a remedy for omissions, and an introduction for the nonspecialist. It provides information on diverse matters, for instance about the functioning of money as related to ethical considerations. Another example is that Keynes's *leitmotif* (human amelioration) is analyzed from the perspective of his coherence as a self-improving thinker. This type of task is undertaken by investigating the nature and applicability of his foundations by means of the study of his world as embedded in an open system, full of dynamism, interrelations, and meaning. Apparently, Keynes's all life task was to solve the economic short-term problem—unemployment—by means of the management of effective demand, that is, by regulating abrupt fluctuations in investment and money, which is what made him create the science of macroeconomics. His means were revision, restructure, extensions, criticism, development, expansion, and the explication of complexities (the results of the proper use of complex methods is simplicity), interdependencies, and flexibility.

However, Keynes offered more than the creation of macroeconomics. This is patent when his work is examined by means of new approaches, balancing principles, comparisons, and attention to practicalities, considering that his objectives were to find new solutions to old problems or even new problems, to outline new challenges in scholarship, to propose new perspectives, and to unearth unsuspected philosophical issues. The strategy is projecting his intellectual history by means of an interdisciplinary view. Keynes had many facets, becoming a figure in the Western cultural configuration. Those facets are philosopher, investor, creator, collector, economist, diplomat, theorist, practitioner, and reformer. This is clear in this book as even if most of its chapters are dominated by a theme, a publication, or an activity, others allow the understanding of the multiplicity of his insights and scope. Depth is now associated to Keynes and this book offers further proof for the sustainment of this contention. For instance, Chapter 11 analyzes the big essay 'My Early Beliefs' of 1938, which is an example of his culture and purposeful complexity.

Finally, Keynes recreated totality by way of the study of multiple interrelations, in terms of organic unities. This book deals with Keynes's central contentions, ancillary points, and semantic differences, by means of many methods, outstanding among them is the Lakatosian approach of *SRPs*, as a demarcation criterion for assessing continuous organic progress. This document thus uncovers both the pensive and expedient characteristics of Keynes's bequest. The means for exposition throughout the book is an argumentation providing new philosophical points by challenging orthodox methodologies, frameworks, interpretations, and possibilities for inquiry. But the argumentation also offers Keynes's intersections, discourses, political theories, and epistemic issues. Keynes's themes are simplified rather than trivialized.

1.5 Table of Contents: A Synopsis of the Chapters

The overview—introduction—outlines the hypothesis of the book: both Keynes's thought and spirit are evolutionary as is the setback of his actions and offers a brief account of the themes dealt with in this book. The purpose is producing a narrative about the outline of the philosophy of a cultural icon which complements specialized biographies and treatises under the perspective of the philosophy of science but also with a life perspective. Philosophy is both a source of knowledge and a way of life. The method is to unify his contributions in both timely and spatial terms for revealing the meaning and inner mechanisms of his work. The framework is Keynes's increasing fame in world culture since many researchers are in favor of reinstalling him as a major intellectual figure (see Appendix 13.1), especially after the financial crisis occurred in 2008 (see Davidson 2009; Backhouse and Bateman 2011; and Skidelsky 2016 on Keynes's return to scientific respect).

Chapter 2 deals with Keynes's *SRP*, paradigm, or complex system which decodes his dynamic and holistic message. Keynes's core is comprised of his views on uncertainty, organicism, a non-regulating system, non-utilitarianism, and the *Laissez Faire*. These elements are the basis for testing the evolutionary argument by supporting the relevance and pertinence of his insights.

1.6 Part I Keynes: The Meaning of Background: 1883–1910

The next step is the identification of Keynes's intellectual debts especially the influence of Classical thinkers, as found in his early writings, on his later philosophy, economics, and multiple intellectual interests.

Chapter 3 goes back to the beginning. It is an analysis of the role of key (received) influences on Keynes; for example: Locke, Hume, and Mill on ethics, epistemology, and political philosophy. It also examines the crucial influence of Burke on Keynes's political philosophy and of Moore's notion of *good* in Keynes's ethics. The chapter attempts to qualify how conservative the foundations of his thought are as a member of the 'Locke connection.' Appendix 3.1 deals with Keynes's view on Newton's grandeur (1933). Appendix 3.2 critically outlines the relation between Keynes and Ancient Greece as a fountainhead, with a note on the relation and between Keynes and some continental Europeans (mainly in the seventeenth, eighteenth, and nineteenth centuries), also treating these cultural epochs as a source. The counterpart, Keynes's influence on Europe, is chronicled throughout the book.

Chapter 4 scrutinizes Keynes's key contemporary—for him—influences. This chapter discerns what factors contribute to Keynes's initial selection of philosophical topics and his subsequent intellectual rebellion, dating from his participation in the groups 'Apostles' and Bloomsbury. The *Keynes Circus* was a group of economists that impacted his thought as well, and the roles of Wittgenstein and Russell are also described, as well as those of Popper and Lakatos but these two in a retrospective form. The meaning of his enchanting youthful philosophical articles (1903–1910, 1921) is addressed in the appendix.

1.7 Part II Keynes's Early Activities: 1913–1935

This section deals with Keynes´s initial professional practices and theoretical efforts. These pages are about his process of becoming an original philosopher informed by his life experience, as his main activity during this epoch was as a practitioner economist.

In Chapter 5 the theme is Keynes's reflection on life—particularly the results of the First World War—drawn from his practical experience and abilities in economics. For that purpose, the *Economic Consequences of the Peace* (1919) is explored in terms of his *SRP*. This chapter ponders whether one should conform to or critically examine learned political views, proposing salvation for the defeated nations by appreciating that Europe is an organic unity. A look at his first economics book *Indian Currency and Finance* (1913) and the analysis of *Revision of the Treaty* (1922) are offered in the appendices.

Chapter 6 constitutes a refreshing change of pace, which is absent in economic treatises. It is about the complex Keynes's theoretical innovative characterization of probability as a logic of choice between propositions (rather than numbers or events) in a natural environment of uncertainty. His work *A Treatise on Probability* (*TP* 1921) tests the relevance of induction, or the departure from the particular to the universal, in human knowledge but overcoming Hume skepticism, producing a new statistical paradigm. This chapter also answers whether Keynes's new conception of probability (both quantitative and qualitative) is useful for understanding the nature of *good*. Everyone is stimulated by somebody else's thought. A summary of Ramsey's influential insights on Keynes (circa 1926) is offered in the appendix.

Chapter 7 goes back to Keynes's social—practitioner—life. It is about Keynes as a first-rate analyst of money in modern systems. Since his early monetary thinking did not fully reveal the innovativeness of his monetary stance, this chapter attempts to answer whether *A Tract on Monetary Reform* (*TMT* 1923) and *A Treatise on Money* (*TM* 1930a) are the evolutionary background to his magnus opus *The General Theory of Employment, Interest and Money* (*GT* 1936), or whether they have a unique value, although this is not a new task (see Dimand 1986), it is done here in philosophical terms. Such intermediate and hence complementary works and notions as the 'Economic Consequences of Mr. Churchill' (1925), the multiplier (1931), and 'The Monetary Theory of Production' (1933) are explored in the appendices.

Chapter 8 is centered on his philosophical piece *Economic Possibilities for Our Grandchildren* (*EPG* 1930b) dealing with his vision of the future in terms of the management of wealth and the fate of Capitalism. This chapter examines whether Keynes was a trans-generational thinker for whom money is only a means for both stability and the attainment of individual goals, and how those characterizations connect with one another. Other writings included in *Essays in Persuasion* (1931) such as 'Am I a liberal?' (1925), 'The end of the Laissez-faire' (1926), the futuristic 'Clissold' (1927), and 'The means to prosperity' (1933) are studied in appendices. Their common thread is the search for better conditions of life, but it is a search not confined to material conditions.

1.8 Part III Keynes's Middle Age Activities: 1936–1939

Part III deals with the topics addressed by Keynes at the height of his creative powers which generate his original mature ideas. Chapter 9 is an *SRP*-type but also a discursive analysis of the literary jewel embedded in Chapter 24 of *The General Theory of Employment, Interest and Money* (*GT* 1936), relating his reflection on the aftermath of a nation's achievement of full employment. This book is acclaimed as the text that exposes the creation of macroeconomics (see Chapter 2), but its aspects also dealt with here highlight the new transition of Keynes's thought from pure economics to the innovation of social and political stances. This last chapter is more philosophical as it depicts the road to human emancipation, leaving money concerns and prejudices aside. Going back to economics, 'The general theory of employment (1937),' as a further clarification of his notion of uncertainty, and the reception of *GT* are outlined in the appendices of Chapter 9.

Chapter 10 indirectly deals with Keynes's frank rebellion against the core of Classical Economics, as represented by utilitarianism, atomism, physicalism, and a self-regulating system, by outlining how his message was misunderstood by subsequent (post-*GT*) Neoclassical economists. This chapter evaluates orthodox Post-keynesianism in his reform of economics, that is, whether Keynes's theoretical stance was betrayed by the faithful subsequent Keynesianism. It thus clarifies in Lakatosian terms whether Post-Keynes's reception (both heretic and faithful) corresponds to what Robinson called 'Bastard Keynesianism' as represented by four schools: Monetarism, the NeoClassical Synthesis, the School of Rational Expectations, and General Disequilibrium. Results are the future was retrograde at that stage as Keynes's core was neglected but his building blocks accepted. Finally, the specific view of Keynes on Friedman (a leading monetarist in the United States in the 1980s), written as a fictional rebuttal as Keynes died in 1946, appearing in the appendix, contributes some insights on Keynes's evolutionary path.

1.9 Part IV Keynes's Late Activities: 1940–1946

Part IV gives an account of Keynes's publications and activities in morals and in the international arena, after his major intellectual—domestic—contributions were realized.

Chapter 11, perhaps the favorite of this author because of its deep and recapitulating character, explains how Keynes further developed his philosophical stances. 'My Early Beliefs' (1938) is an exercise in aesthetics and ethics, wherein he relates how he left behind key Moorean and Bloomsberrian ethical insights. This chapter thus answers how Keynes's life experience influenced the evolution of his core. A complementary essay on the parallels between Keynes's and Nietzsche's elitist notions—mainly in ethics and aristocracy—is the subject matter of the appendix.

Chapter 12 is about his final thinking concerning world events. It is about his design of inflationary remedies after the Second World War (just like *ECP* is written after the First World War), the diversification in topics proving the flexibility of his *SRP*. This chapter is about the extension of his macroeconomics to the international arena where cooperation—a nearly neglected theme in Keynesianology—is critical. Themes addressed are among others lease-loan agreements and the creation of supranational institutions. The first appendix is on development, the second about his inspiration on the design of national accounts and his critique of econometrics, and the third on his esthetic views and activities. The choice of themes is chronological with respect to Keynes's life.

The conclusion in Chapter 13 is an integration of the findings of the mentioned Chapters useful for assessing the nature of Keynes's legacy. This chapter explains how his argument and methodology increased in originality and informative power with some regressions and variants thereby evolving. In other words, it is hereby explained that although his themes were recurrent, they were resolved by means of new methods and views of added significance to his themes. For example, he created an open evolutionary system based on the notion of uncertainty in *GT*. Nonetheless, opposing views are mentioned and the outline of new avenues for research is suggested. Appendix 13.1 is about the use of Keynes for the future. It relates how Keynes's philosophical teachings can be useful for a world struggling with recurrent crisis propitiated by financialized (non-regulated) economies, bearing in mind that Keynes is the monetary economist *par excellence*. It explains how the remedies to crises are Keynesian in spirit. Finally, a non-exhaustive but wealthy list of philosophical books and articles on Keynes is provided at the end of the book.

Note

1. It is continuous, especially in terms of ethics.

References

Backhouse, Roger E., and Bradley W. Bateman. 2011. *Capitalist Revolutionary: John Maynard Keynes*, November. Cambridge, MA: Harvard University Press.

Bateman, Bradley W. (1996). *Keynes's Uncertain Revolution*. Detroit: University of Michigan Press.

Braithwaite, Richard B. 1975. "Keynes as a Philosopher." In *Essays on John Maynard Keynes*, edited by Milo Keynes, Chapter 22. Cambridge: Cambridge University Press.

Carabelli, Anna. 1998. "Keynes on Probability, Uncertainty and Tragic Choices." *Cahiers d'économie politique* no. 30/31, 187–226. Keynes: Économie et philosophie.

Davidson, Paul. 2009. *The Keynes Solution: The Path to Global Economic Prosperity*. London and New York: Palgrave.

Davis, John B. 1994. *Keynes's Philosophical Development*. Cambridge: Cambridge University Press.

Dimand, Robert W. 1986. "The Macroeconomics of the Treatise on Money." *Eastern Economic Journal* 12, no. 1 (October–December): 431–41.

Donnini Maccio, Daniela. 2013. 'On economics and philosophy E Moore's imprint on the Cambridge Apostles: 1903–1936'. Unpublished PhD Thesis. Universita Degli Studi Di Macerata. https://www.academia.edu/17475513/PhD_Thesis_On_economics_and_philosophy_G_E_Moore_s_imprint_on_the_Cambridge_Apostles_ca_1903_ca_1936.

Keynes, John M. 1925. *'Am I a Liberal?' The Nation & Athenaeum*, (Part I: 563–4, and Part II: 587–8).

———. 1926 [2004]. '*The end of Laissez-faire*.' Washington DC: Rowman.

———. 1927 [1931] [1972]. 'Clissold.' In *JMK CW Vol. IX. Essays in Persuasion*, edited by D. Moggridge. London Royal Economic Society.

———. [1931]. 'The means to prosperity.' In *JMK CW Vol. IX. Essays in Persuasion*, edited by D. Moggridge. London Royal Economic Society.

———. 1933. *'The Monetary Theory of Production.' Der Stand und die nächste Zukunft der Konjunkturforschung: Festschrift für Arthur Spiethoff*. Munich: Duncker & Humboldt, 123–25.

———. 1938 [1933] [1972]. 'My Early Beliefs.' In *JMK CW Vol. X. Essays in Biography*, edited by D. Moggridge. London Royal Economic Society.

Keynes, John Maynard. 1913 [1971]. *The Collected Writings of John Maynard Keynes (CW). Volume 1: Indian Currency and Finance*, edited by Elizabeth Johnson (19–28) and Daniel E. Moggridge (15–18). London: Macmillan, for the Royal Economic Society.

———. 1919 [1971]. *The Collected Writings of John Maynard Keynes (CW). Volume. 2: The Economic Consequences of the Peace*, edited by Elizabeth Johnson (19–28) and Daniel E. Moggridge (15–18). London: Macmillan, for the Royal Economic Society.

———. 1921 [1973]. *The Collected Writings of John Maynard Keynes (CW). Volume 8: A Treatise on Probability*, edited by Elizabeth Johnson (19–28) and Daniel E. Moggridge (15–18). London: Macmillan, for the Royal Economic Society.

———. 1922 [1971]. *The Collected Writings of John Maynard Keynes (CW). Volume 3: A Revision of the Treaty*, edited by Elizabeth Johnson (19–28) and Daniel E. Moggridge (15–18). London: Macmillan, for the Royal Economic Society.

———. 1923 [1971]. *The Collected Writings of John Maynard Keynes (CW). Volume 4: A Tract on Monetary Reform*, edited by Elizabeth Johnson (19–28) and Daniel E. Moggridge (15–18). London: Macmillan, for the Royal Economic Society.
———. 1925. *The Economic Consequences of Mr. Churchill*. London: Hogarth.
———. 1930a [1971]. *The Collected Writings of John Maynard Keynes (CW). Volume 5: A Treatise on Money. The Pure Theory of Money*, edited by Elizabeth Johnson (19–28) and Daniel E. Moggridge (15–18). London: Macmillan, for the Royal Economic Society.
———. 1930b. "The Economic Possibilities for Our Grandchildren." http://www.econ.yale.edu/smith/econ116a/keynes1.pdf. Accessed 1 January 2019.
———. 1931 [1972]. *The Collected Writings of John Maynard Keynes (CW). Volume 9: Essays in Persuasion*, edited by Elizabeth Johnson (19–28) and Daniel E. Moggridge (15–18). London: Macmillan, for the Royal Economic Society.
———. 1933. *The Means to Prosperity*. London: Macmillan.
———. 1936 [1973]. *The Collected Writings of John Maynard Keynes (CW). Volume 7: The General Theory of Employment, Interest and Money*, edited by Elizabeth Johnson (19–28) and Daniel E. Moggridge (15–18). London: Macmillan, for the Royal Economic Society.
———. 1937. "The General Theory of Employment." *The Quarterly Journal of Economics* 51, no. 2: 209–23.
O'Donnell, Roderick M. 1989. *Keynes: Philosophy, Economics and Politics: The Philosophical Foundations of Keynes's Thought and their Influence on his Economics and Politics*. London: Macmillan.
Skidelsky, Robert. 2016. *The Essential Keynes*. London: Penguin.

CHAPTER 2

Keynes's Lakatosian Scientific Research Program (SRP) as Outlined in *The General Theory of Employment, Interest and Money* (1936)

This chapter is intentionally placed at the beginning as it offers a methodology for identifying the main tenets of Keynes's philosophy in his Golden Book, also to compare them with other points of reference in his philosophical oeuvre and activities, becoming the benchmark to detect his evolution throughout the remaining chapters.

More specifically, the purpose of this comprehensive chapter in both economics and philosophy is to outline Keynes's Scientific Research Program (*SRP*) from his book *The General Theory of Employment, Interest and Money* (hereafter referred to as *GT* or the Golden Book), which is probably the hallmark of his evolutionary philosophical path, since it signals the creation of macroeconomics. An *SRP* is a methodological concept created by Imre Lakatos (1978a, b) which aids to the comprehension of the gist of theories, to be explained in the following sections. The chapter refers to the academic philosophy of Keynes which is linked in the other chapters to his philosophy of life.

Section 2.1 is a general philosophical context about the methodological relevance of *SRPs* and the background of Keynes's *GT* in the light of *SRPs*. Section 2.2 is an interlude on the relationship between the

J. Muñoz-Bandala, *Keynes's Evolutionary Spirit*,
Palgrave Insights into Apocalypse Economics,
https://doi.org/10.1007/978-3-030-90150-9_2

philosophy of science and methodology. Section 2.3 describes the background of Keynes's *SRP* in 1936, identifying his core in a reading of *GT*. Section 2.4 hypothesizes the 'probable' economic directions that Keynes's *SRP* would have taken after 1936, to trace the evolution of his thought. Section 2.5 deals with a Lakatosian interpretation of these 'probable' directions. Section 2.6 is an excursion into the likely widening of the work of Keynes after 1936. Appendix 2.1 presents Keynes's complex system as an alternative characterization of Keynes's *SRP* in the times of the creation of macroeconomics.

2.1 The Great Philosophical Context as Related to Keynes's Economic Contribution

Imre Lakatos (1922–1994) in 1978 suggests the use of Scientific Research Programs (*SRPs*) for classifying the soundness and evolution of scientific structures. This method entails a demarcation criterion that underlines both continuity in scientific insights and the role of falsification for distinguishing between scientific and non-scientific assessments. *SRPs*, whose components are described in the following section, are thus useful for describing the essence, and variety of a set of interrelated theories; especially for the determination of whether they are either revolutionary or evolutionary. It is very convenient to be used here.

Keynes's *SRP*, extracted mainly from *GT*, is hereby established (see Sect. 2.3, Table 2.1). What explains this selection of the Golden Book at the beginning of this book is that *GT* (1936) portrays the first complete and comprehensive macroeconomic theory on income and employment determination. It does so by using a theory of monetary production in an aggregate economy and the vision of uncertainty along with other philosophical concepts. As Keynes linked philosophical with economic issues in *GT*, this intellectual episode in the field of the history of economic thought offers a great methodological opportunity for the explanation of a unique change of perspective.[1] It also summarizes Keynes's philosophical personality.

2.2 Methodological Interlude

Science is clear, objective, rational, real, systematic, and communicable knowledge about a field, which must be empirically tested *vis-à-vis* reality, and therefore possesses a dynamic character. The goals of science are both

Table 2.1 Keynes's *SRP* in *GT*

Core
• In the search for knowledge, intuitions, conjectures, and inductive processes are relevant—and not simply empirical investigation. Results must be validated by means of verificationism (weak contrast in the face of reality) • Historical rather than logical time is measured. The present is relevant, not being a continuation of the past • The organic (rather than atomistic) economic system lacks a self-regulating mechanism, so market-clearing equilibrium is a special case, and sub-equilibria is the normal situation unlike in the Classical world. Therefore, a transitional method is used, wherein qualitative changes are significant. This method produces piece-meal rather than dramatic solutions • Organicism exists in the form of the 'fallacy of composition.' The universe is complexly organic (the whole is more than the sum of its elements). Consequently, interdependence and irreversibility exist in a unique non-ergodic world (wherein the conditions for observations and experiments are non-repetitive and vary at every moment, and small changes make difference) • Both the objective and the subjective (imaginative) worlds matter. The corollary is that a different concept of behavior is assumed: human beings are not always rational and 'animal spirits' exist. This is because of uncertainty prevails, alongside imperfect information, heterogeneities, and asymmetries in behavior • The result of uncertainty is the need for active and dynamic money sector which affects real variables (especially investment on physical capital) via expectations
Macroeconomics studies the determination of income or output (Υ) and employment (E) at the aggregate level, wherein the public sector must play a dynamic role and investment (I) is unstable and hence must be managed, as a component of aggregate demand

(continued)

Table 2.1 (continued)

Core
Positive heuristics (building blocks)
• Study economic fluctuations and involuntary unemployment (U), and thereby the concomitant decision processes associated with resource allocation under uncertainty at the domestic level. Use the principle of effective demand (ED) as an explanatory tenet, wherein an unstable aggregate demand (AD) is the norm, and aggregate supply is responsive
• Divide the economy into 3 markets: products, labor, and money (both labor and money are non-complex entities in Classical microeconomics). Emphasize the quantification of aggregate interdependent variables, focused on quantity (output) adjustments
• Analyze the components of income (output) or aggregate demand (when aggregate supply is horizontal): consumption, investment, public expenditure, exports, and imports [$Y = C + I + G + X - IM$] as well as money (M) demand and supply, wherein r = interest rate, and f = function of, then:
$C = f(Y)$; $I = f(r)$; $M^d = f(Y)$; M^s = given; $M^d = M^s$
• Analyze the consumption (C) function in aggregate terms
• Consider the pivotal role of investment (I) in the fluctuations of aggregate demand and output (Y), in the face of a constant aggregate supply (AS) which means that the economy has full potential to produce. Uncertainty has a bearing on investment via expectations as captured in r
• If I is insufficient, G must be activated in the short term
• Consider liquidity preference (a part of M^d) and the 'finance motive' as forms of retiring money—on the part of the public—from the circular flow of output as an effect of uncertainty
• The labor market (L) must be in equilibrium: $L^d = L^s$, but wage (w) reductions do not solve the problem of unemployment (U), as in the Classical model. This market is special
Protective Belt (circumstantial and flexible assumptions)
• Intermediate conditions are prevalent in life (GT); however, economic systems are idle as they operate below full capacity as AS is totally flexible. Here Say's Law (supply generates its own demand) is always refuted, which signifies that no auctioneer of prices (Walras) exists
• The propensity to consume (c) is high and relatively constant, unlike the propensity to invest (i)
• There is a liquidity trap at the lowest level, where reductions in interest rates (r) have no bearing on investment (I). The Quantity Theory of Money (MV = PY; 'QTM') is a special case of reality (making Keynes's theory general), wherein V = velocity of circulation of money, M or M^s is given, and price adjustments (P) are not the norm in economies with high productive potential
• Exchange rates (e) are fixed.

explanation and prediction (Machlup 1978). But how is this complex task to be accomplished? Both apriorism and ultra-empiricism are epistemological extreme strands. According to apriorism, the initial abstraction of procedures is the most relevant constituent of knowledge. In accordance with ultra-empiricism, both hypotheses and problem identification depart from observation and results must be tested. The distinction between these two extreme approaches in practice allows for the methodological assessment of the perspectives from which hypothesis formulation arises, also providing the foundations of judgment on the soundness and evolution of a theory.

Methodology is the 'study of logical principles useful for determining if certain proposals are accepted or rejected as valid constituents of the structure of scientific knowledge' (ibid., p. 490), that is, proposals must be falsified rather than verified. Karl Popper (1902–1994) was an advocate of naïve Falsificationism (1945), which is explained in detail in Chapter 4. According to Popper, a theory must be continuously tested, and discarded—at least partially—in the event of not being able to withstand refutations. Hence, Falsificationism, a concept about the automatic rejection of non-scientific theories based on their empirical confrontation, tests the continuous validity and the evolution of theories.

2.2.1 *Lakatos and Scientific Research Programs*

The underlying and departing organizing principle for testing interrelated theories is Falsificationism. For this purpose, the epistemological theories of two successors of Popper are outlined. Thomas Kuhn (1922–1996) proposes the methodology of—sudden—paradigms in 1970, whereas Lakatos in 1978 (a, b) suggests that of—gradual—scientific research programs. Key characteristics of paradigms are that they are dramatically different approaches in terms of problem visualization and their immediate elucidations which are approved or rejected by scientific communities, all of this immersed in a historical setting. In contrast, *SRPs* analyze individual theories or sets of them in terms of the sophisticated falsification of their gradual evolution. The Lakatosian methodology is hereby chosen to assess continuity in the Keynes *SRP* due to its gradual and evolutionary character. Additionally, *SRPs* are an explicit criterion for the detailed comparison of theories, and this comparison gives an idea of Keynes's reach.

The first constituent of *SRPs* is the core, which is not subject to Falsificationism by methodological principle. The second element is positive or negative heuristics, referred to as the guidelines, building blocks, or agenda, scientifically applied to the theories that are undertaken throughout the research. The third constituent is the protective belt, often expressed as parameters, comprised of the auxiliary assumptions of theories, each of which may vary with respect to either time or place. *SRPs* are progressive when the core is solid enough to avoid replacement. In other words, *SRPs* must be chosen if their cores survive falsification, that is if their contributions contain either new theoretical or empirical prescriptions. In contrast, the replacement of some heuristics means that the essence of a theory has not been modified at all. Finally, the replacement of a protective belt only widens the extent of application of that theory, sometimes in an artificial manner if someone aims at keeping the set of theories alive.

The corollary is that the internal history of science is the rational reconstruction of the meaning of an *SRP*, while the external history of science is the description of empirical facts within a field of research. In this context, both consistency and refutation in the explications provided by cores are the main criteria for the acceptance of a *SRP* (Blaug 1980). At the end, if differences between two schools arise only from their cores, both schools are independent *SRPs*. If the differentiation arises only from specific parts of their cores, both schools are independent sub-*SRPs*. If deviations from an original *SRP* on the part of any school do not stem from their cores, these schools are just scientific movements away from the original *SRP* (see Chapter 10 for lively examples). The next step is to describe Keynes's *SRP* for the purpose of identifying its evolutionary characteristics in relation to the outlining of his 'probable' macroeconomics after 1937, that is, after his principal exposition of economic theory has been completed. This exercise helps us to benefit from recent contributions on Keynes's scholarship under the hypothesis that Keynes's *SRP* is a remarkable example in the history of science after he created macroeconomics, for example in Appendix 13.1.

There is a brief interlude before. It must be noted that Falsificationism may reveal some caveats when used for the examination of isolated theories. This is because both observations and results in a *SRP* involve numerous assumptions that do not necessarily belong to isolated theories or fields, but rather arise from interrelated theories or even from outside their fields. This discernment is based on the *Duhem–Quine Thesis* (circa 1951), also known as 'the under-determination argument.' Hence, doubts arise around the functionality of Popper's original (naïve) falsificationism. However, this book avoids this methodological problem by clarifying specific interdisciplinary contentions on Keynes's core throughout all the chapters, but even more importantly by demonstrating Keynes's core notions are original and innovative since he is the creator of a new science: macroeconomics. This is explained in the next section.

2.3 Background: Keynes's Issues in 1936

The two dimensions in economics are quantities produced and prices. Unlike the microeconomists centered upon individual or entrepreneurial behavior, Keynes's research in economics was based on the consideration of aggregate—national—variables. He explains in the Golden Book the determination of aggregate output or national income (Υ) and consequently of employment (E), which was his main scientific and practical concern. The novelty was that aggregate demand was the sole determining factor of Υ, as aggregate supply is totally responsive—flexible, especially in economies with idle capacity. Keynes also had a different view of money as a store of value and used this view to link the real sector with the monetary sector. Other related revolutionary concepts from the Golden—organic—Book are: in a demand-determined equilibrium involuntary unemployment is possible; the ineffectiveness of price or wage flexibility to cure unemployment; a theory of money based on liquidity preference replacing the quantity theory of money ('QTM'); the introduction of uncertainty and expectations; the potential inequality between savings and investment; the downward rigidity of wages; and the marginal efficiency of investment, which breaks Say's law (reversing the savings–investment classical causation). One can ascertain that Say's Law is just an abstraction to be grounded. Avoiding concretion is an epistemic failure. Notice that in Keynes the equality between investment and savings must not be taken for granted (these activities are performed by distinct agents in a modern economy). Instead, it must be induced via economic policy.

How? Keynes's practical contribution is to introduce the possibility of using both fiscal and monetary policies to increase employment which moves in tandem with Υ. These concepts expose the lack of sufficient self-regulation mechanisms on the part of the system to achieve full employment corresponding to Keynes's view of an unregulated (non-Cartesian or Kantian) cosmos. Keynes's issues can thus be classified into theoretical, empirical, and policy related, all of them underpinned by his core. Table 2.1 divides these issues into the—organized?—constituents of an SRP, which are subsequently explained in detail.

According to this table, the most remarkable part of the core embedded in *GT* is that the organic (multi-directionally interrelated) system lacks a self-adjustment mechanism for returning to full employment after a shock due to uncertainty might perhaps be translated into external shocks, and policymakers must make decisions. The implication is tremendous: the system can be permanently in equilibrium without attaining full employment of resources (this is 1936). Further, Keynes introduced the concept of uncertainty linked to irrationality in behaviors, giving rise to the use of money and deeper financial instruments, ascertaining that the future is unknowable. These ontological-epistemological notions break with the former Classical view of a stable universe in economics, which is grounded in a certain atomic world that automatically tends toward self-equilibrium in a predictable future (see Chapter 10). Keynes's insights, as expressed in *GT*, were the gradual result of both his evolving practice and flexible mind.

2.4 'Probable' Directions of Keynes After 1936

Keynes died in 1946 and it is widely assumed that he died too early. Our hypothetical assumption in this chapter is that he would have produced more innovations in economics. Therefore the evolution of Keynes's core after *GT* is hereby assessed, especially in economic thinking, with the advantage of more than 80 years of evidence (a complementary study of Chapter 24 of the Golden Book is offered in Chapter 9). Table 2.2 is a compilation of the most easily discussed themes and issues of a hypothetical research program in economics 'by' Keynes after 1936, alongside possible new directions. These likely salient but specific paths are now analyzed.

2.4.1 'Probable' Keynes Directions: Main Paths

There are more than 1000 interpretations of the message of *GT* (Gerrard 1991). It is widely acknowledged, however, that Keynes's vision centers on uncertainty (see Skidelsky 2010b, 2016). Likewise, the point here is the Lakatosian analysis conducted in the preceding paragraphs suggests

Table 2.2 Keynes's 'probable' specific directions after *GT*

Core (essential notions or activities)
• Analysis of induced equilibrium and sub-equilibrium as alternatives of the Classical system and their self-adjustment properties in a realm of organicism
• Consideration of money as endogenous and interactive via the *Keynes Effect*
• Extensions and clarifications about uncertainty (UNC) and expectations
• Corroboration of his method in a changing world
Positive heuristics (agenda)
• Examination of short-term factors
• Emphasis on the goods market
• Focus on both the difference between saving and investment, and the relationship between interest rates and investment
• Clarifications of the concepts risk and uncertainty
• Discovery of the 'finance' motive
• Concentration on involuntary unemployment, rigid wages, and inflation
• Extension to growth, long-term cycles, development, and financial crises
• Paying heed to aggregate supply (AS)
• Demonstration of interest in income distribution
Protective belt (assumptions on)
• Consumption (C)
• The Marginal Efficiency of Investment (MEI)
• Money demand (M^d) and money supply (M^s)
• The role of governments, especially around public expenditure (G) and institutional issues
• Extensions to the role of exports (X), imports (IM), and foreign investment (FI) in aggregate demand (AD)
• Push-cost (due to devaluations) inflation (π)
- Floating exchange rates (e)

that Keynes would not have changed his stance regarding the lack of self-regulating properties of the system. Otherwise, he would have accepted the Classical conclusions, which assume in an aprioristic manner that full-employment equilibrium is the rule. For Keynes, the theory of effective demand (the positive difference between aggregate demand and aggregate supply) would always be the output theory[2] suitable for explaining economic fluctuations and unemployment. The short-term impact of uncertainty and expectations may be straightforward when placed on money demand (M^d), but it can also be traced to producers (I) affecting effective demand (ED).

Historically speaking, Keynes's focus on uncertainty and expectations is developed in *A Treatise on Probability* (*TP*, 1921) (Chapter 6), but made explicit and ubiquitous in *GT*, and expressly addressed in 'The General Theory of Employment' (1937) (Appendix 9.1). Heilbroner (1999 [1951], p. 275) states that '[u]ncertainty, not assurance, lays at the very core of capitalism,' according to Keynes. A real novelty for that epoch. For authors such as O'Donnell (1982) and Skidelsky (2000, 2016), this is the main feature of the Keynesian revolution. In any event, if uncertainty exists in both physical investment and the money market, it encourages savings (especially in liquid form) and therefore generates depressions according to the standard Keynes theory (see Appendix 13.1). Therefore, Keynes would have refined and quantified his treatment of expectations, noting that uncertainty is a qualitative non-measurable risk.

On the other hand, inflation—a path initially researched by Keynes (1936, 1937)—is as dangerous as depression (its opposite notion) in modern times, especially in emerging economies. According to Skidelsky (1992, p. 116), 'Keynes himself would have said...that at full employment any exogenous injection of demand leads to inflation.' By researching inflation, Keynes would also have provided a more complete theory of prices. Indeed, he studied this problem in the 1940s (Chapter 12).

Finally, the key role of the 'finance motive' for funding investments is justified by the fact that new financial institutions and instruments exist to select from for the purposes of productive—physical—investment, under the Keynes's innovative assumption that borrowers are different from lenders. This issue is related to money demand (the original motive for holding liquid money) and conversely to investment. Whereas investment has psychological roots, saving as the consequence of investment has monetary roots, but it is determined by income. Investment then determines both income and employment. This path has been followed by both Davidson (2002) and Minsky in his 'fragility hypothesis' (1975) among others (see Appendix 13.1), as would have been followed by Keynes himself.

2.4.2 *Secondary Paths*

The concept of uncertainty is still not fully understood not to mention absorbed by most mainstream economists. Indeed, modern finance theory is based on risk (quantifiable uncertainty!), whose main impact is on investors both in the industrial and in the financial sectors. But Keynes would also have conducted research on uncertainty as related to equity finance. This would be a consequence of his acknowledgment of the existence of 'animal spirits,' exemplified by speculators in forward markets, whose existence was envisaged by Keynes in 1930 in *A Treatise on Money*. As Keynes had predicted, failures in capital markets bring about collapses in the overall economy mainly as the consequence of unstable investment. The analysis of stock markets in Chapter 12 of *GT* allows the inference that a reduction in investment due to either 'bubbles' in financial markets or pessimistic expectations is at the heart of recessions. So, a probable Keynes's direction after 1936 would have been research on financial crises (a sample of which are outlined in Appendix 13.1). The emphasis of Keynes after the Second World War was on the financial system, exposing a wider conception of money and its substitutes.

This is not all. Real or tangible investment is also of course at the heart of the performance of domestic economies and especially of that of employment. This variable is the key for industrialization and only industrialized economies—or regions or sectors—have at least partially solved the problem of unemployment in capitalist societies. Hence the insight on the necessary 'socialization' of investment as depicted in Chapter 24 of *GT* favoring the implementation of semi-autonomous institutions would have been explored in more depth by Keynes.

On the key role of investment in the stabilization of economies, according to Skidelsky (1992, p. 555), "[t]he effects of a Keynesian policy depend on expectations." And if investment depends on uncertainty, 'the instability of investment demand emerges as a crucial factor in economic fluctuations' (ibid.). Thus, the control of investors leads to the management of recessions. In this frame of mind, if interest rates are to be lowered by means of a tightening monetary policy, investment (and consequently aggregate demand) must increase rather than the demand for money. The evolutionary heuristics associated to this topic would have been of interest to Keynes had he lived longer.

Moreover, neither his dichotomy between savers and investors, nor his theory of the interest rate, would have been modified by Keynes after 1936, because, in his words, 'the rate of interest [*is*] the inducement not to hoard' (Keynes 1937, p. 110), rather than the incentive for saving as it was considered in the classical *SRP*. Further, Keynes was (perhaps) an exogenous money person, but as the financial system became more complex, he would have become an 'endogenous' money person (to put it simply, when money is managed in central banks). This consideration would have been part of his protective belt.

For some economists, Chapter 19 (related to a new conception of the effects of changes in money wages) is the apex of *GT*. Keynes thought—unlike in the classical system—that downward wages would increase unemployment. In addition, money wage flexibility does not solve the problem of depression as it is stated in *GT*. Keynes also said that nominal wage increases differ from real wage increases, so that if Keynes had analyzed inflation after 1936 he would have produced further insights about the labor market. On similar issues, Keynes would probably have widened both his study of consumption and his examination of liquidity functions, since larger industrial societies are more linked to developed financial systems. Further, no preconceptions would have been held by Keynes about various types of unemployment in industrial societies, but he would always have acknowledged the concept of involuntary unemployment. According to these arguments, Keynes would not have altered his core insights on income determination after 1936. This contention though may be disputable as no one knows the future.

2.4.3 Non-Standard Paths

The resort to such non-Keynes traditional paths as income distribution, growth, aggregate supply, micro-foundations, and open economy macroeconomics seems to have been rather unlikely. Distribution is superficially mentioned in the last chapter of *GT*, but this direction would be followed instead by others. Keynes assumed that distribution was constant just as was the marginal propensity to consume (c), but he would have extended his theory to the analysis of the distributional issues in other economies, a route which might be difficult to imagine, given his concentration on Western Europe and the United States. But as distribution is arguably worse in depressed economies, Keynes would have enlarged his interests to include both growth and income distribution in his conception of development (Appendix 12.2). Nevertheless, it must be recalled that for him an unfair distribution was linked to the savings (S) structures and high interest rates (r).

Concerning growth and aggregate supply (it was totally elastic or responsive for Keynes in 1936), we paraphrase Skidelsky, 'Keynesian growth policy seemed to be what was left when plentiful supply…[*was*]…removed from the picture' (Skidelsky 2010a, p. 130). Keynes would have realized that no gulf exists between dynamic and static macroeconomics, but he was only concerned with the static economy as it was at the heart of economic ills in his time in his demonstration of unemployment equilibrium.

On the other hand, the path of micro-foundations would not have been chosen by Keynes as it contradicts his message in *GT*. Nor had he been interested in imperfect competition. He would have probably, however, made contributions to microeconomics. His interest in international micro-markets would have continued to be limited to their impact on macroeconomic problems. The rationale for this contention is that open economy macroeconomics is one of the most extensive fields for research in economics, especially since 1945. At the end of his life, Keynes was interested in the trade balance, widening his analysis of income (output) determination. Nevertheless, he would have shifted from fixed exchange rates to flexible rates, just as he advocated for adjustable fixed rates rather than adhering to the gold standard in the 1930s. His considerations would have been influenced not only by the evolution of international finance but also by his speed of thought.

Keynes realized that an overvalued currency would be a weak currency. Finally, the work of Mundell in the 1960s on the inclusion of foreign economy considerations would have arguably been accepted by Keynes into his general framework. This is consistent with the fact that Keynes's 'contributions to international economics dealt largely with the financial and monetary aspects' (Minsky 1975, p. 1).

2.5 The Lakatosian Validity of 'Probable' Directions

The affirmation to be tested in this chapter is whether the Keynesian *SRP* in economics would have been modified if Keynes were to be based on new information in the late 1930s, since it was developed based on the prevailing conditions in 1936. In Kuhnian terms, one could investigate whether the paradigm represented by *GT* would likely be superseded by a new one. The most probable answer, when analyzing these directions along the lines taken by the orthodox Keynesians starting from the 1950s,[3] is that Keynes would not have created a new paradigm departing from the original outlined in *GT*.

The basis of this ascertainment goes as follows. According to the discussions above, the main constituent of his core is the absence of self-regulating properties on the part of the system. In addition, in Keynes's core, time is adequately considered in a historical perspective rather than in a logical viewpoint. Further, his picture of human nature, considering irrational behavior as associated to money non-neutrality in terms of its effect on real sector developments, led to his discovery of macroeconomics. Keynes would have stuck to his original theories (before 1936), which explain new observations as well as the functioning of newly expanding aggregate markets (see Appendix 13.1). His most outstanding example is the domestic financial market. Finally, although he was focused on international finance both in the early 1930s and the 1940s, he would have paid attention to domestic finance developments, especially in developed countries. After all, the acknowledgment of heterogeneity and instability in modern domestic financial systems is a proof of Keynes's vision. The *SRP* related to Keynes's macroeconomics after 1936 has been able to withstand refutations at least on most core issues, even experiencing a revival after the crisis occurred in 2007 (Appendix 13.1). Therefore, macroeconomics is a formal science, as it allows both internal history reconstruction and external history refutations.

A caveat to this reasoning is that intellectuals sometimes return to the path followed in their youth. But there is no corroborating evidence to support any of these hypotheses, less in the case of Keynes whose unpredictable mind was prone to improvement. Speed of thought is not the opposite of neither consistency nor accuracy. Hence the details of a comprehensive work are irrelevant, although they appear in the short term as changes in cores. Another caveat is that Keynes was a weak verificationist (Skidelsky 2001), based on minimal self-criticism, but he would have evolved in this sense as he always paid heed to innovations.

2.6 Conclusions on Keynes's Scientific Research Program

Other voices must be heeded, according to Victoria Chick (2018): 'Economics is profoundly not like physics: atoms have done the same things for eons' (Dow et al. 2018, p. 1, Chapter 1). The implication is that for Keynes organic—social—entities are in perpetual change, bringing about uncertainty and evolution; disequilibrium is the norm. The analytical, quantitative, and policy-oriented perspectives embedded in Keynes's theoretical insights in *GT* help both us and the reader to offer conclusions about Keynes's evolution (for a comparison in this respect see Appendix 3.1).

According to the editorial introduction to CW, *Vol. 7*, it is impossible to predict the state of his own revisions of *GT*, but he probably would have updated the Golden Book in heuristic terms—in a sequel? Consistent with the three previous sections, the roots of Keynes's intellectual revolution were already sown in 1936, even though alternative methodological analyses are necessary to confirm this statement by examining the probable Keynesian paths. The world in the aftermath of the Second World War was different, just as the times of *GT* were distinct from those of the *Treatise*.

According to Pasinetti, "[*a*] Keynesian 'revolution', in the strict sense of the word, might as yet remain unaccomplished" (Pasinetti 1997, p. 13). Keynes is evolutionary rather than revolutionary. What is more, it can be argued that most of Keynes's issues were demonstrated once and for all in 1936. This is because of the economic situation prevailing in the nineteenth century was a special case in the history of humankind for Keynes, just as equilibrium is a special case of theories. He would not have widened his original vision of *GT* as the change of vision embedded in the Golden Book was widely accepted, indeed he became orthodoxy. Lakatos' methodology of *SRPs* thus offers an interpretation of Keynes's overall contribution to science. It is also attempted here to be demonstrated that Keynes's *SRP* is articulated. Returning to articulation, this referential chapter has identified the notions of uncertainty, organicism, and the lack of a self-regulating system as the most important in his core. The Lakatosian perspective was useful to comprehend that Keynes's main concern was involuntary unemployment alongside the avoidance of uncertainty in search of a better life. The next step in economic terms is to analyze how the work of those who identified themselves as Keynesians immediately after the publication of *GT* differed from his original work in 1936. In this circular book, the former task is undertaken in Chapter 10, while the specific economic-philosophical insights of Chapter 24 of *GT* are delineated in Chapter 9. Additionally, his preceding insights are described in Chapter 7,[4] and the continuance of these economic insights in Keynes's *SRP* is outlined in Chapter 12. Meanwhile, Keynes's intellectual debts are outlined in Chapter 3.

Appendix 2.1 Keynes's Complex System

The expectations opened in the end of the nineteenth century by the scientific-technical community welcomed rationality but also uncertainty due to the pluralism of perspectives on the part of human beings. Complexity is a notion imported from physics with emphasis on interrelations and dynamism but especially uncertainty and hence may be considered as the science of sciences in the twenty-first century. A complex system is comprised of initial conditions, mobile, interrelations, emerging properties, results, and remedies. Complexity is an approach containing a set of dynamic models depicting the behavior of plural agents (or forces, mainly in physics). An initial example of a system in economics according to orthodoxy is Adam Smith's pin factory, wherein each agent has a specific task, all of them working for a predictable result. As all agents are similar, that model is not really complex, instead reflecting the simplicity of Classical economics. Keynes's open complex ontology reflects the inclusion of such building blocks or categories as heterogeneity, dichotomy, typologies and asymmetries regarding moral choices, epistemological elections, markets, agents, institutions, psychologies, behaviors, variables, and policies. Secondly, he advocates organicism, following Moore and exhibiting an innovative ontic notion, whose purpose is relating—unifying—concepts and categories. Thereafter Keynes traced the complex roots of knowledge, such as the relationship between awareness and justified belief. In this perspective, Keynes's denial of the application of physicalism in social sciences is the 'complex' leading thread running throughout his main book: *GT*.

But dynamism in the form of evolution is also a signal of complexity. Davis (1994) contends that Keynes first believed in both induction and intuition and later in conventions as a device for predicting both our future actions and others' actions in realms as diverse as moral choices, economic policy, or investment selection. Keynes writes in 'Auri Sacra Fames' (1930a [1978]): 'gold has become part of the apparatus of conservatism' (Keynes 1931). This is mentioned here since the usage of conventions is a manner of avoiding complexity. Therefore, Keynes's predominant thought is consistent (although its consistency is not visible at a first glance, especially for the untrained eye), since its concurrent interrelations, motivators, and emerging properties constitute a dynamic complex system. Altogether, the principal issues required for a theory to be qualified as complex are emergence, novelty, evolution, the profundity, and variety of the embedded philosophy, and different intensities of abstraction, which Keynes always make concrete, for example, uncertainty is associated in his writings to the financial market (see Appendix 13.1) but also to the results of political actions (the Gold Standard?). All in all, the salient feature in Keynes's complexity is organic interdependence. This novel concept (specifically in economics) is remarkably applied by him in the distinction between national and individual saving in terms of decision making and hence of their respective origins, but those decisions must be explicated and unified.

We are not alone in our contentions. For Pheby (1989, p. 128), the consideration that systems behave in asymmetric ways is an evolutionary insight on the part of Keynes. Moreover, these behaviors are set for him in historical time, which lends itself to the idea that changes may be either quantitative or qualitative. Evolution, then, is a vision that considers all parts of the process of a phenomenon along with their interrelations and changes in intensity.[5] This forward-looking and cohesive perspective, outlined in the preceding paragraphs, allowed for Keynes's transformation into a macro-monetary economist (see Chapters 2 and 7). Moreover, interdependences (reflected in aggregate variables) and complexities (translated into unexpected turbulences, heterogeneities, and asymmetries) prevail in all real phenomena for Keynes, but he also—unlike Hume—exhibited a curiosity about transitions and not just ends.

The implication is that complex results are over-determined and hence unpredictable. Thus, complexity defines the quality, path, and speed of evolutions, and can be interpreted as order brought about by decentralized action. In other words, complexity can be categorized as a kind of bounded rationality, linking both events and variables in multiple manners, entailing frequent—dynamic—but unpredictable—perhaps irrational—disequilibria. Complexity is also comprised of overemphasis on initial causes (for which initial conditions are especially relevant) and laying stress on interrelations, motivations, emerging properties, or consequences. Complexity thus may portray an evolutionary thought since it may integrate heterogeneous aspects in the holistic visualization of such universals of human conduct as coordination, order, unexpected transformations, and continual change. Complexity then interrelates, arranges, or rearranges the elements of a phenomenon in multidimensional and multi-directional manners.

For its part, evolution is an ordered account of the successive modifications of the characteristics of phenomena, arising in the case of human beings from the diversity of both thoughts and facts, entailing sequences of non-repetitive progress which tend toward a given end. In other words, variety does not alter the ends for organicism. According to Robert et al. (2017) both complexity and evolution offer an idea on the dimensions and attributions of phenomena. Phenomena involved in complex evolutionary trends are thus grounded on dissimilar assumptions but must send unified messages whereas following discontinuing paths may send diverse messages (see Chapter 13). The inference is that coordination for social functioning—or for that matter in ethics—founded on both creative roles and internal changes is required.

How is all this related to Keynes's theories and insights? Keynes's purpose was to remedy the problem of involuntary unemployment, which was caused by fluctuations in aggregate demand due to uncertainty, moved by the interest rate (this was the mobile). The emerging property of the system was money, and the result was instability. The device for restoring equilibrium in a system lacking self-regulating mechanisms is aggregate demand management, in terms of its elements: consumption, investment, and public expenditure (see the Lakatosian-type tables in this chapter). Armed with these complexly—organic—related and dynamic insights, Keynes produced evolutionary ideas in economics, and human amelioration but also associated to *good*, probability, individualism, cooperation, and convention. All these issues are dealt with in detail throughout the following chapters.

Notes

1. Keynes's philosophical development before 1936 is detailed in Chapters 3, 4, 6, and 8, but this chapter outlines his philosophical apex, with speculations on his future work to be contrasted against facts.
2. This is a holistic concept.
3. See Chapter 10 for an analysis of orthodox Keynesians as an additional test of the conclusions of this chapter.
4. Keynes's philosophical evolution is chronologically described.
5. 'Animal spirits' is a novel and dynamic notion, according to Shackle.

References

Blaug, Mark. 1980. *The Methodology of Economics: Or How Economists Explain*. Cambridge: Cambridge University Press.

Chick, Victoria. 2018. "On the Relevance of the General Theory at 80: Economic Change and Economic Theory." In *The General Theory and Keynes for the 21st Century*, edited by Sheila Dow, Jesper Jespersen, and Geoffrey Tilly, Chapter 1. Chentelham, UK and Northampton, MA: Edward Elgar.

Davidson, Paul. 2002. *Financial Markets, Money and the Real World*. Chentelham, UK: Edward Elgar.

Davis, John B. 1994. *Keynes's Philosophical Development*. Cambridge: Cambridge University Press.

Dow, Sheila, Jesper Jespersen, and Geoff Tily. 2018. *The General Theory and Keynes for the 21st Century. New Directions in Modern Economics Series*. Chentelham, UK: Edward Elgar.

Gerrard, Bill. 1991. "Keynes's General Theory: Interpreting the Interpretations." *Economic Journal* 101: 272–87.

Heilbroner, Robert. 1999 [1951]. *The Worldly Philosophers: The Lives, Times and Ideas of the Great Thinkers*. New York: Touchstone, 7th revised edition.

Keynes, J. 1930a [1978]. "Auri Sacra Fames." In *The Collected Writings of John Maynard Keynes*, edited by E. Johnson & D. Moggridge, 161–163. Royal Economic Society, https://doi.org/10.1017/UPO9781139524162.019.

———. 1930b [1932]. "Economic Possibilities for Our Grandchildren." In *Essays in Persuasion*, 358–73. New York: Harcourt. https://assets.aspeninstitute.org/content/uploads/files/content/upload/Intro_and_Section_I.pdf. Accessed 21 March 2019.

———. 1931. "Keynes Rejoinder to Mr. D. H. Robertson." *Economic Journal XLI* 163 (September). In *JMK/EJ/6/7*. Cambridge: Cambridge University Press. https://discovery.nationalarchives.gov.uk/details/r/afc22cbd-5472-49c8-8ba4-a585275185c2. Accessed 15 November 2019.

———. 1936 (1964). *The General Theory of Employment, Interest and Money*. New York: Harcourt.

———. 1937. "Alternative Theories of the Rate of Interest." *Economic Journal* 47, no. 186 (June): 241–52.

Lakatos, Imre. 1978a. *The Methodology of Scientific Research Programmes*. Cambridge: Cambridge University Press.

———. 1978b. *Philosophical Papers*, 2 vols. Cambridge: Cambridge University Press.

Machlup, Fritz. 1978. *Methodology of Economics and Other Social Sciences*. New York: Academic Press.

Minsky, Hyman P. 1975. *John Maynard Keynes*. New York: Columbia University Press.

O'Donnell, Roderick. 1982. Keynes: Philosophy and Economics, an Approach to Rationality and Uncertainty. PhD Dissertaion. Cambridge: University of Cambridge.

Pasinetti, Luigi L. 1997. "J. M. Keynes's 'Revolution' the Major Event of Twentieth-Century Economics?" In *The Impact of Keynes on Economics in the 20th Century*, edited by Luigi L. Pasinetti and Bernard Schefold, Chapter 1, 3–15. Edward Elgar: Chentelham, UK.

Pheby, John (ed.). 1989. New Directions in Post-Keynesian Economics. Gower: University of Michigan.

Robert, Veronica, Gabriel Yoguel, and Octavio Lerena. 2017. "The Ontology of Complexity and the Neo-Schumpeterian Evolutionary Theory for Economic Change." *Journal of Evolutionary Economics* 27, no. 4 (September): 761–93.

Skidelsky, Robert. 1992. *John Maynard Keynes. Volume II: The Economist as Saviour 1920–1937*. London: Macmillan.

———. 1997a. "Chapter 24 Keynes's Concluding Notes: Robert Skidelsky Writing as John Maynard Keynes." In *A 'Second' Edition of the General Theory*, vol. I, edited by Geoffrey C. Harcourt and Peter Riach, Chapter 24, 430–39. New York: Routledge.

———. 1997b. "The Conditions for the Reinstatement of Keynesian Policy." In *The Impact of Keynes in the Twentieth Century*, edited by Luigi Pasinetti, 36–51. Cheltenham, UK and Lyme, USA: Edward Elgar.

———. 2000. *John Maynard Keynes. Volume III: Fighting for Britain 1937–1946*. London: Macmillan.

———. 2001. *John Maynard Keynes. Volume III: Fighting for Britain 1937–1946*. New York: Viking Adult.

———. 2010a. *Keynes. A Very Short Introduction*. Oxford: Oxford University Press.

———. 2010b. "The Crisis of Capitalism: Keynes versus Marx." *The Indian Journal of Industrial Relations* 45, no. 3 (January): 321–35.

———. 2016. *John Maynard Keynes: The Essential Keynes*. London: Penguin.

PART I

Keynes. The Meaning of Background (1883–1910)

Chapters 3 and 4 are about the main inspirations of past and contemporary philosophers on Keynes. Outstanding among them are the epistemological contentions of David Hume along with the ethical views of George Edward Moore and the political perspectives of Edmund Burke (covered in Chapter 3) and the economics of the *Keynes Cambridge Circus* (outlined in Chapter 4). These two chapters provide a better footing for the contentions addressed in Chapter 2 about the strength of Keynes's Scientific Research Program. Chapter 3 includes an appendix on the relation between the philosophies of Newton and Keynes, and another one on the sway of Ancient Greece and Continental Europeans on Keynes. Chapter 4 includes an appendix on the philosophy embedded in Keynes's early papers (before 1911). The purpose of these two chapters is thus to provide an overview of Keynes's past and present—early—influences to offer a qualitative appreciation of his overall work. Further these chapters prepare the groundwork for the description of Keynes's vision on world affairs encapsulated in the *Economic Consequences of the Peace* (1919) undertaken in Chapter 5, and for the creation of a new notion of probability with a sway for uncertainty as depicted in Chapter 6, and so on and so forth.

CHAPTER 3

Keynes's Intellectual Debts and the 'Locke Connection'

This chapter deals with the outlining of the antecedents of Keynes in terms of ontology, ethics, epistemology, and political philosophy. Section 3.1 is about the Irish political thinker Burke, mentioning some of his innovatively exposed but conservative notions, some of which were embraced by Keynes. Section 3.2 is about the key British philosophers who established the 'Locke Connection:' the empiricists John Locke and David Hume, the first one also being an eminence on political philosophy. Section 3.3 deals with the arguments of the creators and disseminators of utilitarianism, Jeremy Bentham, and John Stuart Mill, who was an authority on economics, epistemology, and political philosophy. Section 3.4 is about G. E. Moore and his notion of *good*. This is perhaps the chapter main contribution by providing the analysis of the philosophical excursions of the intellectual who had the noblest influence on Keynes, at least before *GT*, which aided Keynes to shape his early conception of the world. Appendix 3.1 is about Keynes's perspective on the role of Isaac Newton in the formation of the universal conscience. Appendix 3.2 is about the sway of "modern" Continental Europeans on Keynes.

J. Muñoz-Bandala, *Keynes's Evolutionary Spirit*,
Palgrave Insights into Apocalypse Economics,
https://doi.org/10.1007/978-3-030-90150-9_3

3.1 Burke

Now for a brief historical digression of the panorama of Western philosophy before discussing the gist of Keynes's second greatest influence: Burke. For Plato (428–348 BCE), the creator of the theory of eternal ideas, the truth was infinite and ubiquitous, and this enormous insight would have a sway for all subsequent ethical—and religious!—insights and stances. Plato heralded the preponderance of ideas while Aristotle (384–322 BCE) stressed the role of substance (essence?) in ontology (see Appendix 3.2). Much later, René Descartes (1588–1679) with his deductive method and his attention to self-identification moved the epicenter of philosophy from ontology to epistemology (the Cartesian turn). Indeed, Descartes is regarded as the father of both rationalism and dualism between mind and body, stressing the distinction between subject and object in knowledge.

In that philosophical path Emmanuel Kant (1724–1804) became the progenitor of modern idealism, thereby reinforcing the role of apriorism in knowledge. Since Kant's days our transcendental system of knowledge relies on varying mental factors, therefore inferences are no longer automatic, but rather require evaluation, in such a way that data interpretation[1] becomes imperative. The crucial point is that since Kant's days, information deciphering has been based on mental processes rather than on dogmatism. Kant indirectly descends from Hume, whose contributions are analyzed in the next section since he has a major influence on Keynes. Hume's contemporary Adam Smith (1723–1790) created the strand named moral liberalism, and of course formal microeconomics or micro political economy. As an economist and a political philosopher, he championed the doctrines of the *Laissez-faire* (without explicitly mentioning it) and the *Invisible Hand* as ontological visions and the bases of the new social order in the aftermath of the British Industrial Revolution (1760–1840) in *The Wealth of Nations* (1776), enhancing free competition and absolute advantage in the *Homus Economicus* (all men are equal and rationally devoted to profit maximization). However, Smith was regressive with respect to a flexible understanding of the political system and human behavior by advocating that societies move according to physical laws at least in his *oeuvre The Wealth of Nations* (1776), thus discarding the role of human action in problem solving and the effectiveness of policies, except in his treatise *The Theory of Moral Sentiments* (1759), which is now in fashion but is rarely if ever mentioned by Keynes.

Then came Edmund Burke (1729–1797). In accordance to Dostaler (1996), Burke's doctrine of expediency implied that politics is a set of processes to be implemented in the short period rather than a set of received ethical ideals. Burke, who had a foot in the nineteenth century in some respects, was a political utilitarian advocating attention to the present but believing in the power of the *Laissez-faire*. Burke's writings are a source for liberalism since he also criticized democracy, ascertaining that an intellectual—aristocratic—elite is the only appropriate type of institution for governing. Burke was suggesting political and conceptual reforms aimed toward preserving the system so that Burke was a critic of such rationalist theories of natural law as those suggested by Thomas Hobbes (1588–1679). He also rejected the notion of a social contract, as expounded by John Locke (1632–1704) and Jean Jacques Rousseau (1712–1778), for whom neither tyrannical kings nor parliaments must reign, but people. Further, Burke bore in mind that societies evolve gradually. He praised the American Revolution (1776) but perhaps contradictorily condemned the French Revolution (1789) for both its rationalist character and incidental side effect: the destructive rise of Capitalism.

In this frame of mind, while ethical orientation requires an introspective scrutiny of values, political philosophy possesses an outward practical orientation since it demands spontaneous management; that is, politics is a matter of—perhaps discretionary—expediency. According to Dostaler (2007), Burke supports non-violent reform by means of judicious expediency. For Helburn (1991), Keynes became practical as the result of his Burke's legacy. An additional insight, owed by Keynes to Burke, is the relevance of the principle of prudence. Burke represents the gist of the eighteenth century for Keynes in terms of political philosophy (conservatism), human evolution, and the concept of time. Burke also illuminated the theory and methods of politics about reform, elitism, and aristocracy. The Irishman was thus an independent influence on Keynes on the principles of political action; that is, about public duty,[2] which Keynes also respected due to his own British inheritance. To England in the seventeenth and eighteenth centuries we turn.

3.2 Locke and Hume

The advocacy for induction and empiricism goes back principally to Francis Bacon (1561–1626) who wrote on these epistemological tenets, becoming the anti-cartesian philosopher *par excellence*. He was followed by Thomas Hobbes (1588–1679), John Locke, George Berkeley (1685–1753), David Hume (1711–1776), and John Stuart Mill (1806–1873). Apart from Hobbes, the former three philosophers were the pioneer empiricists in the seventeenth and the eighteenth centuries, although the latter one gave a blow to empiricism, which eventually would experience a resurgence in the hands of Mill in the nineteenth century and subsequent thinkers in the twentieth century. These philosophical insights are detailed in the following pages.

3.2.1 Locke

According to Braman (1996), Keynes's philosophical concepts, to some extent originated in the notions of Locke's vision, are: reason, knowledge acquisition, and application, but also democracy (see Keynes's 'The end of the Laissez-Faire'), natural laws, private property, peace, and sustainable development. Locke (the initiator of the 'Locke Connection' according to Keynes's Preface of *Essays in Biography*) is one of the most influential figures regarding the foundation of the modern theory of epistemology, becoming the central figure of empiricism. For Locke, all knowledge comes from experience as well as for both Berkeley (who is considered an idealist by some) and the skeptical—on the relation cause-effect—Hume. This setback describes the foundations for Keynes's notions of probability—who also departed from Hume's insights, but it must be described step by step. Knowledge is for Locke more than belief and the relevant question is whether knowledge as an emergent property of perception exists. The answer is positive, but the understanding of facts must be placed and tested within a social context, which reinforces the role of empiricism as a means for obtaining knowledge. Empiricism thus emerges from induction resulting in Locke's notion of political liberalism, which departs from the analysis of individualism and moves on to analyze societies.

Returning to epistemology, Locke like Newton believed in the prevalence of uniform movements as a source of energy. Hence, he believed in atomism and self-equilibrating trends. In this vein, Locke wrote of associations among ideas, perceptions, experience, sensations, and observation, giving form to human reason. For those purposes, Locke proposed a dichotomy between simple and complex ideas. Locke dropped many lines about the absence of innate ideas and the preponderance of sensitive ideas in the acquisition of knowledge. Sensation is more important than perception as the source for knowledge, but ideas of sensation are unconsciously changed by means of habit into ideas of judgment. Nonetheless knowledge is the perception of the agreement of our ideas based on our experiences. But as there is room for error in the human quest for knowledge, science must address the objects of uncertainty and for that goal, knowledge may be either intuitive or demonstrative. He examined thus the philosophy that propositions are based on probability under a framework of certainty (but despite reading Locke, Keynes was examining uncertainty as early as 1908).

Interrelating the former insights but deepening matters by widening their reach, Locke not only formalized empiricism in *An Essay Concerning Human Understanding* (1690), but also established the foundations for democracy in *A Second Treatise on Civil Government*, the most relevant part of *Two Essays on Civil Government* (1689). This is because Locke did not include in his creed the dogmas of divine and natural rights, believing instead in civil rights (Chapter 8). As the founder of modern democracy, he set the basis of the judiciary and legal systems in England. His liberal political philosophy was based on moderation between the roles of the State and society, superseding the concept of a ubiquitous state (see Chapter 8). Thus, he is a major figure, having influenced on both the creation of the Declaration of Independence of the United States and the writings of both Jean Jacques Rousseau and Voltaire (1712–1778), which ignited the French Revolution. Locke's main ideas also conveyed a different notion on the origin of an individual property; the role of labor as the determining factor of value since every individual owns his (her) body and work; and the categorization of money as an imperishable valuation of worth. Hence, Locke's writing on political philosophy and related issues is also a treatise on the relevance of individualism.

Locke is thus the archetypal empiricist and liberal not to mention his epistemological contributions. The term the 'Locke Connection' refers to the high intelligentsia of England across centuries, wherein Newtonian physics, moral philosophy, and political economy are interrelated. Its other members are Galileo, Bacon, Newton, Hume, Mill, and probably Herbert Spencer (1820–1903) as well as its late adherents who are arguably Moore, Russell, and Wittgenstein among others (Chapter 4), whose inductive orientation would have had an influence on Keynes. On the other hand, the 'Continental Connection' in philosophy as this author has labeled it, is comprised of Plato, Descartes, Spinoza, Leibnitz, Kant, Hegel, and many modern contributors in the tenets of deduction and apriorism. The contention of advocates of the Continental Connection is that knowledge must reconcile reason with experience and that mind is not a passive entity—incidentally the opposite to Locke's notion of *tabula rasa*. The story thus experiences a twist regarding the sources of knowledge in the history of European philosophy, and Keynes was attentive to these former developments. We will see in due time Keynes was not an a-priorist but still accepted the mind is not a passive entity (Chapter 6). The next section shows how one of the most preeminent advocates of empiricism, Hume, was skeptical of induction, which is the basis of empiricism, and this skepticism also had an influence on Keynes's probabilistic work.

3.2.2 Hume

George Berkeley became involved in philosophy through the influence of both Locke and Newton, investigating the existence of matter as related to human perceptions and the knowledge of external bodies. For Berkeley, perceptions and objects were identical, so he was an idealist rejecting Cartesian dualism between the object and the subject. However, for Berkeley every piece of knowledge of the world was obtained through direct perception. Consequently, the goal of science was for him the purification of human perceptions. Berkeley hence took seriously the subjective point of view as an absolute need, enhancing the vital role of ideas in knowledge. Berkeley thus affirmed in a Platonic style that abstract ideas are the source of all philosophical perplexities. He is thereby a bridge between Locke and Hume, who would analyze the essence of both causality and objectivity departing from the contributions of Berkeley.

If Berkeley represents absolute idealism, Hume represents absolute skepticism. For Hume, knowledge progresses from perceptions to beliefs, wherein sequences of perceptions are joined in conjunctions of proposals. Whereas perceptions arise in the form of either impressions or ideas, conjunctions give men and women an idea of the universe, whose elements appear then as interlinked. But objects are not in reality linked to each other, and this is the main tenet of Hume's skepticism. Connections are only a psychological device arising from a logical—humane—necessity, contending that conjunctions relating experience with expectations are due to our minds or senses. In other words, according to Hume causal inference was associated with either instinct or imagination, so that he initially employed habit as an explanatory factor. For Hume, demonstrations, proofs, and probabilities might be used to characterize the nature of conjunctions. The early Keynes would devote an entire book—*TP*—to the investigation of this problem related to the connection of proposals in terms of scientific inference with the aid of formal logic (Chapter 6), and habit in the form of conventions would be relevant in both *GT and* 'MEB.'

Hume's thought, which blends Newton's *SRP* with eighteenth-century French philosophy also relies on mechanic concepts—the price-species-flow mechanism in international trade—because he is a supreme heir of the Scottish Enlightenment, which entails a break with the Greek ideal of science, which considered science possessed a necessary and universal character. Hume enunciated the role of ignorance in problems having a sway on Keynes, for attempting to prove that induction as the connection between cause and effect was simply an illusory process. Hence neither necessity or universality needed to be constrained in their roles as characteristics of formal science and logic.

Science presupposes belief, suggesting that a phenomenon is assumed to be preceded by another one that according to the mind of the researcher will produce the same effects under similar circumstances; that is, science must presuppose fixed logical relations between propositions (Chapter 6). Yet, Hume realized that social sciences must formulate laws based on probabilities instead of rigid predictions based on inflexible connections. His skeptic insight was related to discernments on space, time, cause-effects, external objects, personal identity, and free will. Hume thus ascertained that there is a contradiction in philosophical theories, exhibiting a skeptical position with respect to both focus and extent in both the epistemological and the ontological spheres. He criticized the roles of foundation, belief, and knowledge for assessing the validity of proposals in the orthodox philosophers but did it from an intuitive and pre-theoretical understanding of epistemic concepts rather from an intuitive viewpoint. As the mind draws conclusions from limited experience, reason was contradictory for Hume, and the moral implication is that 'ought' cannot be derived from 'is' influencing economic policies.

Hume's theory of impressions that may be symbolized as a set of perceptions from the self, contradicts Locke's ascertainment on the inexistence of innate ideas. Hume was hence reluctant to believe that sensory impressions are the substitutes of ideas, even though they belonged to the same group. Hume then offered an alternative foundation for practical reason, preparing the way for Kant's critique of reason. Experience for the empiricist Hume was related to evidence, whereas conventions were linked to authority, which made it impossible to explain ultimate principles (an alien idea for the young Platonic Keynes). For Hume, psychology was highly relevant as the basis of habit, an idea that would be championed in Chapter 12 of *GT*. Therefore, according to Hume causation was conventional, but the point is conventions may be misguided since—as causation is a matter of both conjunction and resemblance—conditions in observation and experimentation frequently differ and the human mind may not capture this imperceptible but continuous movement. Altogether Hume was, like Galileo, a believer in the efficacy of the evidence generated by experiments, though he stated that humans have limited possibilities for conducting variated experiments.

Consequently, Hume was more interested in inner processes than in results. Although for him a priori insights must be discarded, this does not automatically signify that induction is a sufficient criterion for drawing useful conclusions.[3] Kant would become the adversary of Hume when attempting to resolve this epistemological problem by placing the mind at the center of knowledge acquisition. However, empiricism—initiated by Locke—and its tenet verificationism persisted as remarkable criteria for the assessment of knowledge at the commencement of the twentieth century at least in the British Isles and followers, which were only improved when new generations of contemporary philosophers ascended into the public eye (Chapter 4), for instance with Falsificationism (Chapter 2). Hume then provided to science a practical foundation for questioning certainty (this is the root of Keynes's uncertainty). Notice since all proposals have only a small degree of certainty, Hume's skepticism must be understood as a call for probabilism. On the other hand, Hume was interdisciplinary; when he rejected the relevance of both reason and evidence in their pure forms, he turned to historical studies to appreciate the experience. In a sense, he was the precursor of the study of human behavior under uncertainty by mingling the use of common knowledge with the tendency to resort to conventions (see Chapters 2 and 9). Perhaps, this is the 'Locke

Connection' as its utmost moment, at least for the making of Keynes's *oeuvre*.

For Locke, arguments are either demonstrative or probable, but for Hume arguments must contain demonstrations of degrees of knowledge for supporting proofs (see Chapters 4 and 6). Hume also considered external factors. Human beings normally ignore dormant forces that may acquire relevance from time to time, even though the future is not a continuation of the present (see Chapters 2 and 6). Nevertheless, the balance between analogy and induction is incomplete in Hume, since he does not consider that variation in experiments (in time, space, conditions, extension, quantity, and quality) may be feasible. But the empiricist tradition relies on the results of repeated observation and experimentation. In this strand, induction may be considered as a relatively reliable guide for selecting theories. Still logic is not guaranteed in thinking processes, making knowledge of the world uncertain. Hence Hume's subjectivist and psychological critique of induction gives rise to irrationality, which has ethical, political, and social repercussions. Keynes would take thus the notions of degrees of belief and irrationality as a legacy from Hume. According to Andrews (1999), in his early years Keynes attempted to answer Hume's skeptical analysis of induction, even in *TP* (Chapter 6), but at the end would accept custom as the guide of life (Chapter 11) at least in some occasions and in some respects.

Hume transformed himself from time to time, by going from speculation to abstract reasoning and thereafter to the test of facts. In political philosophy, he also sustained that property is a convention. Likewise, he had a model of government, and notions about classical political economy with a study on the balance of payments or the prices-species mechanism of international flows of money. Hume was a major influence on Keynes, despite Keynes's ambivalence toward Hume, in terms of both ethics and epistemology (Chapter 2). But Hume was also a moderate inspiration in British political philosophy, partly for being skeptical and partly because of those problems did not seem acute for him.

In summary, Locke was mindful that knowledge was limited in both scope and certainty, as for him we can never know the inner nature of things, only their functioning and consequences. Knowledge comes from the senses through either observation or experimentation, and induction is the preferred method for empiricists. These insights would have an everlasting influence on Keynes, especially in his writings of the 1920s. On the other hand, the influential tenets of Hume's epistemology were the limitations of human knowledge (in this case due to the intrinsic limited character of evidence), the role of imagination, and knowledge as based on convention, influencing Keynes's *TP*. In a word, Hume was an opponent of 'orthodox' rationalism in the quest for the truth. He would shake science foundations, while Keynes would skeptically agitate economic foundations (Chapters 6 and 9). But the difference was that Keynes's revision of foundations superseded skepticism (Chapters 2, 7, 9 and 12), guided by his philosophy of action.

3.3 Bentham and Mill

Empiricism would adopt a new non-inductive direction in the early nineteenth century that would be called utilitarianism (Copleston 1967 [1994]), which is about the pleasure derived from avoiding pain. This latter strand, initiated by the Londoner Jeremy Bentham (1748–1812), related to both ethics and political philosophy, contributed limited epistemological content. The vision of utilitarianism would be refined and deepened, however, by the inductive thinking of John Stuart Mill (1806–1873), and others. To these issues we turn, bearing in mind that Keynes was a non-Utilitarian, unlike many of his countrymen. On the continent, utilitarianism was sometimes dubbed as very simple and unrealistic, for example, by Friedrich Nietzsche (1844–1900).

3.3.1 Bentham

Bentham did not believe in divine rights (like some persons living in the Middle Ages) or in natural rights (like some living in the Renaissance), nor did he appreciate the idea of a social contract (like Rousseau or Locke); rather, he was conscious that the judiciary system was irrational. He thus promoted political reform by making visible the behavioral laws of individuals and societies. At the beginning, Bentham aimed to initiate a political, legal, and judiciary reform. For that purpose, he assessed both the prevailing moral and political ideas and corresponding institutions, questioning the radical and liberal elements of the middle classes. Even more importantly, Bentham proposed utilitarianism which is also an everyday philosophy preaching that men search for pleasure and avoid pain (perhaps the basis of the profit equation: revenues minus costs). Utilitarianism is individualistic but aspires for the welfare of the society, preaching that society is the simple addition of individuals (atomism). He then explained that laws and institutions must be assessed from the viewpoint of utility, which brings about the greatest happiness for the greatest number laying stress upon consequences. This simple principle of utility then became one of the ethical, legal, and political pillars of capitalism. This is the modern—superficial—version of Aristotle's *eudaimonia*, which would be seen by Keynes as linked to democracy (see Appendix 3.2).

Bentham may seem outdated for our modern view, but he discarded the then-prevailing moral theories founded on intuition, arguing that the predominance of the pleasure-pain duality is corroborated in observational terms. This duality was the motivator for human action and the objective of human nature but was built on psychological hedonism. In any event, utilitarianism in the hands of Bentham gained an innovative place in social sciences despite (or due to) its simplicity, also because of Bentham outlined it with the aid of ordinary language. If pleasure and pain define behaviors, there is a chain comprised of causes and effects and this may be applied to all social fields. What is defined as justice for Locke is utilitarianism for Bentham. What is expediency for Burke is utilitarianism for Bentham.

For Bentham, both pleasure and pain conform the equation of 'felicific' calculus. According to Copleston (1967 [1994]) the issues to be measured regarding utility (initially *eudaimonia* for Aristotle, and happiness later for Keynes) are intensity, duration, certainty, proximity, fecundity, and purity. Utilitarianism is thus a guide for action, presupposing atomism, rationalism, and harmonization in interests (see Chapter 2). On the other hand, the elimination of legal restrictions and the acceptance of the doctrine of *Laissez-faire* contribute to the long-term utility or happiness of the community (see Chapter 8). Benthamism is thus atomistically democratic. For all these reasons, when advocating both individual and common *good* through the implementation of reforms, Bentham promotes the quantitative analysis of ethics, a highly questionable premise in epistemic terms except when money is analyzed. At any rate, Bentham's discernments were soon elevated to the status of natural laws as they were akin to the notions proposed by such economists as Smith, the main supporter of the *Laissez-faire*; David Ricardo (1772–1823), a backer of free trade; James Mill (1773–1836), a promoter of liberal ideas; and some of their successors,[4] including his son. Keynes was still far away.

3.3.2 *John Stuart Mill and His Formidable Intellectual Context*

Now a little detour. Perhaps the main economic insight of John Stuart Mill is the explanation of how an economy arrives at a stationary state. If profits in perfect competition are small, they may be diminished even more up until they turn zero. This condition produces stability, but capital accumulation would be exhausted. The only manner to get out of this state is the creation of technology, and perhaps the finding of new markets as in colonialism (Mill lived in the epoch of Eastern Indias Company). Mill believed in a—modern-type—wage fund to prevent the impact of oscillations on wages. But Marx and Keynes would have much to comment about stationarity. Keynes would see this condition as demand deficient. Hence Mill might have some influence on Keynes's writings.

Indeed, John Stuart Mill was a prominent philosopher-economist—one of the last of this kind (see Skidelsky 2016). Returning to Bentham's teachings, Mill confused the concept of *good* with that of pleasure in the realm of utilitarianism but had the merit of offering a qualitative separation of short-term and long-term pleasures which relied on a subjective but advanced standard of *good*. Mill had a great impact on the fields of ethics and political philosophy, especially his idea on the limits of freedom for the individual (the 'harm principle': my rights are valid if and only if I do not interfere with yours). Mill also proposed social, legal, and political criticisms, but championed liberalism while suggesting moderate—in scope—reforms. He even left a legacy in epistemology with his positivistic approach akin to those of Auguste Comte (1798–1857) and Herbert Spencer. Like them, and most philosophers in the 'Locke Connection,' Mill left no room for innate ideas, and hence examined the inductive logic of both proof and causation. Unlike Hume, he saw induction laws as valid. For Mill, intuition is the source of knowledge and induction a device for processing it. However, he ascertained that induction is not better than empiricism when studying the essence of inferences on propositions[5] (Chapter 6).

Here propositions are statements on the predicate of a subject, whereas scientific inference is the practical element in a universal proposition. Further inductive inferences, corroborated with experience, become predictions, not to be confused with interpretations. In addition, variability in social phenomena across space and over time impedes the automatic confirmation of propositions; plus, repetition does not prove validity (see Chapters 2 and 6). At the end, inductive generalizations possess partial validity for Mill, but this is a step away from Hume. Thus, quantitative induction is mythical in the sense no probabilities can be attached to events if the pertinent empirical arguments are lacking (Chapter 6). Conversely, empiricism is insufficient because explanations must be grounded in reasoning, and empirical generalizations must be deduced from principles of conduct, which is not always the case in practice. These subjects will be attractive for the early Keynes, at that stage interested in both knowledge and the truth.

On the other hand, the Libertarian in political terms Mill (*On Freedom*, published in 1859, is still a lively treatise) framed Benthamism into the context of its consequences for individual freedom both in the short and long periods. But these insights on utilitarianism would be rejected by Keynes whose ethical perception of *good* was based on virtue rather than on consequences. Nonetheless, a detainment on Mill may prove to be fruitful. In Mill's view happiness is only attained while pursuing one's own objectives, provided that the objectives are not happiness (Copleston 1967 [1994]). He criticized some of the premises and results of Classical Political Economy but accepted the Classical Core. He ascertained Utilitarianism (benefits minus costs) is more than egoism, although he sided with Bentham in that the principle of utility cannot be proved by means of deduction. This brings back the political thought of Mill. If collective happiness is the objective, then all people have a right to education and liberty. In other words, the social nature of individuals must not be neglected.

Mill though distinguished, not in organic terms but grounded on considerations associated to political philosophy, between individual and communal happiness. Accordingly, Mill launched an objection to the limited character of the utilitarian theory in terms of communal duty. The State then must take control of such social variables as income distribution (determined by tradition) and wages. Mill also wrote on the liberty of indifference. Hence for Mill human liberty also has political components. While Bentham thought he developed an a priori rationalization of social and political (and individual) relations, Mill was attentive to founding moral sciences by means of objective causal relations. This is due to the idea that the mind is—for Mill—an organic entity which captures empirical data, yet it is capable of reasoning, and hence induction is in Mill the bridge between empiricism and apriorism.

As the upshot of all this admixture of apparently disconnected insights, Mill also presented utilitarianism as an appropriate definition of moral consciousness. However, there are other perspectives on utilitarianism. The life of Francis Ysidro Edgeworth (1845–1926) is the subject matter of a chapter of the cultural historian Keynes's book entitled *Essays in Biography* (1933). Edgeworth promoted the use of mathematics in political economy with contentions akin to those made in physics when searching for an epistemological foundation for the social sciences. Everything was quantifiable, why not? According to Baccini (2007), Edgeworth adopted the notion of man as a pleasure machine to solve the maximization problems in ethics and economics, thereby setting the mathematical bases of utilitarianism while broadening the frequency approach to probability. These discernments preceded Keynes's aim at merging utilitarian ethics and the logical theory of probability (Chapter 6). No wonder Edgeworth was the favorite proto-economist of Keynes—perhaps of the young Keynes, after Malthus. In Edgeworth's reading of utilitarianism, the ethics of the individual and of the society appear as two progressive—not organic—stages of an activity. There also were opposite views. Herbert Spencer declared that evolutionism is the principle behind the essence of both natural and social sciences, being critical of utilitarianism. Keynes was evolutionary but not of the Spencerian-type.

Moderation always exists in science. There were suggestions on subtle modifications to the initial bases of utilitarianism. Henry Sidgwick (1838–1900) was representative of ethical philosophy in the Victorian era, offering an introspective explanation of moral motivation. Sidgwick's account of *good* is predominantly naturalistic. He also combines ontological with epistemological comprehensions, perhaps laying the groundwork for the changeover to political philosophy via the ethical consideration of rights. A great contribution. Sidgwick was a visitor to the Keynes house when Maynard was young and represents the culmination of the utilitarian strand but Sidgwick eventually departs from traditional aprioristic Benthamism and rather grounds its ethical insights on intuition. This can be attributed to the idea that he, according to Copleston (1967 [1994]), perceived a divergence between psychological and ethical hedonisms. The latter must search for its core outside human psychology, and this part is fulfilled by 'metaphysical' intuition in the quest for the fundamental moral issues. At the end Sidgwick returned to the external philosophy of common sense in morals. His discovery also had a bearing on his conception of political duty. Indeed, he wrote about the principles of prudence, justice, and benevolence as applicable to human decisions. In this view, utilitarianism is thus universal hedonism. But Bentham had not differentiated among its ethical, political, and behavioral connotations. Choices were ambivalent (dyadic) for him, and thus were not subject to the use of probabilities in decision-making processes (see Chapter 6).

In summary, utilitarianism is akin to a strand of atomism suitable for undertaking both individual and public decision-making by increasing revenues and reducing costs, comprising a Scientific Research Program that would be straightforwardly rejected by Keynes (Chapters 8 and 11). Among many of its flaws, pleasure is difficult to be measured. Instead, Keynes advocated only the extreme version of act utilitarianism, stressing specific contexts, as he privileged discretion and an ethics of value. But for Keynes, utilitarianism was also a superficial account of what we must do with an impact on our moral perspective. Instead, the Moorean question of what is *good* would be eventually of interest for Keynes, who was searching for the essence of ethics in the form of virtue (Chapter 2). For while Bentham, Mill, and Sidgwick represent morality without religion, Moore stands for religion without morality (Dostaler 2007). For understanding this dichotomy, we turn to Moore's search for the foundations of morality.

3.4 Moore

The Cambridge philosophers founded analytic philosophy around 1912 in part against Kantian-type idealism and in general metaphysics. It is the set of philosophical strands denying reality to the object of knowledge, that is, they negate the existence of entities which are independent of consciousness. George Edward Moore (1873–1958), Keynes's mentor in philosophy and especially in ethics, was among those founders of analytic philosophy. *Good* was, for him, an indeterminate intuition which brings about complex states of mind. In addition, he was a believer in intrinsic merits rather than in virtue. Thus, he was a consequentialist as he aimed to demonstrate that doing *good* was the same as being *good*. To begin with, Moore provided an intuitionist conception of *good*. For him, a non-natural property was one that can exist in time (not beyond the times). Moore then defended an unanalysable notion of *good*, involving its non-natural and a non-metaethical view which is normative, since he endorsed ideal consequentialism.

There are rules in Moore's morals. By considering the existence of non-natural properties in ethics, he brought a robust metaphysical side to a field that became intuitive. Moore accentuated two elements of nonnaturalism: Realism and a commitment to the autonomy of ethics, advocating the awareness of impersonal consequentialism grounded in the principle of organic unities. Yet there is a calculating angle in Moore's consequentialism—like in the Classical Utilitarianism—since in his view the effects of both goods and evils may be accumulated. Nevertheless, it is now acknowledged that moral principles can only be understood using preference orders.[6]

Moore was perceived as very theoretical and hence inexpedient in academic communities, in addition to non-materialistic, unworldly, and spiritual. Other than that, he stands out within his circle at any rate as the master who clarified many neglected essential epistemological and ethical problems. During the process, he contributed to the collapse of idealism in Britain, supplanting such conceptions as 'idea by concept,' and 'judgment by propositions' (referred to as relations between concepts, see Chapter 6).

In *Mind* (1899, p. 180), Moore states that 'concepts are the unique objects for apprehending knowledge.' He then disapproves of the idea of general propositions. A thing is what it is and is not definable by its relationships to other things. Moore then rejects idealism by investigating the weight of the arguments of propositions in his aim of explaining the world. Being means being perceived and thought denotes being experienced. In other words, sensations derived from perceptions of different *fit* objects[7] are united by means of conscious processes. But consciousness for Moore is more than an object.

3.4.1 Deepening Matters

Once again for Moore, questions are the basis of his open method of enquiry. His first point of attention is *good*. Moore distinguishes between what is *good* and what it is to *do good*, and this is the essential question of his. To generate these contentions, Moore exhibited an attitude grounded in the use of common sense related to sense data, especially in his study of sensation and perception. Common sense[8] is the ultimate test of Realism in propositions, even though differences of opinion may emerge. For this reason, Moore's philosophy in this issue falls just short of empiricism. But Moore launches two correlated vital questions: What is *good*? and What actions must be performed for doing *good*? (see Chapter 11). For the first, he concludes that *good* is a simple notion. *Good* is neither a non-natural quality nor a metaphysical property of things. According to Copleston (1967 [1994]), the notion of a super-sensible reality in ethics has no worth for Moore. *Good* does not exist for its own sake and hence is not suitable to be expressed as an assessment. Hence only moral philosophy can reveal the qualities of the things possessing a high level of *good*.

As for the second question, the fact that *good* is indefinable does not mean that it is subjective, such that our duty as individuals is to ponder the *good* in the actions to be undertaken and at the same time investigate the truth of a given moral proposition.[9] The implications are twofold: that *good* has been eliminated from the category of intrinsic qualities, and that Moore is a consequentialist in ethics. Here (and this is very relevant) ideas mean universal meanings rather than individual states of mind, a contention that will be questioned by Keynes (Chapters 8 and 11).

On the other hand, the analysis of the explanations of the quality and evolution of an entity are implicit in Moore's rejection of idealism. Moore related things to their causes relying on (yes) organicism, an ontological notion formally defined as the purposeful unity of things in both time and space in a distinct manner to addition (as seen in Chapter 2).[10] Moore was also troubled by the relationship between sensations and sensible data, while sensations are defined in the conventional form sensible data refers to the immediate objects arising from direct perception, which are different from sensations because the latter are more complexly perceived. Beyond that contention, in accordance with Copleston (1967 [1994]), Moore dealt with the phenomenological exploration of the essence of sensible perception. For that objective, he posed questions focused on the nature and implications of *good*, its intrinsic moral qualities, and the distinction between object and subject in terms of perception, paving the road for the musings of the young Keynes, who was interested in finding the meaning of propositions[11] (Chapters 6 and 8).

With respect to perception, what accounts for the differences in our states of mind is the presence of separate external objects prompting universal states of mind, contending that common sense beliefs are more reliable than metaphysical—idealist—statements. However, the interpretation of such beliefs brings about difficulties. Moore affirmed that to discard beliefs it is necessary to provide more evidence on both quantitative and qualitative grounds. His aim was however the elucidation of enigmatic propositions, moving away from simple propositions. In addition, he approached the notion of *good* with the aid of moral intuition, wherein right and duty are examined in terms of their possession of *good*.

Yet Moore was a non-skeptical empiricist in the sense of being reliant on experience but with concern for consequences. He can be classified as an impersonal consequentialist since for him moral laws deal with the effects of human actions, wherein ethics is about fulfilling by ourselves the universal mandate.

Moore relies on common sense, ascertaining that even though we have an internal life, we live in contact with the external world (he was rather shy, though). For example, he challenges Hume's skeptical phrase 'will the sun rise tomorrow?', rejecting Hume's psychologism, since physics predicts that the sun will continue to rise. The non-skeptical Moore was perhaps the greatest intellectual influence on Keynes, especially because in his early years, the former advocated common sense. Further, the Moorean dichotomy between doing *good* and being *good* (which Keynes eventually solves by distinguishing the two elements but unifying them in practice, see the ensuing paragraphs) forms the basis for Keynes's subsequent analyses of intuition, probability, uncertainty, and social habits (duty), and becomes a solid ethical foundation for his *A Treatise on Probability* (Chapter 6).

3.4.2 Yet Moore and Keynes Differed

Moore departed from traditional consequentialism in deontological terms (deontology being the normative ethical position that judges the morality of an action based on rules), sometimes described as duty-based ethics. For Keynes, however, moral rules are not consequentialist and therefore must not be subjected to the empirical investigation as fundamental—causal—values exist. This is the Platonic Keynes. In a word, Moore advocates that *good* is an ideal state of mind, automatically identifying doing *good* with being *good*, but Keynes, and this is an extremely relevant point, detached them by including the power of action in his philosophical vision (Chapters 8 and 11) but affirming they can cohabit after the effort of identification has been made. Fortunately, the dichotomy between being *good* and doing *good*, for Moore, requires a piece-meal causal consideration, since organic events are complex (Chapter 2). Moreover, since *good* is embedded into organic unities, the truth, personal affections, and esthetics and aesthetics are interrelated. Moore then provided the bases for ethical teleological intuitionism. However, Keynes reasons, if practical reason is introduced into ethics, there is no room for the naturalistic fallacy (an informal logical fallacy which argues that if something is 'natural' it must be *good*, for instance pleasure). This line of ethical thought goes from metaphysics (like in Kant) to empirical realism (like in Hume). Contrarywise, Moore was interested in value as based on moral convictions and especially on reflective reason.

In *Principia Ethica* (1903), Moore's Golden Book, *good* is thus an end as well as a means. Duty is an ethical (and a political) concept, and ethical thought and judgments of intrinsic value are irreducible, such that individual commitments and social identifications are interconnected. Moore's truth is conceptual, but ethics is embedded in everything since there is not a value-free comprehension of human needs. Another theme connected with the organic *good* is its interrelation with other notions. Moore's ethics is thus substantive, but perhaps contradictory. For example, he deprecated rationalist psychology, but his conception of duty is still utilitarian,[12] which has rational psychological bases. Where general utility cannot be defined, he suggests assessing individual considerations. Moore thus evolves from moral skepticism to conservatism, proposing an ethical conditional analysis.

In Moore's Golden Book he brings arts and love into the framework of his rational utilitarian ethics, which deepens the intrinsic value of *good*. Ideals (not in the sense of German idealism, but in that of aspiration) are the purpose of human action and set the criteria for progress as well as states of consciousness. Therefore, only things with intrinsic value provide gratification for consciousness, leading to a better external world. Moore's theories dealing with the essence of values and the irreducibility of ethical concepts are the basis for Keynes's ethics and decision-making criterion but under uncertainty, a concept arisen from epistemology—Hume—not from ethics.

A hallmark of Moore is that he distinguished between causal and ethical truths when attempting to identify the foundations of ethical intuitionism. Interestingly enough, the ontological belief in the existence of organic unities is the basis of propositions for the identification of the truth (witness the impact of this ascertainment on Keynes's core in Chapter 2). Yet propositions must be treated as if they were intuitions, which can neither be proven nor disproven at the beginning (Chapter 6). Conversely, values are objective and multiple and come from intuition. Thus, and this is of utmost importance, propositions and values are interlinked. If moral consciousness is a synergetic unity of the two, the ontology embedded into organicism can be applied to questions of value (*good*), epistemology (organic systems), and esthetics aesthetics (beauty, friendship, love, and art). In summary, Moore creates an intuition-based moral, personal, but consequentialist ethical view (from which the causally-oriented ethics of Keynes took exception), which ultimately suggested the adherence to conventions (Chapter 2).

Principia Ethica (1903) by Moore examines in its first chapter whether ethical judgments are grounded in *good* when applied to conduct, but Moore is no practitioner. He wonders how much *good* a thing or a whole possesses. In this chapter he criticizes those ethical theories which consider that *good* exists relative to time and those that only define *good* in relation to other things. Moreover, *good* must never be mixed up with pleasure or progress. In Chapter 4 Moore treats hedonism as an intuition, but also as both egotistic and utilitarian, concluding that hedonism is a variant of naturalistic ethics, hence rejecting hedonism. Further, he hereby highlights the fallacy of confusing means with ends. One can add that egoism and utilitarianism are not necessarily contradictory. In Chapter 5 Moore states that some describe the supreme *good* in metaphysical terms, but metaphysics can have no bearing on defining *good* itself, since metaphysics affirms eternal reality as the sole *good*.

In Chapter 6 he affirms that neither volitions nor feelings can be related to *good* since they are not analogous to awareness, and awareness is critical to Moore's notion of *good*, even though awareness is silent on the definition of *good*. Determining whether an object is *good* is not the same as understanding how it is cognized. In Moore's ideal perfection, both the defense of moral claims and intuitive moral judgment are still appreciated. This Moorean chapter about the essence of *good* as a concept and as a form of action was considered as progressive by the Bloomsbury Group (1902–1930). Yet some critiques ascertain that Moore overstates the distinction between moral and scientific truth. According to Dostaler (2007), in Moore's view *good* ties ethics with politics, whereas beauty connects ethics with esthetics aesthetics. For Moore, and this is a crucial notion of his, *good* may either be a means or an end, and this may be the reason why he equates doing *good* with being *good*. The tie between these two entities must not be taken for granted, at least for Keynes who was a fine distinguisher. The scenario is as follows. For Moore, being *good* is organic, whereas doing *good* is related to rules, since doing *good* is accomplished by actions with organic results. Keynes accepted the first part but not the second one (rules), since he also supported rebellion, at least in his early years (see Chapters 4 and 11 of this book). In Chapter 6 of *Principia Ethica*, Moore finally categorizes which things are *good* (not

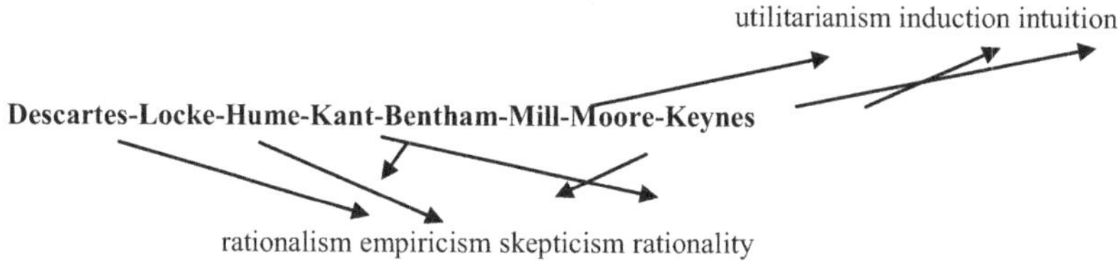

Fig. 3.1 Keynes and his immediate philosophical branches

good itself): states of mind which are perceived through intuition, such as beauty, truth, and friendship. This is the essence of Moore's ethics, and that of Keynes but modified (Chapter 11).

Moore was arguably the most influential figure for Keynes, especially since their relationship went back to Keynes's early years, and the early Keynes was in some sense sensitive to initial conditions. But late Keynes's approval would not be conceded without reserves (Chapters 8 and 11). The outline of the epistemological-ethical connection envisaged by Moore is hereby contrasted with Keynes's view. But this contrast can also be put in context with other philosophical branches in Europe as illustrated here (Fig. 3.1).

This chapter is a chronicle of the foremost contentions produced by Keynes's predecessors in political philosophy (Burke, Locke, Mill), epistemology (Locke, Hume, and Mill), and especially ethics and ontology (Moore). The consequence of the examination of these philosophical strands, mainly the Moorean version of the doctrine of organicism, is Keynes's investigation of the essence of the philosophical generality of economics. Finally, the concept of *good*—originally dealt with by Moore—appears in every thought and action of Keynes along with the shadow of Burke's notion of expediency in the short term. The next chapter expounds crucial philosophical contentions made by Keynes's contemporaries rather than by his past influences, highlighting the mutual influence among them.

Appendix 3.1: Keynes and Newton

Both John Locke and Isaac Newton (1642–1726) accepted the principle of atomism and the existence of homogeneous movements (that is, the principle that all movements have the same quantitative pace and effect). Contrarily, Keynes advocated the principle of organic uniformity in nature and in the social realm with a heterogenous impact on the part of its elements. In this vein, Keynes's Eton unpublished papers, or *JMK/UP* (1902–1910 [1921]), especially 'Miscellanea Ethica' (Chapter 4) criticize both determinism and atomism since for Keynes the universe was inherently disorganized. Nevertheless, the stimulus provided by Newton to members of the 'Locke Connection' is associated with his deductive and introspective method grounded in his peculiar absolute view of the cosmos. Newton only needed to verify what he already knew, incarnating scientific intuition. While Keynes did not believe in apriorism, deduction, or physicalism, he conceded that Newton gave sense to a mechanical world in a universe wherein according to Newton absolute knowledge, certainty, atomism, and homogeneity prevail in his quest for an eternal truth. Keynes recognized Newton's *SRP* as an overall contribution to later generations based on its atomism but 'organic' magnificence.

In 'Newton the Man,'[13] Keynes writes that the last of the magicians had one foot in magic and the other in rationality, and he benefitted from both of those great perspectives. For him, Newton's gift was that of an intuition full of conjecture. Newton's imagination was a laboratory, suitable for experimenting with different complex orders grounded in hidden but accurate mechanisms and connections. Newton follows, in Keynes's words, a continuous esoteric tradition with a perspective of generality. Newton, the founder of modern physics and one of the three most important mathematicians,[14] was a genius of fruitful reflection. Perhaps following Newton, Hume examined the nature of knowledge by inspecting the essence and implications of induction, which was eventually defied by Kant's idealism. The legacy of Newton to science, knowledge, and the truth is incalculable, both in terms of his method, and his insights into the function of the universe. We will examine whether Keynes's philosophy is closer to Einstein's relativity and generality, especially when conceiving the spirit of *GT*.

Appendix 3.2: Keynes, Ancient Greece, and the Continental Europeans

Eternal Europe. The present time regression demonstrates Keynes's multiplicity of sources since such notions as intuition, judgment, convention, logic, knowledge, rational belief, precariousness, credibility, and fragility can be traced out to philosophers in Ancient Greece. To say the least, they had a sway on Keynes's conception of uncertainty as exposed in *TP* (see Brown-Collier and Bausor 1988). A part of Keynes's roots comes from Plato and Aristotle, mostly absorbed during his juvenilia years. Keynes acknowledged the relevance of moral figures, for example: 'Plato's absorption in the good itself' (1933 [2013], p. 442). Or, 'We existed in the world of Plato's Dialogues' (1933 [2013], p. 445). Keynes's early idealism was a form of Platonism inherited from Moore (Fitzgibbons 1988 [1990]). Perhaps the consequence of the influence of Plato was that for Moore and Keynes *good* is only discernible by intuition.

On the other hand, 'Keynes's notion of happiness is connected with Greek Tragedy…with [*overcoming*] indecision and uncertainty. It is associated with virtue' (Carabelli 2019, p. 215). Further, in a Nietzschean-type of statement, Keynes paraphrases the Greek tragedy: 'There is an element of happiness in most heroic states of mind' (1905, p. 8). 'Keynes's…is an ethics of virtues' (Carabelli 2019, p. 215). But [his]'view of the good and happy life is really close to Aristotle's' (Carabelli 1998, p. 12). Keynes considered Aristotle's *eudaimonia* may prove to be a basis for solving real ethical problems (Carabelli 2019, p. 224).[15] If *eudaimonia* is akin to Keynes's happiness as the activity of the soul, it is linked to the dichotomy being *good*-doing *good*, especially after full employment is conquered (Chapters 2 and 9). In addition, Keynes's philosophy deals with organicism, an idea originated by Aristotle. Surprisingly, [*Aristotle is*] 'the first to…identify how an economy at the macro level could fail' (Brady 2017, Abstract). The conception of moderation is associated to the supreme philosopher as well. The distance between ethics and political philosophy is short. Indeed, *Eudaimonia* and human amelioration also require a just and expedient government. It is easy to discern the continuity of these ancient concepts in the development of European ideas. As a matter of fact, the Ancient Greeks pioneer the idea of democracy, the basis of the Swiss-born Rousseau's and Locke's conceptions leading to the *Laissez-faire* (Waligorski 1994). Last but not least, money is a social creation rather than a natural entity. This is an obvious antecedent of the message of *GT*.

Finally, Keynes also had some late prominent Continental philosophers and economists as nurturing springs. The idea of Happiness reappeared in the Enlightenment, being replaced by utility in Neoclassical theory, which was rejected by Keynes. Additionally, Rousseau is an inspiration for Keynes regarding the latter's critique of rationality, but considered by Keynes as an advocator for the *Laissez-Faire* (Chapter 8). The Irish thinker—obviously a non-continental philosopher—Burke has already been mentioned in this chapter. Keynes would also criticize the stances of Marx, Lenin, Trotsky in the field of political philosophy, especially in 'The end of the Laissez Faire' (1925). On the other hand, some critiques and experiences associated to Frenchmen (Etienne Mantoux, Georges Clemenceau) and inspirational sources from Germany (Carl Melchior) are chronicled in Chapters 5 and 8. Additionally, the Austrian philosophers Wittgenstein and Freud, and the economists: the Italian Sraffa, along with the Austrians Hayek and Schumpeter are mentioned in Chapters 4, 7, or 8. The Polish economist Michal Kalecki is briefly mentioned as a simultaneous creator of macroeconomics (according to Joan Robinson). Interestingly no continental influences—which aided to the making of Keynes's milieu, especially in his younger days, except that by the universal Plato, are mentioned in 'MEB,' perhaps Keynes's main philosophical *oeuvre* (Chapter 11).

Notes

1. Explanatory data in this context may either be quantitative or qualitative.
2. Moore will write about private duty, which is outlined in the final part of this chapter.
3. This is the Hume's problem.
4. The core of the Classical political economy will be disputed by Keynes on the grounds of uncertainty, organicism and non-self-regulating systems.
5. The young Keynes attempted to solve these problems by grounding the logic of propositions (Chapter 6) in probability.
6. Keynes would reject the exclusive emphasis on quantitative calculations (see Chapters 6 and 11).
7. A 'fit' object is one the contemplation of which ought to give rise to a state of mind which is *good*.
8. Coupled with the sobriety of statements and the concomitant clarity in proposals.
9. Keynes will investigate the distinction between logical and moral propositions.
10. The property of multi-directionality belongs to the realm of complexity.
11. Keynes would add the study of political philosophy and aesthetics, both fields directly related to ethics.

12. It is also for this reason why Keynes's political philosophy is based on expediency.
13. 'Newton the Man' was written in 1933, but read publicly by his brother for the first time in 1946.
14. The other two were, arguably, Archimedes (287–212 BCE) and Karl Gauss (1777–1855).
15. The literature on the role of happiness in Keyenes's philosophy is now a subfield, mainly dealt with by the authors Anna Carabelli and Mario Cedrini (several dates).

References

Andrews, David R. 1999. "Continuity and Change in Keynes's Thought: The Importance of David Hume." *The European History of Economics Thought Journal* 6, no. 9: 1–21.

Baccini, Alberto. 2007. "Edgeworth on the Foundations of Ethics and Probability." *The European Journal of the History of Economic Thought* 14, no. 10 (March): 79–96.

Brady, Michael E. 2017. "From Keynes Back to Smith and Aristotle: Liquidity Preference, Hoarding, and Speculation," December 23. https://ssrn.com/abstract=3092485.

Braman, Chuck. 1996. "The Political Philosophy of John Locke and Its Influence on the Founding Fathers and the Political Documents They Created." In *My General Views on Philosophy, Politics and Economics*, blog Chuck Braman. https://www.chuckbraman.com/political-philosophy-of-john-locke.html. Accessed 15 June 2015.

Brown-Collier, Elba K., and Randall Bausor. 1988. "The Epistemological Foundations of the General Theory." *Scottish Journal of Political Economy* 35, no. 3: 227–41.

Carabelli, Anna. 1988. *On Keynes's Method*. Basingstoke: Macmillan.

———. 2019. "Keynes's Aristotelian 'Eudaimonic' Conception of Happiness and the Requirement of Material and Institutional Preconceptions: The Scope for Economics and Economic Policy." *Anualli della Fundazione Luigi Einaudi* LIII, 213–26.

Copleston, Frederick. 1967 [1994]. *A History of Philosophy. Volume VIII: Modern Philosophy: Empiricism, Idealism, and Pragmatism in Britain and America*. New York: Image.

Dostaler, Gilles. 1996. "The Formation of Keynes's Vision." *History of Economics Review* 25, no. 1: 14–31.

———. 2007. *Keynes and His Battles*. Chentelham, UK: Edward Elgar.

Fitzgibbons, Athol J. 1988 [1990]. *Keynes's Vision: A New Political Economy*. Oxford: Clarendon Press.

Helburn, Suzanne. 1991. "Keynes and Burke." In *Keynes and Philosophy: An Introduction*, edited by Bradley W. Bateman and John B. Davis, Chapter 2. Aldershot, UK: Edward Elgar.

Keynes, John Maynard. 1902–1910 [1921]. Keynes's Unpublished Eton Papers, JMK/UP 1902–1910, 1921. https://archiveshub.jisc.ac.uk/data/gb272-jmk. Archive Search. Archive Centre, King's College, Cambridge. https://archivesearch.lib.cam.ac.uk/repositories/7/archival_objects/285279.

———. 1905. "Miscellanea ethica." In *JMK/UA/21*.

———. 1925. *The Economic Consequences of Mr. Churchill*. London: Hogarth.

———. 1933 [2013]. The Collected Writings of John Maynard Keynes. In *Volume X: Essays in Biography*, edited by Austin Robinson and Donald Moggridge. Cambridge: Cambridge University Press.

Moore, George E. 1899. "The Nature of Judgment." *Mind* 8, no. 30: 176–193.

———. 1903. *Principia Ethica*. Reprinted in Prometheus Books' Great Books in Philosophy Series. http://fair-use.org/g-e-moore/principia-ethica/. Accessed 8 January 2015.

Skidelsky, Robert. 2016. *The Essential Keynes*. London: Penguin.

Waligorski, Conrad P. 1994. "Keynes and Democracy." *The Social Science Journal* 31, no. 1: 79–91.

CHAPTER 4

Keynes's Horizontal Connections

Proper feedback stimulates the application of intelligence and sensitivity. This chapter deals with the influence of Keynes's contemporaries on him and his sway for them, a reaffirmation of the evolutionary trait of his philosophical path. This is due to the idea that reciprocal influence is sounder than unilateral influence (meaning from the past to the present like in Chapter 3). Keynes was a strong individual partly because he always believed in cooperation and the consideration of others' opinions, especially in both academic and practical matters. In his case these matters were related to ethics and epistemology, and—since the 1920s—he linked political philosophy to both ethics and economics.

Section 4.1 outlines his teamwork with the 'Apostles'[1] in the 1920s. Section 4.2 deals with his philosophical cooperation with the Bloomsbury Group in the 1920s and 1930s. Section 4.3 describes his crucial collaboration in economics with the *Keynes Circus* (the Robinsons, Sraffa, Kahn) in the 1930s. Section 4.4 details his philosophical feedback with his contemporary Cambridge professors (Russell and Wittgenstein) in the 1920s and 1930s. It also reviews the relevance of the late academicians in the footsteps of the 'Locke Connection' (1950s and 1960s): Popper and Lakatos

J. Muñoz-Bandala, *Keynes's Evolutionary Spirit*,
Palgrave Insights into Apocalypse Economics,
https://doi.org/10.1007/978-3-030-90150-9_4

for providing a methodology for the post-assessment of Keynes's philosophy. The importance of Keynes's early papers is explored in Appendix 4.1 since they were one of the backbones of his evolution. Notice that unlike in the former chapter the influences on Keynes preponderantly come from Britain.

4.1 The 'Apostles'

Burke shaped Keynes's advocacy for action in the present and denial of the future's influence, and Moore influenced Keynes's beliefs about the notion of *good*, but John McTaggart Ellis McTaggart (1866–1925)[2] delineated Keynes's relative and almost unconscious views on time.[3] Time is highly relevant in economics and finance. But this is only a prelude for narrating that the first group to influence Keynes was the 'Apostles' (1820–1970), an association of intellectuals whose connection deepened as the result of Moore's teachings, and this group would become the forebear of the Bloomsbury Circle (1905–1930). According to Dostaler (1996), Keynes studied in Eton between 1897 and 1902 while personally pursuing the rewards of including philosophy in his cultural activity. Then he was accepted as an 'Apostle' in 1902, becoming an 'Angel' in 1911. His 'Apostles' membership would be one of the biggest milestones in his life.

The 'Apostles,' also known as the *Cambridge Conversazione Society* (1820–1970), with its heyday occurring in the 1910s, was an elitist association for intellectual discussion comprised of selected Cambridge University members from four of its colleges. They met to debate many topics but especially those related to God, belief, ethics, and politics, conceding special importance to the pursuit of the truth. This group influenced Keynes's views on capitalism in terms of both its morality and fragility. The 'Apostles' were a group of bohemians oriented toward triumph and public relations with interdisciplinary concerns for the application of their insights and Moore's. Such orientations would later be extended by the Bloomsbury Group, who sustained similar contentions on such apparently disconnected themes as the First World War, the futility of human nature, imperialism, elitism, dynasties, existentialism, and free style in expression (in literature or painting, see Chapters 8, 9, and especially 11). They chased the truth in knowledge with authenticity, enhancing the power of the intellect. Keynes would share their discernments on the consequences of ignorance. Keynes was formed in the 'Apostles' as an economist-philosopher, their insights founding his practical activity undertaken in the 1920s, 1930s, and 1940s. The 'Apostles' were also humanitarians voting against utilitarianism (Chapter 3), affirming that it is the environment and its organization that shape the human mind and spirit rather than the dual pleasure-pain principle, which also precluded the role of imagination. For them, utilitarianism assumed equality in values but at the price of considering men as machines who were artificially rational and democratic. They also defied materialistic societies, guided instead by the idea of duty, obligation, and the liberal man.[4] A favorite topic of theirs was love and the properties of beauty. They were skeptical about induction, also considering that knowledge may be fallible.

They distinguished between the two worlds: the real for undertaking action and the phenomenal for accomplishing individual progress. Keynes would combine these two worlds but in successive stages because of the evolutionary character of the requirements of their tasks. The 'Apostles' always searched for the many-sidedness of the truth and discarded the employment of pure opinion, but paradoxically maintained secrecy with respect to their objects and principles while filtering propagation. Their thoughts were focused on the innermost nature of things, being incidentally involved in the analysis of religion.

In their intellectual emancipation they considered the outside world as one of the decays but simultaneously opined that maintaining growth is about being in contact with the outside world. They were therefore open-minded, exhibiting common sense, perception, and charm but also intellectual wandering. In their war of ideas (brainstorm sessions, in modern wording) they professed belief and conscience, but also entertained doubts and confessed dislikes. They were concerned about words, generated inter-generational friendships, and considered that tolerance strengthens character; after all, their personalities were not uniform. They shaped Cambridge philosophy from outside the classrooms giving form to the epistemology of modernism in Britain underpinned in Moore's examination of general ethics. This would also be the concern of the young Keynes, who took this task to a high level of accomplishment as can be seen in his concerns about the results of both World wars (Chapters 5 and 12) and the writing of 'My Early Beliefs' (1938). The 'Apostles' was a group comprised of undergraduates, graduates, and professors. Among their exceptional devotees previous to the Second World War, at Keynes's time, were not only George E. Moore, but also the philosophers

Bertrand Russell, Ludwig Wittgenstein, and Frank P. Ramsey (1903–1930) (Appendix 6.1); the economist Gerald Shove (1887–1947); and the critic Desmond McCarthy (1877–1952).

4.2 The Bloomsbury Group

The Bloomsbury Group perpetuated the Apostles' beliefs and disquietudes but reformulated and deepened their inquiries. The intellectualism and artistic orientation of the Bloomsbury Group (1905–1930) were prominent during the whole first half of the twentieth century. Its adherents produced profound discernments with worldly interests in literature, esthetics, criticism, pacifism, sexuality, and feminism. Bloomsbury was Cambridge in exile—the site of such old 'Apostles' as the biographer Lytton Strachey (1880–1932), who maintained a nurturing correspondence with Keynes, affirmed; the author Leonard Woolf (1880–1969); and Edward Morgan Forster (1879–1970), who wrote *A Room with a View* (1908) on the effects of unemployment on an individual. Recall unemployment would be the main concern and the basis of Keynes's heuristics in *GT* (Chapters 2 and 11).

Other members were the author Virginia Woolf (1882–1941), the arts critic Clive Bell (1881–1964), the founder of the Thursday evening gatherings Thoby Stephen (1880–1906), the writers David Garnett (1892–1981), and Gerald Brenan (1894–1987), the poet Vita Sackville-West (1892–1962), and the painters Roger Fry (1866–1934), Vanessa Bell (1879–1961), Duncan Grant (1885–1978), and Dora Carrington (1893–1932). Most of them had a foot in the Edwardian Era (1901–1910), employing their social networks and relying on self-confidence for the demonstration of rebellion against conventions as formulated in the Victorian Era (Chapter 11).

The Bloomsbury Group excelled in arts by contributing insights and works to art, biography, history, politics, economics, and international affairs, among other fields (Appendices 11.1 and 12.3). The Group resulted from the joining of the Strachey's and the Stephen's families. Their focus was on Post-impressionism in many facets of life, adding both color and clarity to many topics, in great part because Post-impressionism was not favored by the establishment. Their moral standards were high and influenced their general life-view more than in the case of the average person.

In 1905 the Bloomsbury Group started an activity known as *The Friday Club*, where participants gathered in informal meetings to read something—substantial—together. In 1920 *The Memoir Club* was born, adding regular lectures with the proviso that they should always tell the truth about their thoughts, experiences, and discoveries. The members of these groups also maintained correspondence with one another in the years to follow. They were not utilitarians since for them morality, which is of course superior to pleasure, must be the key element associated with the increase of the variety of *good* things, thus augmenting happiness, not utility. Their ethics were about friendship, happiness, and the products of the intellect. They also rejected those moral systems consisting of commands or based on customs, traditions (see Chapter 11), or orders. However, their vision may be considered as the adult extension of that of the 'Apostles,' being both ethically oriented and wide-ranging as well as far-reaching, perhaps because the Group comprised sensitive individuals. They were always launching questions on such topics as agnosticism, beauty, irreverence, and *good*. Yet their discussions had the purpose of nurturing creativity rather than fostering aspiration as in the 'Apostles.' Queen Victoria (who reigned between 1837 and 1901) was the ideological symbol of the nation, later succeeded by her son Edward (who reigned between 1901 and 1910). The Bloomsbury exhibited radical styles of life between 1905 and 1930 which would not be seen again until the 1960s in other latitudes but were conservative on matters related to money—unlike Keynes—(Chapters 8 and 11) and poverty. The Bloomsbury Group consolidated the shaping of the development of British Modernism, but they did not believe in radicalism as a form of revolt, and would rebel against some of the traditions of this epoch as symbolized by the belief in hierarchies, families, and social classes, which in their view impeded progress in both morality and the economy.

But rebel morality must also be organized. Fortunately, Moore's book (1903) succeeded in codifying an ethic for Bloomsbury, partly taking as a starting point the discussions of two generations of 'Apostles,' blending political ideal goods, such as democracy, with common sense. Recall that for Moore *good* was a non-material property and we intuit its presence. This is so because the supreme *good* is an organic unity. *Good* is an end in itself taking the forms of the truth, aesthetic emotion, and friendship. *Good* is simply referred to as affection in the topic of the nature of love. This ethic thus ascertained that *good* must be tested in experience after being felt in accordance with Moore's philosophy of individual consequentialism (Chapter 3). In this respect, the Bloomsbury Group was engaged in practical experimentation with open-mindedness. The Group distinguished themselves by their enthusiasm in the search for a new civilized society, propounding the radical transformation of a threatened civilization. Their means for overcoming moral decay and recurrent economic depressions were the enhancement of the arts and thinking in the 1920s–1930s, and the reasonable move toward tradition and convention in the 1940s (Chapter 11).

4.2.1 *The Bloomsbury Group and Keynes*

Keynes would read papers in *The Memoir Club* (see Chapter 11). Keynes's philosophical attentiveness soared after the publication of *Principia Ethica* in 1903. For the Bloomsbury Group, being *good* was as important as doing *good*, although Keynes contended that the link between these realms could not be taken for granted but instead had to be sought in practice. According to Davis (1991a, b), for Keynes objects must be *fit* to generate good states of mind, noticing that universal *good* is not necessarily superior to individual *good*. He was eventually able to distinguish between the truth and knowledge. The former was his motivation in his younger days, but the latter would be more valuable for him in his activities as a policymaker and a pamphleteer in the 1930s. Bloomsbury also reaffirmed Keynes's acknowledgment of intellectual debts—restricted to Britons (Chapters 8 and 11), which would turn him however more conservative and rationalist in the late 1930s as he became more interested in the real world at this stage. Keynes's worries in that same decade echoed his contention that national *good* in the form of employment and wellbeing was not being appropriately pursued (Chapter 9), just like in the 1920s and the 1940s when he considered that international *good* in the form of peace and stability was not being practiced (Chapters 5 and 12).

The Bloomsbury Group, along with the *Keynes Circus* (1930–1931), made *The General Theory of Interest, Money and Employment*, or *GT* (1936) possible and philosophically grounded and oriented (Chapter 9). Keynes's membership in the Bloomsbury Group made clear for him the weight of evidence in proposals. Bloomsbury also propelled his talent for the writing of biographies in the forms of either psychological portraits or cultural achievements (Appendix 3.1, Chapters 7 and 9) and served as the root for his aesthetical and practical visions on the arts (Appendix 12.3). In addition, Keynes would become the Director and stockholder of the Theatre of the Arts of Cambridge (founded in 1936) after being a sponsor of the Bloomsbury Group and an investor in the arts, mainly in Continental paintings (see Appendix 12.3 on CEMA).

4.3 The *Keynes Circus*

The third influence on Keynes and particularly on the making of *GT* (1936) was the *Keynes Circus* (also referred to as the *Cambridge Circus*), aiding Keynes to consider money—and its by-product notion the interest rate—as the mobiles of the economic system, and shaped his attitude to money, seeing it as a means. This is of course an ethical insight (Chapter 8). The Circus consisted of Keynes's younger colleagues focusing mainly on the birth of macroeconomics, at the time an intuited but diffuse and elusive core concept. The members of the *Keynes Circus* were his former pupils Richard Kahn (1905–1989), James Meade (1907–1995), Austin (1897–1993), and Joan Robinson (1903–1983), and the Italian-born Piero Sraffa (1898–1983). This intellectual movement emerged after the publication of *A Treatise on Money* or *TM* (1930) (see Chapter 7). The motivator of their polemics was to elucidate the meaning of the twin insights of the metaphors the 'Widow's cruise' and the 'Danaid jar' (recession and inflation) as adjustment mechanisms—but also upshots—of the economic system.

The *Keynes Circus* helped Keynes liberate from his unconscious theoretical shackles, but also made patent that *TM* did not offer a coherent theory for the determination of both output and employment (Chapters 2 and 7). Sraffa, for example, defied many of Keynes's heuristic concepts, such as liquidity preference, labeling it as vague and not useful for everyone. He also challenged the notion of marginal efficiency of investment (he was an adversary of marginalist economist to reinstate Classical Political Economy) along with Keynes's protective assumptions of an exogenous money supply or a fixed supply of consumption goods. Based on these concepts, Sraffa stated that Keynes was too classical in his contentions. However, this was just a case of infighting. Sraffa defended Keynes against the Austrian-born Friedrich Hayek's (1899–1992) criticism of *TM* by proposing that the interest rate is the theoretical foundation of capital. This occurred in 1931. Sraffa, a tremendous theorist in his own right, would suggest a set of heterogeneous interest rates across industries which would provide a foundation for Keynes's linkage between the real and the monetary systems (a sample of a complex system), making him move away from the contentions of Swedish-born Knut Wicksell (1851–1926) for whom a 'natural' interest rate existed. The Polish-born Michal Kalecki (1899–1970), another creator of macroeconomics (according to Joan Robinson, see below), was not accepted into the *Keynes Circus*, perhaps because of his ideology oriented to excessive planning and perhaps because of his deficiency in the command of the English language. Keynes was obviously a master of the English language and this included a distaste for deviationists.

Returning to Sraffa, he affirmed that Keynes backed past marginalist (microeconomic) criteria, which he saw as incoherent, thereby contending that Keynes was still an orthodox economist, unaware of the evolution followed by Keynes at that moment. However, he admired Sraffa's talent: 'for whom nothing is hid' (1933a, 'Thomas Robert Malthus,' p. 97). Sraffa critically examined the metaphysical notion of value. Keynes did not rely on the Classical theory of value on which all previous economists have relied, but eventually Sraffa's stance on this issue played a special role in the shift from *TM* to *GT (Chapters 7 and 9)*. As Sraffa critiqued the neutrality of money advanced by Hayek, Keynes progressed with respect to his conception of liquidity, letting go of his former notion of 'bearishness-bullishness' in *TM*, which was more heuristic and intuitive. Finally, Sraffa shared an appreciation for the role of history in economic analysis along with Keynes.

In addition, the Italian economist was against unrealistic assumptions; for example, the assumption corresponding to the natural interest rate as championed by Knut Wicksell (1851–1926) (Chapter 7). With this contention in mind, Keynes could then be more focused on the mutual movements between the interest rate and liquidity giving support to his contention that monetary productive economies differ from real-world economies, paving the way for the explanation of variations on the part of the main variable: output. This would be consistent with Keynes's consideration that the short—non-natural—interest rate is the best device for expediency purposes. Joan Violet Robinson befriended by Sraffa would become a defender of *GT*, long after it was published, even dimensioning later contributions to macroeconomics (Chapter 10). Her stance was highly relevant due to her world reputation as a theorist and an expert on economics philosophy. Robinson, despite her multiple interests, sources, and contributions, remained faithful to Keynes's core. However, she commented that the idealistic contentions posed by Keynes in the 1930s have gone too far.

The other motivator—technically, the mobile—proposed for Keynes's complex system would be the Kahn-Hawtrey multiplier, a heuristic hydraulic-type device relating the effect of injections (and leakages) on output. Richard Kahn was the major contributor to this multiplier in 1931 (Appendix 7.2). Kahn also wrote (1984) that *TM* had not assumed away an inelastic aggregate supply, partly validating the message of *TM*. Both thinkers, Kahn and Sraffa, affirmed that *TM* was too abstract, perhaps because of Keynes still assumed there that output was constant, hindering the gist of his own later discovery in *GT* (Chapter 2). These suggested heuristic improvements on the part of the *Circus*, however, would help make Keynes's static model complex and organic in *GT*. A conclusion from these insights is that *GT* was conceptualized as early as 1932.

4.3.1 After the Storm (1936)

After *GT* was published, Meade was a simplifier of Keynes's theory whereas the Robinsons were propagators of the Keynes revolution. Joan Robinson would integrate the Classical and Keynes's ideas (1940–1970). The Robinsons and Meade would become post-reviewers of *GT*. These contentions are outlined here—before the foundations of *TM* are described in philosophical terms in Chapter 7—if only because they make clear how Keynes's thinking evolved by taking notions from multiple specialists and philosophers (horizontal connections), which was typical of his partly extroverted way of doing science. In other words, these paragraphs highlight the virtues of cooperation and consensus when making science. The Quixote required to hear external voices.

4.3.2 Keynes Self-Defense in the Transition Between TM *and* GT

The *Keynes Circus*[5] became a large continuous seminar discussing *TM* and hence serving as a benign filter of ideas. Keynes would also debate at this epoch against the dissenting economists Arthur Cecil Pigou (1877–1959), Dennis Robertson (1890–1963)—to whom Keynes acknowledged his intellectual debt in the Preface—and Ralph Hawtrey (1879–1975) about his 1930 (*TM*) book. This has a historic importance because Keynes would give the final blow to orthodoxy some years later (1936), in part because of the feedback resulting from the *Circus*. He reconsidered the problem of stagnation as laid upon entrepreneurs' phenomenal expectations instead of real profits, ridiculing hoarding as the source of the latter. According to Johnson and Johnson (1977), the *Circus* also exhibited disagreements with other monetary theory specialists, for example, Hayek whose debates are well-known and chronicled, highlighting the fact that they had distinct philosophies, for example, that of Hayek who was strong defender of the self-regulating mechanisms of the market system and an advocator for private money. In all cases, Keynes's evolution—transition at this epoch—would improve orthodoxy.

The *Circus* had other side effects. Concurring with O'Donnell (1992b), Keynes's project on the road to *GT* included two intermediate books that were never written: *Footnotes to the General Theory (a short explanatory sequel)* (see Harcourt and Riach 1997; Muñoz 2008) and *A Treatise and Introduction to Economic Principles*. These works would reinforce the understanding of Keynes's core with respect to two key issues: Uncertainty for explaining the mechanisms for the determination of national income (Chapter 9), and Conventions about its adherence on the part of former irrational agents facing uncertainty (Chapters 11 and 13).

At a later stage (after *GT* was published), the *Circus* would progressively offer both intuitive and practical arguments for supporting Keynes's insights on the role of money and business cycles, specifically defending Keynes's heuristic idea of liquidity preference. There also were immediate associates of the *Circus* (Keynesians) acting after 1936 with multiple interests but demonstrating in many cases a misunderstanding of Keynes's philosophical foundations (not the formal schools studied in Chapter 10). They were Roy F. Harrod (1900–1978) (Chapter 12), Michał Kalecki (1899–1970), Maurice Dobb (1900–1976), Abba Lerner (1903–1982), George L. S. Shackle (1903–1992), John Hicks (1904–1989), Nicholas Kaldor (1908–1996), Lorie Tarshis (1911–1993), Richard Stone (1913–1991), and Evsey Domar (1914–1997). Ironically, this admixture of followers and contenders comprised a further generation of revisers inspired by Keynes's outspoken philosophy: His core. Some of them combated Keynes or followed distinct directions in Keynesianism armed with Keynes's principles! Keynes was thus a heir of (and the inspirator for) people who in some cases covered relevant themes for Cambridge University, not only about political economy but also related to moral philosophy and modern history.

4.4 The 'Later' Philosophers: Russell, Wittgenstein, Popper, and Lakatos

In his late 30s, Keynes connected mainly with Bertrand Russell (1872–1970) and Ludwig Wittgenstein (1889–1951) (part of the formerly mentioned groups) in terms of their awareness on atomism and the philosophy of language, respectively. Russell and Wittgenstein belonged to Cambridge University in times when philosophical stances were changing: Cambridge University was turning his attention to analytical philosophy moving away from traces of idealism. Russell, as the first characteristic philosopher of the aftermath of the 'Locke Connection' (if Keynes is now the departure point), used a scientific approach for backing his vision of logical atomism, contributing it to epistemology. He was not interested in results, claiming that the methods belonging to formal sciences such as logic and mathematics must be assigned to all sciences. In this frame of mind, a formal logical analysis of expressions must be undertaken since ordinary language does not show its structure, so the formal arrangement of its expressions must be identified, wherein expressions consist of logical propositions (see Chapters 3 and 6).

For Russell, propositions were clusters of sensible expressions in the search for meaning, being of two kinds: atomic and molecular. The former type emerges when objects have a given—detached—relation among them while the latter type arises when words express logical connections among quantities. But Keynes stated that the relevant relationships are those between qualities (see Chapter 6). Russell—like Moore—was interested in accuracy but contended that expressions are seldom accurate in social sciences in which time and space are relative due to the dynamism of human conduct. Going backwards, Russell started his philosophical path with Bacon and continued to Moore, affirming that neither induction nor empiricism must be utilized for assessing the role of methods or the results of theories, advocating instead a logical formalistic analysis of science. Russell co-authored with Alfred North Whitehead (1861–1947) *Principia Mathematica* (1910–1913) about the foundations of mathematical logic, advocating the analysis of an ideal language which must be the goal of humankind. This book was the third *Principia* relevant to Keynes after those produced by Newton and Moore.

Russell, as an aprioristic atomist, believed in universals and atoms as the basic unit for analysis. Regarding apriorism he defended objectivity, the truth, and absolute knowledge. Moreover, Russell contended that morality is about thinking in a straightforward manner, aiming to reduce all philosophical insights to mathematical forms which means to deduce the truth from symbols. But he elevated his scope by stating that the relationships that matter most are the ones between proposals. While reasoning must be about objects, abstraction is about ideas and requires higher thought levels.

He promulgated education as a scientific pattern. For him, these two great types of sciences—physical and social—possess different assumptions. As a result, Russell considered that social changes are difficult and slow, but this stance generated contradictions for him, particularly given his opposition to private property. Russell's affirmations on the nature of propositions (not on atomic unities) are partially akin to Keynes's epistemological insights. Russell's philosophy is outlined here to make Keynes's contentions visible (see his core in Chapter 2), demonstrating that he was aware of the philosophical establishment, but that he had his own contentions, influenced by his practical activities and his rejection—or eventual acceptance—of received concepts. Russell, a first-rated brain himself, explicitly admired Keynes's intelligence.

4.4.1 Wittgenstein

Wittgenstein was an original philosopher, and this quality was assuredly appreciated by Keynes. Wittgenstein saw philosophy as an activity (but also as a means for attaining personal comfort), thinking of the world as ordered (an alien thought for Keynes), and is the archetypical philosopher of language. Initially, Wittgenstein considered language as a logical structure to be investigated (*Tractatus* 1921). Later he realized language is a way to grasp the essence of reality but contending the structure of language is a puzzle. Eventually he became aware language refers to ordinary life and can be understood by means of language games (*Philosophical Investigations* 1953). Consequently, he restricted the mission of philosophy to the analysis of language rather than to logic, mathematics, physics, or probability. He contended elements that do not represent atomic facts lack sense, although there are here examples in him of the relationship between realities and propositions giving space to organic unities. Therefore, language is relevant for the scrutiny of the truth as embedded in philosophical assertions but also in real-life situations. However, ethical statements are simply pseudo-propositions as for Wittgenstein no values exist. Hence language is not suitable for the expression of ethics, after all *good* is indefinable according to Moore. Thus, the structure of propositions must project the structure of facts, and neglect both normative and ethical propositions. For all these reasons ordinary private language is imperfect. In sum, in the *Tractatus Logico-Philosophicus*, language is descriptive and follows objective rules but in 1953 Wittgenstein considered language games as subjective reversing to some extent his initial stance but giving language a more dynamic characterization. Keynes died in 1946, but in his work this subjective but social view of language—about which both philosophers had some conversations—was acceptable which is reflected in his stance that discretion prevails over rules in the practice of economics and politics,[6] and persuasion through language is crucial for the accomplishment of economic goals.

Wittgenstein affirmed that aesthetics tells what words cannot. His general idea in this sense was that all philosophical problems imply a bad understanding of language. In other words, logic has a sense, but is a set of tautologies. Then he wrote about certainty, wherein doubts could be eliminated by the praxis of language (but uncertainty is a fact of life for Keynes). This was Wittgenstein's evolutionary approach for unveiling the foundations of thought. The presupposition in both books is that language is both a map of reality and a way of life, and Wittgenstein's letters are relevant for understanding these two principal stages of his philosophy. His comprehension of the roots of knowledge is useful for understanding the power of Keynes's writing and eloquence and focus on praxis. Moreover, this change in the epistemological atmosphere of Cambridge, partly enriched by the late Wittgenstein, would have a straightforward influence on Keynes in the 1930s and 1940s. Keynes thus took to practicing the power of ordinary language both for understanding philosophical entities and as a form of propaganda. Perhaps partly due to Wittgenstein's influence, Keynes used a new framework defined by new inter-relations in his novel conceptions in macroeconomics, especially in *GT*.

Summarizing, Wittgenstein (admitted in Cambridge with the aid of Keynes, just like Sraffa and Hayek, as Keynes believed in amity) is relevant for Keynes as the latter made use of language artistry in *TP*, *ECP*, *GT*, and 'MEB.' Both Russell and Wittgenstein were relevant for strengthening Keynes's notion of knowledge, but Keynes criticized their ordered—logical—conceptions of the world, especially that of Wittgenstein: 'A ... piece of scholasticism is Wittgenstein's view that all our everyday propositions are ... in order' (1933b 'Frank Ramsey,' p. 343).

4.4.2 *Karl Popper*

Perhaps one of the final but invisible consequences of the 'Locke Connection' was the Circle of Vienna (1907–1938), a movement that championed Logical Empiricism in the search for a criterion of undisputable meaning and the unification of sciences, with verificationism as its yardstick, justifying induction by means of intuition. This somewhat conventional association investigated the epistemological and ontological essence of the natural and social sciences, logic, and mathematics, chaired by Moritz Sclick (1882–1936) and Rudolf Carnap (1891–1970). They preached the non-existence of metaphysics, the defense of natural sciences, and the ubiquitous and unrestricted use of mathematics (also criticized by Keynes in *GT* and the 1940s), but imposing the laws of natural sciences to social sciences (physicalism). Yet verificationism is an insufficient demarcation criterion since events vary and a simple verification does not suffice as in physics (if something exists now it can be gone in a few hours), especially in the social realm. Nonetheless, this extreme version of the originally British tradition in epistemology affirmed that all knowledge comes from sensible experience (Chapter 3). We will soon see why Keynes belonged to another realm.

Eventually, Falsificationism with its insistence on permanent proof entered the stage. For Karl Popper (1902–1994) and Imre Lakatos (1922–1974), results are more relevant than method, the implication being science progresses through the enterprise of theory falsification, which is a tighter criterion than verification. Falsificationism was for Popper the radical solution to Hume's problem of induction. For supporting this contention, Popper penned insights on the insufficiency of inductive logic, wherein statements must be falsifiable since observation delivers neither universally valid nor definitive laws. Popper thus advocated Critical Rationalism as the justification of scientific propositions according to facts, stating that science advances through conjectures and refutations. Hence Falsificationism captures evolution in science. His insights may be useful for capturing the evolution of Keynes's insights (for instance, in Chapters 2 and 4). Skepticism is not useful since all that is needed are falsifications or meaning, as Wittgenstein had contended.

For Popper, then there must a critical discussion of those ideas and facts comprising theories. He did not include a historical dimension in his scientific tests of the truth when he suggested the contrast of theories against reality. Thus, Popper's methodological analysis advocated logical rigor for designing interconnected and testable hypotheses.

Popper wrote the *Logic of Scientific Investigation* (1934) against logical positivism, contending that knowledge only advances through 'healthy' criticism. For Magee (2000), Popper's explanations comprehend knowledge in both the human and natural worlds and thus guarantee epistemological certainty.[7] According to Magee, Popper contended that a logical asymmetry exists between verificationism and falsificationism, the latter being a method for generating reformulations that consider new contexts and experiences (Chapter 6), capturing dynamism. The implication is knowledge goes beyond human thinking and this contention backs the insights produced by the former members of the 'Locke Connection.'

Furthermore, proposals must be informative, and hypotheses must not be ad-hoc. Thus, Popper's verdict was that science must be a guide for innovation, not for confirmation as in pure physics. He also insisted that observations are full of theories to be falsified. Hence Falsificationism is the demarcation principle between science and non-science. Errors become an advantage for the society since the knowledge obtained through imagination is subject to criticism and improvement. For Popper unproven ideas must be avoided especially as a guide for scientific practice. Experience made through observations or experimentation is the sole norm to be used in Falsificationism. Popper, like Hume and Keynes, was not convinced that a scientist could derive universally valid laws by departing from pure observation, and even less so in the social sciences. Keynes, like Newton, selected theories that departed from intuition (Appendix 3.1). But Newton was a physicist. Keynes instead found it impossible to initiate social research without an ideological basis. The point here is not the assessment of the contribution of Popper but considering Keynes's theories have stand Falsification.

4.4.3 Lakatos

Popper's theory would require of more gradual sophisticated criteria than automatic—naïve—refusals of single theories. This contention validates the usefulness of the Lakatosian methodology heralding sophisticated Falsificationism for enunciating Keynes's evolutionary vision in this book

(Chapter 2). To understand Lakatos's insights in terms of Keynes's endeavors it can be stated that the enigma of the relation between intuition and induction is relevant for Keynes since he advocates its use in ethics and epistemology in the 1920s and the 1930s along with probability as a further step for the attainment of knowledge, but instead he was a fragile verificationist (Chapters 2, 6, and 9).

Popper's critical rationalism and (naïve) falsificationism overcame the (naïve) principle of verification vocalized by the Vienna Circle in the 1920–1930s. But thereafter Lakatos (1970, 1976, 1978) exchanged naïve for sophisticated Falsificationism. Popper got rid of isolated theories wherein a single refutation was sufficient for discarding them, considering them as devoid of sense or despised as 'metaphysical' after being refuted. More realistically, Lakatos focused on Scientific Research Programs or *SRPs* (Chapter 2), which rejection by evidence against reality must be gradual, implying that that set of theories is no longer progressive, but it can evolve or even return (Chapter 13). For Drakopoulos and Karayiannis (2005), Popper's naïve Falsificationism, Kuhn's paradigms, and Lakatos's Scientific sophisticated Falsificationism set the foundations of post-positivist philosophy of science. Their methodologies may examine the nature and progress of interrelated theories. *SRPs* are also expedient because they are interdisciplinary. For these reasons, we borrow Lakatos' methodology, even though this book is a narrative of Keynes's own methodology (Chapters 2, 3, and 6). The Keynes's aspects evaluated by Lakatos' methodology are findings, influence, criticism, impact, and ultimately evolution.

To put matters in context, British philosophy in the twentieth century was initially dominated by Moore and the analytical philosophers, then by Russell and the first Wittgenstein, thereafter by Logical Positivism, and finally by the second Wittgenstein. Then Popper stepped into the scene and Lakatos would continue his work. The methodologies of the latter philosophers are brought here because they constitute a stimulus for the investigation on the nature of growth in economics with the aid of interdisciplinary material, being appropriate for analyzing the contributions of individuals or schools in terms of both theory and practice, namely Keynes.

This chapter deals with three of the breakthrough and progressive Keynes's associations that shaped Keynes's life when he was a Cambridge Don. The first two were philosophically oriented (The 'Apostles' and Bloomsbury), while the third one was economically tilted (the *Keynes*

Circus). These groups strengthened Keynes's individualism focused on creativity in his most receptive years, the 1920s, the 1930s, and the 1940s, when he became influential in both academic and public policy circles. Summarizing, this chapter outlines the contentions produced by two contemporaries of Keynes (Russell and Wittgenstein) and the perspicacity of two Post-Keynes methodologists for assessing the evolutionary character of Keynes's scientific work (Popper and Lakatos).

In a refreshing change of pace, Chapter 5 deals with Keynes's philosophy of action as an economist responding to the challenges posed by the aftermath of the First World War, namely payments and recessions, on which he would produce *The Economic Consequences of the Peace* in 1919 and its sequel in 1922. Yet Keynes displays at this epoch his gift as a writer and as persuader about political matters in the international arena with a philosophical grounding: organicism. The theoretical and practical essence of the 1919 book is identified according to its Lakatosian core. The result is Keynes attains no less than the unification of Europe underpinned by his economic and moral footing.

Appendix 4.1 The Magic of Keynes's Early Papers (1902–1910; 1921)

Magic is about the powerful display of imagination and inspiration at the appropriate moment. Keynes early philosophical disquisitions are one of the most remarkable accomplishments of his life, although they were relatively neglected until the 1980s. The characteristics of his papers are originality, depth, curiosity, and innovation. They are also peculiar and personal even though the 'Apostles' were to some extent the inspiration for Keynes's unpublished articles (*JMK/UA*) and some published papers (*JMK/PP*). Keynes entered Eton College in 1897 and left there for King's College, Cambridge University in 1902. The creation of these writings started circa 1900 and gained momentum in King's College circa 1908.

In this phase he also produced juvenilia writings, family papers, and correspondence. His philosophical interests were still quite varied at this point, and he used his internal background, intuition, and experiences for sharing his knowledge, values, and emotions by means of both writing and debating as a liberal thinker. Around 1900 he penned articles praising the intellect of peculiar historical figures, for example, 'The character of the Stuarts: How far was it responsible of their misfortunes'

(JMK/PP/31/3, 1900), focusing on that family dynasty of the seventeenth century. Other papers, some of them about Continental authors, written for the Eton Literary Society are: 'Cromwell' (JMK/PP/31/5, 1901), who gained artificial political power, but was a non-conformist in religion; 'Essays on Bernard de Morlaix of Cluny' (JMK/PP/33, 1902), who lived in the twelfth century; and 'Essays on Peter Abelard' (UA/16, 1902–1903), who lived in the eleventh century. Abelard was a scholastic who fought against the political and religious dogmatism of his time, rejecting violence in favor of words as a piece-meal solution to problems. Keynes would eventually do the same in economics by means of persuasion.

The unpublished articles (1902–1910; 1921) archived in the library of King's College, Cambridge University, are relevant for the identification of the road followed by Keynes as a juvenile philosopher. Their rationale, nature, and significance are enormously varied, but they are mainly devoted to ethics and epistemology (seldom to ontology and political philosophy), also giving an idea of how Keynes became concerned with social matters. Skidelsky (2016) analyses[8] 'Ethics in relation to conduct' (JMK/UA/19/2, 1905), 'Miscellanea Ethica' (JMK/UA/21, 1905), 'Egoism' (JMK/UA/26, 1906), 'The political doctrines of Edmund Burke' (JMK/UA/20/3, 1901), 'Virtue and happiness' (JMK/UA/24, 1905–1906), 'On the principle of organic unity' (JMK/UA/35, 1910; 1921), 'A theory of beauty' (JMK/UA/23/3, 1905), and 'Science and art' (JMK/UA/32, 1909). Skidelsky's analysis makes evident the depth and reach of Keynes's thought.

'Ethics in relation to conduct' is about Keynes's core, specifically how Keynes conceives doing universal *good*, a quest related to the conflict between personal and temporary values, setting the bases for the evolution of Keynes's ethics (Chapter 11). Moore's distinction between being *good* and doing *good* was a concern of the highest relevance for Keynes in this epoch, when he affirmed that they must be balanced for taking the appropriate ethical stance. Eventually Keynes would conclude they can be mixed but that they are two separate entities, even though he is not ready yet to undertake this giant task on demonstration. Skidelsky (2016) ascertains that 'Miscellanea Ethica' consists of transitional notes on Moore's ideas about the multiplicity of recipients of *good* and the *fitness* of objects for the sake of *good*. *Good* is objective, but there is an asymmetry between *goodness* and *fitness*. Keynes's metaphysical assumptions about the characteristics of reality in this *oeuvre* will be the core of his *magnum opus* and beyond. His assumptions result from his acceptance of Moore's theory of organic unities but from the optics of a young man.

In addition, Keynes argues in some papers that probability relationships are objective, which implies that knowledge must be based on experience. But here Keynes goes beyond Moore's sense data and Hume's sensations, arguing that no subjective appearances exist, a contention that he modifies only circa 1926, after Ramsey's advice for considering the subjective dimension of probability choices (see the making of *TP*, Chapter 6). On the other hand, Keynes writes, in 'A Theory of Beauty,' that there is general uniformity in human sense organs (the 'principle of uniformity') in terms of perception, which makes the case for an objective consequentialist ethics, but also may support utilitarianism and democracy. This is the young Keynes. At the end, since the 'principle of organic unities' is applicable to the goodness of individual minds, *good* is universal and *fitness* applies only to perceptions, leading to *good* states of mind. However, Keynes would later affirm perhaps contradictorily in a Nietzschean or a Freudian style that actual and rational thoughts are distinct[9] (Chapters 6, 8, and 11).

According to Skidelsky (2016), in 'Ethics in relation to conduct' Keynes affirms that Moore relied on a utilitarianism of the type of impersonal consequentialism, whereas Keynes initially advocated act utilitarianism, although he later changed to embrace virtue ethics. Keynes also advocates the *Principle of Indifference* for neutralizing the effects of the unknown (Chapter 6), but since ethics is associated with epistemology, these Keynes's views also explain his opinion on the limitations of forecasting (Chapters 6, 10, and 12). Hence Keynes extends here his ethical assertions into other spheres, broadening his analysis of themes in knowledge such as uncertainty (Chapters 6 and 9).

Davis (1991a, b) states that according to the paper 'Egoism,' the universal *good* and the *ought* are disconnected, unlike in Bentham, Smith or Moore. This is a variant of Hume's contention that the 'ought' is not derived from the 'is.' The implication is that rationality and moral perfection do not exist on their own but must be gained. This is a first clue for understanding the Keynes's lack of belief in the existence of a self-regulating—certain—economic system (Chapter 2). Keynes also states there that egoism is superior to altruism since one's *good* today is preferable to one's *good* tomorrow (with an accused influence from Burke, see next paragraph). However, this quandary launches the question of what is preferable: to save our soul or to save others? Keynes eventually solved this problem by turning his energies to social and international endeavors, but this was an expedient decision, rather a philosophical one.

Another paper setting the bases of Keynes's subsequent philosophy is 'On the principle of organic unity,' which makes the case for an organic universe that perhaps destroys the absolute belief in methodological individualism and atomic certainty. The latter concepts support rationality, self-regulating systems, and democracy which happen to be the tenets of the Classical core (Chapters 2 and 10). In the paper 'The political doctrines of Edmund Burke,' Keynes progresses from the *Principle of Indifference* to the political doctrine of prudence in expediency after modifying his formerly rational perspective on the evolution of humankind. His focus on short-term problems was formed at this time when he followed Burke's assertion that short-term expediency is vital (Sect. 3.1).

Following Skidelsky (2016), the paper 'The adding-up problem' (1904) tells that Moore's organic unities were inspired in Hegel's organicist philosophy. This is highly relevant and means that *good* (in action and beauty) is not additive but rather holistic, for example, in the case of an individual. As synergy or the fallacy of composition exists, the world is 'organic' (every atom is multi-directionally and dynamically interrelated with others). In practical terms, our decisions and acts affect other people in a dynamic setting and vice versa. Hence, the Classical—Smithian—core assumption of the independent and individualistic *Homo Economicus* is false. Aggregates (and the relevance of total outlooks) are thus the unit of analysis for Keynes, and this insight would found his notions of European unity in 1919 (Chapter 5), his creation of macroeconomics in 1936 (Chapter 1), and of course his conception on international unity in the 1940s (Chapter 12).

According to Skidelsky (2016), the paper 'A treatise on probability' (TP/A/1–2, 1904) demonstrates that Keynes likens the Classical logic on probability to the methodology of the physical sciences. This logic artificially validates induction and advocates the automatic belief in orthodox contentions. But induction was for Keynes only a psychological process (like in Hume), attaching artificial weight to evidence. Instead, probability for Keynes was undefinable (like ethics), though it can be formulated as a relationship between proposals in open and dynamic systems (Chapter 6).

According to Moggridge (1992, p. 115), Keynes's preeminent early papers are 'Truth' (JMK/UA/18/1, 1904), 'Modern civilization'

(JMK/UA/22, 1905), 'The present position of metaphysics in the society' (JMK/UA/33, 1909), and 'Have we a panacea?' (JMK/UA/37, undated). These papers result from his collaboration with the 'Apostles' and are informative on the identification of ethical and social problems from a novel perspective, related to the gleaning of insights.

'Miscelanea Ethica' (1905), 'Egoism' (1906), 'Ethics in relation to conduct,' and 'A scheme for an essay on the principles of probability' (1908) address issues raised by Moore's *Principa Ethica*, basically states of mind depend upon the principle of organic value.

To sum up, the magic of these texts lies in Keynes's ability to overcome inherited contentions and expectations. Moreover, Keynes's core contentions on ontological, epistemological (chiefly on uncertainty), ethical (especially on moral intuition), and political philosophy problems are formed at this time. Still, they will be refined and unified posteriorly, thanks to his lesser introspect attitude assumed from 1913 (Appendix 4.1). In these papers he demonstrated that evolution is more than an escape from classical thoughts. The only remaining major amendments in his ethical philosophy will appear in 'My Early Beliefs' (Chapter 11) when Keynes's realized that the meaning of his life had changed. For Keynes states of organic consciousness have nexuses with real activities.

Notes

1. It was founded by G. Tomlinson (1794–1863) in 1820.
2. For McTaggart, time is unreal. His insight is akin to Kant's conception: Time is a product of consciousness. Nevertheless, McTaggart rejected idealism since for him the world must be restored to reality.
3. Time is relative in terms of its connection with change.
4. Perhaps following the route of the 'Locke Connection'.
5. It must be distinguished from *Keynes's Club* (1909–1937), which was comprised of undergraduates.
6. The use of different levels of complexity in language permitted Keynes to persuade politicians and communicate with the masses. Further, he used subjective forms and emotions in his writing.
7. Statements based on tradition, speculation, prejudices, habits or the like pertain to the realm of insecure knowledge.
8. The orders of both *UA* and *PP* follow that of 'The papers of John Maynard Keynes' in *Janus*, an online catalog of the Library of King's College (see References).

9. Our desires and aversions as human beings are not rational (Freud, Nietzsche, Dostoyevski, etc. in the times of Keynes).

References

Sources

Davis, John B. 1991a. "Keynes's Critiques of Moore: Philosophical Foundations of Keynes's Economics." *Cambridge Journal of Economics* 5, no. 1 (March): 61–77.

———. 1991b. "Keynes's View of Economics as a Moral Science." In *Keynes and Philosophy: Essays on the Origins of Keynes's Thought*, edited by Bradley W. Bateman and John B. Davis, 89–103. Aldershot, UK: Edward Elgar.

Dostaler, Gilles. 1996. "The Formation of Keynes's Vision." *History of Economics Review* 25, no. 1: 14–31.

Drakopoulos, Stavros A., and Anastassios Karayiannis. 2005. "A Review of Kuhnian and Lakatosian Explanations in Economics." *History of Economics Ideas* 13.

Harcourt, Geoffrey C., and Peter Riach (eds.). 1997. *A 'Second' Edition of the General Theory*, Volume I. New York: Routledge.

Johnson, Elizabeth S., and Harry G. Johnson. 1977. *The Shadow of Keynes*. Chicago: Chicago University Press.

Kahn, Richard F. 1984 [2011]. *The Making of Keynes' General Theory*. Cambridge: Cambridge University Press.

Keynes, John M. 1933a [1972]. 'Thomas Robert Malthus.' In *JMK CW Vol. X. Essays in Biography*, edited by D. Moggridge. London Royal Economic Society.

———. 1933b [1972]. 'Frank Ramsey.' In *JMK CW Vol. X. Essays in Biography*, edited by D. Moggridge. London: Royal Economic Society.

———. 1938 [1933] [1972]. 'My Early Beliefs.' In *JMK CW Vol. X. Essays in Biography*, edited by D. Moggridge. London Royal Economic Society.

Lakatos, Imre. 1976. *Proofs and Refutations*. Cambridge: Cambridge University Press.

———. 1978. *The Methodology of Scientific Research Programmes: Philosophical Papers Volume 1*. Cambridge: Cambridge University Press.

Lakatos, Imre and Alan Musgrave (eds.). 1970. Criticism and the Growth of Knowledge. In *Proceedings of the International Colloquium in the Philosophy of Science, London 1965*, vol. 4. Cambridge: Cambridge University Press.

Magee, Bryan. 2000. *Popper*. México: Colofón.

Moggridge, Daniel E. 1992. *Maynard Keynes: An Economist's Biography*. London: Routledge.

Moore, George E. 1903a. *Principia Ethica*. Reprinted in Prometheus Books' Great Books in Philosophy Series. http://fair-use.org/g-e-moore/principia-ethica/. Accessed 8 January 2015.

———. 1903b. "Refutation of Idealism." *Mind New Series* 12, no. 48 (October): 433–53. https://es.scribd.com/document/163302582/Moore-G-E-The-Refutation-of-Idealism-1903. Accessed 20 January 2015.

Muñoz, Jesús. 2008. "Keynes the Keynesian. A Lakatosian Insight into 'Keynes's' Probable Theoretical Contributions to Macroeconomics after 1937". In *Keynes and Macroeconomics after 70 years. Critical Assessments of the General Theory*, edited by Randall Wray and Matthew Forstater. Chentelham, UK: Edward Elgar.

O'Donnell, Roderick M. 1992a. "Keynes's Weight of the Argument and Popper's Paradox of Ideal Evidence." *Philosophy of Science* 59, no. 1: 44–52.

———. 1992b. "The Unwritten Books and Papers of John Maynard Keynes." *History of Political Economy* 24, no. 4: 767–817.

Skidelsky, Robert. 2016. *John Maynard Keynes: The Essential Keynes*. London: Penguin.

Wittgenstein, Ludwig. 1921 [1922]. *Tractatus Logico-Philosophicus*. New York: Harcourt.

———. 1953 [2009]. *Philosophical Investigations*, 4th ed. New York: Wiley.

PART II

Keynes's Early Activities: 1913–1935

Some years after being a civil servant in India circa 1911, Keynes served as an adviser to the government of Great Britain in the negotiations for the peace after the end of the First World War. Nonetheless, he was not satisfied neither in economic nor in moral terms with the plans of the Allies for the reconfiguration of Europe after that war. Thus, he resigned from his position and wrote the *Economic Consequences of the Peace* (*ECP*) in 1919.

Chapter 5 deals with his reflections on the future of Europe according to selective philosophical fields, mainly political and ethical from an informed ontic perspective. Section 5.1 is about Keynes's thinking circa 1919. Section 5.2 is an introduction to the topics studied in the *ECP*. Section 5.3 is a literature review of Keynes's general philosophy around 1919 (partly based on the insights described in the first three chapters of this book). Section 5.4 is about the general philosophy expressed in the *ECP*. Section 5.5 is an original and detailed account of specific philosophical insights of the *ECP* in terms of Epistemology, Ethics, Ontology, and Political and Social Philosophy. Both Sects. 5.4 and 5.5 give added value to the contentions of many authors on Keynes's philosophy. Section 5.6 concludes by means of offering an encompassing perspective on the young adult Keynes. Appendix 5.1 chronicles his earlier stage as an official in India circa 1913, as captured by the book *Indian Currency and Finance* (*ICF*). Appendix 5.2 reviews his contentions about the practicalities of the remedies of the war undertaken after 1919, expounded in *A Revision of the Treaty* (1922).

Chapter 6 deals with Keynes return to academics in the early 1920s with a logical writing: *A Treatise on Probability* (*TP*) published in 1921, which is the refined result of his early papers on the subject, attempting to link epistemological innovations on knowledge and uncertainty with the search for *good* and departing from the logical links between proposals, not between numbers. Appendix 6.1 is on the contributions of Frank P. Ramsey (1900-1930) about the subjectivity element to Keynes's objective-subjective core in probability circa 1926.

Chapter 7 explains how Keynes diverts his attention in 1923 to such breakthrough writings as *A Tract on Monetary Reform* (*TMR*) (1923) and *A Treatise on Money* (*TM*) (1930), the initial bases of his economics. The philosophical analysis of these books as a subject matter in itself includes two appendices about the transition of these two books toward *The General Theory of Employment, Interest and Money* (*GT*) (1936), namely 'A monetary theory of production,' and the contributions of Richard F. Kahn (1905–1989) circa 1931.

Chapter 8, on the 'Economic possibilities for our grandchildren' (1930), is more philosophical in essence relating a diversion from economics since Keynes explains there how the overstated loveof money was formed and how it can be overcome for the spiritual betterment of mankind, including appendices on the futuristic analysis of civilization such as 'The end of the Laissez-faire' (1925), 'Clissold' (1927) and others.

CHAPTER 5

The Philosophical Foundations of *The Economic Consequences of the Peace* (1919): The European Keynes

The purpose of this chapter is to synthesize the philosophical background and meaning of *The Economic Consequences of the Peace* (hereafter *ECP*) to follow the foundations and implications of Keynes's evolutionary legacy during these years. The connection of this chapter with Chapter 4 lies in that in both chapters Keynes makes a plea for the transformation of a threatened civilization, but in this case from a less contemplative viewpoint.

5.1 Keynes's Thinking circa 1919

Keynes's critique of the Treaty of Versailles (1919–1937) is conceived in terms of both its ethical foundations and consequences and viability. His methodological approach is especially suitable for this purpose as it is related to the coordination of theory and practice as well as to the use of both rationality and intuition, wherein his economic thought is the automatic materialization of his philosophical vision. The study of the complex social interrelations of the European system in 1919 is at the heart of the *ECP*. As every happening in Europe affected most of its countries and sectors, Keynes's belief in the lack of a natural order highlighted the need for practical and ethical intervention throughout the region in the form of respecting nationalities but at the same time recommending them

J. Muñoz-Bandala, *Keynes's Evolutionary Spirit*, Palgrave Insights into Apocalypse Economics, https://doi.org/10.1007/978-3-030-90150-9_5

remedies for turning their conditions as either debtors or defeated nations into situations of progress. Thus, in 1919 he championed practical cooperation since expediency in reparation was for him the road to freedom. He realized that the then-current situation in Europe—an organic whole in political, economic, and cultural terms—was a turning point in world history and this vision anticipated his overall legacy.

5.2 The Topics in *The Economic Consequences of the Peace*

The economic dimension of the *ECP* as well as the economic context and implications of the Treaty have been widely studied by many authors (Moggridge 1992; Skidelsky 1983; Hession 1984; Harrod 1951). The focus adopted here is synthesizing Keynes's underlying philosophy on this subject. In the *ECP* Keynes describes a mature European economy facing the payments of reparations and the effect of pronounced cycles but also suffering stagnation due to an excess of savings relative to investment opportunities, the latter being a topic later studied and refined in both *A Treatise on Money* (1930) and *The General Theory of Employment, Interest and Money* (*GT*) (1936). Inequality in the statuses among victor and losers is particularly relevant in the *ECP* since the objective of that moment was 'to achieve the economic reconstruction of the continent' (*ECP*, p. 113). In addition, the British economist was interested in the financial aspect of reparations to avoid human suffering.

Allegedly the effects of the Versailles Treaty were related to the ensuing conditions of growth, trade, and borders, whereby reparations were planned, but in practice the Treaty was based on revenge and irrationality. Keynes, realizing this, had a counterproposal about the economic and moral implications of the Treaty, as if unimproved it would bring about fragmentation, pauperization, and isolationism in Europe in the aftermath of the victory of the Allies in the First World War (this is 1919). The practical (Keynes's philosophy was eminently practical most of the time since 1919) result that he foresaw was that Germany would be unable to pay for the reparations of the damage caused in that war. In other words, for Keynes the so-called Carthaginian Peace (cf. Mantoux 1946) generated by the Versailles Treaty was going to be unfair for Germany and Eastern Europe, with systemic and perhaps unexpected economic effects, and would be detrimental in moral terms. The Treaty was solely the result of transitory, and myopic economic and political considerations and the

ECP is simply Keynes's answer. The book is still relevant particularly because of Keynes's philosophical understanding of humane conditions and permanent weaknesses. For him, the problem was that the Treaty was created under misleading—irrational and selfish atomic—bases.

He always had foresight and a gift for prophecy supported by intuition, which also generated qualitative predictions (Skidelsky 1996). Hence practicalities, intuition, and philosophy are linked, and it is convenient to associate the above-mentioned economic and political issues with the so-called Keynes's philosophic 'Universals' such as time, uncertainty, money, equilibrium, and organicism in the present analysis.

5.3 Literature Review of Keynes's General Philosophy

Writers on Keynes's philosophy are Sheila C. Dow, Victoria Chick, Anna M. Carabelli and Mario Cedrini, Roderick O'Donnell, Bill Gerrard, Tony Lawson, and Athol Fitzgibbons. Biographers of Keynes are Roy F. Harrod, Charles Hession, Daniel E. Moggridge, and Robert Skidelsky. Economic commentators on Keynes's work are Axel Leijonhuvfud, Don Patinkin, Milton Friedman, Friedrich A. Hayek, Jacob Viner, and Paul A. Samuelson. This list is obviously non-exhaustive.

The reading of those authors inform that the philosophical analysis of Keynes's writings was re-initiated in the late 1980s along with a new interest in his life and accomplishments, especially about his early days, reflecting a complementary interest in his economic thought which returned with enormous strength in the 2000s. According to Gerrard, the 'recent emergence of the "new" Keynesian fundamentalism associated with Carabelli (1986), Fitzgibbons (1988) and O'Donnell (1989), amongst others, represents a shift of weight in favour of Keynes's early philosophical papers' (Gerrard 1991, p. 99). However, this author contends that Keynes's philosophy matured or at least entered to a new stage during the *ECP* years. The validity of this ascertainment is patent in the next Sections. But who is Keynes the active thinker at this stage? Let's take some authorized opinions. The voice of the author appears in the synthetic choice of authors and contentions.

5.3.1 *A Bibliographical Summary of Keynes's General Philosophy*

For Harrod (1951), Keynes's principles are constructive. His contribution is related to method, vision, and approach, where uncertainty is pervasive, thereby impacting money, investment, and output. In the *ECP* he handles quantitative affairs that have been taken for granted, rejecting impractical principles, and contemplating transitory stages—not only ends—considering that interrelations among economic agents must lead to action. According to Davis (1994), the 'task of those who seek to explain Keynes's philosophical thinking …is, to demonstrate how Keynes resolved problems specifically in economics as a philosophical self-conscious thinker' (p. 158). Themes in the *ECP* are judgment, behavior characterization, induction, interdependence, uncertainty, and intuition.

For Carabelli (1998), Keynes's practical rationality is embodied in experience, whereas criticism is referred to logic. For him, investigation must not be empirical or rational. Keynes rejects certainty, perfect knowledge, and universal causation. He aims to achieve the art of reasoning in uncertainty. The truth is the objective and rationality as a means, complemented by intuition, must be practical and contingent—for example as associated to the remedies for reparations in *ECP*. Keynes's use of intuition with persuasion is linked to both convention and practice. For him theory must be operative and the choice of models an art. Uncertainty can modify stances, whereby events are non-repetitive. Presuppositions are linked to conclusions; that is, assumptions have practical consequences.

For Keynes, there is no such thing as logical independence (Carabelli 1992). Hence his issues are organicism, openness, and complexity. The British economist advocates the use of ordinary and non-demonstrative language, especially in the *ECP* (Chapter 4). There is also pluralism as phenomena are variable. He criticizes lack of clearness and generality as well as independence of events, but emphasizes relevance, being against the permanence of social forces and exhaustiveness. Non-isolated elements require open systems (our Chapter 2). He envisaged relative perspectives within the contingent situation because he was interested in the way things work. The mere consideration of these philosophical factors reflects evolution in his philosophical ideas, at least from 1921 to 1936, especially because Keynes's philosophical enquiry is refined when he participates in the Bloomsbury Group.

Marzola (1994) identifies Keynes's reconstruction of the psychology of the society in the *ECP*. She states that argumentation in Keynes's writings is both semantic and methodological. For her, Keynes conducts dissociations within a single thought, which generates a re-organization of elements. Rhetorical figures delineate distinctive content in the *ECP* (prefiguring *GT* Chapter 8).

Fitzgibbons (1988, 1992), when addressing Keynes's early philosophical work, states that he believes in what is probably true, wherein both art and reason must be used in investigation. Keynes represents a middle way between nihilism and quantification. Probability judgments arise from either convention or emotion, and rationality supposedly contains them as a law of thought. But a wider notion of rationality must be used according to Keynes, for example when examining the expectations of 'animal spirits.' Indeed, he rejects conventional knowledge wherein no excessive abstraction must be used; for him theory is a framework for intuition. Then, he enlarges the scheme of reasoning to both problems and policies, and thus his philosophy is inspirational. Keynes's issues, according to Fitzgibbons, are theoretical, methodological, and political, whereby ethical virtue concerns are ubiquitous (Chapters 5 and 7). This perspective stems from considering ethics as the basis for both political economy and public duty (Chapter 2), especially in the *ECP*. Nevertheless, there is no universal Keynes theory, and he does not fall into epistemological excesses. For him, the truth is the rational basis for action and uncertainty—its veil—is related to imperfect knowledge. In other words, Keynes's essentials are constant, but their application varies. Yet stated differently, Keynes is aware that theory is different from reality.

Fitzgibbons (1992) also writes that Keynes emphasizes intentionality in terms of *good*. He rejects mechanical views as they do not anticipate the complexity of politics. Instead, rational intuition must guide politics, based on the old right but this may be a return to a pre-enlightenment system of thought. His philosophy is about practical wisdom mixed with ideals, with an interest in both liberty and equality. For him, Keynes is relevant because of his recently discovered methodological roots, making sense in a wider context.

O'Donnell (1982, 1989) analyses rationalism, intuition, conventions, realism, and assumptions in Keynes. O'Donnell (1989) focuses on Keynes's early philosophy, whose issues are uncertainty, probability, information, public policies, practical principles, and social goals, with emphasis on clarification. O'Donnell sustains rationality. Rationality—arguably for this author—is the method for unification of knowledge in Keynes, but the issues of influence and continuity are also relevant. In this view, the British economist is also interested in induction, statistics, and aesthetics. The evolution of Capitalism into an ethically rational society is the middle way in all issues. Indeed, Moore's theory of *good* is a cause of Keynes's turning to the study of probability (recall that the multidisciplinary Keynes publishes *TP* in 1921), exploring the relationships between probable and ought, quantity and quality, and the parts and the whole.

For O'Donnell, Keynes's pursuit is philosophical up until 1908, but there is continuity—not evolution as for this author—in his philosophy from 1904 to 1921 and from 1921 to 1941. He investigates the foundations of certainty by means of a logical analysis, whose implications are the critique of the assumptions of perfect information and foresight, and the resolution of the problem of knowledge. Political economy or economics is for Keynes a moral science, a branch of logic, and a method. Shifting and complex elements are interrelated and interdisciplinarity is necessary. There must be evolution toward an ideal commonwealth. In this view, Keynes searches not for partial formulations (O'Donnell's wording), rather aiming for a synthesis at higher levels of generality, bringing about practical orientation (highly pertinent in *ECP*), whereby criticism is against premises, an insight forgotten by later economists (see Chapters 2, 6, and 10). There is symbiosis between diagnosis and cure and the objective is the truth. Keynes—arguably—holds an objectivist tradition.

Philosophy 'provided the foundations of Keynes's life' (Skidelsky 1983, p. 133). Skidelsky's Keynes is a non-conformist, writing with successive overemphasis. His aims are the truth, purpose, moral commitments, individualism, and the examination of social and intellectual traditions. The *ECP* is an elegy of a vanished age, and Keynes exhibits there his typical middle-way attitude (according to Skidelsky's great portrait).

Clarke (2010) thinks that uncertainty is the *leitmotif* of Keynes, evidenced by the behavior of economic agents. For Keynes the immoralist[1] arguments are more significant than rules. Thus, probability is an epistemic theory. In this sense ethics is consequentialist, as Keynes believes in an ethics of virtue. This contention is pertinent for framing the notions of *ECP*. Lawson (1994) considers that Keynes analyses the nature and mutability of social reality, witness the circumstances analysed in *ECP*. Indeed, Lawson refers to Keynes's realism in terms of both the subject of study and assumptions. Lawson and Pesaran (2009) also state that Keynes is interested in ontology. An example of this is Keynes's approach to organicism.

According to Dow (1991), Keynes's views on method and theorizing vary from poetry and intuition through lawyer-type arguments to formal logic and mathematics. He is also a pluralist in terms of categories, definitions, and language. For Dow, the impulse-convention dichotomy is relevant in Keynes's analysis of agents' behavior. In addition, the author of the *ECP* relies in terms of method, on personal interpretation, states of confidence, and 'animal spirits.' Motives and psychological uncertainties—for example in *ECP*—are also important, wherein complexity has its own logic. Austin Robinson (1947) considers that Keynes doesn't believe in the privacy of arguments. Keynes goes beyond his former ivory tower.

According to Chick (1992), 'Keynes's revolution consists in the choice of method.' Chick claims that, according to Keynes, deviations from equilibrium are the rule, with the consequence that Keynes's view is a framework of thought. For the British economist, constructiveness, intentionality, and prevalence are pivotal, which is related to the creation of a new science and the distinction of organic entities (like in *ECP*). For Andrews (2010), both Keynes's politics and economics are subsets of his ethics. Keynes represents reaction against tradition, dogma, superstition, and both economic and financial restrictions, his objective being a return to proper moral values. Last but not least, Harcourt (2001) writes that Keynes's economics is full of social purpose. He advocates real-world observations—for example after the First World War, rather than axiomatic approaches such as profit maximization (an a-prioristical conception), being innovative about the nature and method of theorizing,[2] not necessarily purely empirical in spirit. Further after knowing evidence, he eventually comes back to real-world problems.

5.4 The Philosophy of *The Economic Consequences of the Peace*: Problem, Hypothesis, Objectives

Keynes heuristically demonstrates how difficult it is to exhibit a stable path for growth in Europe in 1919. But his aim is to appeal to the wisdom of the few—persuasion is at his core, and his hypothesis is that the building of a real new order is imperative. Keynes's affirmations on the Treaty of Versailles (hereafter the Treaty) are about evolutionary justice and morality, but they can be considered as his Hegelian Owl, since relief for Germany would come too late.

According to Marzola (1994), in the *ECP* puritanism is the structure of capitalism. The implication is that capitalism should be preserved in a new era, but the momentary problems of that order are instability and—alas!—unemployment. Remedies are appropriate monetary schemes, government intervention, and international cooperation, based on organic interdependence and the consideration of an open-ended system. The aims of the *ECP* are practical, in terms of policies; philosophical, as forced reflection; and scientific. Keynes could see through problems by going straight to their centers.

For Heilbroner (1951), the Treaty (1920) is a vindictive process of peace. The *ECP* is an analysis of the harm that had been done, a Bloomsbury-style critique of society (Chapter 4), and a novelty as rebellion against international institutions. For Andrews (2010), the *ECP* advocates material progress, which leads to a state of mind in which people can proceed to the nobler exercises of their faculties. Skidelsky (1992, p. 542) writes that in 'the ECP…Keynes depicts a society whose capacity for enjoyment is crippled by the duty of non-consumption.'

5.4.1 *General Objectives of the* ECP *(First Chapters)*

Keynes states in Chapter 1 of the *ECP* that in the Treaty 'a large part of the addresses is concerned with spirit, purpose, intention, and not with concrete solutions' (Keynes op. cit., p. 24). He is a practical re-constructer of Europe in the *ECP*, his concern being to set the actual conditions for recovery. Europe is devastated but still conforms an organic unity. Goals are peace and stability and the objectives are a new civilization, freedom, and prosperity (Chapter 3 of the *ECP*). At a lower level of abstraction, rebuilding, compromise, and reconciliation are relevant. For Keynes, the Treaty broke the existing order without adding either content or practicalities. Hence the hypothesis of the book is that future disasters can be prevented by using appropriate methods which is underpinned by the selection of the proper assumptions. Overall—organic—improvement is therefore what is sought (Chapter 1 of the *ECP*). Before 1870, Europe 'was self-subsistent' (p. 4) but this process is reversed when the golden age comes to an end in 1914 (Chapter 2 of the *ECP*).

The renewal of life via the creation of realistic expectations is the purpose. History at that moment is concentrated on four individual—Northern?—leaders, but no eternal conditions exist and the deeper tendencies which were to govern the future could not be overlooked.

Hence realistic foundations would have to be set. For this purpose, it is necessary to depart from the actual course of events (Chapter 3 of the *ECP*). Critiques of Keynes (cf. Mantoux 1946) talk about the existence of an integrated economic order, even below the surface. This self-regulating and non-chaotic stance deserves no comments. Others would claim that Chapter 234 of the Treaty of Versailles is flexible about the burden imposed to Germany, but neither the Council of Four nor Keynes himself paid heed to it.

5.5 Specific Philosophical Insights from the *Economic Consequences of the Peace*

The rationale for the breakdown of philosophical topics into the branches of epistemology, ethics, ontology, and political philosophy in this section is that it allows the re-identification of Keynes's core as introduced in Chapter 2, with the purpose of making the evolution in Keynes's thinking visible.

5.5.1 Epistemology

Keynes's method is holistic realism, that is, he is interested in the organic problems of his time and place within limits. As praxis must arise from realism, both foundations and viability must be relevant in ethical and pecuniary terms, also assuming that time is historical rather than logical.[3] In Lakatosian terms, the inexistence of a self-regulated system, organicism, and uncertainty as perceived in expectations are at the core of *ECP*. Thus, he writes about uncertainty (like in Chapters 2 and 6) but at this stage applied to Germany's and Continental Europe's future. Yes, future written in singular. He is thus stuck on ends as he aims for external consistency, an issue not considered by others among the potential consequences of the Treaty.

In the *oeuvre* in question, he generates predictions, relying on observation, intuition, analysis, and interpretation, and using both persuasion and reasonableness as relevant means. Keynes's emphasis on epistemic organicism is confirmed in Chapter 1 of *ECP*, particularly in terms of interrelations, remedies, and consequences, particularly when he contends that the 'statistics of the economic interdependence of Germany and her neighbours are overwhelming' (p. 7). There existed the risk of common ruin in Europe as an organic entity, worse than the sum of national disasters. This does not come as a surprise since both uncertain and relative situations, knowledge, and qualitative predictions analysed with objectivity pervade his writing, under the core assumption that the system lacks self-regulating mechanisms. This ascertainment is consistent with the dissection of Keynes's core (our Chapter 2).

Consequently, he preaches action in Chapter 1 of *ECP*, since natural and permanent plans are at play and consciousness in the form of concrete action in the face of the lack of self-regulating mechanisms must be a living reality. This relates to the analysis undertaken in Chapter 2 of *ECP* on 'the actual character of the peace' (p. 10), because it is necessary to select such chief unstable elements as population, religion, property, government, classes or psychological instability, and not focus solely on ideal or abstract elements or "universals'."

According to Chapter 3 of *ECP* both irrationalism and selfishness reign during the unfolding of the Treaty. But practicing economists must possess a thorough understanding of processes and institutions with realism, not ruling out scientific imagination. Furthermore, no unreal questions must be introduced, that is, logic must be coupled with intuition. Keynes's psychological critique of the Main Four, the leaders of the core negotiating nations, is illustrative. For example, in Chapter 3 he writes that Wilson 'was not sensitive to his environment' (p. 17). Success entails 'resources, fertility and knowledge' (p. 18); therefore, a concrete application of knowledge to the state of Europe must be undertaken.

In Chapter 5 of *ECP*, uncertainty replaces scarcity—scarcity had been the leitmotiv of economists during centuries, anticipating the core of *GT*. What is more, proposals must be concrete, considering scientific data. Figures must be precise, and it would follow calculations must be realistic. The 'method, apparently contemplated by the treaty…is evidently impractical' (p. 62). Of course, details must always be contemplated. He avoids undertaking unsupported assumptions as his epistemology is about essence: we 'shall lose ourselves in mere hypotheses unless we return…to first principles' (p. 72). Moreover, foundations based on past expectations are impractical since the world evolves. It is relevant to let go of impressions about things that never occurred. Inadmissible issues must be ignored. Vagueness and uncertainty in the Treaty of Versailles are excessive for him.

In Chapter 6 of *ECP* Keynes states that a new era means the dawning of a more complex world. In addition, he rules out the usage of spurious variables. Clear things need no analysis, however 'the power of ideas is sovereign' (p. 104). This insight anticipates the closing lines of *GT*. In Chapter 7 he writes about the role of prognosis after identifying causes. The effects of problems are not necessarily immediate, but the remedies must be timely. All in all, intuition plays a role, clarifying means and ends in the *ECP* by envisaging the whole from the beginning, and this method is superior to a step-laden rationality. He re-interprets data, aiming to resolve unsettled questions grounded in incomplete hypotheses. Keynes condemns pure rationalism, following Hume, as well as deduction, mechanism, hydraulics, and atomism.

5.5.2 Ethics

Economics is a moral science with value judgments (Chapter 3 in this book), which signifies that the pursuit of the truth is above all the investigations about ideal and mechanical worlds. On arriving to this point, Keynes escapes from Benthamism, the Victorian and Kantian moralities—via Moore, and the Cartesian geometry. He is aware that the Treaty of Versailles could bring a clash of values because he sees inevitable consequences for the unfairness and unfeasibility in the treatment of Germany such as insolvency and lack of opportunity for future generations. He sees the harsh treatment of Germany as vengeful and unnecessary, perhaps based on conceptions of 'human nature...always the same' (Keynes 1919, p. 15). Dialogue is therefore the remedy, rather than imposition, according to Chapter 1 of *ECP*. His examination of the deconstruction of a non-natural peace is an issue related to ontology.

An appeal to humanism is the solution for softening the consequences for Germany. Keynes thinks as a European and above all as a human being. In Chapter 2 of *ECP* he expresses an idea of progress related to the security of mankind. He is against conventions and bad persuasion, especially at that turning point in history. He is interested in transition (see Chapters 7 and 9 of this book). Chapter 3 analyses, in a Schopenhauerian or Tolstoyan style, whether the action of a single individual matters. Those post-war times require compromise and commitment, and institutions must be fair and practical. The Treaty assumes 'to assure a settlement of justice and magnanimity and a fair hope for a restoration of the broken current of life' (p. 16). However, the restoration of justice is imperative as international morality must be behind the right governance of Europe.

In Chapter 4 of *ECP* he examines the effects of political immoderation on final consequences, perhaps leading to revolution. Reconciliation is also relevant and both discrimination and prohibition should be avoided. Keynes's ethics are about common interest, wherein the human spirit must prevail. In Chapter 5 he writes that scruples are not useful. Neither false statements nor unjust claims should predominate (p. 65). No room must be allowed for ulterior—one can suspect, hidden—motives. Both restoration and happiness matter, and justice is the means for avoiding suffering, but it 'is not so simple' (p. 86). Encouragement must be a precondition for the entry into a new age. In Chapter 6 of *ECP* Keynes is apparently pessimistic about the results.

In Chapter 7 Keynes opines that no room for naiveté must be allowed, 'modern society is not immune from the very greatest evils' (p. 106). He continues, [*s*]'olutions exist, since solidarity is not a fiction' (p. 112). For him, there is a universal element in every soul, hence essentiality—attention to causes and deep motivations—must exist in the reconstruction of Europe. The inductive Keynes always presents a sort of middle way (in Skidelsky's terminology) between skepticism and rationalism, but he is moved by reasonable passion in 1919. His attitude to the fallacies described by Moore in *Principia Ethica* (1903) is a key point for his own evolution even in *ECP*. Moore is a utilitarian with respect to ethical consequences, but Keynes is in favor of virtue as the supreme ethical end value in the footsteps of the philosophers of classic Greece. The point is to give a practical sense to the ends of virtue ethics in terms of freedom, happiness, the truth, *good*, justice, equality, efficiency (yes, efficiency is a value), and utility.

5.5.3 Ontology

Everything is sequentially interrelated in Keynes's organicist vision of the world. In Chapter 1 of *ECP* he focuses on the unstable nature of the European economic organization. Put differently, he is aware social conditions are not perpetual as they arguably are in the physical sciences. These insights allow him to unearth the false foundations of the Treaty, if viewed as a complex system. This is 'true of Europe as a whole' (p. 7). Keynes consequently writes about an application of organicism in Chapter 1, affirming that Europe's 'structure and civilization are essentially one' (p. 1). He must have said 'must be.' Moreover, Europe is experiencing an involution in the sense that events are marching on to fated conclusions as institutions would be destroyed if left to their own course. Human adaptation is the key to survival and the implication is that ethical planning is always required.

In Chapter 2 of *ECP* Keynes expresses that equilibrium is threatened and that such nations like France regard the then-current state-of-affairs as normal, certain, and permanent, contradicting Keynes's dynamic notions of time, asymmetries, and heterogeneity of effects (our Chapters 2 and 4). For him, internal organizations are related to industrial orders which are transitory precisely because they are organic. In fact, there is 'economic interdependence of Germany and her neighbours' (p. 7), and even more between Germany and Western Europe. This reality is distinct from the atomism assumed by the proponents of the Treaty. In Chapter 3 Keynes ascertains institutions must be devoted to human ends and must be preserved, bringing to a close that no destruction of organized economic life can be permitted. For example, in Chapter 4 of the *ECP* he concludes that 'the treaty strikes at organization' (p. 37). Likewise, in Chapter 6 heuristic order is relevant. For instance, there 'must be imports before exports' (p. 104). Finally, in Chapter 7 attention is paid to transition. The conclusion is that *ECP* contains an ontological investigation associated to epistemological discernments which is useful for detecting the essence and dynamics of both events and the remedies of the problem in hand.

5.5.4 Political and Social Philosophy

Keynes was a Liberal in the sense of rejecting the *Laissez-faire*, a stance that he further supports in the 1930s (our Chapter 8). His—international—political vision in Chapter 1 of *ECP* is that national individualism prevails: 'European history is to be a perpetual prize-fight' (p. 14). Hence stability and justice are the antidotes for this 'immutable' state-of-affairs. In other words, post-war conventional policy is disguised as a measure for the attainment of freedom and international equality, but this is false according to Keynes's informed political philosophy.

In Chapter 3 of *ECP* the economist criticizes the 'suggestion that the Germans should not be heard' (Keynes 1919, p. 22), as this would bring about undesirable geopolitical effects. New-generation Europeans would also suffer from inadequate political measures brought about by the Treaty. The message of the *ECP* is thus that political and social philosophical insights must be rooted in considerations associated to ethics, epistemology, and ontology. Thus, he wonders about the fate of the Treaty: 'what…was the substance…to which the Allies had bound themselves?' (p. 24). He distinguishes between political and social philosophy, as can be seen in his statement that 'the property and persons of private German nationals, as distinct from their government, are also injuriously affected' (p. 27). In Chapter 4 (Keynes 1919, p. 44) he gives an example of an unsettled political fate.

In Chapter 5 of *ECP* Keynes writes that solutions and the choice of questions must be settled on their merits. In contrast, 'the British Prime Minister had perceived that the conclusion of hostilities might soon bring with it the break-up of the political bloc upon which he was depending' (p. 55). This insight is related to ethics; indeed, rules must not prevail, but Keynes makes clear the Main Four blindly follow—their own—traditions. As he contends about German reparations: [i]'n order to re-establish her economic life, or as to the degree of liberality with which the Allies will exercise their discretion' (p. 71), payments must follow a rational path. The preference for discretion would also be a rule in both *TM* and *GT* (Chapters 7 and 9 of this book). Keynes wonders why politicians' lies are credible, since he is aware that motives are related to the *Laissez-faire*, but intervention is necessary. Finally, it is mentioned in Chapter 7 of *ECP* that fundamental tendencies must be redirected by means of a specific program avoiding misleading positions.

A critique of *ECP* is undertaken by Thorstein Veblen (1857–1929), who wrote that Keynes takes the Treaty clauses at face value, ignoring such hidden factors as the Bolshevik menace (Veblen 1920). Prior to the eighties and the nineties, few investigators go beyond the economic dimension of Keynes's insights in *ECP*.

5.6 Conclusions on the *Economic Consequences of the Peace*

For any *oeuvre*, a researcher can investigate its reception, impact, origins, foundations, and meaning. This compilation of Keynes's core insights as expressed in *ECP* is relevant as Keynes's work is based on insights which leave an imprint in the social sciences, specifically his qualitative predictions originated by intuition supporting his vision in *ECP*.

As affirmed in Chapter 2 of this book, for Keynes there is no *deus ex* machine (a self-regulation universe) in human events which is the basis for the statement that the moral sciences are different from the natural sciences. This implies that Keynes's methods and scope differ from the establishment of his epoch, especially regarding political events. Both history and future can be found in *ECP*, wherein method, language, and expediency are integrated by means of a mixture of rationalism and intuition. However, his view of human nature is the key for understanding his message in 1919, which signifies that ethics is the end of *ECP* due to his impression that there is moral decay in Europe during those years.

Keynes's epistemological ideas in *ECP* are the critique of core assumptions and heuristic management of the consequences of the First World War on the part of European and American leaders, but he thinks in terms of the core of their misleading scientific and epistemic views. Economics as a part of ethics is for him a precondition of *good* as early as 1919, a stance he reaffirms in 'The Economic Possibilities for our Grandchildren' (1930) (our Chapter 8). In ontological terms, Keynes exhibits in the *ECP* his conception of time as historical rather than logical. He also advocates interdependence in events, which is spatial continuity. His practical concern about organicism starts in *ECP*, wherein he pursues the truth while attempting to transform energy into action. In political philosophy, he advocates reconstruction since his experience in terms of rebellion indicates that a disintegrating Europe was the result of anarchy. He addresses this problem with a plurality of discourses but always emphasizing the relevance of organicism in the culturally unified Europe.

Altogether, this chapter narrates how Keynes creates in the *ECP* a doctrine with new hopes, being against convention and hypocrisy. Skidelsky's reading of Keynes, wherein 'order has to be created; it is not natural' (Skidelsky 1992, p. 410), must be right. This issue is at the core of Keynes's vision: disease is the rule and health the exception, for which Keynes advocates intervention based on analysis and intuition. His political philosophy, characterized by reasonableness, propaganda, and persuasion in action, is not devoid of strength and contempt. On the other hand, the aftermath to *ECP* is for him an awakening to life: greed prevails, and hoarding is nefarious (our Chapter 8). He exhibits there evolutionary thinking in his search for universal *good* (as preached by Moore) and the truth (as championed by the 'Apostles' and Bloomsbury), demonstrating his interest in expedient public duty (following Burke). Carabelli (1986, 1988) and O'Donnell (1982) argue that Keynes's ideas show an essential continuity. Fitzgibbons (1988 [1990]) and Braithwaite

(1975) advocate the opposite perspective. Nonetheless Keynes is an evolutionary truth seeker in our reading of the gist of the *ECP*, at least as compared to his contemplative stance before the First World War.

Although this hypothesis must be proven or demonstrated, his evolutionary outlook can be visualized in the following Keynes themes on the logic of proposals: intuition, induction, the weight of the argument, subjective judgment, and conventions (in the face of both epistemological and ontological uncertainty and whose material manifestation is self-interest) as exposed in the next chapter. These last themes are the background for the investigation of the significance of probability (conceived as the relation between propositions) under an uncertain organic environment, both themes ultimately being related to ethics[4] We close this chapter by citing Zanini (2003, 2008), for whom the normative horizon links uncertainty and rationality; yet not only 'animal spirits' but also political and economic institutions are irrational, for example from Versailles to the Treasury in Britain to Washington. The next chapter outlines an apparent change of intellectual focus since now Keynes produces a novel theoretical treatise.

Appendix 5.1 Indian Currency and Finance (1913)

Indian Currency and Finance or *ICF* (1913) is written by Keynes as a young official about the financial effects of old imperialism on India and other emerging countries. He had started working for the India Office in 1906. Keynes's work on these issues is undertaken as if he is conducting an experiment, the result being that Keynes was recommended in 1914 as a member of the Royal Commission on Indian Currency and Finance to establish an Indian central bank, due to both his public relations and the novelty of his discernments. The theme is how a country may benefit practically from a transition from a silver to a gold standard with India as an example. During the process, he proposes an international system with the aim of providing easy access to money without generating instability. Keynes maintains that activist domestic monetary policies must be combined with managed exchange systems, an innovation for that time signaling one of the cornerstones of the origin of international finance.

Keynes had written on philosophy between 1905 and 1910, but he changed the approach: now his economics book on India further contributes to molding his philosophical development. This treatise enhances global independence predating some of his similar contentions in 1940 (Chapter 11). Yet another topic is the poorly regulated Indian banking, but Keynes steadfastly contemplates the coinage of gold as the solution for both challenges, ascertaining that hoarding brings about excessive fluctuations to the Indian money market. He aims to reduce the risk—not yet uncertainty—emerging from British foreign domestic investment.

Therefore, the original Keynes book dealing with central bank policies and international financial patterns is *ICF* not *TM*, but he would recurrently be in interaction with policy circles which widened his philosophical armour (unlike other philosophers who either felt uncomfortable in practice or detained their philosophic careers). The gold standard had been suddenly halted in Great Britain by the war (1914–1918), and thereafter India was for Keynes an example of a fiat currency management system for the sake of rejecting the gold standard.

Appendix 5.2 The Sequel to the *Economic Consequences of the Peace* (1922)

Keynes writes *ECP* referring to the terms imposed on Germany as impossible to be fulfilled. Austerity would never work (see Appendix 13.1) because it withdraws money from the circular income flow. With this and similar contentions, *ECP* influences world affairs. There Keynes affirms that integration ought to be achieved (organicism). His principles are the basis of treaties (ethics), and practicalities must rule (expedient political philosophy and heuristics). He also supports the cancellation of inter-ally debts and a loan for Britain from the United States in the 1940s. Further he contends payments on reparations and war debts should be paid by United States loans, leaving no one better-off in terms of credit payments. The upshot is that *ECP* and its sequel are qualitatively successful as a revelation since, in the end, a small part of the reparations would not be paid by Germany, who therefore becomes resentful. Emotions matter in macroeconomics.

Aftermath to the Treaty

Keynes's revelation may prove to be insufficient at least in the short period in practical terms. This was the case of a philosopher possessing however, a talent for expediency but with a vision. Indeed, Keynes writes in *ECP* that the prevailing situation in Europe in the aftermath of the First World

War is an opportunity to begin a new era. But the powers representing the Treaty were conservative.

The Paris Conference had as its major outcome the creation of *The League of Nations*, as proposed by the American delegation aimed at the settlement of the bases for world development, and its main result was the Treaty of Versailles (1919–1920) aimed at the accomplishment of world peace. Its sequels were going to be the Paris Peace Treaties of 1947. *The League of Nations* was an inter-governmental organization ideated by the United States founded in 1926 that lasted for 26 years but was incapable of preventing a regression by the Axis Powers in the 1930s. Its proposed 14 Points on the part of Wilson referred to the peace negotiations for ending the First World War (1914–1918). Even more importantly, the United States failed to ratify the Treaty wherein the French delegation aimed at achieving peace but annihilating Germany, which was eventually considered as a long armistice. France was adamant about reducing the payment of reparations on the part of Germany. Moreover, many of these domestic peace ideas were unsuccessfully translated into orthodox foreign policy such as free trade and self-determination. The key upshot is Germany defaulted the Treaty in December 1922, and the United Kingdom became a debtor while Americans rebuilt Europe. These historical paragraphs constitute a framework for Keynes's sequel to the *ECP*. Enter Keynes.

The Sequel

During the aftermath Keynes realized that his premonitory insights—which gave him universal fame as a writer based on informative data about reparations—would not be followed so that he wrote a reprimand in the form of a sequel. *A Revision of the Treaty, being a Sequel to the Economic Consequences of the Peace* (1922) contains an analysis of facts, practices, and expediency in the aftermath of the Treaty of Versailles. It is a continuation of the debate over German reparations, and the division of those reparations among allies. It also proposes the management of inter-ally generated debt. Its realism demonstrates that Keynes—not Veblen who affirmed Keynes took the Treaty literally—is right since he makes no mistakes in interpretation: in 1922 the chapter on reparations of the Treaty proved to be unsustainable. Keynes was also correct when analysing the 'organicist' context of long-term welfare in Europe.

Keynes broke again with the Victorian value of self-restraint and postponement at the aggregate level (our Chapter 9), as exemplified for him by the austerity measures proposed for Germany. Recall that the unit of analysis in macroeconomics is the country level. Moreover, in transitions one must remain open. Thus, Keynes maintains that real wealth is originated by capital accumulation which lies at the heart of both inequality and the established order, which signifies that investment must be leaked into the system. Hence a new order was mandatory with productive and financial investment at its center, especially in that new phase of capitalism.

Keynes's core in *ECP* is left without amendments in this follow-up. He is still defending Europe from the *Treaty of Paris* by resorting to powerful arguments. Now he affirms that in politics the truth is inconsistent with expediency, but it is also a privilege of powerful circles. Thus, democracy is considered a fallacy (see Appendix 11.1 on aristocracy). *A Revision* is written in an eloquent style full of common sense, verifying facts, journalistic communication, and opinion. This way of doing analysis reveals a philosophy of both knowledge and action. The scope of a journalist must be realistic, supported by data.

Finally, Keynes also edits in that same year with the same philosophy 13 pieces resulting from the *Genoa Conference* about the financial reconstruction of Europe. These 13 academic pieces also upheld in 1922 deal with Europe's financial situation, having Gustav Cassel (1866–1945), Maxim Gorki (1868–1936), and Luigi Einaudi (1874–1961) as contributors. He listened to others' opinions and this contributed to his evolution. Keynes's own 'A contribution to reconstruction' provides clues about the relationship between war and cyclical trade exhibiting an overarching view about the consequences of the First World War while undertaking a critique of atomicism: The problem is now [*s*]'ocial conflict...[*related to*]...nationalism' (p. 12).

Notes

1. See Chapter 11.
2. This section is also the basis for Chapter 9.
3. They exist solely in the minds of rational individuals.
4. Further explorations arising from this chapter are conducted in Chapter 11 of this book.

References

Sources

Andrews, David R. 2010. *Keynes and the British Tradition, the Moral Purpose of the Market*. New York: Routledge.

Braithwaite, Richard. 1972. Editorial Foreword. In *A Treatise on Probability, Collected Writings of JMK, Volume VIII*, edited by D Moggridge and Johnson. London: Macmillan.

———. 1975. "Keynes as Philosopher". In *Essays on John Maynard Keynes*, edited by Milo Keynes. London: Macmillan.

Carabelli, Anna. 1986. On Keynes's Method. PhD Dissertation, University of Cambridge.

———. 1988. *On Keynes's Method*. Basingstoke: Macmillan.

———. 1992. "The Method of the Critique of Classical Theory: Keynes on Organic Interdependence." In *John Maynard Keynes, Language and Method*, edited by Alessandra Marzola and Francesco Silva, 128–52. Chentelham, UK: Edward Elgar.

———. 1998. "Keynes on Probability, Uncertainty and Tragic Choices." *Cahiers d'économie politique* no. 30/31, 187–226. Keynes: Économie et philosophie.

Chick, Victoria. 1992. "On Money, Method and Keynes." In *Selected Essays of Victoria Chick*, edited by Philip Arestis and Sheila Dow. Basingstoke: Macmillan.

Davis, John B. 1994. "The locus of Keyne''s philosophical thinking in The General Theory: The Concept of Conventions". Chapter 9 in *Perspectives on the History of Economic Thought*, edited by Karen Vaughn, 157–78. Chentelham, UK. Edward Elgar.

Dow, Sheila C. 1991. "Keynes's Epistemology and Economic Method." In *Keynes as Philosopher-Economist*, edited by Roderick O'Donnell, 144–67. London: Macmillan.

Fitzgibbons, Athol J. 1988 [1990]. *Keynes's Vision: A New Political Economy.* Oxford: Clarendon Press.

———. 1992. "From Keynes's Vision to Keynesian Economics." In *Recent Developments in Post Keynesian Economics*, edited by Philip Arestis and Victoria Chick, 17–26. Cheltenham, UK: Edward Elgar.

Gerrard, Bill. 1991. "Keynes's General Theory: Interpreting the Interpretations." *Economic Journal* 101: 272–87.

Harcourt, Geoffrey C. 2001. "Is Keynes Dead?" In *50 Years a Keynesian and Other Essays*, edited by Geffrey C. Harcourt, Part I, Chapter 2. Basingstoke, UK: Palgrave.

Harrod, Roy F. 1951. *The Life of John Maynard Keynes*. New York: Harcourt.

Heilbroner, Robert. 1951. *The Worldly Philosophers: The Lives, Times and Ideas of the Great Economic Thinkers*. New York: Simon & Schuster.

Hession, Charles H. 1984. *John Maynard Keynes: A Personal Biography of a Man who Revolutionized Capitalism and the way we Live*. Old Tappan, NJ: Better World.

Keynes, John Maynard. 1913 [1971]. Indian Currency and Finance. In *JMK CW Vol. I Indian Currency and Finance*, edited by D. Moggridge. London: Royal Economic Society.

———. 1919 [1971]. *The Collected Writings of John Maynard Keynes (CW)*. Vol. 2: *The Economic Consequences of the Peace*, edited by Elizabeth Johnson. London: Macmillan, for the Royal Economic Society.

———. 1922 [1971]. "A Revision of the Treaty. A Sequel". In J*MK CW Vol. III A Revision of the Treaty*, edited by A Sequel. D. Moggridge. London: Royal Economic Society.

———. 1930 [1971]. "A Treatise on Money". In *JMK CW Vols. V and VI A Treatise on Money*. edited by D. Moggridge. London: Royal Economic Society.

———. 1936 [1964]. *The General Theory of Employment, Interest and Money*. New York: Harcourt.

Lawson, Tony. 1994. *Why Methodology?* Cambridge: University of Cambridge. https://heterodoxnews.com/ajes/readings/Lawson5-why-methodology.pdf.

Lawson, Tony and Hashem Pesaran. 2009. "Methodological Issues in Keynes' Economics: an Introduction". Chapter 1 in *Keynes' Economics (Routledge Revivals) Methodological Issues*, edited by Tony Lawson, Hashem Pesaran. London: Routledge.

Mantoux, Étienne. 1946. *The Carthaginian Peace: The Economic Consequences of Mr. Keynes*. Oxford: Oxford University Press.

Marzola, Alessandra. 1994. "Rhetoric and Imagination in the Economic and Political Writings of J. M. Keynes." In *John Maynard Keynes: Language and Method*, edited by A. Marzola and F. Silva, 192–223. Aldershot: Edward Elgar.

Moggridge, Daniel E. 1992. *Maynard Keynes: An Economist's Biography*. London: Routledge.

O'Donnell, Roderick. 1982. Keynes: Philosophy and Economics, an Approach to Rationality and Uncertainty. PhD Dissertaion. Cambridge: University of Cambridge.

———. 1989. *Keynes: Philosophy, Economics and Politics. The Philosophical Foundations of Keynes's Thought and Their Influence on His Economics and Politics*. London: Macmillan

Robinson, Austin. 1947. "John Maynard Keynes 1883–1946". *The Economic Journal* 57 (225): 1–68.

Skidelsky, Robert. 1983. *John Maynard Keynes. Volume I: Hopes Betrayed 1883–1920*. London: Papermac.

———. 1992. *John Maynard Keynes. Volume II: The Economist as Saviour 1920–1937*. London: Macmillan.

______. 1996. *Keynes. Past Masters*. Oxford: Oxford University Press.

Veblen, Thorstein. 1920. "Review of John Maynard Keynes, the *Economic Consequences of the Peace.*" *Political Science Quarterly* 35: 467–72.
Zanini, Adelino. 2003. "Un capitalismo incerto. Incertezza e normazione nel pensiero di J.M. Keynes (1921–1939)." Working Paper 194, Universita' Politecnica delle Marche (I), Dipartimento di Scienze Economiche e Sociali.
———. 2008. *Economic Philosophy: Economic Foundations and Political Categories.* Bern: Peter Lang.

CHAPTER 6

The Epistemology of *A Treatise on Probability* (*TP*) (1921)

The issues of probability and decision-making belong to the field of epistemology but also to that of logic. It is in this sense that Keynes's economics was always grounded on logic, but what kind of logic? This chapter outlines Keynes's novel concept of probability, which sees at least initially probability as a logical (objective) relationship between propositions rather than between numbers or events. This concept is outlined in Sect. 6.1. Section 6.2 is about how this concept becomes also subjective and thereby the basis for some of Keynes's contentions; especially uncertainty, which will be the backbone of his later theories on economics and finance, epistemology, ethics, and political philosophy. Appendix 6.1 deals with the contribution of the late 'Apostle' philosopher Frank P. Ramsey (1903–1930) to Keynes's work on probability. He convinced Keynes of the relevance of the subjective dimension to the selection of criteria apt for decision-making, which would become vital for the Keynes depiction of agents interacting in a realm dominated by uncertainty.

6.1 A New Conception of Probability

Keynes writes in *TP* in 1921 that decisions do not rely on mathematical expectations but rest on logical grounds. He parts company from Hume's claim that induction is an insufficient method for knowing something

J. Muñoz-Bandala, *Keynes's Evolutionary Spirit*, Palgrave Insights into Apocalypse Economics,
https://doi.org/10.1007/978-3-030-90150-9_6

by departing from its premises. Thus, Keynes is involved in the study of probability to identify the logical steps connecting assumptions and implications in proposals, which is useful for decision-making in epistemological, moral, economic, and political terms. Keynes contributes to the founding of logical probability since he does not believe in Moore's individual act consequentialism (Chapter 3). This has a bearing on assumed knowledge, which must not be reduced to the calculation of quantities via the use of mathematical methods, as in physics. For Keynes, acts have another type of consequences, most of them unpredictable. Then he attempts to elucidate moral issues (of consequences) by identifying the proper methods for obtaining knowledge. For Keynes true methods must lead to certainty in the face of initial uncertainty, thus avoiding multiple, undesired, or hastened results and consequences. Keynes creates thus a criterion wherein probability is useful for measuring consequences. He believes in human logic rather than in formal logic (Fitzgibbons 1990), so uncertainty and expectations are highly relevant in decision-making. In that sense he opposes the rational and certain world of apriorism in Descartes and Kant, or the continental route from the truth to cogency, which was opposed to the Locke connection embedded in the usage of empiricism.

6.1.1 Probability

The next task is presenting some history of the field. The first approach to probability is the Classical, suggested by Jacob Bernoulli (1654–1705) and Pierre Simon Laplace (1749–1827), based on the principle of indifference or of insufficient reason. According to them, opposite events can proportionally happen without uncertainty, with an approaching limit of 50 percent probability of occurrence, and repetitions can occur under similar conditions. They are ergodic in Davidson's terminology (Davidson 2003). No choices exist since the sampling of events is mechanical. Probabilities are represented in a normal-type distribution, wherein their numerical probabilities ($1/n$; n = number of events) approach the mean (μ) and the variances (σ^2) are small and infrequent. The numerical results of their sampling are comparable since this Classical vision assumes homogeneity in events (notice heterogeneity of effects in happenings is enunciated by Keynes, see Chapter 2). Thus in orthodox statistics, the probabilities of occurrence within a single event are added up and their total addition must amount to one. The Gaussian or normal curve of probabilities distribution is the reflex of this classical conception where the mean (μ) is the norm, and variances (σ^2) are the exception and are corrected either in large samples or in the long period. Welcome to the world of certainty and atomism as borrowed from the physical sciences.

The second method of measurement for probability is suggested by John Venn (1834–1923). It is akin to the Classical view, but it is preponderantly related to the limit of relative frequencies of occurrences of an event (for instance when throwing dice in an experiment), which also results in equi-proportional expected values amounting to 16.6666%. This method relates to probabilities between events rather than between numbers. However, this more flexible conception is still apt for the physical world.

Keynes proposed an alternative logical notion of probability in which probability ties propositions. He criticized the formerly explained static and deterministic standpoints, especially for the examination of probability in social events. At the very end, his perception of probability is logical and has a subjective dimension (Appendix 6.1). Returning to the objective beginnings, Keynes suggests the use of a non-additive and non-linear approach for measuring probability with a mathematical foundation (Brady and Arthmar 2012), but it is not a mathematical relationship which makes probabilities function in a way that is fitting for decision-making. According to Keynes, in most cases a non-objective probability or a logical probability are 'frequently' non-numerical. For Keynes in 1921, epistemic (objective, but not mathematical) probability is associated with inductive (and latter, intuitive or subjective) probability.

Keynes (1921) thus suggested a third approach: the logical-objective interpretation of probability (at a first moment). In this case, events exhibit asymmetries and heterogeneities arising from objects and results of either observation or experimentation; that is, sampling is not repetitive in the sense that conditions and results are different in each experiment (as happens in the social sciences). This approach is related to probabilities between proposals and is logical in the sense that the truth is independent of opinion. The idea is to draw conclusions from premises but also from arguments, assuming strong evidence.

6.1.2 *Reasoning in Keynes's Approach to Probability*

Hume attacked induction affirming that the number of samples in an experiment is finite and transient, and hence it does not allow us to tell if a result is definitive at any given point, as subsequent observations or experiments can deny the former truth. In other words, there are not definitive truths. Keynes initially justified the validity of statements by means of induction, but this leads to personalism or overstated subjectivism. Aware of that, he aimed to solve the problem of inability of inferences in induction by stating that probability is a relationship between proposals with a varying degree of evidence.

Thereafter Keynes contended that if the evidence in any proposal is augmented, probabilities are higher, and induction may be justifiable, albeit provisionally. This was his logical standpoint. To put matters in context, later Keynes included the subjective dimension after Ramsey's critique to his objective approach in 1926 (Appendix 6.1). In the end he validated inferences by resorting to convention (that is certain probabilities) both in 1936 and 1938 (Chapters 9 and 11).

Let's go step by step. Returning to Keynes's logical (objective) initial approach, the roles of intuition, certainty, convention, and context are relevant to examine when investigating induction. Unlike Hume, Keynes was not skeptical about the role of inductive logic in knowledge. For Keynes, the cause–effect dichotomy was related to both sensation and association. Hence no empirical reality could be the foundation of a universal law as in Hume who affirmed that the relationship between cause and effect is not more than the result of custom leading to the blind application of universal laws for the verifiability of results.

However, for Keynes intuition is an internal faculty that must be followed by intelligence, capturing the dynamics of organic unities. But induction is also a posteriori knowledge, being asymmetrical. Thus, the insecure inductive method is akin to uncertainty which does not mean it must be ruled out. To begin with, induction backs a-posteriorism (empiricism) and is conventionally linked to intuitive knowledge, empiricism, falsifiable models, experience, sensation, observation, concreteness, rigor, and praxis. But Keynes was not an empiricist since, among other reasons such as he followed an ethics of virtue, he did not believe in Classical probability. Probability theory for him is a logical interpretation based on degrees of belief as the tool for inductive logic overcoming skepticism. His probability thus is cardinal, wherein induction drives and makes causal reasoning flexible. Further, for him the process of reasoning is also based on analogy.

Probability and expectations (based on the consideration of uncertainty and organic unities) are linked. Keynes, in a Kantian-type of stance, defied both Locke's *tabula rasa* and Hume's skepticism by ascertaining that the mind is active in perception, attempting to find a foundation for knowledge but (alas!) starting with probability, thereby explaining the steps leading to knowledge. The first step was to consider that all events are probable, which signifies that the mere notion of probability must be widened. According to his effort to assimilate the foundations of probability to logical prescriptions, he stated that probability is at first objective and then subjective, capturing the degree of belief in a proposition, given inconclusive evidence.

The second step—actually a leap—undertaken by Keynes was to destroy the applicability of the frequentist quantitative approach by contending that quantification—or average stances—neither explains nor justifies the core of Classical probability. Heuristic explanations of probable events based on numbers are only suitable for deterministic cases confined to closed systems, such as card games. This was a standard probable reasoning process ruling human conduct in a pre-designed setback of limited knowledge. The repercussion is that numerical probability, as a non-logical relationship between evidence and hypotheses, possesses only a degree of partial implication. Realizing about these pitfalls, Keynes thus progressed from finding the truth to grounding knowledge, albeit only in terms of method since knowledge and information always vary.

Probability is hence—according to Keynes—the degree to which arguments are provisionally conclusive. This is important to logic since probability is visualized by Keynes as non-deterministic but objective with some part of subjectivity. This is also the reason why rules and functions are different in probability[1] (deductive) from those belonging to other statistical procedures such as hypothesis testing or confidence intervals (inductive).[2] But probability is also a degree of partial inference as well as of rational belief. Thus, Keynes's type of probability calculus represents a step beyond both pure intuition and pure induction, since these two methods of knowledge are intrinsically aprioristic, despite (or because of) their Kantian or Cartesian sophistications which assume certainty in knowledge and order in an atomic Newtonian universe.

6.1.3 Deepening Matters for Visualizing Keynes's Contribution

In the basic relationship between hypothesis (premise, '*a*') and conclusion (evidence, '*h*'), the issue is how to conduct in a proper form a valid inference process (between cause and effect), a doubt first raised by the skeptical Hume. According to Maher (2010), Keynes would extend the difficulty (or the complexity) of this process by asserting that all phenomena can add new information at every instant. Probability—and this is highly relevant—then is non-demonstrative, being correlated thus to expectations and hence to uncertainty. *TP* is therefore embedded at the root of Keynes's complex and fuzzy epistemology, becoming the foundation for his later developments in many fields.

For Runde and Mizuhara (2003), at the time of the initial writing of *TP*, probabilities are objective for Keynes, but he never claims that universal induction yields certainty, just like he did not believe in universal *good*. Induction is the estimation of the validity of observations as evidence for a proposition. But since social science faces the problem of generalization from observations: a proposition can never be definitively demonstrated. For Brown-Collier (1985), in *TP* Keynes sets the principles for justifying the use of induction by means of either the method of analogies or pure induction (the multiplication of experiments). However, induction is only valid in a universe with finite probabilities, which is (arguably for this author) seldom the case in real life.

Whereas organicism is a philosophy of complexity and evolution and is the basis for Keynes's methodological general stance, probability molded his vision of how to obtain knowledge. Keynes initially advocated for intuitionist epistemology since he considered it more relevant to knowledge acquisition than Locke's or Moore's sense experience. Thus, he overcame the two basic stances for understanding phenomena (in their pure forms): the empiricist view, wherein external coherence, post-interpretation, and open systems play a vital role; and the aprioristic stance, wherein internal coherence, pre-interpretation, closed systems, invariant laws, and analogies exist—a courtesy of the physical sciences.

Further, in 1921 Keynes did not believe in the unsophisticated Benthamist calculus of benefits and costs, which is also a form of action grounded in the Classical frequentist approach to probability. Instead, he decisively considered both the objective and subjective conceptions of probability with the purpose of shaping knowledge acquisition and application, especially that which captures the impact of uncertainty by means of tying up logical propositions. According to O'Donnell (1991), Keynes focused upon the weight of the argument rather on plain evidence.

In *TP*, Keynes contends that probabilities clarify how agents may conduct decision-making in the face of uncertainty, thereby criticizing Mill's categorization of hedonism as a variant of utilitarianism but especially as a form of knowledge (Chapter 4). He started by analysing the role of introverted judgment in the acquisition of knowledge, objectively, as grounded in both the intuitive and inductive approaches. Keynes's logical consideration became a benchmark for detecting the appropriate actions and theories since high-quality choices must have an ethical background. He then turned to subjectivism (see Appendix on Frank Ramsey). From that point forward he was in favor of intersubjective objectivism, wherein conventional extroverted judgment is explicit.

Keynes used logical axioms of causality for understanding the essence of probability. For him—and this is very—relevant—causality depends on induction which is in turn reliant upon probability. Both Moore and Keynes promoted organic *good* in objective but intuitive terms. This is mentioned now since for Moore common sense is grounded in certainty, while for Keynes it is based on probability and subsequently on uncertainty and irrationality. Probability is thus linked to both *goodness* and efficacy. Hence, *TP* offers insights into the nature of the spontaneous actions conducted by 'animal spirits' (not yet under that name), who may avoid unexpected—non-ethical—results by measuring logical probabilities.

Intuition has the characteristic of not being susceptible to proofs. But Keynes rejected accepted, illogical, or inherited arguments and categories at this stage. Hence, he placed individual judgment (discretion, see Chapter 2) at the core of decision-making at the expense of rules, by creating a behavioral theory for facing uncertainty, rejecting maximization under certainty as in Classical Political Economy. Moreover, judgments and beliefs based on probability are connected to action—entailing movement, unlike in the quiet Moore's metaphysical vision. Perhaps Moore considered that probability cannot be connected to applied knowledge due to the existence of certainty. But probability is based on frequencies that exist only in closed systems, and that assume ergodicity, repetition, homogeneity, and continuity, categories which were denied by Keynes.

According to Zappia (2012), *TP* provides theoretical content to non-numerical probabilities, deals with Hume's problem of the shaky foundations of induction, attempts to avoid 'physicalism' in knowledge, and gives sense to moral principles. *TP* is thus a characterization of uncertainty, using weights on evidence and decisions, particularly when errors in probability measures arise. For Zappia a second critique Keynes had of the frequentist approach is associated with the magnitude of the probability of the argument as related to its degree of confidence. The implication of this critique is that information must be both efficiently obtained, processed, and interpreted (which is seldom the case in reality), but also that the difference between a probability assessment and its degree of confidence cannot be found in a Bayesian setup.

Confidence ranks at a higher level in the realm of epistemic knowledge than frequency.[3] For Zappia (2012) the third part of Keynes's criticism is his own refusal to use mathematical expectations, which is identical to rejecting Bentham's calculus or the mere concept of risk as a calculated measure. Simply put, Keynes realizes mathematical expectations ignore the weight of evidence. Mathematics does not predict social choices since not all events possess the same level of frequency in terms of occurrence ($\mu^2 s$ fluctuate across experiments). But whenever information is vague the frequentist approach is inappropriate, and the 'weight of the evidence' must be used. Keynes is aware probabilities may be unknown, unreliable, or multiple, but they are non-Gaussian and non-Bayesian. Instead, Keynes relied on qualitative orders, wherein non-numerical probabilities (representing most events in real life) are analogous to probability weights. This core-heuristic understanding led him to prefer choice-moderation and hence discretion (which may lead to an aristocratical management of the economy).

For Zappia (2012), 'normal' probabilities are represented by the formula: $E = pA$, while Keynes's formula for understanding probability is: $E = cA$, where E = expectations; A = event; p = probability; q = non-probability; $c = p/1 + q$. Thus, Keynes's criterion classifies the orthodox maximization of expected utilities as a special case and as a transient one. Its origin is his rejection of Moore's analysis of the appropriate behavior rules to be employed in ethics, objecting (at this time) to Moore's assertion that conservatism is the adequate behavioral norm (Bateman 1988; Raffaelli 2006). Further the orthodox expected value is a valid guide only when confidence is at a maximum. Keynes thus employed degrees of belief in the place of what used to be called a-priori possibilities in orthodoxy.

On the other side of the epistemic spectrum, empiricists assume that facts supported by observation or experiments substantiate hypotheses and may support the making of future decisions. Keynes goes a step further with the degree of belief for making probabilistic choices because it covers a spectrum rather than being restricted to the dual decision of the robotic world,[4] or even simply to numbers. The degree of belief assumes intensities of intentionality in a world dominated by uncertainty. His contentions in 1921 (1908) thus considered the role of intentionality which presupposes an active mind and a flexible conception of both time and space.

The 'Apostle' William Ernest Johnson (1858–1931) influenced Keynes with respect to inference. But Johnson assumed homogeneity among events and emphasized the relevance of calculus. He referred to exchangeable sequences of 'random' variables (such as risk) wherein future observations behave like earlier observations, meaning that there only is a finite sequence of them, like in atomism. However, this contention sets limits to the use of independent and identically distributed random variables (σ is assumed to be constant throughout an experiment), and the inductive hypothesis may fail. This potential failure may emerge if the inductive method is also based on analogy so that mechanisms may provide invalid results in the presence of organicism and its elements: heterogeneity and asymmetry.

In his youth, and because of his Classical influences, Keynes relied on the principle of indifference when designing the scheme of logical probabilities among proposals, but this was corrected in his logical method when he considered the weight of evidence rather than simple evidence. Since people do not make mechanical choices, he ultimately takes a double-sided approach: intersubjective-objectivism (Appendix 6.1). He arrived at this approach for two reasons: first, because objectivity implies mechanical choices; and second, because of his eventual acceptance of Ramsey's subjective bets, wherein the rules of probability are logical deductions from one's own perspective rather than from primitive or deterministic axioms, as Keynes had originally presupposed. To sum up, for Keynes proposals must be logically related to make sense under uncertainty, but the concomitant choices have a subjective element in active minds. Thus, his probability inference process goes beyond both intuition and induction as well as beyond robotism—as represented in dyadic stances, also overcoming Hume's skepticism about both the acts of obtaining and processing knowledge in closed systems. But what is the use of these concepts?

6.2 The Interlinkages and Repercussions of Keynes's Novel Concept of Probability

TP on non-numerical probabilities is the culmination of Keynes's early philosophy (Bateman and Davis 1991). The book is about judgment in human affairs, giving rise—and this is highly relevant—to the analysis of behavior under uncertainty.[5] But at this stage he still believed in certainty when trying to find a parameter for undertaking rational action by means of the analysis of probabilities. Other contentions in *TP* are that probability (as indefinable as *good*) is irreducible to other concepts such as risk, and that probabilities cannot be compared since events are different. For example, two stocks markets may not be comparable since they differ in terms of both size and composition, not to mention origin.

Keynes studied the practical worth and roles of expectations, knowledge, beliefs, intuition, induction, experience, evidence, pure arguments, unguaranteed assumptions, conventions, and values in the field of epistemology in *TP*. He also examined intuition leaps and debated against certainty. He was not satisfied with empiricism. This suggests that investment choices in foreign exchange markets, for example, must consider qualitative effects and not just trends or recent evidence. Moreover, for him the justification of intuitionism must be examined when judging our moral behavior. The conundrum of the validity of induction was thus left to Keynes. He agreed that each impression is a separate experience which justifies the existence of non-repetitious behaviors (non-ergodicity). Whereas Hume's distinction between mathematics and life may be valid, Keynes amplified the spectrum by including weighing evidence throughout the whole spectrum of sciences (from the natural to the physical to the social sciences), thereby making finite samples more operational, meaning that if induction is a matter of belief, its qualitative premises must always be significant. For instance, in economics cycles must be studied in terms of the causes of their seasonality.

Keynes only rejected pure induction when referring to Hume's experiment of causality in terms of the relation between cause and effect. But he went beyond Hume's skepticism by suggesting new forms of evidence leaving room for optimism, being more extensive though perhaps less profound (which is sometimes necessary). What is more, for him, both context and the 'weight of the argument' matter in induction, not only evidence. Keynes also inspected the roles of tautology, analogy, and the scope of generalization. Perhaps his key finding was that certainty is about analytical propositions (those analysing the concept of the subject), unlike uncertainty whose existence arises from daily challenges and which is about synthetic propositions (those which are true in terms of its relationship to the world).

In Keynes's *TP* objective theory, proposals must also be analysed from a social point of view as well as in subjective terms (which he did at the end of his analytical examination). His approach to probability has thus the advantage of being more subject to change with varying evidence by considering a wider spectrum of social phenomena. In other words, the contact with social events in a wider world makes his approach more robust than Hume's physicalist consideration of induction.

6.2.1 Keynes's Conception of Probability in Practice

TP is about the reliance on personal choice, which is the opposite to rule-deterministic abeyance, and this is relevant in policymaking or even in the pursuit of an objective *good*. The reason is that individuals are irrational, entertain multiple goals, and possess different degrees of belief about the future, which produces heterogeneous responses to shifts in events; for example, the design of discretionary policies after depressions,[6] whereas discretion possesses the advantage of flexibility. *TP* comes from an early Keynes's paper about probability written in 1904, in which he advocated for the use of practical reason supported by 'act consequentialism,' since at that moment he was not yet interested in the ethics of virtue nor he was thinking about irrationality. His advocacy for 'act virtue' and the overcoming of irrationality were more fully revealed at the end of *GT* (his Chapter 24, our Chapter 9) and in 'MEB' (our Chapter 11).

According to Garner (1982), Keynes was a pioneer in the understanding of the role of uncertainty in the strengthening of inferences. He grasped the sense of uncertainty in his activities as a financier and government adviser, although he was conscious of the preeminence of the subject of uncertainty partly because of his familiarity with the work of the German physicist Heisenberg (1927). Here, paths cannot be easily predicted by departing from the initial certain conditons of phenomena. Keynes's intersubjective probability fuses epistemology with ethics, wherein extroversion is mixed with introspection. Probability detects the truth based on the quality of evidence and the 'weight of the argument' and this may be useful in macroeconomic management as the impact of policies is dynamically uncertain.

But Keynes was critical of notions themselves especially regarding their assumptions and hidden mechanisms. Probability is a core atomic concept whose importance cannot be minimized. It is counter-intuitive in the sense that it is imperfectly inductive, and its evidence is only partial and not totally reliable as those in a deterministic or atomic world. Uncertainty—a realm in which the use of probability is crucial—changes rapidly of concrete disguise; otherwise it would become certainty, probably abstract certainty. In other words, the inference of a general solution arising from certain aspects of knowledge is problematic, since homogeneous evidence is limited (like in financial decision-making); unlike in most mathematical problems, which possess general-type solutions. Yet another way of stating this problem is the contention that behavior is unpredictable since human actions vary across space and through time (Chapter 2), but in any event Keynes attempts to reduce this uncertainty by diffusing—and taking advantage of—knowledge and elucidating moral conduct. He realized that large systems are subject to both dynamic and—interrelated—external influences.

The notion of probability relates to a body of knowledge that differs for every person but must be objective to be evaluated. For Keynes, it was conventional wisdom that the probability of an argument's veracity is contingent on 'a balance between what may be termed the favorable and the unfavourable evidence' (*TP*, p. 77). But an imbalance in evidence was not sufficient to discard an observation, witness the holding of a share in our investment portfolios. Instead he considered that the weight of the argument is not fixed as it might be in physics. The objective part of probability in Keynes (E_1) corresponds to logic whereas the subjective part (E_2) concerns the fragile character of human events which are always non-repetitive and non-ergodic. There is a trade-off between E_1 and E_2, since the former symbol contains more information, but the latter is more varied. All of this abides by Hume's argument that induction requires total evidence. This train of thought about probability and its relevance can be seen in Keynes's treatment of economic cycles. The 'frequentist' classical theory is a special case since nothing can be aprioristically known in open systems. Not even the knowledge of social patterns guarantees that events may take on previous probability values. But probability (values within ranges) is a different notion from uncertainty (unknown qualitative values), though both reflect changing social conditions even in certain environments. Later, based on these contentions,

Keynes reaffirmed that agents are heterogeneous and produce asymmetrical information. For instance, foreign exchange markets differ from one another as each is influenced by thousands of diverging perspectives and factors.

For Davis (1991a), most of Keynes's early unpublished articles expose a criticism of Moore's *Principia Ethica* (1903a) (Appendix 4.1), but Moore's insights found their way to have an influence on both *TP* and elsewhere. What is more, according to Davis (1991a), 'Miscellanea Ethica' (1905) contains seminal notions on probability. The connection between ethics and probability is evidence that proposals must be logically grounded, whereas judgments relate to right conduct and duty, for instance in policymaking (Chapters 9 and 11).

Those acts that lack rules may be based on intuition[7]; additionally, as Hume ascertains, induction might be invalid. Keynes solved this problem by widening the spectres of validation. This is mentioned again since events are organic in his probability relationships. For Davis (1991a), in *TP* Keynes coherently made use of Moore's ideas, extending their realm of application. He started by considering that probability is both rational and objective, but the existence of expectations, perspectives, and perception turn the result of judgments on rational probability into subjective. Human acts are not exact, measurable, homogeneous, symmetric, repetitive, or static, exactly as markets and economic policies are not ideal (Chapter 9). For example, while resorting to conventions may remedy the problem of imperfect markets, investors do not believe in them in times of crisis, and disequilibria reinforce the presence of subjectivism in decision-making. The conception of uncertainty is also fleshed out in the example of the distinction between nominal and real wages (which are nominal wages but divided by prices) in *GT*.

Regarding practicalities, the complementary treatises dealing with probability and uncertainty are *GT* and the paper 'TGE,' where the problem is that uncertainty provides no scientific basis on which to form any calculable probability whatsoever (Keynes 1937). He is thus the founder of the non-additive approach to probability, which signifies that arguments are complexly—organically—related (their associations represent more than an addition), a contention based on both Moore's insight that *good* is non-additive and his concept that organic unities are associated to ethical choices, as values are interlinked. Hence axiological (both ethical and aesthetic) ideals are related to methodological norms.

According to Davis (1991a), Keynes went from intuition in his unpublished manuscripts of the early 1910s to conventions after *GT* (1936), but his intermediate work on induction and probability led him to present new theoretical constructs and linkages in his views with impact in his activity as an economist. Davis asserts that a moral science employs introspection and value judgments, hence Keynes evolved after he wrote *TP* in his views on ethics and the foundations of political philosophy. He considered, for example, that some societies are more inclined to elect aristocratic regimes due to the existence of heterogeneous criteria. At the end, flexibility is the ideal strategy for obtaining either successful ethical choices or economic decisions since uncertainty prevails; requiring discretion, for example, when choosing financial options in the struggle against an uncertain future. *TP* as a general theory of belief under uncertainty in the field of probability matches with Keynes's experience, which brought him to affirm that financial markets can act perversely even in the short term. Uncertainty will lead him to comprehend the role of money in the generation of disequilibria and the implementation of policies. However, thanks to Keynes the consequences of economic policies may be probable but also organically uncertain. Organicism is the basis for uncertainty.

Keynes passes judgment on both the ontology and the epistemology of probability with the aim of applying this knowledge to real-life episodes. According to Werle (2011), for Keynes the atomic character of natural law precludes the envisagement of organicism. Organicism is the upshot of complexity and its concomitant interactions in systems, thereby introducing the dimension of openness in systems, which is a precondition for the existence of logical cardinal probabilities as Keynes sees them.

For Werle (2011), aggregate (Keynes's) variables are irreducible to summations of individual decisions as in *GT*, just like probabilities are non-additive as in *TP*. In other words, Keynes's belief in organic wholes becoming apparent from the interactions of complex systems is initially demonstrated in his work on probability. Furthermore, *TP* is an attempt to reject both utilitarianism[8] and rationality by considering human spontaneity and creativity. Keynes realized that induction is in contradiction to certain knowledge, immediate equilibria, and logical time. All told, his critique of frequentist probabilities will be the backbone for supporting discretion both in ethical and policy actions, for example when counteracting investment cycles (Chapters 7, 8, and 9). On the other hand, in the insights penned in Chapters 2, 22, and 25 of *TP* he relates his introspective past reflections to his future undertakings, and to *good* (our

Chapter 11). A consequence of his notion of probability is that when events are improbable 'animal spirits' emerge and become ubiquitous, since their behaviors are based on instinct.

Keynes's uncertainty[9] will be thus an epistemic-ontological concept prevalent in open systems (Chapter 9). And the controversy related to the question whether uncertainty is ontological or epistemological is idle since the core of philosophical insights—revelations or discoveries—must be reduced to unity. What is more, uncertainty is vital in practice as it may play a role in the use of money (Chapters 7 and 9) and may result in misunderstandings (Chapter 11), economic instability, or even economic wars (Chapter 12). Uncertainty also means that systems are not able to self-regulate since their functioning cannot be equilibrated, except by chance (Chapter 9). This is highly relevant for financial practices. Finally, while the basis for uncertainty and the use of probabilities are ontological, their consequences are epistemological (see Chapter 2) and ethical (see Chapter 9), and ultimately practical. Keynes is thus proposing the conformational holism of interrelated hypotheses for explaining phenomena (Chapter 7), as it will also be evidenced by his treatment of economics in *GT* (Chapter 11).

According to Zappia (2012), *TP* pioneered a wider structure for managing probability comparisons, entailing indirect knowledge. Still Keynes's theory of probability is logical in the sense that he relies on judgements based on preferences and the principles of indifference and relevance. His notion of probability thus may influence moral, financial, local policy, and international policy decisions. The weight of the evidence, grounded in breadth of knowledge, may support choices of probabilities aimed at avoiding ambiguity, for example in policymaking.

On the other hand, rejecting the frequency theory in a social world is akin to revising Benthamism while challenging the rational prescriptions of Mill and the Classics (Chapters 4 and 10). The modern explanation of the existence of unknown probabilities is that non-ergodicity is the basis of irreducible uncertainty (Davidson 2002). Non-ergodicity may be interpreted as heterogeneity coupled with the absence of repetition in economic events. All of this goes hand-in-hand with Keynes's desire to move away from atomism to organicism in proposals (Chapters 8 and 11) and discarding microeconomics in favor of macroeconomics.

According to Van Der Hauwe (2011), Keynes has a monistic interpretation of probability. What is more, his macroeconomics is grounded in his ideas on probability, uncertainty, and expectations formation

(Chapter 9), an understanding born from the elements of his *SRP* (Chapter 2). Keynes's logical reading of probability thus went beyond the acts of intuition or induction, transforming the notion of probability in terms of a duality: its essence and operationality. But probability must be based on evidence, which must be worthwhile, important, or frequent but above all probable. If something is not probable (and this is a highly relevant point), then it is uncertain and must be either avoided or fought. For instance, he struggled against uncertainty by relying on probable convention in the beauty contest depicted in Chapter 12 of *GT* (Chapter 9).

The points of departure for understanding the essence of uncertainty are the concepts of both variance (σ^2) in the Classical conception of probability and its economic orthodox version: risk as exposed by Frank Knight (1885–1972) in 1921. Notice risk is often mistaken for uncertainty, giving way to confusion about how financial markets function, thereby leading to bad financial decisions (Appendix 13.1). For Keynes risk was associated to numerical probabilities whereas uncertainty was qualitative. Further, the atomistic concepts of a self-regulating universe, a-priori moral duty, the *Homo Economicus,* and the Laissez-faire (Chapters 8, 9, 10, and 11) were also discarded by Keynes's conception of probability. Instead Keynes's contentions are suitable for a dynamic and heterogeneous world, but he had other reasons for supporting his conception of probability. In a Keynes world, transitions bring about social changes after structural breaks occur even under stable conditions. Furthermore, frequent variations across space and through time are neither homogeneous nor symmetrical, and variables, lags, and breaks are not constant. Moreover, constants do not exist in social sciences and errors play a role. This explains why policymaking is a complex task, an issue highly relevant in *TM* (Chapter 7).

The first part of this chapter deals with the creation of an objective conception of probability by Keynes which is useful for an uncertain world, although he later adds the subjective element as inspired by Ramsey (Appendix 6.1). The second part explores the interrelations and implications of this notion of probability on decision-making for investors, financiers, or policymakers. Thus, Chapter 6 in this book outlines Keynes's refusal to rely on determinism in both knowledge and morals by connecting probability with uncertain information from an intersubjective-objective perspective. Summarising, on probability Keynes goes from the classical view to the frequency approach to an objective account to a subjective viewpoint, ending up with an amalgam of the two latter approaches. This realization led him to find a resemblance among the concepts of behavior, probability, conventions, discretion, and uncertainty. By leaving behind the frequency approach to probability, Keynes overcomes some parts of Moore's certain (conventional) ethics (see Chapters 8 and 11).

Before that, Chapter 7 is about economic theory as treated in both *TMR* (1923) and *TM* (1930). They represent a continuation of Keynes's pioneer notions on probability but in economics. From the times of *TP* on, he undertakes the collection, interpretation, and dissemination of both qualitative and quantitative theoretical and empirical information, aided by intuition and imagination to recommend suitable policy decisions for uncertain economies.

Appendix 6.1: A Precocious and Transient Genius: Frank Plumper Ramsey (1903–1930)

Ramsey's critique of Keynes's logical approach to probability is considered an underpinning of Keynes's subjective and objective dichotomy between the roles of the mind and facts in the decision-making process of probabilities calculus, which arguably makes Keynes the precursor of information economics. Since information is uncertain, all that humans can do is be reasonable in an irrational world. But Keynes's uncertain factors affecting human behavior may be captured by understanding the subjectivity embedded in probability choices. How is it?

For García Duarte (2007), Ramsey's distinction between formal and human logic[10] had an influence on Keynes thereafter. Ramsey was, arguably, more interested in perceptions than in evidence both as the origin and proof of knowledge. Keynes accepted Ramsey's subjective notion of probability in the weight of the argument since objective knowledge is related to judgment but both introspection and values matter as well. Since the individual mind is an organic unity for Keynes, he does not accept universal *good*. But individual thought may be representative of other thoughts according to both the notion of inter-subjectivity and the principle of uniformity; conversely, individuals are dissimilar in experience and circumstance generating unexpected behaviors and intentions around events. Keynes hence questioned the theory of the representative individual in economics (in favor of aggregates)—but accepted it as the unit of analysis in probability, epistemology, and ethics in 1921.

In that vein, Keynes wondered at this epoch what the sense of the principles of intuition and induction is. Eventually he embraced to a certain extent Ramsey's subjective approach to probability believing that logic in terms of associations of proposals denies the possibility that algorithmic logic could represent the way in which human beings think going far beyond utility maximization. Human choices are qualitative, as exemplified by degrees of belief. Ramsey wrote on uncertainty based on subjective probability. He was a member of the 'Apostles' (1921–1929) and attended the sessions upheld in Keynes's Political Economy Club, being influential in Keynes's partial demise of logical rationality. According to García Duarte (2007), Ramsey wrote his first criticism of *TP* in 1922 on philosophical judgment, based on Moore.

Ramsey also affirmed that mathematics need not be used at every opportunity. For him, the results delivered by numerical models must be simple, interesting, and not obvious. He writes that weight of evidence, information, and knowledge could come at a reasonable price. The best alternative is to gamble with expectation; in other words, he championed a subjective ex-post approach to probability. For reciprocity, Keynes explained to Ramsey the advantages of intuition. The upshot of this scientific exchange is in *TP* Keynes delineated a wide notion of rationality when modelling choice under uncertainty. Radical Uncertainty destabilizes economies and prevents them from rapid recoveries. What unifies these contentions? Since lack of knowledge translates into a lack of efficacy, the remedy is to rely on probability. Hence, for some writers the foundation of Keynes's philosophical thinking is outlined in *TP* as a reaction against Moore's notions of common sense, utilitarianism, rationality, and implicit belief in frequentist probability.

How does the ensuing story go? Keynes was to some extent a rationalist. Ramsey criticized Keynes's Kantian-type logical probability relations, supporting the view that even in the light of objective facts individuals may attribute different probabilities to distinct events. Ramsey was correct. Keynes however was right to acknowledge that probability is related to the logic of proposals. According to Roncaglia (2009), Keynes argued that the Classical and the frequentist approaches are non-applicable in a complex world. In his non-Classical perspective, Keynes's weight of the argument is backed in the theory of groups, which renders it intersubjective. Oddly enough for this author, Ramsey's subjective approach ultimately serves as a basis for conventional Bayesian statistics. Such Ramsean continuators as Bruno de Finetti (1906–1985), Leonard

Jimmie Savage (1917–1971) and Milton Friedman (1912–2006) would support expected utility functions in decision-making, but that is another matter. Ramsey also sent a letter to Keynes in 1928 about the latter's work on monetary economics, contending that inflation is a tax on money holdings, and that optimal policies must be used for management. Finally, Ramsey also distinguished between individual behavior and collective welfare. Last but not least, he applied his talent to ethical problems considering that the love of saving is based on the misunderstanding of the differences between means and ends, a contention coming from the Moorean dichotomy between being *good* and doing *good*. This analogy closes this chapter.

Notes

1. Hence, Keynes advocates discretion in the use of policies, discarding (deterministic) rules.
2. Keynes is critical of statistics for its reliance on the interrelated premises of atomism in variables, data independence, random errors, and that the present is a continuation of the past. No Gaussian curve of probabilities exists for him (Appendix 12.2).
3. Keynes still sustains in 1921 that individuals undertake personal choices, just like in the 'atomist' Classical and Marshallian schools, without internalizing information on social conditions and preferences (Chapter 10).
4. The black-and-white view of the world corresponds to either physical facts or paranoid minds.
5. This would be useful, for instance, in finance.
6. Nevertheless, rules and conventions are not examined by Keynes at this stage (Chapter 11).
7. However this realm of knowledge may also be subjective and aprioristic.
8. The Benthamist calculus is frequentist as well as atomist, besides being both rational and democratic (see Chapter 3).
9. Not to be confused with asymmetries in information or heterogeneities in agents' behaviors, which only reinforce uncertainty.
10. It is captured in the notion of conventions for him since 1936.

References

Sources

Bateman, Bradley W. 1988. G. E. Moore and J. M. Keynes: A Missing Chapter in the History of the Expected Utility Model. *American Economic Review* 78, no. 5: 1098–1106.

Bateman, Bradley W., and John B. Davis. 1991. "Introduction." In *Keynes and Philosophy: An Essay on the Origins of Keynes's Thought*, edited by Bradley W. Bateman and John B. Davis, 1–5. Marquette University Faculty 141. https://epublications.marquette.edu/marq_fac-book/141. Accessed 17 August 2017.

Brady, Michael E., and Rogerio Arthmar. 2012. "Keynes, Boole and the Interval Approach to Probability." *History of Economic Ideas* 20, no. 3: 65–84.

Brown-Collier, Elba K. 1985. "Keynes' View of an Organic Universe: The Implications." *Review of Social Economy* 43, no. 1 (April): 14–23.

Davidson, Paul. 2002. *Financial Markets, Money and the Real World*. Chentelham, UK: Edward Elgar.

Davidson, Paul. 2003. "Is 'Mathematical Science' an Oxymoron When Used to Describe Economics?" *Journal of Post Keynesian Economics* 25, no. 4: 527–545.

Davis, John B. 1991a. "Keynes's Critiques of Moore: Philosophical Foundations of Keynes's Economics." *Cambridge Journal of Economics* 5, no. 1 (March): 61–77.

———. 1991b. "Keynes's View of Economics as a Moral Science." In *Keynes and Philosophy: Essays on the Origins of Keynes's Thought*, edited by Bradley W. Bateman and John B. Davis, 89–103. Aldershot, England: Edward Elgar.

Fitzgibbons, Athol. 1990. *Keynes's Vision: A New Political Vision*. Oxford: Oxford Clarendon Press.

García Duarte, Pedro. 2007 [2009]. "Frank P. Ramsey: A Cambridge Economist." *History of Political Economy* 41, no. 3 (July): 445–70.

Garner, Alan, C. 1982. "Uncertainty, Human Judgment, and Economic Decisions." *Journal of Post Keynesian Economics* 4, no. 3 (Spring): 413–24.

Heisenberg, Werner. 1927. "Über den anschaulichen Inhalt der quantentheoretischen Kinematik und Mechanik". *Zeitschrift für Physik* 43, no. 3–4: 172–198.

Keynes, John Maynard. 1937. "The Ex-ante Theory of the Rate of Interest." *Economic Journal* 47, no. 188 (December): 663–69.

———. 1921 [1973]. *The Collected Writings of John Maynard Keynes (CW)* Vol. 8: *A Treatise on Probability* , edited by Elizabeth Johnson (19–28) and Daniel E. Moggridge (15–18). London: Macmillan, for the Royal Economic Society.

Maher, Patrick. 2010. "Keynes Concept of Probability." *Scientific Thought II* (Spring).

Moore, George E. 1903a. *Principia Ethica*. Reprinted in Prometheus Books' Great Books in Philosophy Series. http://fair-use.org/g-e-moore/principia-ethica/. Accessed 8 January 2015.

———. 1903b. "Refutation of Idealism". *Mind New Series* 12, no. 48 (October): 433–53. https://es.scribd.com/document/163302582/Moore-G-E-The-Refutation-of-Idealism-1903. Accessed 20 January 2015.

O'Donnell, Roderick M. 1991. *Keynes as Philosopher-Economist*. Proceedings of The Ninth Keynes Seminar held at the University of Kent. London: Macmillan.

Raffaelli, Tizziano. 2006. "Keynes's Interaction with Cambridge Philosophers." In *The Cambridge Companion to Keynes*, edited by Roger E. Backhouse and Bradley W. Bateman, Chapter 6. Basingstoke: Palgrave.

Roncaglia, Alessandro. 2009. "Keynes and Probability: An Assessment." *The European Journal of the History of Economic Thought* 16, no. 3: 489–510.

Runde, Jochen and Sohei Mizuhara (eds.). 2003. *The Philosophy of Keynes' Economics: Probability, Uncertainty, and Convention*. London and New York: Routledge.

Van Den Hauwe, Ludwig. 2011. "John Maynard Keynes and Ludwig von Mises on Probability." *Journal of Libertarian Studies* 22: 471–507.

Werle, Nicholas. 2011. "More Than the Sum of Its Parts: A Keynesian Epistemology of Statistics." *The Journal of Philosophical Economics* 4, no. 2: 65–92.

Zappia, Carlo. 2012. "Re-reading Keynes after the Crisis: Probability and Decision." Department of Economics, University of Siena, Quaderni del Dipartamento di Economia Estadistica No. 646. https://ideas.repec.org/p/usi/wpaper/646.html. Accessed 19 October 2017.

CHAPTER 7

The Bronze and Silver Books: *A Tract on Monetary Reform* (1923) and *A Treatise on Money* (1930)

Keynes's activities in those formative years establish the bases for macroeconomics and modern finance, especially in his transitional stage to *GT*. Section 7.1 analyses *A Tract on Monetary Reform* (1923) or *TMR*, a still conventional and orthodox but illuminating book. Section 7.2 deals with the influential and modern *A Treatise on Money* (1930) or *TM*, which constitutes a proof of Keynes's knowledge on both finance and economic policy, full of elucidating concepts and metaphors, but still lacking the spark that initiates modern macroeconomics. Yet, discussions and criticism on both *TMR* and *TM* led to orthodox Post Keynesianism, as conventional economists visualized them as unadventurous contributions, especially the latter book, not realizing that this succession of books entails new interrelations and generates new discernments. Lets' follow this story. The appendices outline the surrounding events of these three books. Appendix 7.1 is about 'The Economic Consequences of Mr. Churchill' (1925), where he reconsiders the implications of Britain's return to the gold standard making it a practical companion to the theoretical *TMR*. Appendix 7.2 is about 'The monetary theory of production' (1933), the prototype of *GT*, mentioning his letter to Roosevelt. Appendix 7.3 is the chronicle of the making of the 'heuristic' multiplier by Keynes's lieutenant: Richard F. Kahn (1931).

J. Muñoz-Bandala, *Keynes's Evolutionary Spirit*,
Palgrave Insights into Apocalypse Economics,
https://doi.org/10.1007/978-3-030-90150-9_7

7.1 *A Tract on Monetary Reform*: The Initial Exploration with Borrowed Concepts

TMR, *TM*, and *GT* (the latter analyzed in Chapters 2 and 9 in this book) comprise Keynes's constructivist-type trilogy in economics, each work entailing an evolution from previous conservative scientific attitudes. *TMR* argues against the re-implementation of the gold standard and analyses facts to assess the effects of an unstable value of money. Keynes thus was setting the standard for the appropriate management of monetary activities on the part of central banks. Macroeconomic management must impart order to the system. Then he attempted to find a stable measuring rod of value, in terms of purchasing power at the international level, since the First World War had brought economic disorder. But he was not convinced that *Laissez-faire* was the solution for development, so the monetary system must be reformed from the inside.

TMR, then, is about the impact of the time fluctuations of money within an orthodox framework requiring management. Here he was still influenced, in terms of content, by both Marshall[1] and Pigou. *TMR* is the first book on fluctuations, wherein both profits and investment affect price stability and produce investment swings, which in turn generate business cycles. But the problem was that under a fixed gold standard orthodox rules must be followed, an alien thought for Keynes. This philosophy also pushed against an anachronism: the gold standard (1925–1931), which had made a comeback since having been suspended in Britain in 1919.

The bronze book is also Keynes's contribution to the gist of monetary policy: the Cambridge version of *QTM*. The Cambridge version of *QTM*,[2] grounded in the role of money as a store of value for emergencies, is symbolized as: $M \bullet V = P \bullet \Upsilon$, where M = money supply; V = velocity of circulation of money; $k = 1/V$, the proportion kept in cash; P = price level; and Υ = output, gross domestic product, income, or the level of activity. This equation focuses on the demand side (short-term) of the money market indicating that some portion of money is preserved in cash (liquidity) rather than in assets. In contrast, the Fisherian long-term version of *QTM* (from the American economist Irving Fisher [1867–1924]) is focused on the money supply-side and based on the role of money as a medium of exchange. It is represented as: $M \bullet V = P \bullet T$, where T is the number of transactions and money is immediately spent. Keynes was moved initially by the Cambridge adaptation, but in the end he dismissed both versions based on his own conception of money as an alternative to financial assets. Even more importantly, he considered that interest rates (r) play no role in those versions and wanted to remedy this omission considering r as the fuel for his theory of price fluctuations, but not yet of output fluctuations (as in *GT*).

TMR is on the instability of the standard of value bringing about the notion of financial risk and outlining the applicability of currency reforms to reduce monetary instability in the early twenties. The implication is that the return to the gold standard should be avoided as an old-fashioned foul.

7.1.1 The Purpose of the Tract

Capitalism must have a stable standard of value. In this context, *TMR* relates fluctuations in the money supply (M^s) and uncertainty to both inflation and deflation. Moreover, movements in wages (w) are either larger or smaller than movements in prices and this affects both profits and investment (I), bringing about instability. The heuristic rules in the old macroeconomy were threefold before Keynes: the gold standard, balanced budgets, and free trade. But *TMR* rejects these guidelines proposing new ones such as a monetary policy based on interest rate management.

Keynes provided data on fluctuations in the value of money since 1914, but also suggested that such elements as exchange rate control and the increase in confidence may halt these fluctuations benefitting wage owners, investors, and businessmen. To ensure stability he did not trust in the gold standard, since gold is prone to fluctuating. Instead, he recommended policies suitable for both the United States and Great Britain for stabilizing both the value of the dollar and domestic prices. He was still in 1923 an orthodox philosopher, considering that all evils proceed from the instability of the value of money which poses risks (yes, risks) for investment.

According to Brad de Long's review (1996), *TMR* sets the agenda for monetary management by introducing: monetary instability as the cause of economic evils, sound monetary principles for diminishing risk, the public sector's ability to provide the private economy with a measuring rod, and the heuristics for the accomplishment of a stable economic framework. But *TMR* is also an investigation into the economic problems of post-WWI Europe.

For de Long the first chapter of *TM* is a summary of the effects of deflation and inflation on the distribution of income, activity, and attitudes toward risk and reward. The second chapter introduces the idea that inflation is a hidden tax on holdings of real money balances, perhaps following Ramsey. The third chapter is an introduction to *QTM*. It contains the line: 'In the long run we are all dead,' meaning that economists must concentrate on short-term expediency in the footsteps of Burke but more than that no ideal or imaginary benchmarks exist in economics. The second part of the chapter is an introduction to exchange-rate determination, the purchasing-power-parity theory, and why there might be deviations from purchasing power parity.

According to de Long, Chapter Four deals with Keynes's affirmation that currency values must be in line with national price levels to force the latter into consistency. This is under the framework of pre-WWI exchange rate parities but indicates that no past values must prevail as only present conditions are relevant. He preferred a stable exchange rate (at this stage only) as a precondition for the elimination of fluctuations in price levels. He argued that modern central banks can maintain price stability if they are not tied to gold. His arguments are suggestions to reform practices on the part of central banks for improving their functioning. Continuing to follow de Long, the last chapter of *TMR* is full of conventional guidelines such as the use of monetary policy to stabilize internal prices. The value of money must be managed, but both savings and investment must still be left to market forces. The core of *TMR* is thus an orthodox belief in the ability of the system to self-regulate (see Appendix 10.1). As such, imbalance is only temporary, and regulation brings about accelerated recovery. End of story.

Nevertheless, the Great Depression would destroy Keynes's faith in the proposition that economies only generate small transient business cycles. From then on, he was concerned about the management of the effects of depressions—output and employment swings; the former he still assumed to be fixed in *TMR* (1930). But the book lacks a leading thread for linking all macroeconomic realms, providing only worthwhile isolated insights. Let's see how this occurred.

7.2 *A Treatise on Money* (1930): The Silver Book

Keynes states in *TM* that monetary stability is at the heart of an explanation of depression so that the book is also a financial interpretation of the business cycle. *A Treatise on Money* or *TM* (1930) is about windfalls (fluctuating earnings), investment, expectations under uncertainty, and unemployment (U) as the joint products of market sclerosis as generated by an investment (I) that is inferior with respect to savings (S). *TM* thus offers a treatise on the function of money. Keynes presents new views, letting the classical assumptions go and leaving aside the effects of the gold standard since in 1930 he was interested in explaining the price level. Here profits and interest rates drive capitalism but stability in *GDP* or Y is the objective.

His aim was to explain macroeconomic stability and autonomy, with a focus on Britain.[3] The heuristic contentions characterizing *TM* are the differences between savings and investment as well as between nominal and real wages, thus representing an evolution from his former treatise in economics. At this stage Keynes became the discoverer of the impact of investment on the credit cycle. Instability in prices must be related to fluctuations in the cycle due to uncertainty. However, he was still under the influence of Ralph George Hawtrey (1879–1975), who was a former 'Apostle' but a traditional economist supporting a managed gold standard.

TM examines the relationship between unemployment, money, and prices in the 1920s. This is his first (imperfect) attempt to explain the dynamics of investment, stating that instability in production arises from price fluctuations. The classical theory had preached that the system is immediately self-adjusting, with output fluctuations being inoffensive but in 1930 price stability was the most pressing concern. If savings is larger than investment this has an uprising effect on the interest rate, which generates unemployment. Then recessions occur and policies for solving this problem become crucial. Keynes prefers discretion in policy conduction as he foresees an open system, rejecting conventions in terms of policy conduction. For instance, the closed-system solution to unemployment proposed by Ramsay MacDonald (1866–1937), who was Prime Minister from the Labor Party between 1929 and 1931, was traditional: wages (w) must be lowered. Instead, for Keynes the problem is related to the mentioned difference between savings and investment.

The conception of uncertainty and its by-product instability are captured in *TM* in the form of circumstantial fluctuations in interest rates and asset bubbles that affect productive investment. Thus, in *TM* the interplay between financial variables and asset speculation is an integral part of the account of the business cycle (Ertürk 2008). Keynes enunciates that the economy functioning is essentially monetary. Yet here the engine of enterprise is profit which implies price instability, and the secondary concern is employment via stabilizing investment through money management. But *TM* also attempts to solve the problem of unemployment by means of counter-cyclical public expenditure and credit provision for enhancing profits.

Keynes was the Chairman of the Economic Advisory Council in the early 1930s, so he disseminated his Silver Book but was soon regretful about its theoretical incompleteness. The reason was that the multiplier or m (Appendix 6.3) is absent, which signifies that neither the cause nor the path of recessions is explained. Further, he was aware that the use of a balanced budget is not the key for accomplishing stabilization (this is a novelty); indeed, stabilization is impossible along the extreme points of the business cycle. Also, the austerity measures of tight monetary policies and the enhancement of saving (S) implemented by rules represent conservatism, and such measures are not always useful in an uncertain world.

Wood *TM* depicts early elements of *GT (see Chapter 2)*, but in the former savings is passive and must be a fortiori and rapidly (automatically) equal to investment. Robert Dimand (1986) states that *TM* deals with disequilibrium dynamics[4] after using Keynes's two fundamental equations, each a variant of Fisher's *QTM* (1911), one at the macro level and the other at the micro level (see below). In those equations the subtraction of profits from the costs of investment determines price levels, both at the micro and the macroeconomic levels, whereas the simultaneous management of interest rates and the prices of capital goods (through a portfolio balances approach) restores equilibrium. However, a misleading monetary policy or the return to gold standard would bring about unemployment.

In the Silver Book, changes in output (Y) still result from fluctuations in the price level (P) as in the Classical view. Keynes is still concerned with credit or business cycles but also with 'windfall' profits (π) or losses, and this type of dynamics forces the model to be only suitable for static and equilibrium-oriented economies. Something is missing. He did not still see uncertainty as the basis of both finance and macroeconomics. Further, he did not explain the adjustment mechanism that constituted the credit cycle in *TM* (Chase 1991; Davis 1989) since he assumed constant output (Y) throughout the process. His theory of the interest rate (r) is another flaw. But he desperately needed a more complex framework than *QTM* since this former specification still links changes in output to changes in prices. The upshot is *TM* lacks a motivator—a subject—since money is fully absorbed by industrial production due to the excesses in the price level that are only eliminated in equilibria. Thus, *TM* explains the direction of the influence of aggregate demand on output, not the varying levels of the latter. In *TM*, he also started to outline the outcomes of deflation, which is worse than both inflation and restricted trade. *TM* is thus a dinosaur's but dynamic study of the flow of incomes and expenditures and hence the forerunner of the model of injections and leakages set up in *GT*. The consequence of this nascent view is that *TM* introduces the ghost of involuntary unemployment, but the world still lacks a connection between investment and saving.

For Giuseppe Fontana (2003), *TM* is an exploration in money matters written by a practitioner. Instability is due to the divergence between investment and saving. This is due in turn—not yet to uncertainty—but to the—Marxian?—possibility that 'windfall' profits may be larger than the normal remunerations to entrepreneurs. However, disequilibria eventually will require correct interest rate management to reduce unemployment in the absence of abnormal profits. In addition, the proper workings of financial systems—banks, assets, and currencies—are required for attaining stability; but unemployment is still not a monetary problem for Keynes in 1930. Inflation (the opposite) matters are at the top of the agenda. The point is that Keynes needs now to build his own home.

For Dimand (1986), the cause of fluctuations in prices in *TM* is investment but the offspring is 'windfall'[5] profits (Q). The point is savings do not guarantee investment, but profits do. If $Y = C + I$ (or $O = R + C$, in the notation of the second fundamental equation) turns out to be different from $Y = C + S$ (or $E - R = S$, where E = earnings of a community or cost of production), then production and expenditure decisions must be reconciled via movements in the price of consumption goods. Again, if I is distinct from S there will emerge either booms, or vice versa, and banks must stabilize the purchasing power of money by controlling credit. In addition, the market and natural (Wicksellian) rates of interest still must be equal. The novelty lies in that the public sector must encourage investment as no invisible hand exists. The conundrum is that profits disappear in the ensuing Keynes's writings.

7.2.1 Depicting the Fundamental Equations

The two fundamental equations (Eqs. 7.1 and 7.2 here) link investment with savings, tracing their causes and effects for building a monetary theory of production (Appendix 7.2). They explain price fluctuations at both the micro-consumption sector and the macroeconomy levels as follows:

$$P = W_1 + Q_1/R \qquad \text{in the consumption goods} \qquad (7.1)$$

$$\pi = W_1 + = Q/O \qquad \text{in the whole economy} \qquad (7.2)$$

where: Q = windfall profits for the economy ($Q_1 + Q_2$); W = rate of earnings per unit of human effort, so that its inverse $1/W$ is the labor power of money; $W_1 = E/O$.

The price of consumption goods is equal to the rate of earnings of the factor of production plus the rate of profit per unit of consumption goods at the micro level, and the same dynamic happens at the macro level. Price fluctuations resulting from profit fluctuations are traceable to differences in savings and investment, the basis—still here—for inflation. But credit swings also affect the relationship between investment and savings via *QTM* since money supply developments directly affect prices in $P \bullet Y = M \bullet V$ (Y and V are constant here). Inflationary pressure generates underemployment, or 'stagflation.' A finding which is forgotten in conventional Keynesianism. Forgetfulness about stagflation is what provoked the Keynesian counter-revolution, led by Milton Friedman around 1978 or perhaps even earlier (Appendix 13.1).

Keynes further hypothesized on the problem of failing (not fluctuating yet, or shifting as in the moderns) output bringing about depressions, which would invalidate the notion of a 'Widows' cruse' (an adjustment via quantities). The converse term is the 'Danaid's jar' (an adjustment via prices), which is never filled. Keynes's systematic effect of r on I—which is the central tenet of macroeconomics—is still not consolidated at this time, and the real and the monetary sectors are still separate. However, he linked instability to unsystematic movements in both interest rates and the prices of securities, hinting for the first time that uncertainty plays a pivotal role in the functioning of price and output systems. Since the psychological manifestations of entrepreneurs, as captured in uncertainty, are more acute at the highest and lowest phases of the trade cycle, *TM* concludes that investment/saving (I/S) is the motivator of the system. This innovation is great for the early 1930s.

According to Stamp (1931), *TM* is a masterpiece in the explanation of dynamic economics,[6] in which the *Fundamental Equations* permit the proof of the argument. Under this framework, banking policies provide an understanding of the monetary world economy wherein credit creation is important. This is due to the idea that the short-term *r* is the key (occasional) variable for the requirements of domestic policy rather than M^s (but occasionally as in the Neo Classical model) which might not be free from developments in the price of gold. Hereafter the liberal remedy for the inequality between *I* and *S* is firstly real and then financial. Moreover, financial volatility brought about by asset diversification intensifies swings in the productive sector (witness recent financial crises taking place at the beginning of the twenty-first century). Nonetheless adjustment mechanisms keep economies flowing: economies must be managed.

To put matters in context for the non specialist, it must be mentioned that for Smithin (2010), the issues in contention in monetary theory are: ontology of money, endogenous vs. exogenous money, interest rate determination, and the choice of policy instruments. At least at the beginning, however, *TM* does not deal with money non-neutrality in the sense that effects are seen in prices rather than in output via investment. *TM* is also about balance between the domestic and international macroeconomic autonomies, as increases in prices affect other economies via exchange rate developments. According to Seccareccia (2002), Keynes's analysis of price formation in *TM* is original but still based on classic presuppositions. In any event, *TM* is about controlling the intensity of the fluctuations by creating his version of the Wicksellian[7] theory of the trade cycle by means of tracing the relationship between money and prices. This is the first mention of fluctuating output and unemployment levels, but Keynes at this point still treats these elements with a static framework. Transitions fuse contradictory elements.

Wicksell defines the *natural rate of interest* as that compatible with a stable price level. Departing from the Swedish Wicksell, the Austrian School then hypothesizes that a boom happens when *r* falls short of the *natural* rate, and *I* and *S* differ. An expansion (depression) occurs, and prices rise (reduce). Increases in M^s also lead to price rises. As credit and deposits constitute part of money supply, the central bank can create money. Then disequilibrium leads to an increase in the money supply. Given a constant velocity of money (V), then in terms of $M \bullet V = P \bullet Y$, a rise in *M* (money supply) leads only to a rise in prices (P). Keynes did not adopt this part of the story based on *QTM*. He considered *r* as the fundamental mechanism for rehabilitating economies (like the Austrians) but only contingent upon social circumstances, not as a 'natural' constant as $\pi = 3.1416$. For Wicksell, Say's Law telling that supply generates its own demand—another favorite straw man of Keynes—is also violated by the introduction of money into the picture. The supplies of capital goods and inputs are constrained thus factor and goods prices increase. Inflation is hence brought about by a rise in aggregate demand above constrained aggregate supply. Wicksell's endogenous creation of money and its bearing on the goods markets is a breakdown of the Neoclassical theory, according to which the monetary and real sectors are separate, and money is neutral. These contentions are obviously non-Keynesian but as stated before Wicksell still believes in a natural interest rate.

According to Temin and Vines (2016), *TM* is an early *GT* wherein expectations are quasi-rational. Still *TM* is futuristic since it informs that under the then prevailing gold standard there were not opportunities for conducting independent domestic policies in 1931. For Kregel (2012), the tools for Keynes for achieving stability at this epoch are a zero-interest rate policy and quantitative flexibilization—a very modern concept (see Appendix 13.1). Under this framework, Keynes is the father of unorthodox monetary policies, but he still placed no emphasis on the need to provide an external source for demand enhancement through government expenditure (G).

The novelty of *TM* is that problems are endogenously caused (see Appendix 13.1, especially with reference to Minsky). If high interest rates inhibit investment, generating unemployment, not even foreign saving must prevail. This statement is modern. *TM* also deals with the rules of currency credit, reforms to monetary policy, and the value and dynamics of price levels. Then again, output (Υ) changes in the short period are still on the horizon. Still in *TM* Keynes explains what a monetary economy is since money is not a veil.

7.2.2 *Special Issues and Implications of* A Treatise on Money

The theory related to money as a sporadic driver of the system (Appendix 2.1) takes elements from Dennis Holme Robertson (1890–1963) and Hubert Douglas Henderson (1890–1952), contemporaries of Keynes. These contributions motivated Keynes to envisage in the 1930s that free monetary management is possible, favoring it against an international standard such as gold or the dollar. A problem might be a shortage of international liquidity, but this could be solved by lending to countries with balance of payments problems, an idea that anticipated Keynes's stance on international cooperation in *How to Pay for the War* (1940).

According to Moggridge (1992), for Keynes in the early 1930s directed public investment could be increased, thereby augmenting employment through loan-finance public works or capital development schemes for investment; nonetheless, his preferred instrument was still monetary policy (unlike in *GT* when he evolved to prefer interest rates or fiscal policy). In addition, he was still concerned about profits (π) as he considered the special position of Britain during those years: low profits and high unemployment.

In *TM* Keynes was concerned about transitions (unlike Hume who was always concerned with points of departure and arrival) not reform, an insight he learned in practice and one that is based on his philosophy related to organicism, in which interrelations and dynamic changes are crucial. The remedies are considered separately from intermittent interest rate (r) management propelling increases in investment (I), to wage controls, and improvements in the foreign balance. Moreover, he dismissed the 'Treasury View' (that fiscal policy has no effect on activity and unemployment) concerned with rationing public expenditure,[8] as he was reluctant to accept rigid—non-discretionary—principles of action. Conversely, the 'Treasury View' practitioners were skeptical about Keynes's proposals for using short-term domestic monetary policy to mitigate slumps. On the other hand, Keynes realized that the local interest rate cannot go down in the presence of high international interest rates, but also that the remedies must include coordination between the central bank and commercial banks, international cooperation, and attention to both foreign investment and savings; in the process, he envisaged the relationship between international trade and international finance. All this is related to Keynes's practical philosophy of action underpinned by his notions of organicism and the non-existence of a self-regulating system, but still lacking the key mechanism: a varying output in the face of uncertainty.

Also, according to Moggridge (1992), *The Macmillan Report* appears in 1931 revealing Britain's debtor position. After these monetary disorders, Keynes advocated long-term programs for industrial reconstruction to avoid both structural and involuntary unemployment and he backed short-term protection at least until the gold standard prevailed, thereby proposing a revenue tariff with duties on certain goods, foodstuffs, and raw materials. His vision of liberty was restricted to the management of British economic affairs. *TM* unveils the dynamic laws behind the passage of time between any two equilibria in monetary economies. This insight on transitions allowed Keynes to investigate the methods of spontaneous monetary management. In this sense, Keynes's discernments were evolving from the contentions of *TMR* (1923). Nonetheless, some parts of the book are not harmonic, in part because he was straying from mainstream ideas, such as that the economy is intrinsically static possessing automatic forces, except in cases of prolonged depressions. But the progress lies in that *TM* affirms that humans can control their destiny by means of selecting expedient policies.

7.2.3 Economic History in A Treatise on Money

Keynes re-outlines known historical episodes for exemplifying the repercussions of a savings rate being larger than the investment rate (Chapter 30, Volume II) based on his objective distaste for savings, as he was against Victorian notions. Since the idolatry for *S* has implications for the financial system, he was inspired to find new monetary patterns to explain the changeover from booms to busts and vice versa. For that purpose, he relied on his knowledge of the mechanics of Capitalism, contending that the solution is a decreasing long-term interest rate. For Keynes, the Middle Ages could be considered as an enormous depression and the Renaissance as a boom. This contention anticipates those made in *GT* (1936), when adventuring the idea that India's ancestral poverty is the result of hoarding. In these examples Keynes's methodology is holistic, dynamic, observational, comparative, complex, and characteristically self-reflective.

7.2.4 Financial Investment in the Epoch of TM

At the micro level, Keynes's *contango* and *normal backwardation* theories of speculation (going long) and hedging (going short) over financial instruments in forward markets, respectively, are depicted in Chapter 29, Volume II. At the macro level, it is explained that asset speculation may exacerbate the difference between saving and productive investment thereby producing depressions (Appendix 13.1). He illustrated the operational characteristics of the forward markets contending that speculation has an influence on fluctuations, since speculative money is artificially withdrawn from the circular flow of income. In other words, the mere possibility—yes, possibility as the phenomenon is being reflected in market movements—that future prices could be larger than spot prices generates perverse incentives for productive—not only financial—investment. Productive investment is thus funded here with liquid capital and prefigure the theory of liquidity preference. The assumption is that the system abhors non liquid capital, as it is normally invested in the financial markets and is not useful for the sake of stabilizing the economy. The essence is that these artificial developments in financial markets may either breed or magnify uncertainty, ultimately impacting employment.

The forward market may thus generate crises that unveil deficiencies in the real sectors of economies (see Appendix 13.1). In the best scenario, the forward markets may be used for temporary either hedging or speculation. But for Keynes, enterprise must prevail over either savings or speculation, and hence profits must originate in and be directed to real (physical) investment. For him, crises are the corollary of his application of the organic principle ('fallacy of composition'): savings (speculation) are beneficial for individuals, but not for the stability of the system (see Appendix 13.1). The point is the forward market magnifies market happenings; being analogous to those great episodes when price fluctuations are exaggerated, such as the Spanish Gold galleons or the Dutch Tulips in the seventeenth century, or the depression that occurred in the 1890s. Hence, he helped to diffuse the idea that the foundations of capitalist society are shaken by the emergence of slumps (Keynes 1931), and many of them were unnecessarily provoked (see Appendix 13.1). This was organicism at its best taking account of uncertainty will only be dealt with in the *GT*. The implication in *TM* is financial investment requires a philosophical background to be sustainable.

This chapter has dealt with the philosophy embedded in Keynes's *TMR*, his first exploratory book about economic reform still under a setback of certainty whereas *TM* is about his thoughts regarding economic stability. The legacy of *TM* (and to a lesser extent *TMR*) is that it makes clear that shocks are primarily internally caused, preparing the ground for the core ontic contentions expressed in both *GT* (Chapters 2 and 9) and 'MEB' (Chapter 11) with reference to ethics. Both books, *TMR* and *TM*, still possess a great influence on policymakers, financiers, and investors; and lay the groundwork for the making of *GT*. Both *TMR* and *TM* and their contemporary pamphlets and events (Appendices) may also give the impression that Keynes did not produce philosophy between 1923 and the early 1930s. However, he applies his philosophy and does write philosophical pamphlets, articles, and biographies in that epoch, and this is the subject matter of Chapter 8. There it is explained how Keynes delves into moral themes in the early 1930s, partly returning to the topics addressed in Chapter 6.

Appendix 7.1: 'The Economic Consequences of Mr. Churchill' (1925)

The controversies of 1920s Britain were about the aftermath to the treaty of peace and war debts in Europe, but also about the policy of deflation and the return to the gold standard. All are associated with Keynes's return to the public arena. Specifically, he counseled on employment policies and the dangers of depression when criticizing the entry of Britain to the gold standard in 'The Economic Consequences of Mr. Churchill' (1925). For Keynes the return to the Gold Standard (1925) reveals avoidable asymmetries in the adjustment mechanism supporting an unnecessarily fixed exchange rate. The gold standard as an exogenous currency not only involves a fixed exchange rate but imposes the same monetary and fiscal policies to countries facing different unemployment conditions in a post-war world in which coordination policies were inexistent. He predicted that this uncertainty would not endure instead searching for a clarification of slumps, aiming thus for a basis for both the design and conduction of policies.

Keynes argued in the 1925 pamphlet (a long article) on Churchill that committing to the pre-war parity would ultimately prove to be deflationary. His analysis proved to be prescient. The arguments of Chapter I are against the Gold Standard in conditions which require a readjustment of money values. Britain then was committed to forcing down money wages and money values under the guidance of Churchill's experts. But they miscalculated the misalignments of money values resulting from restoring Sterling to its pre-war gold parity as they chose irrelevant price indices.

The Treasury used to compare the wholesale index numbers in Britain and in the United States, since at least two thirds of these comprise the raw materials of international commerce. Hence it was visible that Churchill's experts also underrated the difficulty of bringing about a general reduction in internal money values. According to them there would be no repercussions if there was some way to bring about a simultaneous reduction in all money payments. For those pundits, the necessary adjustments followed from the Bank of England's policy could bring about depression in the export industries, coupled with tight monetary policies, which would have even consequences throughout the community. However, if the exchange rate is fixed at the gold parity, the alternative was to bet on a rise in gold prices abroad, which would induce foreigners to pay a higher gold price for Britain's exports, or to adopt a policy of forcing down nominal wages (w) and the cost of living to the necessary extent. The officials would choose the first option as for them U still depends on w rather than on profits (or in the future *GT*'s aggregate demand).

According to those officials, the advantages of the Gold Standard were secured at the cost of depression in the export industries. They said that this would generate a reduction in wages, but the cost of living would also fall. Keynes always having other spectacles contended that the cost of living would not fall enough, and that the export industries would not be able to reduce their prices sufficiently, since wages would fall only in the sheltered industries and prices would be on the rise. In addition, for him w would not fall in sheltered industries because there was U in unsheltered industries. For him, hence these actions would only intensify unemployment until wages would fall, but the result would be worse than the original evil. Then again Keynes did not buy standard theory, informed by his experiences. He had the stature to create and diffuse his own conceptions.

Further Writings on Liberal Proposals

Keynes followed the progress of reparations and war debts after the adoption of the *Dawes Scheme* in 1924 (Moggridge 1992), but its successor the *Young Plan* (1929) emerged to give more time to Germany. Moggridge (1992) writes that 'The German Transfer Problem' (1929) about the international denomination of German payments, ignited a controversy between Keynes and the Swedish economist Bertil Ohlin. For Keynes, the problem of German recovery was serious, and the alternatives were inflation in the world or deflation in Germany. Additionally, according to Moggridge (1992), Keynes's comments circa 1929 on the intensification of the Great Depression paved the road for the creation of *TM* in 1930. Keynes also participated in the *Economic Advisory Council* in 1931, which included inquiries into banking, finance, and credit with an international perspective. He believed in protectionism (Chapter 4 of *TM*) as a necessary condition for conducting policies whenever inexpensive money is insufficient for enhancing investment or *I*.

Keynes wrote the liberal 'Can Lloyd George do it? The Pledge examined,' (1929) co-authored by Hubert David Henderson (1890–1952), a politician in the Liberal Party. The pamphlet is about the financial positioning of Britain, especially about the post-war difficulties which were more pertinent at that moment for Keynes than the then-current preoccupation with the impoverishment left by the war. The idea was to enhance employment through a policy of national development. Nevertheless, Lloyd George opined that post-war unemployment would solve itself, like in the nineteenth century, by implementing microeconomic schemes. Lloyd George exposed his view in a letter addressed to *The Nation* in 1924, supported by a survey made to economists and businessmen. The results were published in the Yellow Book: 'Britain's Industrial Future' (1928), but the Keynes's pamphlet 'We can conquer unemployment' (1928) captured its gist. Keynes analysed the Pledge in terms of its common sense, facts and projections on unemployment, the liberal framework, and the situation of Britain's government in terms of budget freedom, timing costs, indirect job creation, and employment diversion. He concluded that the Pledge was a product of conservative philosophy applied to an unconventional problem related to growth. A new watershed had emerged in 1931, when Britain was out of the gold standard as Keynes had foreseen, and the connection with the United States had to be reformulated.

Appendix 7.2: A Letter to Roosevelt, and a Superb Transition Toward *GT*: 'The Monetary Theory of Production' (1933)

Keynes was also active at the international level again in 1930 but focused on Britain's future. As a context, the *New Deal* promulgated in the United States included both laws and executive orders during the first term of Franklin Delano Roosevelt (1933–1937). It was a response to the Great Depression (1929) and was focused on relief for the unemployed and the poor (unsystematically), recovery of the economy to normal levels, and reform of the financial system. Keynes's response is 'An Open Letter to President Roosevelt' (1933). He saw that the post-war United States might confuse recovery with reform in terms of timing. Short-term recovery only would imply increasing both output and employment by means of consumption, investment, lower interest rates, and public expenditure (*G*). Here particular items of *G* must be chosen, with preference for large-scale public investment (Keynes 1933). This means expenditure is not futile as was supposed by superficial disseminators of his insights. According to Keynes, recovery requires increases in purchasing power, though this happens at the expense of recovery lags due to price lowering. Yes, prices were still the preoccupation not unemployment. Keynes wrote at a stage when managing the quantity of money had limits unlike expenditure. He disagreed with the sanctification of gold as the base good for prices, suggesting that Roosevelt conduct exchange depreciation as the result of a domestic price-raising policy, as the latter policy must serve the purpose of increasing *GDP*. The issue was 'the maintenance of abundant credit and the reduction of the long-term rates of interest' (Keynes 1933, p. 6). He thus linked at last the real with the monetary economy via the effect of decreasing *r* on the enhancement of *I*, but, notice, still not systematically, still as the upshot of an intuition. Keynes thus suggested here an interaction of policies. *GT* was approaching.

Finding Gold Mines: 'The Monetary Theory of Production' (1933)

In the meanwhile, a draft of the index of 'The Monetary Theory of Production' (1933) penned in 1932 (in *JMK CW* Vol. 30, p. 49) contains a section on the interest rate but it is still empty of content. This temporary omission perhaps demonstrates that the connection between the real and the financial sector was still waiting for more reflection. At any rate, the first 'informal' draft of *GT* (1936) is 'The Monetary Theory of Production' undertaken with the auspice of the German citizen Arthur Spiethoff (1873–1957). Keynes was in a transitional stage in terms of envisaging his macroeconomic core while fighting orthodox thought, especially their vision about a long-term self-equilibrating system. For him, the long run depends—at this time—on the decisions undertaken in the short run. In 'The Monetary Theory of Production,' money at last—but imperfectly conceived—affects the nature of transactions. This view partially came from the circuit approach in the early German and

Swedish literatures. Keynes's version was an analysis of money circulation like in *TM* (Graziani 2003). But in 1933 money is clearly seen by Keynes as providing a benefit when held as a store of value, a new formulation of monetary economics. Money then becomes the missing link between the short and the long terms but also between the real and the monetary sectors. That is, money affects r, which in turn has an effect on both I and w (unlike in Pigou[9]), causing systematic fluctuations in output (Y).

Hence in Keynes's document of 1933, unlike in *TM* or the writings of Marshall, cash money is different from credit. The corollary is that money (in the form of M_1 in money supply $= M^S$) is also a tool for dealing with booms and depressions, which are more than real productive—monetary exceptionally—tribulations. Knowing that booms and depressions are always latent, policymakers must be able to manage interest rates (the price of money, not its quantity) to avoid them. Hence in this proto-version of *GT* the solution can no longer be found in—private—banking policy, like in *TM*, since Keynes at last realized that problems arise whenever money is non-neutral and this is a matter belonging to the central bank. Therefore, the monetary theory of production goes beyond the real-exchange (Classical) paradigm in which money is a veil (just a means of exchange). The correct expression for this Keynes's innovation is an entrepreneur (monetary) economy (*CW* Vol. 29, p. 81). This is highly relevant for the history of economics. But going backwards, Keynes's developments of the monetary theory of production as a concept were partly a rationalization of the Marxian sequence: *M-C-M'* (Graziani 2003), where: M = initial money for producing commodities, C = commodities, and M' = final money after selling commodities in a non-self-subsistence economy. Money is a commodity that reproduces itself but is more than a commodity: it is the commodity. Thus, Marx's sparking insights were crudely related to the role of aggregate demand, but the full effect of money on investment (via interest rates) will only be described explicitly in Keynes's Golden Book (1936).

At this stage Keynes's primary goal, still not understood by his contemporaries, was to avoid 'unsystematic' slumps as Keynes had a foot in the Classical world. Perhaps for this reason apart from his busy life, he never penned the article he planned around 1933, which would have been named 'Footnotes to the General Theory.'[10] There the notions of both the absence of a self-regulating system and uncertainty would explain why fluctuations in r have a bearing on effective demand, employment, and instability. The time is ready for *GT*. Whereas *TM* is about the transition between two disequilibria, *GT* is grounded in a disequilibrium approach. Thus 'The Monetary Theory of Production' encompasses an application of organicism in which everything is internally, inter-dimensionally, and reciprocally related (see 'Miscellanea Ethica' 1907). On the other hand, his activities in the early 1930s also included the Keynes-Henderson Plan and his participation in the World Economic Conference. At that time, he also found the energy to preach the 'good life' (see Chapter 8). He even challenged some assumptions about Soviet Russia (1925) and British unemployment doles, criticizing the latter in favor of construction work and restricted trade for remedying *U*.

Keynes Revisits Financial Investment

His long-term investment philosophy contradicts his advocacy for exercising short-term expediency (Chapter 9) but he created one of the earliest mutual funds with uncorrelated investment options: the impressive but volatile *Chest Fund* of King's College (1924–1946). There he favored concentrated but balanced (conventional) portfolios since at this moment he was a believer in following assets with intrinsic value, based on his ethical beliefs in virtue (Chapter 4) and his knowledge of probability (Chapter 6). However, he was aware that fundamental values do not matter if financial investment is going to be practical, especially in the short term. Moreover, an investor must anticipate others' reactions, advancing insights that predate game theory (conceived by Von Neumann and Morgesten in 1944), which considered two rivaling scenarios: the bull and the bear dichotomy. According to that dichotomy he recommended avoiding risks by the distinction between borrowers' and lenders' risk; the examination of both yields and commercial values; the speculation after the assessment of psychological and political events; and the dissimilarity between small and large investors.

Keynes practiced his version of the principle of action, possessing a practical visualization of financial markets, including futures (Sect. 7.2). For him both uncertainty and transitions were the clue for understanding the workings of both those markets and the system. He might have considered that a financial market operating in a certain environment would not be interesting or profitable for anyone and that it would be unrealistic in any economy due to the existence of fluctuations. Later, Keynes (1937) criticized his own over-investment attitude for not acting more drastically on the expectation of trouble ahead, proving that ex-ante probabilities must be considered when investing. On the other hand, he stated that successful investment also depends on holding back shares even in troubled times. He avoided second-class investments and the anticipation of busts, being conservative about the long term by not losing sense of proportion (which is pertinent in nineteenth-century Britain). He distinguished between intuition and inside information and suggested analysing our principles and activities from time to time.

Appendix 7.3: Keynes's General: Richard Ferdinand Kahn (1905–1989)

The first legacy of Kahn is the multiplier in 1931, the second is his participation in the *Keynes Circus* between that year and 1936 by providing ideas leading to the making of *GT* (Appendix 4.3), and the third is the co-generation of the idea of a clearing union in Europe as early as 1932. The philosophy of the multiplier (*m*) and Kahn's role in convincing Keynes of its usefulness—in his article 'The Relation of Home Investment to Unemployment' (1931)—are indispensable for capturing the gist of the evolution in the heuristics (the building blocs) of *GT*. The multiplier would become, along with interest rates, the motivator—mobile—of the theory of investment-driven cycles, control of which leads to full employment. Keynes, at the time of writing *TM*, was a supporter of new statements in economics.

Kahn discovered the uneven relationship between a given element of aggregate demand (*AD*): Consumption (*C*), investment (*I*) or public expenditure (*G*), and the increase in output (*Y*). If *G* was doubled, output would increase tenfold, if m $(1/1 - c)$ amounted to 5, where c = marginal propensity to consume was less than 1. The effect of *m*—due to the interaction among all elements of *AD*—dwindled after some iterations, a case of Taylor's imploding series. For Moggridge (1992), Kahn's heuristic tool ended the controversy around the increase of domestic investment versus public expenditure, the crowding-out effect, since now the effects of *C*, *I*, or *G* could be measured and hence managed. Both Joseph Schumpeter and Joan Robinson (a rival and a supporter of Keynes, respectively) recognized the role of *m* on the envisagement of *GT*. As *m* provides flexibility to *AD*, the remaining rigid variable for Keynes was now the monetary wage (w) since the labor market depends on institutions and the classical wage flexibility is not the solution to slumps or unemployment.

But a free exchange rate is not viable either. Kahn saw Europe as a mini area requiring stability by means of a complex monetary arrangement which could be akin to the inter-war monetary system. The objective of Keynes and Kahn was the accomplishment of regional stability. Both men were preoccupied by both internal and interregional imbalances in 1933. According to Kregel (2017), they produced a joint plan about a multi-faceted clearing union subjected to a unit of account and an internal settlements system. It was a mini Bretton Woods accord for enhancing policy management including internal exchange flexibility, by enabling symmetric adjustments but distinguishing the effects of dis-adjustments on creditor and debtor countries.

Ceilings would be accumulative aggregates. This was the essence of Kahn's discount dynamic method. Keynes wanted to set things up so that no further arrangements were required. In the Keynes-Kahn plan, revisions would occur every six months, creating symmetries through incentives, functioning as offsetting mechanisms. In modern terminology, the United Kingdom was expected to be the lender of last resort in a context of free trade. They knew that the success of any clearing scheme depends both upon the relative sizes of the extreme countries and the method of settlement balances. This was far better than the alternative—atomicist—method of respecting national sovereignties.

More specifically, Keynes and Kahn proposed an international alternative to the locally focused policies prevailing in the world at that moment. Keynes advocated grouping countries in Europe; for example, the Germanic, the Scandinavian, and the Latin countries (Keynes 1940–1944 [1980], quoted in Kregel 2017). But he rejected the application of uniform fiscal and monetary policies among countries since they might have imparted asymmetries to adjustment processes. Keynes wanted homogeneity in diversity rather than equality, in this case in terms of the conditions for managing problems arising from currency and export–import imbalances. Paradoxically, regional harmonization would generate regional independence and diversity but bringing about political integration in Europe in the late 1940s. International adjustments would balance recessions with no effect on internal aggregate demands, which then could be managed domestically. Kregel (2017) writes that Kahn foresaw at this epoch the creation of the European Payments System or *EPU* (which could start in the 1950s). It must be recalled that Keynes's advocacy for a united Europe is an evolutionary remnant of Keynes's notion of organicism and international uncertainty in a non-self-regulating system subjected to heterogeneities and asymmetries, exactly as exposed in *ECP* in 1919. The difference is that Keynes was now more informed because of his experience as a practitioner economist.

On the other hand, Kahn became an additional collaborator of Keynes in the revision of *GT*, along with Ralph C. Hawtrey, Roy F. Harrod, and Nicholas Kaldor (1908–1986). Keynes had witnessed harsh reviews of the Golden Book, such as those of Jacob Viner (1892–1970) and Joseph Schumpeter. The trans-generational Kahn would later reject the *Neoclassical Synthesis*, a rebirth of traditional economics under 'Keynes's' name which reigned during the 1960s and the early 1970s (Chapter 10), realizing that they misunderstood Keynes's message on both uncertainty and equilibrium. Kahn also wrote on Keynes's notion of liquidity preference circa 1954, while joining others in the empirical critique of the rediscovery of the anti-Keynes 'QTM' circa 1971. The bottom line of this analysis of collaboration is that evolution is also comprised of temporary returns; that is, relevant insights might be re-signified.

Notes

1. Alfred Marshall (1842–1924), Keynes's famous mentor in Cambridge.
2. The construction of Keynes's professors: Alfred Marshall and Arthur Cecil Pigou (1877–1959).
3. His international co-operative spirit is not there yet, except in 1919. It re-emerges after the Second World War (Chapter 12).
4. For traditionalist economists, equilibrium is the rule. For non-orthodox economists, such as Dimand, equilibrium is seen as an exception.
5. This is a renowned Keynes term.
6. *TM* is at this time well thought out as the depiction of a static scheme since it does not consider output fluctuations.
7. Knut Wicksell (1851–1926) was an economist in the Stockholm school who was instrumental in the creation of the first central bank in the world.
8. This orthodox view can be traced back to Says' Law: Supply generates its own demand (Jean Baptiste Say, 1767–1832).

9. A.C. Pigou was a Keynes contemporary who represented in Keynes's mind the Orthodox way of thinking.
10. 'The general theory of employment' (1937) comes closer to Keynes's explanation of the role played by uncertainty (Appendix 9.1).

References

Sources

Chase, Richard X. 1991. "Keynes's Dichotomy: A Methodological Escape for a Theoretical Revolution." *Methods* 3, no. 2 (December): 79–85.

Davis, John B. 1989. "Keynes on Atomism and Organicism." *Economic Journal* 99, no. 398 (December): 1159–72.

De Long, Bradford. 1996. *Review of John Maynard Keynes: A Tract on Monetary Reform*. London: Macmillan. http://www.j-bradford-delong.net/Econ_Articles/Reviews/monetaryreform.html.

Dimand, Robert W. 1986. "The Macroeconomics of the Treatise on Money." *Eastern Economic Journal* 12, no. 1 (October–December): 431–41.

Erturk, Korkut A. 2008. "Why Keynes' A Treatise on Money Might Have Greater Relevance Today Than His General Theory?" *Middle East Technical University Studies in Development* 35, no. 1 (August): 101–20. https://www2.feas.metu.edu.tr/metusd/ojs/index.php/metusd/article/view/216. Accessed 15 September 2018.

Fontana, Giuseppe. 2003. "Keynes's Treatise on Money". In *The Elgar Companion to Post Keynesian Economics*, edited by John E. King, 237–41. Cheltenham, UK: Edward Elgar.

———. 2005. "Mr. Keynes and the 'Classics' Again: A Methodological Enquiry." *Atlantic Economic Journal* 34: 161–74.

Graziani, Augusto. 2003. *The Monetary Theory of Production*. Cambridge: Cambridge University Press.

Kahn, Richard F. 1931. "The Relation of Home Investment to Unemployment." *The Economic Journal* 41, no. 162 (June).

Keynes, John Maynard. 1931. "Keynes Rejoinder to Mr. D. H. Robertson." *Economic Journal XLI* 163 (September). In *JMK/EJ/6/7*. Cambridge: Cambridge University Press. https://discovery.nationalarchives.gov.uk/details/r/afc22cbd-5472-49c8-8ba4-a585275185c2. Accessed 15 November 2019.

———. 1933. "A Monetary Theory of Production." *Festschrift for Arthur Spietoff.* https://web.archive.org/web/2010121813158/http://homepage.newschool.edu/hot/profiles/Keynes.htm. Accessed 21 February 2017.

———. 1937. "The Ex Ante Theory of the Rate of Interest." *Economic Journal* 47: 663–669.

———. 1940. How to Pay for the War. A Radical Plan for the Chancellor of the Exchequer. In *CW, Vol. 9: Essays in Persuasion*, 367–439. London: Basingstoke.

Kregel, Jan. 2017. "A Two-Tier Eurozone or a Euro of Regions? A Radical Proposal Based on Keynes's Clearing Union?" *Policy Brief 144 The Levy Economics Institute*, September. https://www.levyinstitute.org/publications/a-two-tier-eurozone-or-a-euro-of-regions-a-radical-proposal-based-on-keyness-clearing-union. Accessed 23 September 2019.

———. 2012. "Was Keynes's Monetary Policy, à outrance in the Treatise, a Forerunner of the Model of ZIRP and QE?" *Ensayos Económicos* 1, no. 12 (September): 7–22.

Moggridge, Daniel E. 1992. *Maynard Keynes: An Economist's Biography.* London: Routledge.

Seccareccia, Mario. 2002. "Aspects of a New Conceptual Integration of Keynes's Treatise on Money and The General Theory: Logical Time Units and Macroeconomic Price Formation," April, Department of Economics, University of Ottawa. https://aix1.uottawa.ca/~robinson/english/wp/keynestreatise.pdf. Accessed 16 February 2018.

Smithin, John. 2010. "Keynes's Theories of Money and Banking in the Treatise and the General Theory." *Review of Keynesian Economics* 1 (April): 242–56.

Stamp, Josiah C. 1931. "Mr. Keynes Treatise on Money." *Economic Journal* 41, no. 162 (June): 241–49.

Temin, Peter, and David Vines. 2016. "Keynes and the European Economy." *Review of Keynesian Economics* 4, no. 1 (Spring): 36–49.

CHAPTER 8

The Future as Portrayed in the 'Economic Possibilities for Our Grandchildren' (1930)

A major issue in the historical recreation of Keynes's work is investigating whether his ethical and associated political views in the early 1930s are original as well as stable or evolutionary, specifically his stance on the issues of *good* , welfare and duty. This is especially pertinent because he advocates the ethics of virtue against a variants of the ethics of ends such as individualistic utilitarianism in economics or blind practicality in policy management. This topic is expounded in detail in this chapter by means of the analysis of the meaning of 'Economic possibilities for our grandchildren' or *EPG* (1933).

But he also produces similar futuristic documents in this epoch. Appendix 8.1 is about the transitional pamphlets 'Am I a liberal' (1925) and 'The end of the Laissez-faire' (1926). The first one questions the irreflective adherence to parties in Britain, whereas the second is judgmental on the foundations and viability of the *Laissez-faire* at the beginning of the twentieth century. Appendix 8.2 examines 'Clissold' (1927) and 'The means to prosperity' (1933). 'Clissold' is a futuristic landscape about a society in its quest for a freer life. 'The means to prosperity' is about the attainment of full employment by means of the participation of the public sector, preparing the ground for *GT* (1936).

J. Muñoz-Bandala, *Keynes's Evolutionary Spirit*,
Palgrave Insights into Apocalypse Economics,
https://doi.org/10.1007/978-3-030-90150-9_8

8.1 Predictions in 'Economic Possibilities for Our Grandchildren' (1930a)

1930 was not only a monetary year for Keynes. Keynes was 47 years old and perhaps his rebellion was dissipating. Hence, he started to recognize his intellectual debts in 'EPG', as he would scarcely do in *GT* (Chapter 9) and 'My early beliefs' or 'MEB' (Chapter 11). More specifically, after analysing probability, in both objective and subjective terms (Chapter 6), and economic issues (Chapter 7), he would analyse moral concerns in 'EPG,' leaving room for induction and intuition with the purpose of conducting personal judgments.

Keynes started 'EPG' by rejecting economic pessimism. This did not impede his recognition that progress, to the nineteenth century mind, was changing direction. He contended that the improvement in the standard of life and in technological terms would slow down (at least in Great Britain), and that there would be a decline in prosperity in the next decade (by 1940). Furthermore, he wrote that there would remain such challenges as labor absorption and an insufficient fall in the interest rate with respect to equilibrium.[1] He ascertained that depression and unemployment generate the two opposed errors of pessimism: extreme right or extreme left. He realized that the situation in the early 1930s was only a readjustment between one economic period and another, however, neither catastrophe nor blessing or godsend. But being Keynes, he was in depth expecting to put faith in progress.

Then he wondered in 'EPG:' what are the economic possibilities for our grandchildren? Writing as an economic—or cultural—historian, Keynes explains that well before the eighteenth century no changes in life standards took place due to the lack of technological improvements and slow capital accumulation. But capital started to be accumulated in the sixteenth century due to rises in prices and their concomitant profits (recall his narrative on the gold impact on Europe in *TM*, Chapter 7). Hence, during the previous 200 years, science and technology had taken form augmenting life standards in most of the North-western Hemisphere, even though population grew uncomfortably large.

In accordance with 'EPG,' changes in some areas of the goods market were noteworthy during the last ten years (during the 1920s) and this progress entailed such temporary problems as technological unemployment. But Keynes notoriously affirmed that humankind was on the verge of solving its economic problem. If this would come true, the ethical habits of humans would be discarded within a few decades and money-makers would turn to cultivating the art of life. Keynes considered that humans must feel comfortable in existential terms. Money also alienates both the middle and the high classes, but due to economic progress the behavior of wealthy people changes at the end. They begin to do more things for themselves outside of work, taking on only small duties and thus reducing job shifts. This will bring about a change in morals since people will be able to assess the money motive at its true value: as a possession (or even as an asset of value, that is a generator of more money), but nothing more in existential terms. Further, money practices associated to profits and thence to income distribution would promptly change. Finally, Keynes affirms in 'EPG' that the new conception of money will result from a gradual process that has already started, but that will end when relations among people are able to evolve after freeing themselves from superficial constraints (was he talking about himself?). The pace will depend on population control, the avoidance of conflicts, the reliance on science, and capital accumulation. Nevertheless, humans must not wait to experience the art of life and purposeful activities.

Keynes thus contributed to reform regarding such ideas as utilitarianism in ethics by ascertaining that money is a means and in political philosophy contending that the State is a key element for liberalism. He saw money adoration is simply the by-product of the quest for both profitability and capital accumulation at the micro level. So far so good. But love of money may be translated into saving and economic halts at the macro level, bringing about also decaying ethical terms since it permeates human relations in areas where no financial calculus must be resorted to. Moreover, money fulfills unconscious fantasies becoming the basis for neurosis (here Keynes widens his analysis of his notion of the love of gold conducted in Freudian terms, according to Skidelsky). The alternatives for devoting energies different from money generation in the search for a *good* life are creativity and art, which is visibly an ethical legacy from the Bloomsbury Group (Chapter 3, Raffaelli 2006). Keynes's supreme ethical aspiration is not mysterious, education and attitudes broaden mental horizons and change the mere notion of *good* life. Does it sound elitist?

From a post-modern perspective, Keynes is a trans-generational thinker (Raffaelli 2006). His question is: what is left in moral terms for the next generations once the economic problem has been grasped? The question is open, but clearly Keynes's objectives were the attainment of full employment and individual liberty. Then he sacrificed many things.

He despised the ideology of middle-class entrepreneurs in their search for profits, as it does not necessarily lead to equilibrium or serve the purposes of liberty; the latter being the goal in life along with happiness. His contentions were based on methodological topics associated with his assumptions, life experiences, history, and interactions with other disciplines. In sum, money is a matter of time, and useful but only as a transitional device.

Keynes made the passage from ethics to political philosophy inspired by varying motivations. As an ethical philosopher, Keynes was oriented to virtue, but as a political philosopher he was tilted to ends. This already-mentioned double standard may mean in this context that ethics and political philosophy are conceived by him at distinct levels of abstraction which he also did when he distinguished between micro and macroeconomics. He examined the implications of the money motive—one must be a *connossieur* or at least a practitioner before criticizing something. Money idolatry was for him the moral inconvenience of his age (and ours, see Appendix 13.1), but also an example of the naturalistic fallacy in utilitarianism as rejected by Moore (Chapter 3). For Keynes, *good* depended on states of mind, but objects must be *fit* for applying the qualities of *good* to them (Chapter 3). This outline changes subjects very rapidly but it is the manner how Keynes's mind functioned. The point is: What is the appeal of these reflections for Keynes? Keynes concluded at this stage that states of mind are more various than he—or Moore—had previously thought, and that money does not generate ideal enduring states of mind as it is neither a natural nor a *fitting* object for *good*. Thus, his ideals were neither utilitarian nor hedonistic centered on immediate pleasure. In parallel, he was becoming a more extroverted man, which means he gained in his understanding of earthly things and social realms, with his abilities not restricted to contributing insights to elitist or intellectual circles.

The upshot is that in 'EPG,' the economic motive was only a preliminary step in the universal pursuit for *good* states of mind gained after undertaking informed, intentional, and ethical action. This is a basic concept for scrutiny in 'EPG.' Money must not be considered as an end. The corollary is that people must take short-time jobs for the sake of devoting themselves to nobler non-pecuniary tasks,[2] but, and this is very relevant, in the presence of economic progress. Even more importantly, intuition, induction, qualitative uncertainty, expectations and forecasting, all of these concepts being explained in Chapter 6, are now connected as the intellectual products of Keynes's psyche and soul. With the consequence in 'EPG' he gave way to the 'Republic of his Imagination' by propositioning social and ethical environments free of such passions as the exaggerated love of money, wherein rentiers would disappear (see Chapter 9, Appendix 13.1). A critique is that Keynes never wonders whether emerging countries may solve problems in the way that developed countries have done nor does he mention that Capitalism may involve.

Where are we now in the analysis of Keynes's own evolutionary path? According to Dostaler (1996), Keynes wrote about reforms in his early treatises (1901–1913). He then evolved into becoming a conservative elitist in the footsteps of—or despite his—Bloomsbury's ethos (Chapter 4). But one finds him fighting against inherited views in the early 1930s,[3] mainly but not only in Britain. For the atomicist Austrian citizen Rothbard (1992), Keynes's attack on traditional economic values focused on specific issues. The first was the Great Depression (1929), which gave him an opportunity to disagree with the Classical economists, especially on the role of money. The second was thrift, which impedes progress (production is more important than consumption or saving for Keynes, unlike for the Neoclassical economists). Notice these are heuristic issues.

On the other hand, but still examining the—core—role of money in ethics, Keynes condemned Moore's contentions that there are multiple objects subject to the application of *good* rather than just three or four such as beauty, friendship and the like[4] (the Keynes's *fitness* issue), but money was not among those multiple objects in Keynes's view. The qualitative implication is that if money is not a state of mind, values and human interrelations are non-pecuniary. All in all, Keynes's discernments in 'EPG' separate him from ordinary thinking. Likewise, when Keynes criticized the love of money and the adoration of gold, he was also judicious on the epistemological part of utilitarianism, which contended that the only important part of things is their results. Money is only the result—or mobile—of production, consumption, and distribution. He was always involved with the functioning of things[5] and this is the reason why he studied the concrete function of money. But Keynes the insider comprehended that loving money is a misunderstanding of its true social function. In this sense 'EPG' produces guidelines for extending freedom by overcoming the fetishism of money even once full employment is achieved.

In other words, Keynes as a monetary policymaker and an investor was aware of the performing role of money, so he refused to categorize money as an end in the analysis of human behavior. For Mini (1994), Keynes was a realistic contender of nineteenth century Benthamism, which entails the questioning of the relevance of his learning in Eton, Cambridge, and—to a lesser extent—in Bloomsbury for the aim of creating a new story in the adventure of thought. Keynes thus conducted in 'EPG' an examination of values and outlook. He believed in ethical virtue. This means that if virtue is above all, money preoccupations are artificial and pathological. Nevertheless, and apparently in contradiction, one of the meanings of 'EPG' is that no liberties exist until economic problems are conquered (Chapters 9 and 11), which would force us to infer for the sake of solving this contradiction that the love of money is reminiscent of an antique unsolved material difficulty (generating leftovers in the form of neurosis). Indeed, money is advantageous as a unit of account, for conducting transactions and as a store of value for coping with uncertainty (taking several forms, for example bonds or stocks), but nothing else in metaphysical terms.

Money is a creation dating from the times of the ancient Egyptians, used subsequently by the Babylonians, the Assyrians, the Jews, the Indians (who systematically hoarded it), the ancient Greeks, the old Carthaginians, the Roman Empire, the bankers of the Renaissance, the American natives, and the makers of the Industrial Revolution, always overvalued by the middle classes. The point is that adoration for either money or gold pervert human relations. Moreover, money is not indefinable like *good* or irreducible like probability, it is simply the lubricant in economies (its abundance reducing the interest rate) within advanced financial systems, where it is impossible to exchange commodities for commodities as in a barter system. This means that the relationship of money with real production must be understood rather than overstated. Overstatement is usually an upshot of confusion.

Much has been written on the fulfilment of Keynes's qualitative predictions almost one hundred years after 'EPG' was penned (cf. Pettifor and Tilly 2015; Carabelli and Cedrini 2011, 2013, 2016; Pecchi and Piga 2008). But unlike what Keynes accurately predicted, our desires for leisure must wait. Leisure has become more common in quantitative terms but although wealth standards (measured by *GDP* growth) have been improving during the last 80 years in some regions, the levels foreseen by Keynes have not been achieved due to such interrelated factors as wars, upheavals, inequality, crises, and uncertainty. Keynes saw that progress was taking place but also that social sciences must evolve more to comprehend the complexities in human behavior. This signifies that the time scenario of his predictions is not accurate. People cannot yet devote their energies to the pursuit of non-economic tasks and still overstate the role that money plays in their lives, although today money in the form of capital accumulation along with technology are the bases for producing wealth and work is for some a means for self-realization.

'EPG' is optimistic in some of its contentions for understanding the past and the immediate present in moral terms. Under this view, 'EPG' is a plea for revolutionizing values in Capitalism which exalts individualism. He was also correct when affirming that money adoration comes to some extent from confusion. But his own notion of money is clear since he passes from an understanding of the functioning of money in social systems in *TM* to its ethical critique as a form of alienation in 'EPG.' Altogether, the significance of this pamphlet is that the negative consequences of the love of money find an analogy in the contention that hoarding is lethal for economies because it generates stagnation.

Finally, for Keynes (1931a), the choice of gold as a standard of value is based on tradition, proposing that the principles and consequences of traditions be revised. In 'Auri Sacra Fames' (1930b), also printed in *Essays in Persuasion* Part III The Return to the Gold Standard, Chapter 2 (1931a), Keynes stated that Sigmund Freud (1856–1938) contended that there were deep instincts at the heart of this choice. Furthermore, the love of gold also has a sway for political philosophy standards. Even in Keynes's times gold was owned by a few hands or countries and this concentration impeded freedom in policymaking.

8.2 Population

Will the world of our grandchildren be overpopulated? Material progress must take account of overpopulation. The Benthamite calculus might be linked to a declining or stationary population in a hypothetical closed system. But for Keynes happiness was the end, and his categorization might be linked to changes in habits propitiated by an evolution in economics wherein money in the form of wealth was related to population in conceptual terms. For Toye (1997), Keynes thinks that excessive population growth should be halted. Perhaps he thought that an uneducated person would suffer and would not generate benefits. He served as the Director of the British Eugenics Society between 1937 and 1946.

Moreover, Keynes detects a link between population growth and deteriorating terms of trade. His 1914 Oxford lecture on 'Population' discusses his engagement with the Social Darwinist doctrine of the 'rapid multiplication of the unfit' and its relationship with eugenics. But what can be more elitist than suggesting the qualitative selection of population? (See Appendix in Chapter 11).

Let's bring together all these insights. Zanini (2003, 2008) investigates the relationship between the economic and political writings in Keynes. The former writer underlines how in Keynes's works (among others') the nexus between ethics, economics and politics has produced an exemplary solution. By reconsidering the insufficiency of free-market competition according to Keynes, Zanini shows how the evolution of economic ideas is the result of a complex connection between theory and policy. According to Zanini (2003, 2008), economics and politics should go together, combining rationality and irrationality. Nothing new, Keynes's category of uncertainty underpins his critique of the *Laissez-faire*. Further, unethical Darwinism is the basis for economic foundations (biologism?). But is the love of money a biological function?, certainly not for Keynes.

This chapter deals not with technicalities about money but with the ethical analysis of the social and individual roles of money, the adoration of which will diminish as humankind moves closer to solving its economic problems over the next hundred years in Keynes's view. This is the argument exposed in 'EPG' and the four related futuristic writings analysed in the Appendices 8.1 and 8.2. 'EPG' constitutes an approximation to Keynes's ethical mature philosophy as exposed in Chapter 11. In the meantime, Chapter 9 deals with the philosophical contentions exposed in the last chapter of *GT* (1936). Its connection with Chapter 8 is the emphasis on the quest for a better life once the main economic or material problem (unemployment) is resolved.

Appendix 8.1: 'Am I a liberal' (1925) and 'The End of the Laissez-Faire' (1926)

Keynes's concern in both the late 1920s and the 1930s (exception made of the creation of *GT*, see our Chapters 2 and 9) was the turmoil brought about by war, peace, and the world's economy, placing emphasis on Britain as the European Keynes is confined to the early 1920s and the 1940s. Throughout the compendium *Essays in Persuasion* (1931b) he states that public expenditure must be administered by an intellectual aristocracy, and this collection of essays is permeated by prophesy (the croaking of Cassandra) on social developments. Among the conventional themes examined by Keynes at that time are the superfluity of the classic gold standard, the foundations of diatribes among the political parties, and remarkably the history and essence of the *Laissez-faire*.

'Am I a liberal' (1925) appears in *Essays in Persuasion* (1931b) in Part IV Politics, Chapter 4. Keynes deals with his eventual affiliation to a political party, which makes him examine the core of the three parties in Britain: The Liberal, the Conservative, and the Labor. It seems that he did not believe in fixed adherences due to the prevalence of fuzziness in human decisions. In other words, for him no party can fulfil the complete aspirations of anyone, and its tenets are not absolute. Above all, he was concerned about the expansion of horizons in this transitional period of Britain.

He examines the term liberal. Political philosophy is about the adherence to the rights of life, liberty, property, and civil society, but the undirected market economy's capacity as the benchmark in liberalism is hereby questioned. Keynes then assesses his distaste for the Labor Party, also analyzing the leadership characteristics of both the Conservative and the Liberal Parties. He elects not to be a Conservative, as it is not safe to preserve that degree of civilization. On the other hand, the Labor Party was subject to an autocratic control. The Conservative Party ought to be adapted to the new conditions and is not different from the Liberals. The Liberal Party may entail progress if they conduct the right program. All parties adhere to old guidelines. But such issues as unemployment for which the Liberal Party fought are achieved, obsolete or common for all parties. Moreover, for Keynes free trade will flourish due to the force of circumstances in an open system.

For Keynes, the reason for intellectual poverty in parties lay in the transmission of wealth and the control of business. The Labor Party was a party of hatred, but possessing moral and intellectual respectability, like the Conservatives. But those are extreme stances, and there must be a classless party apt for constructing the future. Keynes then outlines the philosophy of practice of such an ideal party: it must emancipate itself from old-fashioned individualism and the *Laissez-faire*, the bases of the success of nineteenth century Britain. Its doctrines must deal with matters of urgent importance, connecting them with the notion of expediency in Burke.

On peace, the process of disintegration of the empire was now almost complete. The government must undertake neglected duties and be decentralized by establishing semi-independent corporations and organs of administration, without impairing democracy. The sex questions were not addressed by any party. Some of the partisans were deeply involved in the solution of economic questions. For Keynes, the then-current law about birth control and similar topics was medieval. The question of whether wages should be fixed in accordance with the theories of the *laissez-faire* was relevant. Keynes wrote about the economic questions, explaining that John R. Commons (1862–1945) recognized a transition in three phases. The first is the era of scarcity, which took place in the fifteenth or sixteenth centuries. Next came the era of abundance with the maximum of individual liberty and the minimum of coercive control through government in the seventeenth and the eighteenth centuries but culminating in the nineteenth century due to the triumph of the *Laissez-faire* and historic Liberalism. Nonetheless, and this is Keynes's contribution, Britain was not living anymore in the nineteenth century. He notices in the era of stabilization, there is a reduction of individual liberty, enforced in part by governmental or private collective sanctions. The extremes are Fascism and Bolshevism. The transition from anarchy to a directed regime in terms of social justice and stability is tough, but New Liberalism must find a solution. Instead, the Treasury and the Bank of England pursued an orthodox nineteenth century policy sanctifying market forces.

But Keynes always fought against unguaranteed or past core assumptions. For him, the State was not an obstacle for progress and policies must avoid interferences with social stability. His critique of entrepreneurial behavior is restricted to the consideration of animal spirits. Returning to political philosophy, it is not a set of opinions, it must be focused on monetary policy management, which may affect the price level, whose fluctuations may be softened by modern institutions. The conclusion was that a new party program must be developed in terms of its core but also results. The clue for answering the question of whether Keynes was a liberal is that he contended that liberalism must be modernized, otherwise it was disguised traditionalism. Whereas he was still not attentive to the possibility that instability may arise from static output or employment and be cured by fiscal policy, he defined the direction and the functioning of appropriate policies for the next years and in this sense the pamphlet is visionary.

A Related Investigation

'The end of the Laissez-faire' (1926) can be read in *Essays in Persuasion* (1931b) in Part IV Politics, Chapter 3. It is about the relationship between economics and political philosophy. Keynes analyzes the political ideas of Locke, Rousseau (yes, including a continental thinker), Bentham, and Smith, placing the notion of utilitarianism in its transitional role. But Keynes also ascertained rather conventionally that what unites political economy with political philosophy is the role of the government. The corollary is that public policy must reduce unemployment, noticing full employment was not yet part of the formal agenda in that moment of Keynes's life.

In Part I, Keynes explains that individualism and the *Laissez-faire* had prevailed for more than one hundred years. At the end of the seventeenth century natural liberty and tolerance were overcome by the worldly calculations of utility. With Locke and Hume these doctrines were fused into rational self-love. According to Keynes, the effect was an ethical contract enhancing the notion of property. How? Bentham accepted utilitarianism in the form of hedonism but widened it into social utility, by means of a mathematical law of indifference preaching the greatest happiness of the greatest number. Rousseau transformed Locke's Social Contract into the General Will with an emphasis on equality. Thus, conservative individualism was harmonized with democratic egalitarianism in the late eighteenth century and the early nineteenth century. Notice Keynes was a fine distinguisher before forming new arrays of ideas.

For Keynes, the political philosophers not the political economists gave a scientific basis to the thought that the government had no right to interfere and that its meddling was inexpedient. But the political economist took over. Smith even stated in the eighteenth century that only individual efforts improve personal conditions. Further, the incompetence of eighteenth century governments survived into the nineteenth century and the solution then was thought to be the *Laissez-faire*. Keynes explains in this pamphlet that growth between 1750 and 1850 came from private initiative and free competition. Moreover, the Darwinians affirmed that free competition had built humankind, and the survival of the fittest became a generalization of Classical economics. In Part II, Keynes contends that this is what the economists are supposed to have said, but instead it is what the utilitarians believed, and the doctrine became popular among the political philosophers. Lately, the Manchester School with its heyday occurring between 1825 and 1845 stuck with the *Laissez-faire*, which has undiscerning free trade as a counterpart, as their practical conclusion. As a writer, Keynes exposes his own political philosophy.

According to Keynes's pamphlet, the *Laissez-faire* became a dogma by 1850 and a common place in the nineteenth century. For the Frenchman Frederic Bastiat (1801–1850) the equalization of individuals was the only form for general amelioration, perhaps ignoring the principles of organicism. But since the arrival onto the scene of the moderate John Stuart Mill, economists dimensioned those ideas. John Elliott Cairnes (1823–1875) considered the *Laissez-faire* as a practice, whereas Alfred Marshall elucidated cases in which private and social interests differ, accepting that the *Laissez-faire* is a benchmark. Nevertheless, the dogma prevailed, in Keynes's wording.

In Part III of 'The end of the Laissez-faire,' Keynes nicely affirms that economists select the hypothesis because it is simple. Perhaps many want to hear profit-makers reach the top, which supposedly will endure forever. This assumption is accompanied by those of automatic efficacy and the sanctification of individualism. Hence the individualist invokes the love of money as an upshot of natural selection. But this hypothesis is, among many of its traits, incomplete since the processes of production and consumption are organic and uncertain. Others contended that the *Laissez-faire* is ideal, departing from the naturalistic fallacy. Still, individualism lends itself to the fantasies of businesspeople, whose first reaction in the face of attacks to their beliefs is moral.

In Part IV, Keynes explains that no natural liberty exists in the conduction of private activities. He also insists that private and social interests do not always coincide. Further, enlightened self-interest does not necessarily operate in the public interest, and 'it is not always enlightened.' In sum, he contends that the *Laissez-faire* may not be beneficial in the sense that some individuals take advantage of the uncertainty and ignorance of terms. In parallel terms—ethics and political philosophy interact, Keynes affirms that Burke considers that the State must intervene wisely in some areas and leave others to private action, unlike in Bentham's core in which interference is needless (Chapter 3). Perhaps Keynes was thinking that in an open heterogeneous system all elements must interplay. Keynes also proposes a return to semi-autonomous corporations. But he also outlines trends in joint stock institutions, which in the event of growth may approach the status of public corporations. There was thus a trend in big enterprises to be 'socialised'; eventually shareholders would be dissociated from the management, especially if their activities affect national wealth. Because big business is uncertain, income inequalities and unemployment arise, also due to disappointing expectations and investment. The partial solution cure is the control of the currency and of credit, but neither savings nor investment should be left to private judgment (Chapter 7).

In Part V, Keynes's reflections are associated to improvements as carried upon by collective action, which may be compatible with the money-making instincts. This is a link with 'EPG'. Capitalism must be efficient and morally viable, but he states that no party is pursuing the right reforms. If poverty provides the incentive to change, prosperity removes the incentive so that policies must be selected through discretion. In terms of both categories of the truth and knowledge, Keynes was revolutionary and traditional at the same time. Keynes was a liberal, 'but not in the conventional sense of the term' (Lambert 1963, p. 1). This ambivalence left an imprint on the character of his expedient vision in political philosophy. Recall that Keynes's ethics is not related to consequences or expediency but is an ethics of virtue (causal). However Keynes also adopted Moore's metaethical intuitionism, linking ethics to politics, which made him realize that the *Laissez-faire* was an illusory visualization of the world.

For Mann (2019), the constant renewal of Keynesianism by radicals and liberals, is today built into both liberal and Left thinking, a product of two centuries of political thought in the face of existential threats to the very notion of 'civilization.' We contend Keynes has nothing to do with the Left, but for Mann Keynes's roots may be traced out to Hegel, perhaps ignoring the role of the Locke Connection and the Bloomsbury tradition. In his rebellion, Keynes celebrates government intervention in 'The end of Laissez-faire,' also disbelieving in self-regulating systems. In his view thus the *Laissez-faire* is the conclusion of orthodox political thought as the outcome of the paradigm represented by liberty, democracy, free markets, and individualism. He questions the merits of the *Laissez-faire*, as he accepts aristocracy interference though he never questions the assumption of perfect competition. The former contention is thus contrary to his statement that many agents must interact with one another in modern economies which must be open-ended. An open system must have both internal and external interactions taking the form of monetary flows and information under a free evolutionary framework, which takes us to the analysis of the 'future' by Keynes.

Appendix 8.2: 'Clissold' (1927) and 'The Means to Prosperity' (1933)

'Clissold' (1927) appears in *Essays in Persuasion* (1931b), Part V: The Future, Chapter 2. Here Keynes reviews the novel *The World of William Clissold* (1926) penciled by Herbert George Wells (1866–1946). Keynes was amazed at Wells's message in a book filled with educational ideas. The message primarily analyzes English businessmen, and then also the women; he examines their potential relationships in the modern world, to themselves and, for the women, to men of Clissold's type.

The first theme deals with Keynes's and Well's protest against Conservatism, laying stress upon the necessity and rapidity of change in industrial societies, wherein the mistakes are to look backwards or to be inadaptable. The contrast comes from the failure of conservative ideas, conventions, and prejudices to keep up with the pace of material change. But Keynes explains that the environment moves faster than people. Indeed, Wells criticizes the modern man, whose career moves with the times unlike his way of life. The contrast between the activity of commerce and the dullness of private life is enormous. This is a critique of the 'plastic' essence of modern social life. Beyond that, it is not enough to be efficient in our jobs and happy in our private lives, we must also be ethical by concerning ourselves with others and the political system. Therefore, Keynes gives added value to Wells's prescient analysis of the then-modern life, especially the behavior under Capitalism.

In Clissold, Keynes calls attention to the fact that we are older than our ancestors in the phase of maturity. Wells contends that the average age of a rapidly increasing population is inferior to that in a stationary population. In the twentieth century the age in power may have risen 15 years with respect to that in the nineteenth century. In accordance with Keynes, Wells preferred an adult world. But the margin between old men and men in the stage of making money was fuzzy, which indicated that men were living in a transition which complicated the panorama for reaping material fruits. However, Keynes states that Wells also outlines his disappointment with Socialism, searching for an alternative to economic construction. Clissold reacts against the Socialist Party considering that creators must serve both science and business. Wells describes himself as a

Liberal, but he claims that political Liberalism must be reformed in terms of both methods and purpose. Although Wells does not explain why men are involved in making business, Keynes knows that it is the upshot of a monetary economy. Hence the rapid development of the industrial and financial systems goes hand in hand with the development of Keynes's ideas about economics.

Keynes becomes conscientious, alongside Wells, that Capitalism permits the advancement of work, money, and technology, but impedes progress in the ethical and existential side of man, who in the case of Keynes's Britain is stuck in the past with a foot in the arena of technological change. But Keynes sees Wells's perspective as tilted toward Socialism, conducting his own critique of modern ethics under the framework of Capitalism. This criticism of extra-curricular activities goes well with Keynes's contention that money is an alienating means, refining Wells's statements about the alienation of the middle classes. The futuristic vision of Keynes about a world without work is astonishingly utopian in both 'EPG' and 'Clissold.' Keynes's vision of future work is dissimilar in this sense from that in the Bible, even though he may be right in stating that rationalism is absent in non-economic activities.

Keynes's importance as far as this stage concerns may lie in his politically sound stance (related to a solid ethics). The implication is that a liberal policy may be conducted in the face of a non-self-regulating system. Keynes thus produces heuristic strategies after overcoming misleading concepts and contexts. A corollary is that Capitalism entails economic success but social and ethical—initial—failure, requiring human intervention. Beyond that money is not a veil but economics is certainly a veil being only the surface of human essence.

Another Reflective—Yet Purely Economic—Text

'The means to prosperity' (1933) appears in *Essays in Persuasion* (1931, 1972, 2010) in Part VI Later Essays, Chapter 4, as a later addition. This pamphlet brings together economics and politics, a process leading to sensible policymaking in the upcoming years. The idea is to persuade people that the government must spend without crowding out private expenditure, which goes against the principles of the 'Treasury View.' Keynes's half-futuristic 'The Means to Prosperity' includes recommendations for tackling unemployment in a global recession, chiefly by implementing counter-cyclical public spending with the aid of the multiplier effect on output and its concomitant reduction in unemployment. While it is addressed to the British Government, it contains advice for other nations affected by the global recession. The pamphlet is permeated by unconventional idealism in the concern about the attainment of stability. A summary of this transtional pamphlet ensues.

Chapter I: The Nature of the Problem. It is necessary to increase national income. Keynes proposes a policy based on loan expenditure, beginning with domestic affairs, and proceeding to the guidelines recommended in the World Conference (1933).

Chapter II: Internal Expansion. The reluctance to support capital expenditure is based on both the scarceness of the employment created, and the strain on budgets created by subsidies. If new expenditure is added, the increase of employment will not stop there. The additional wages and incomes paid out could be spent on additional purchases, which would be reflected in higher prices and increased imports. Keynes's estimate makes the multiplier (see our Chapter 7) at least two. Small changes may have ample repercussions (see our Chapter 2 on organicism). An additional loan would increase national income by more than that amount. There is no need for balancing the budget as in conventional proposals.

Chapter III: The Raising of Prices. The Exchequer aims at raising the prices of commodities, but for the community it would reduce demand. Organicism is present. How could they raise prices? If the public were to spend a larger proportion of the incomes, it would partly raise prices and partly employment. Aggregate spending power within a country could only be raised by increasing the loan expenditure of the community. The means of raising world prices is thus increasing loan expenditure.

Chapter IV: A Proposal for The World Economic Conference. Increase of loan expenditure throughout the world could be conducted as follows: Through direct foreign loans, or even stronger countries could increase loan expenditure at home. If it leaks into expenditure on home-produced goods, the repercussions of the initial loan expenditure on employment would be multiplied. The only possibility for a rise in world prices is a simultaneous relief of taxation and increase of loan expenditure in different countries.

Chapter V: The International Note Issue and the Gold Standard. The creation of an International Note Issue may give incentives to central banks. The increase in loan expenditure would improve international practices. Also, exchange restrictions must be abolished along with quantitative trade restrictions. Strong financial centers must re-open their money markets to foreign loans. It is necessary that each participating country adopt a de facto parity between gold and its national currency. An unchangeable parity would maintain gradual adjustment between national and international conditions.

Chapter VI: Conclusion. To put one man to work for a year, an increased loan expenditure plus an increased foreign balance are both necessary, until world recovery sets in. Thus, annual primary expenditure and increased loan expenditure are both required. The policies of protecting the foreign balance and the stimulus to loan expenditure must be combined with the expansion of international reserve money.

Great summary but what is the importance of this pamphlet? The two dimensions in economics are prices and production, and Keynes led a movement to focus on production and hence on employment rather than on prices, everything at the macro level. This is a heuristic movement (prefiguring the enormous relevance of the notion of the multiplier). Being in the recovery from the international crisis of 1929 and in the transitional phase between *TM* (1930c) and *GT* (1936), Keynes was still preoccupied with rising prices but in the transition, he became focused on revising other problems: output and employment. His policy purpose of increasing employment in 1933 was still conventional and his remedy static. He believed in heterogeneous paces and asymmetric effects in the interactions of a complex—macro—system (Chapter 2). Thus, in his 'British-focused' stage he relied on discretionary piece-meal approaches as far as policy concerns. Unsurprisingly his aim was to strengthen local employment, as the precondition for the attainment of future prosperity in the same vein as the more qualitative 'Economic possibilities for our Grandchildren'. His proposed heuristic methods were innovative as they were based on an open ontology, demonstrating the heretofore unnoticed link between core and heuristics. It is precisely domestic unemployment—not inflation—the topic of the last part of Keynes's *magnum opus (GT)*, offering a new non-economic core, to which we turn in Chapter 9.

Notes

1. Perhaps Keynes still believes in the existence of a natural rate of interest (Chapter 7).

2. These insights will be refined in the ethical standards set forth in 'My Early Beliefs,' with convention as a tenet (Chapter 11).
3. The mature Keynes would have great respect for ancient traditions in the 1940s (Chapter 11).
4. He is writing about such objects as beauty, friendship, love, or knowledge. See Chapter 11 about Keynes's rebellion against Moore's ideology and the uniqueness of fit objects.
5. Modern philosophers would state that Keynes is a realist, due to his interest in the hidden mechanisms of phenomena.

References

Sources

Carabelli, Anna M., and Mario A. Cedrini. 2010–11. "Indian Currency and Beyond: The Legacy of the Early Economics of Keynes in the Times of Bretton Woods II." *Journal of Post Keynesian Economics* 33, no. 2: 55–80.

———. 2013. "This Time Is... Complex. Keynes on Time". Università del Piemonte Orientale "Amedeo Avogadro" and Università di Torino. Campus Luigi Einaudi. https://www.postkeynesian.net/downloads/downloads/events/Carabelli_and_Cedrini_This_Time_Is_Complex_-_final_version_2_lhXhVbE.pdf.

———. 2016. "Great Expectations and Final Delusion. Keynes and the Ultimate Values of Capitalism." Conference: 40 Years of the Cambridge Journal of Economics, 12–13 July. https://www.cpes.org.uk/dev/wp-content/uploads/2016/06/Carabelli_Cedrini_Great_Expectations_and_Final_Delusion.pdf. Accessed 14 December 2019.

Dostaler, Gilles. 1996. "The Formation of Keynes's Vision." *History of Economics Review* 25, no. 1: 14–31.

Keynes, John Maynard. 1925. "Am I a liberal." In *JMK CW Vol. IX Essays in Persuasion*.

———. 1926. "The end of the Laissez-faire." In *JMK CW Vol. IX Essays in Persuasion*, edited by D. Moggridge. London: Royal Economic Society.

———. 1927. "Clissold." In *JMK CW Vol. IX. Essays in Persuasion*, edited by D. Moggridge. London Royal Economic Society.

———. 1930a. "Economic Possibilities for Our Grandchildren". In *JMK CW Vol. IX Essays in Persuasion*, edited by D. Moggridge. London: Royal Economic Society.

———. 1930b. "Auri sacra fames." In *JMK CW Vol. IX Essays in Persuasion*, edited by D. Moggridge. London: Royal Economic Society.

———. 1930c. "A Treatise on Money." In *JMK CW Vols. V and VI A Treatise on Money*. edited by D. Moggridge. London: Royal Economic Society.
———. 1931a. "Keynes Rejoinder to Mr. D. H. Robertson." *Economic Journal XLI* 163 (September). In *JMK/EJ/6/7*. Cambridge: Cambridge University Press. https://discovery.nationalarchives.gov.uk/details/r/afc22cbd-5472-49c8-8ba4-a585275185c2. Accessed 15 November 2019.
———. 1931b. "Essays in Persuasion." In *JMK CW Vol. IX Essays in Persuasion*, edited by D. Moggridge. London: Royal Economic Society.
———. 1936. "The General Theory of Employment, Interest and Money." In *JMK CW Vol. VII The General Theory of Employment, Interest and Money*, edited by D. Moggridge. London: Royal Economic Society.
———. 1933. *The Means to Prosperity*. London: MacMillan. https://archive.org/details/in.ernet.dli.2015.227329. Accessed 17 June 2017.
Lambert, Paul. 1963. "The Social Philosophy of John Maynard Keynes." *Annals of Public and Cooperative Economics* 34, no. 4 (October): 483–515.
Mann, Geoff. 2019. *In the Long Run We Are All Dead. Keynesianism, Political Economy, and Revolution*. London: Verso.
Mini, Piero V. 1994. *John Maynard Keynes: A Study in the Psychology of Original Work*. Basingstoke: Palgrave.
Pecchi, Lorenzo, and Gustavo Piga. (eds.). 2008. *Revisiting Keynes Economic Possibilities for Our Grandchildren*. Cambridge, MA: The MIT Press.
Pettifor, Ann, and Geoffrey Tilly. 2015. "What Are the Economic Consequences for Our Grandchildren." *The King's Politics Society at King's College Chapel*, November. Cambridge: Cambridge University. https://static1.squarespace.com/static/541ff5f5e4b02b7c37f31ed6/t/564a1bc0e4b06fd62eb2453a/1447697344068/Keynes.pdf. Accessed 17 May 2018.
Raffaelli, Tizziano. 2006. "Keynes's Interaction with Cambridge Philosophers." In *The Cambridge Companion to Keynes*, edited by Roger E. Backhouse and Bradley W. Bateman, Chapter 6. Basingstoke: Palgrave.
Rothbard, Murray N. 1992. "Keynes, the Man." In *Dissent on Keynes: A Critical Appraisal of Keynesian Economics*, edited by Mark Skousen, Chapter 11. New York: Praeger.
Toye, John. 1997. "Keynes on Population and Economic Growth." *Cambridge Journal of Economics* 21, no. 1 (January): 1–26.
Zanini, Adelino. 2003. "Un capitalismo incerto. Incertezza e normazione nel pensiero di J.M. Keynes (1921–1939)." Working Paper 194, Universita' Politecnica delle Marche (I), Dipartimento di Scienze Economiche e Sociali.
———. 2008. *Economic Philosophy: Economic Foundations and Political Categories*. Bern: Peter Lang.

PART III

Keynes's Middle-Aged Activities: 1936–1939

The mature Keynes unifies his main former concepts in the fields of economics and philosophy to form a new core, which is visible in his creation of macroeconomics in *GT* (Chapter 2). In a variant of focus, Chapter 9, also about *GT,* chronicles Keynes's main contentions on unemployment and human freedom, specifically about the analysis of the last Chapter of the Golden Book (Chapter 24) which provides suggestions related to both ethics and political philosophy for future generations. But Chapter 9 also contains an appendix on the accompanying document 'The general theory of employment' (1937), wherein he clarifies his notion of uncertainty, and another appendix on the reception of *GT*.

Chapter 10 gives an idea of how these notions, especially but not solely economic contentions, evolved after being absorbed into subsequent orthodox *SRP*s since the 1950s, supposedly representing the theories of Keynes. It includes an appendix on the contributions of the American monetarist—but also a philosopher—Milton Friedman (1912–2006) to macroeconomics, written as a fictional account of Keynes's thinking. Friedman is chosen since he led the influential revolt against Keynesian economics that took place in the 1970s (see the Monetarist SRP in Chapter 2). Both Chapters include Lakatosian-type analyses of Keynes's theory, especially the second.

CHAPTER 9

The Philosophical Foundations of Chapter 24 of *The General Theory of Employment, Interest and Money* (1936) (GT); The Envisagement of Human Destiny as the Essence of Keynes's Evolutionary Vision

This chapter deals with two of the most important linked concerns in Keynes's life; especially in the last chapter (Chapter 24) of the Golden Book, which is about the pursuit of a better life in an uncertain world after full employment has been attained outlining a concrete portrait of his wishes as expressed in 'EPG.'

Section 9.1 is a preliminary text on *GT* philosophy, especially focused on its last towering chapter. Section 9.2 is an introduction to innovative issues extracted from *GT*. Section 9.3 is an analysis of Chapter 24 of *GT* in the specific philosophical fields of Epistemology, Ontology, and Social Philosophy, with an emphasis on Ethics and Political Philosophy.[1] Section 9.4 is an analysis of special issues in *GT*. Section 9.5 is a conclusion on the relevance of Chapter 24 as a representative expression of Keynes's multidimensional thought, putting ethical concepts into practice. The first appendix clarifies the concept of uncertainty (the pivotal concept in Keynes's *SRP*) whereas the second outlines the initial responses to *GT* concluding that perhaps dissenters have not evolved.

J. Muñoz-Bandala, *Keynes's Evolutionary Spirit*,
Palgrave Insights into Apocalypse Economics,
https://doi.org/10.1007/978-3-030-90150-9_9

9.1 Philosophy in the *General Theory of Employment, Interest, and Money* Especially Its Last Chapter

It is difficult to advance a point beyond what Keynes himself comments about his own vision in Chapter 24 of *GT*.[2] It is also arduous to express a deeper thought than what Robert Skidelsky, Keynes's leading biographer, wrote about Chapter 24 of *GT* (cf. Skidelsky 1997). The purpose of this chapter, then, is to identify whether the end part of *GT* is the gist of Keynes's legacy, having set the core foundations of macroeconomics in the previous 23 Chapters. Relevant topics included in Chapter 24 are the consequences of full employment, the fate of income distribution, the future of overall wealth, the notion of expectations, the role of the State in economies, the future of financial markets, and the interaction between economics and other disciplines. With its multifaceted vision, this piece may be considered as a justification for Capitalism. Keynes sees there the State as both the spender and the employer of last resort, thereby proposing a new role for the government (Skidelsky 1997). He also suggests a new function for the private sector reconsidering the interrelation between it and the public sector, viewing this relational issue with an evolutionary viewpoint.

In addition, Keynes blurs the distinction between economics and sociology, advancing new interdisciplinary methods in his thinking. He is also concerned about the epistemological relevance of assumptions when obtaining defensible conclusions. In addition, *GT* is grounded in new psychological laws and motivations; that is, in a new vision of humankind, especially in Chapter 24. He highlights in a few pages new roles for interest rates; savers and 'rentiers'; and at a higher level the relevance of such concepts as ideas, interests, and power.

A debatable topic dealt with by Keynes in Chapter 24 of *GT* is the 'socialization' of investment. This is, in the words of Skidelsky, only a shift in the balance of social power, being consistent with his former critical attitude with respect to the *Laissez-faire* but never advocating socialism or totalitarianism. Keynes is thus in Chapter 24 of *GT* an idealist, a reformer, and a trans-generational thinker but not a political revolutionary. He is also advancing explanations for financial crises in terms of speculation when he criticizes the passion for thriftiness along with its explosive results and aims for the setting of reasonable financial rewards from financial instruments (see Appendix 13.1).

GT is cited to give encompassing evidence for the re-interpretation of Keynes about economic systems as well. An example is the Preface to *GT* p. XIV: 'The relation between this book and my *Treatise on Money*...is...clearer to myself than it will be to others; and what in my own mind is a natural evolution in a line of thought...may strike the reader as a confusing change of view,' or a mutant (Samuelson 1946).

9.2 Key Issues in the *General Theory of Employment, Interest, and Money*

Therefore this subsection complements the epistemological insights found in Chapter 2 proving evolution. *GT* is considered as the analysis of economic decision-making under uncertainty. Alternatively, it is about the existence of underemployment equilibria in economies, demolishing the concept of a self-attainable full-employment equilibrium. The point is unemployment is its main concern (Chapter 4) which arises from the inequality between savings and investment and a non-self-regulating labor market. The distinction between the real and the monetary sectors is overcome and a new role for the monetary variables is identified. This notion heralds the beginning of macroeconomics, wherein phenomena are to be studied in organic terms, and uncertainty (translated into money holdings) is pervasive, unveiling societal weaknesses and generating unstable systems.

There is consensus, after Keynes, that unemployment is the result of deficient aggregate demand (expenditure), a notion which opens frontiers in knowledge. The economic framework, context, and implications of the famous book, which demolishes the Classical concepts especially that of unemployment coming from the labor market only, have been studied by thousands of authors, perhaps more holistically by Keynes's biographers: Moggridge (1992), Skidelsky (1992, 2000), Hession (1984), and Harrod (1951). Nevertheless, Chapter 24 of *GT* is special since rarely has a contribution contained—at its end—such a relaxed vision, in this case once full employment has been attained. Thereafter everything is possible. As Skidelsky states, Keynes here displays the power of his imaginative life—the 'republic of his imagination.' It is also a literary jewel. Moreover, like in many of his writings, but especially in *The Economic Consequences of the Peace* (*ECP*) and in the final part of *GT*, Keynes exhibits a gift for prophecy,[3] which generates qualitative predictions (Skidelsky 1996). His forebodings are based both on his theoretical and practical insights, which are supported by his usage of intuition and life experience as analyzed in former chapters. The theme is so important that a literature review of Keynes's specific philosophical insights on the end of his magnum opus follows to deepen matters.

He considers that social elements are necessary for a thorough understanding of economic issues and their consequences, such as peace and happiness. Many views on Keynes's thinking can together be taken to suggest that Chapter 24 contains the gist of Keynes's mature philosophical thinking, confirming that for him attitudes are one of the most relevant issues in life. Altogether Chapter 24 displays Keynes's genius as a social philosopher, following the tradition of *The Economic Possibilities for our Grandchildren* (1930a), but now he is examining his landmark product with some distance, as did Phillip II when observing the construction of his castle *El Escorial* in seventeenth-century Spain.

9.3 Specific Philosophical Insights in Chapter 24 of the *General Theory of Employment, Interest, and Money*

Keynes's interrelated philosophical issues are hereby studied in terms of categories, as is done in Chapter 5 in the study of *ECP*. But now the theme is to find out what is known about Keynes's post-*GT* thinking.

9.3.1 Epistemology

Keynes relies on both intuition and induction at the beginning of his philosophical career, and on conventions in the latter part of his life (Davis 1991a, 1994). The late 1930s represented a practical advancement in Keynes's career like in 1919 when he wrote *ECP*. This is because, according to Lawson, his scientific method is one of Realism coupled not only with intuition—as in the early 1930s, when he was dealing both theoretically and practically with the underlying problems of his time and place—but also with imagination.

Further, foundations and viability are relevant at the end of Chapter 24 in both ethical and epistemological terms. An example of Realism in Keynes at this stage is his position on wealth distribution. He wrote: 'there is social and psychological justification for significant inequalities of incomes and wealth, but not for such large disparities as they exist to-day

(Keynes *GT*, 1936 [1997], p. 374).' But there are more important issues for Keynes here. The existence of a non-self-regulated system, organicism (along with heterogeneity and asymmetry in events), and uncertainty (reflected on expectations, liquidity, and non-neutral money) are at the epistemic core of *GT* (Chapter 2). The novelty is he wrote about uncertainty in Chapter 24 as continuously applied to the events in the whole society, even after the urgent economic problems are resolved, namely involuntary unemployment.

Keynes's investigation in *GT* is also cultural and historical. He aimed to achieve external consistency in terms of social ends. In that vein he also generated predictions about society's destiny, relying on observation, analysis, and interpretation, considering language, persuasion, reasonableness, and propaganda as highly relevant for convincingly expressing his insights. He succeeded. His emphasis on epistemological organicism while creating macroeconomics has been confirmed in Chapter 24 of *GT*, particularly on interrelations, remedies, and consequences. Moreover, relative situations were analyzed with objectivity by him based on conventions (this will be the later Keynes), but based on intuitionism (Keynes at the beginning). He preached optimism and action (knowledge is just the means for conducting practical activities) in Chapter 24, wherein natural, permanent, and operational plans must be identified, and consciousness must be a living reality. This is the continuation of the British empirical tradition started by Locke as can be deducted from a reading of the portraits of some members of this connection in Keynes's *Essays on Biography* (see Chapter 3 of this book).

Keynes's scientific method is above everything else, since 'no subject matter is more than its own method' (Robinson 1932). A part of Keynes's method is to consider such unstable 'mezzo' socio-economic elements (from the protective belt) as population, religion, property, government, classes, or psychological instability as given. Therefore, not only core elements or 'universals' are analyzed. He turned from analyzing Europe's destiny in *ECP* to that of humankind in *GT*. The early Keynes was centered upon personal and human considerations, in the 1920s Keynes lies emphasis upon Britain's monetary issues, but the mature Keynes was concerned with general theories and world affairs, anticipating his late interests in the 1940s (Chapter 12 in this book).

Economists must set real—core—hypotheses for understanding processes. For Keynes, no inaccurate core issues must be introduced (for instance, uncertainty replaces scarcity). Logic is hereby coupled with intuition in the sense that concrete and clear knowledge must be applied to the understanding of current states of affairs. This is necessary because misunderstandings prevail; for instance, there is 'confusion on the public mind on the matters of low employment and the growth of capital (Keynes *GT* 1936 [1997], p. 374).'

For Keynes, a new era emerges within a more complex world after full employment is attained. He was aware of the power of ideas; however, according to Joan Robinson, Keynes 'very much over-estimate[s] the power of reason (Robinson 1983, p. 397).' This is presumably in the sense of reasonableness not of rationality. Finally, Keynes is a constructivist in modern parlance. For instance, he writes '[o]ur criticism of the accepted classical theory of economics has consisted... in pointing out that its tacit assumptions are seldom or never satisfied (ibid., p. 378).' That is, he conducts a critique but offers new coherent integrated insights suitable for economic and social policies.

9.3.2 Ethics

Epistemology and ethics are interrelated in this case since economics is a moral science with value judgments. In other words, economics must not be supported by irrationality or by empty or utopian ethics. Recall that for orthodox thinkers, knowledge is to be found only in rational action or thought, but certainly not for Keynes. This assessment is based on Keynes's belief in intrinsic ethical values, in an ethics of virtue (Chapters 3, 4, and 6 of this book). Just like in his Apostles' days he placed the pursuit of the truth above all ideals. Keynes was implicitly critical of utilitarianism when exposing his ethical goals and epistemologically oriented policy recommendations. In arriving at this point, he also escaped orthodox Marshallian Economics, partly devoid of values.

Freedom arising from employment is the remedy for human suffering in *GT*.[4] This consideration is an appeal to Humanism. Keynes still opposed conventions in the sense that in Chapter 24 he rejects irrational—and selfish—behaviors such as savings and puritanism (Keynes offers a visible nexus between his economics and philosophy). For that purpose, he analyzes the effects of extreme immoderation on thriftiness and contends that interest rates must be kept humanly low to reduce the incentive for saving as well as uncertainty. Keynes's ethics is about the pursuit of common interest, whereas economic justice is the initial means for avoiding discontent. He signals culprits of inequality when condemning 'the euthanasia of the rentier...of the capitalist to exploit the scarcity-value of capital' (p. 376). Take a look at Appendix 13.1.

Chapter 24 is almost Hegelian with respect to the emphasis laid upon the viability of the evolution of human spirit (idea or consciousness). There, progress can only be accomplished by means of ethical and pensive actions. The crucible for some readers is that in Keynes means are ethically revolutionary, but ends are conservative. Keynes was a moderate revolutionary, but more than a reformist (as in 1923 for example). As he contends, 'the foregoing theory is moderately conservative in its implications' (ibid., p. 377). For example, the result of filling gaps in the classical vision is not to dispose of the 'Manchester System' (ibid., p. 379)—oriented to Classical market-enhancing measures—but rather to maintain focus on social justice. Chapter 24 of the Golden Book hence analyses how to identify which situations are suitable for ethical action on the part of humankind. To acquire wealth and to be *good* (not just to triumph) imply individual progress, but wealth creation is brought about by social organic unities. In other words, doing *good* as the complementary step to being *good* is something eminently practical and organic.

9.3.3 Ontology in Keynes?

Ontological visions shape evolution and Keynes's envisagement is organicist. Everything is timely and spatially interrelated in Keynes, especially in Chapter 24. This 'definitive' chapter, but still not the last song of the swan, starts by stating that '[t]he outstanding faults of the economic society in which we live are its failure to provide for full employment and its arbitrary and inequitable distribution of wealth and income' (ibid., p. 372). Here Keynes assumes a conciliatory position. Therefore, he is the third alternative (dialectically moderated) for understanding the economic universe. Smith was the first and Marx the second.

Once again, he contends that the conditions of human affairs are not perpetual as in the physical sciences (he was not a determinist), and all facets in human life are sequentially integrated, like in the *ECP*. For instance, an epoch—the age of unemployment—was over in 1936 at least in conceptual terms. This has practical consequences since he identifies false assumptions in the Victorian world, especially an overstated individualism. He demonstrates in *GT* that the macroeconomy is a complex system whose ontological unity is national economies. The next step is his concern with stabilization after both individual liberty and life options have been achieved.

There is no self-equilibrating system which means that organic systems cannot be left to their own course, requiring practical action. Thus, his beliefs evolved from the advocacy of reform in 1923 (Chapter 7 in this book). For the Classical economists, problems would eventually be solved by themselves. Keynes's vision of reality is thus distinct from that assumed in the Classical atomism, and this insight pervades Chapter 24.

But this ascertainment is also associated with path dependence among events. In the case of Keynes time is irreversible and historical; that is, non-ergodic (an insight clarified in recent Keynes scholarship: Davidson 2007). Attention on the part of Keynes is paid not only to subsequent periods but also to transition (not only to final or stationary states, as in John Stuart Mill[5] for instance), especially in times of either change or turbulence. An ontological investigation is thus useful for identifying the essence of life in Keynes's view, which generated the conclusion that ontology and epistemology are integrated in Keynes's core.

9.3.4 Political and Social Philosophy in Chapter 24

As Skidelsky states, Keynes is in depth an optimist in terms of future wealth, the potential of the government, and the evolution of Capitalism. He writes: 'I see, therefore, the rentier aspect of capitalism as a transitional phase which will disappear when it has done its work' (p. 376). The implication is institutions must be fair and timely and must be devoted to human ends. In addition, Keynes distinguishes between political and social philosophy in some themes in Chapter 24. According to Lambert (1963), the book is the keystone of Keynes's social philosophy. What matters is Keynes was a Liberal in the European sense of acknowledging that no automatic equilibrium exists. Thereby he envisages a new type of Liberalism when stating that 'the political problem of mankind is to combine economic efficiency, social justice and individual liberty' (*CW* IX p. 311). According to Streeten (1954), Keynes wanted to inherit the doctrine from the philosophers of natural law, but we contend that Keynes does not descend in that sense from pre-Lockian philosophers (Chapter 4). Keynes was a Burkean conservative by advocating expediency and focusing on the short term in a complex non-physical world. Moreover, his political philosophy deals with the search for the truth and this line of thought proceeded from his time with the 'Apostles' and the Bloomsbury Group.

But the truth is not written in stone, less in the social sciences or in post-warring times. Keynes was always searching for political freedom, in this case at the national level (rather than at the personal level as in the early 1920s, or at the British level as in the late 1920s or early 1930s). This was 1936. In the social philosophy of *GT*, the assumption is that an innovative world configuration should bring about a new state-of-affairs but the task starts at home. Then new-generation citizens would benefit from adequate institutions. Hence Keynes's political and social philosophical insights were rooted in his ethics, epistemology, and ontology, especially the ethics.

The elitist—organic—preference for discretion is also the rule in *GT* like in *TM* (Chapter 7 in this book, Appendix 11.1). The universe is a chaos, and the system lacks a self-regulating mechanism. Nothing can be done at the cosmic level, but economic intervention was necessary for attaining not only full employment (as in the first 23 Chapters of *GT*) but also both political and social stability (including reparations in *ECP*), all of which will eventually result in both human development and freedom. The means for attaining those goals in a social system dominated by uncertainty are full employment and an egalitarian wealth distribution, but this is related to interest rate management and the 'socialization' of investment,[6] although the latter must not affect private activities since it entails cooperation between the private and the public sectors: semi-autonomous institutions like in the Middle Ages.

This is both a political and an epistemological solution. Keynes then states that the 'socialisation of investment will prove the only means of securing an approximation to full employment...[b]ut beyond this no obvious case is made out for a system of State Socialism' (ibid., p. 378). A salient heuristic point is that when he analyzes long-term possibilities, hoarding is the hurdle as in the *ECP*. The point is better social institutions must spend to lead investment, which in turn must result in growth and social advantage (see Appendix 13.1). Thus, both common *good* and social security must result from quantitative planning, which does not rule out individualism or free competition (including the search for profit). The implications are crucial. If the *Laissez-faire* philosophy was considered as archetypical for the economies in the nineteenth century, Capitalism must be propelled by deliberate state policy in the twentieth century, indeed most companies are prone to be socialized in terms of ownership. But what is a semi-autonomous institution? This characterization of the corporate world must not be vilified since in this variant conjunction of interests it is less prominent than influencing actions.

For some economists Keynes was an advocate (*gato pardo*-type) of the system of free enterprise, never analyzing the issue of justice in terms of social classes. According to other dissenting—naïve?—views, Keynes advocated a totalitarian role for the State with consequences on individual liberty, for example in the writings of both Milton Friedman and Friedrich Hayek. Nonetheless, in Keynes's system conventions, traditions, social institutions, and social norms are respected, as he was not a political liberal (Fitzgibbons 1988). Are these views fair? 'Keynes's social philosophy is complex and heterogeneous' (Lambert 1963). For others, his message is simple: Government functions must be enlarged but still preserve freedom. In Keynes's words 'there will still remain a wide field for the exercise of private initiative' (ibid., p. 380). Once the economic problem is solved the government must step out of the scene. The objective is only that effective demand attain an adequate level, reducing uncertainty to achieve peace and prosperity.

According to Dostaler (1996), Keynes was involved in the Liberal Party, and his middle stance allowed him to be a great negotiator, except when the future of Britain was at stake or theoretical discernments were misplaced, but he ended up concerned about the future of mankind as in 'Economic possibilities for our grandchildren' (Chapter 8). The upshot is that the final volume of the Golden Book (Chapters 22–24) blurs the distinction among economics, history, utopianism, and literature. Depth and interdisciplinarity go hand in hand. In addition, the ordinary person thinks that the future is a linear continuation of the past. Keynes's rejection of this type of determinism in human behavior —including utilitarianism—has a sway on decision-making in economics. His conception of the future of humankind assumes that humans must control their individual and social destinies. This is a central tenet in liberalism, democracy, macroeconomics, and Capitalism.

9.4 Further Issues and Related Chapters in *The General Theory of Employment, Interest and Money*

Keynes was individualistic but at the same time preoccupied with social and public policies and contexts. Freedom and relative leisure are the by-products of 'full employment,' after Keynes designed a panacea-type recovery policy for this stage of Capitalism, wherein Keynes's focus on the short term is modern (Chick 1983).

According to Keynes, the creed that the world is comprised of atomic facts (Chapter 4) is a philosophical argument applicable to the natural but not to the social world. The corollary for this author is that perspectivism is inoperant in physics but useful in social sciences. A further consequence of the difference between organicism and atomism (main example is the paradox of thrift, wherein he distinguishes the individual from the national level) is Keynes's innovative dichotomy macro-microeconomics. In the former (the science of aggregates, see Chapter 2) expectations and uncertainty are relevant for implying that monetary variables affect real variables. Moreover, due to both organicism and uncertainty prevail there is no reason for investors to be equal to savings, or for considering that wages will equilibrate the labor market (Chapter 2) and there emerge disequilibria and an insufficient aggregate demand bringing about involuntary unemployment. These ontic nuances underpin the relevance of macroeconomics.

In the end, once full employment is attained, the atomic hypothesis may be used with discretion (Smith, Chapter 4, makes a comeback). This proves the validity of Keynes's early philosophical investigations in logic, ethics, and epistemology. Put differently, his philosophical past permitted him to integrate various elements of his thought into a new open framework. According to Wood (1982), *GT* is full of new concepts and macroeconomics is an organicist theory of income determination.[7] In this book, Keynes focuses upon effective demand as the motivator of the system registering its impact on movements in output, wherein domestic investment conducted by 'animal spirits' is the crucial variable, the mobile (Chapter 2). Here investment depends on both interest rates and uncertainty, which explains cyclical instability and underemployment equilibria but also the relationship interaction between the real and the monetary sectors, that is the *Keynes Effect* operates, which makes that the lowering of interest rates propel investment but acquire also a moral angle in the last Chapter of *GT*. Indeed, usury impedes human development.

For Davidson (2002), who has knowledge of the physical science, *GT* is a treatise about the impact of fluctuations in effective demand on output and employment in a non-ergodic world. In Keynes's view liquidity disequilibria and diversions in the prices of financial assets are the ultimate cause of involuntary unemployment. This has been confirmed in recent crises (Appendix 13.1). *GT* is the place for reaffirming that no natural forces exist in the (human) economic cosmos. Those natural forces had taken in the Classical orthodox past the following interconnected metaphysical—rational—variants: *Deux ex machina*, perfect rationality, Cartesian internal perfections, Kant's moral law, Newtonian forces, Walras's neutral auctioneer, Smith's invisible hand, market homogeneity, agents' symmetry, or Say's Law.

Keynes's economic evolution may thus be discerned from the philosophical analysis of *TMR* (1923), *TM* (1930b), and *GT* (1936), and the passthroughs, but this awareness took some time. *TMR* is about pattern identification in cycles for the prevention of the return to the gold standard and a plea for international cooperation in monetary reform. *TM* is the work of an erudite on finance, whose prescription is that price fluctuations are due to discrepancies between investment and savings. The less conservative *GT* provides a more open framework with emphasis on unemployment, sub-equilibria, liquidity, and sundry social issues (including social improvements), when the mercurial mind of Keynes (this author's wording) allegedly breaks with orthodoxy (Pasinetti 2007).

According to Davis (1991a), the insights on the essence of both *good* and probability have an indirect impact on two of Keynes's major heuristics topics in *GT*: liquidity preference and unstable productive investment. In terms of financial investment selection, judgments reflect subjective expectations on prospective yields as people are heterogeneous[8] (an idea akin to Nietzsche's doctrine of perspectivism[9]), and this heterogeneity also applies to the preference for liquid assets. In Chapter 13 of *GT* both conventions and judgments founded on numerical evidence are objective, but the states of confidence used for decision-making are subjective (see Chapter 6 of his book). Chapter 13 in *GT* uses the metaphor 'A Theory of Beauty' (1905b) for outlining the subjective dimension of long-term expectations. He breaks up with orthodoxy which tends to believe that long-term judgments and situations are objective and rational.

In that same vein, Keynes criticizes 'profiteers,' and thereafter 'rentiers' in Chapter 24 for supposing (they do!) that money is the means toward happiness.[10]

Keynes's treatment of financial markets in Chapter 13 of *GT* is related to convention in the face of uncertainty and fuzzy knowledge, notions which widen his original vision on the functioning of agents. His 'chair game' is another metaphor employed in that same chapter of *GT*. Both metaphors are about a selection based on inference from one's knowledge of public perceptions, being examples of the effects of uncertainty via expectations on the economy. His figure of 'animal spirits' in *GT*, which renders investment unstable, is considered the backbone of modern behavioral finance. *GT* resembles the *Treatise on Probability* in terms of method and its dominant object of study: uncertainty; as well as the *Treatise on Money* regarding the policy actions of a monetary economy. *GT* summarizes Keynes's previous economic and philosophical insights where his aphorism is 'the problem is primarily a monetary one' ('The economic consequences of Mr. Churchill' 1925, p. 228), but the problem in *GT* has an ethical dimension as well.

For Harcourt and Riach (1997), the last chapter of *GT* is about outlines, issues, extensions, developments, vision, methods, research paths, interpretations, historical accounts, novelties, and theoretical loans and dispatches. They contend that the long-run implications of a successful full-employment policy for the accumulation of capital constitute the greatest topic in Chapter 24. For Harcourt and Riach, Keynes also examines the complexities and interdependencies of the real world, especially those related to income distribution after full employment is attained, and prices are fair. In Keynes's pensive and sensitive—but financially tilted—view fair price is a low-interest rate. For Aspromourgos (2004), Keynes's wide idea is to systematically reduce the interest rates. But however ethical this redistributionist awareness is, it is impossible to be implemented in the absence of management after assuming the deficiency of a self-regulated mechanism, wherein the public sector must step into the scene by leading expenditure.

A related topic is the consilience between private and public advantages, dismissing the Classical prescription of null government. *GT* thus departs from appropriate (realistic) assumptions for arriving at defensible conclusions, recalling that the Golden Book is created as a departure from the interpretation of Keynes's previous footnotes in 1933 (Appendix 7.2). Keynes thus backs an administered type of Capitalism, because of the inefficacy of the *Laissez-faire* Capitalism in managing short-term fluctuations and immoralism regarding egalitarianism. According to Patinkin (1987), the attainment of long-term full employment has implications on capital accumulation, interest rates, income distribution, the future of *laissez-faire* (Chapter 8), and the prospects of war and peace.

For Zhang (undated), Keynes writes against Smith, Darwin, and the prevalent political thought in the seventeenth and the eighteenth centuries, based (Keynes) on a realistic understanding of the functioning of social and physical procedures. The contention embedded in this insight is that physicalism is a simplified hypothesis (see Chapter 2) which only reflects what is natural and therefore ideal and abstract. Instead, Keynes was as concrete as a financer. A high long-term interest rate brings about unemployment and an uneven income distribution, which is why he was suspicious about the role of 'rentiers' in modern societies. Freedom at the individual level entails getting rid of this type of agent by means of euthanasia. Hence Keynes uses liberal means for arriving at conservative implications (a *gattopardo* attitude). Crises of insufficient demand arise from collapses in the Marginal Efficiency of Capital (MEC); that is, from decreases in investment; but the turning points in economic activity may also be provoked by diminishing rates of consumption. Once again, crises finally generate rising unemployment which can only be reduced by managing aggregate demand in Keynes's terms (again Appendix 13.1). This is only a tool, in fact, he argues that when the objective of full employment has been attained, there is room for implementing the Classical theory, but this only occurs to him in early 1946.

9.5 Conclusions on the Visionary Chapter of the Golden Book

This chapter has analyzed Keynes's philosophy as expressed in Chapter 24 of *GT* for investigating the reception, impact, origins, foundations, and meaning of his bequeath. How visionary is Keynes in Chapter 24? As he writes 'the power of vested interests is vastly exaggerated compared with the gradual encroachment of ideas' (ibid., p. 383). Perhaps, as Joan Robinson suggests, Keynes is simply following an illusion. Nevertheless, ideas lead to visions, especially in modern and virtual societies. Keynes was a visionary with respect to the role of the public sector in 1936.[11] But there may be some caveats. As Wray writes: 'attempting to maintain full employment by stimulating private investment would shift the distribution of income toward owners of capital, worsening inequality and thereby lowering the society's propensity to consume—one of the problems addressed by Keynes in Chapter 24 of the *General Theory*' (Wray 2007 p. 6).

Further, Keynes's intuitive quantitative predictions have left their imprint on social sciences constituting a progressive *SRP*. Lakatos stated that evolution exists in the theoretical world of economics. Blaug (1980, 1991) stated his preference for the Lakatosian application of philosophy of science in economics. Then, in Lakatosian terms, the Keynesian theory is the general case of Classical economics since Keynes considers heterogeneity in people's behavior, non-ergodicity, and historical time. Nevertheless, the innovation introduced by Keynes is at the core level. There is neither *deus ex machine* nor natural laws in social and political activities—this may come from Moore's revolt against the naturalistic fallacy, which assumes natural things are intrinsically *good*. A parallel core result is that moral (political or social) sciences are distinct from natural sciences, so their methods and scope differ.

The result of new ethical contentions after the economic problem is addressed so he depicts—at least partially—how a new civilization will emerge (and its future, Chapter 8). Chapter 24 of *GT* is thus a contribution to the understanding of future Capitalism. Whereas a historical introduction of economics for the sake of demolishing old ideas is the goal of Chapters 2 and 3 of *GT*, the outlining of the intertwining of both human history and future is found in the final chapter of *GT*. Economics for him was a precondition for *good*. These humanitarian insights are based on Keynes's mix of rationalism[12] and imagination, just like his theory of knowledge is a blend of subjectivism and objectivism in *A Treatise on Probability* (1921). The man of the middle stance is also the man advocating for the juxtaposition of notions. Thus Keynes's plural methodology is a key element to understanding his message in Chapter 24. There he re-interprets information for resolving unsettled questions by offering innovative directions, being against outmoded paradigms just as he condemns hypocrisy in *ECP*.

According to Skidelsky (1992) in 'the Banana Parable' (TM) it is outlined how a shock produces cumulative reactions, as opposed—we would add—to a once-for-all effect. But the cumulative upshot does not bring about equilibrium except by chance. Organicism is thus the ontological foundation of *GT*. In Chapter 24 of *GT* Keynes addresses this ontological problem of no-nonsense togetherness by means of interrelated discourses for doing *good*. The result is that he proposes a new society fed by new hopes, tying up his philosophical insights from distinct fields. Dissenting views would state that Keynes disguised conventions to save the destiny of Capitalism, but we have described his core for denying Keynes is a simply short-term pamphleteer advocating for platitudes.

Keynes also demonstrates his interdisciplinary vision in his quest for the truth. Liberty is to be gained in a world where heterogeneous disequilibria are the rule. Keynes's deep reflections thus guide the writing of his famous book departing from philosophy to delve into political economy and returning to philosophy.[13] The main issue of Chapter 24 is hence the consideration of means for overcoming uncertainty. This is a permanent task for him, entailing behavioral evolution. In this sense, Chapter 24, 'Concluding notes on the social philosophy toward which the General Theory leads,' is the philosophical counterpart of Chapter 13, 'The state of long-term expectations' in *GT*,[14] which explores the effect of long-term expectations of agents on economics.

The final paragraph on the power of ideas is an invitation to ponder our future as persons. If freedom is about responsibility, Keynes's idea in Chapter 24 of *GT* is that conditions will be suitable for growth and high levels of life once the problem of unemployment—our main responsibility and duty as societies—is solved, but this paradise must be gained through proper knowledge oriented toward action. Keynes preaches action instead of contemplation, but in Chapter 24—a holiday-type chapter in appearance—he resorts again to contemplation. Perhaps Keynes follows the spirit of his early paper 'Modern Civilization' (1905a) where he supports Burke's contentions on expediency in political philosophy but contending that there are new worries (see Moggridge 1992, p. 126), also echoing Burke's contention that self-government is just a means. Evolution also requires going back from time to time.

Finally, Keynes affirms in 'Egoism' (1906) that Moore had assumed away the idea that ought and universal *good* are interrelated (see Moggridge 1992, p. 129), instead Keynes attempts to prove the existence of a link between these two realms in Chapter 24 of *GT*. He also proves in the Golden Book that ethics has a practical significance, but one related to reaching an end as related to virtue. Utilitarian ends are restricted to the short term throughout *GT* with some exceptions, but Chapter 24 of *GT* is about both the attainment and enjoyment of wealth in the long term which is based on virtue. Keynes is consistent herewith his ethical milieu.

This chapter is about the closing part of a book dealing with a new conception of monetary economics wherein cycles can be reduced in terms of intensity and unemployment can be resolved. It then delineates the human landscape when the economic problem leaves its place to humanistic concerns. Appendix 9.1 outlines 'TGE' which clarifies Keynes's message about uncertainty. Appendix 9.2 tells the story about the immediate reactions to *GT*. In that vein, Chapter 9 assesses the characteristics of subsequent macroeconomic ('Keynesian') theories, which resort to dissimilar (Pre-Keynesian) core and methods and send a different message by ignoring uncertainty, organicism, and the absence of a self-equilibrating system, treating again macroeconomics as a simple extension of microeconomics. History is cyclical as some repressed elements re-emerge at unexpected times, or new notions are embedded into new forms of development.

Appendix 9.1: 'The General Theory of Employment' (1937)

Some relevant papers by Keynes dealing with the expansion of his theories and the responses to his critiques to *GT* are mentioned here. The first, 'Fluctuations in net investment in the United States' (1946), is a numerical characterization of the components in aggregate demand (consumption, investment, and public debt), which is the basis for the design of national accounts and is an appendix in some editions of *GT*. The second paper whose subject matter is the clarification of uncertainty is 'The General Theory of Employment' (1937a) or 'TGE,' outlined in this Appendix. The third article is 'Alternative theories of the rate of interest' (1937a) where Keynes confirms that the interest rate is a measure of uncertainty (he makes economic uncertainty operational), defining its mechanical role in the attainment of stability. The fourth paper is 'The ex-ante theory of the rate of interest' (1937b), where he expounds that the transitions toward stability may be attained by putting low pressure on the demand for liquidity and the rate of interest. The fifth article, 'Relative movements of real wages and output' (1939), contends that movements in nominal wages increase unemployment contradicting the microeconomic lapidary rule established by the Classical economists.

The second paper is the one to be analyzed in this Appendix as Keynes's immediate response to his critiques and skeptics after *GT* is undertaken in this philosophical piece by re-emphasizing his concept of uncertainty. His core notion of uncertainty—arising from Hume's skepticism—is that it is a qualitative variable, and hence its effect is a matter of degree (Chapter 6), the highest degree being Hume's notion of ignorance. Notice uncertainty is non-existent in orthodoxy: In Ancient Manichaeism, Cartesian dualism (Rene Descartes 1596–1650), Spinoza's geometry (Baruch Spinoza 1632–1677), Leibnizian optimism (Gottfried Leibniz 1646–1716), and Kantian Idealism (Emmanuel Kant 1724–1804). However, these binary contentions are only worthwhile in closed atomistic (predictable) systems.

Now recall *GT* is about the analysis of a credit-monetary economics with cautious expectations in the face of uncertainty, wherein money is a store—asset—of value and hence movements in interest rates are the cause of output—income—fluctuations in the face of consumers,' investors,' and policymakers' uncertainty (see Appendix 13.1). This phenomenon is revisited in this post-*GT* heterodox piece, for improving its explanation which is addressed to impatient readers or newcomers. The effect of uncertainty on interest rates as a critical element of Keynes's theoretical stance therefore originates as a reasoning thread that runs formally from *TP* and addresses the confusions of those 'Keynesian' economists apart from the *Keynes Circus* (Chapter 4).

Uncertainty generates complex and diverse expectations and guides 'animal spirits' via affectations on both liquidity preference and the marginal efficiency of capital (these changes being unequal and discontinuous), thereby impacting the level of aggregate demand through modifications in investors' moods and actions. These effects presuppose agents are heterogeneous (different from the homogeneous *Homo Economicus* of Smith) since uncertainty arising either by foolishness or purpose is magnified in the presence of dissimilar expectations. Keynes's crucial key words in his 'TGE' are: about the consequences of the future 'we simply do not know' (CW XIV, p. 13) to distinguish between uncertainty and risk. Uncertainty also changes in intensity rapidly in terms of its causes, interrelations, and effects. It is not only about both the future but also about others' reactions in a complex economic-financial system (Chapter 3). This hints at the then unconventional idea that interest rates may fluctuate without a discernible order, and money must be regulated for managing investment in a coordinated fashion in the realm of aggregate economies.

Therefore 'TGE' is also a response to his late critiques and is now considered to be the 'official' article in the field of the philosophy of uncertainty, the bible for the Heterodox Post-Keynesians, a school which is faithful to the consideration of uncertainty as to the original message of Keynes. However, according to Fitzgibbons (1988), the mere meaning of uncertainty raises problems. What is certain is that uncertainty is neither a risk nor a probability since logical propositions are not related to future events but the 'weight of the argument.' According to Darity (1995), an inspirator of uncertainty for Keynes was Silvio Gesell (1862–1930) mentioned in the final part of *GT*, perhaps because of his peculiar advocacy of the use of stamped money for the avoidance of future difficulties and the understanding of changes in money values (see Chapter 9). The latter contended that the uncontrollable money-interest rate system constitutes a barrier to continuous full employment, whereas Wicksell for example assumes that interest rates are totally manageable as they automatically tend to equilibrium, to their 'natural' level. Gesell also writes about some relevant properties and uses of money but fails to see liquidity preference, which for Keynes is the main manifestation of uncertainty: an emerging property of an open system. In a nutshell, uncertainty is the basis of both modern economic policies and finance, being ubiquitous in its impact on businesses (especially in the financial sector) as well as political events (then again see Appendix 13.1). If we are perplex about the last events in the 2000s, we can assuredly ascertain Keynes belongs to the twenty-first century. Conversely, the Classical core concept (epitomized by Smith's works) was scarcity, which is only appropriate for an economy entering for the first time into its industrial phase.[15]

Appendix 9.2: The Immediate and Unfavorable Reactions to *The General Theory of Employment, Interest and Money*

The main aspects regarding the acceptance of *GT* are diffusion, scandal, acceptance, revisions, and fusions (see Chapter 10). The enduring influence of *GT* can be partly appraised by assessing the responses, acceptance, criticism, reviews, misunderstandings, disagreements, sequels, accords on the heyday, demise, and resurgence of the Golden Book. There were immediate favorable reactions to *GT* mainly coming from the *Keynes Circus* (1931) and other followers and converts. But not only Kahn and the remaining members of the group had a sway for disseminating *GT* (they had had a role in the making of the book, see Appendix 7.1), but also such contemporaries as Nicholas Kaldor (1908–1986), among others, participated in this task during the 1940s. Joan Robinson subsequently devoted some years to defending and clarifying the Godspell of *GT*, while Leijonhuvfud famously made a distinction between Keynes's economics and Keynesian economics in 1968, criticizing Hicks's artificial model *IS-LM* as it did not include insights on uncertainty. In Hicks's[16] model *IS-LM* (1937) equilibrium schemata depict the relationship between output and interest rates to explain how fiscal and monetary policies lead to full employment. Other contemporary reviewers of *GT* only made comments about heuristic details (Chapter 10).

Ralph C. Hawtrey (1879–1975) was adamant about some contentions of *GT* and this soured their relationship. However, Keynes paid special attention to the contrary opinions of Jacob Viner (1892–1970) more than to those of the more famous Joseph A. Schumpeter (1883–1950), demonstrating in his attention to Viner both his commitment to science and his altruism. Viner (1936) affirmed that the role of liquidity was a strange material in the Golden Book, but perhaps he did not follow Keynes's line of reasoning: that liquidity is a haven from uncertainty but also an element blocking the efficacy of interest rates to activate the economy. Schumpeter maintained the view that *GT* was co-authored by Kahn (Chapter 7), elevating the heuristic notion of the multiplier to a core assumption. Friedrich Hayek never reviewed *GT* contending that Keynes changed his mind from time to time. Roy F. Harrod (1900–1978) thought of Keynes's system as an engine of economic growth, extending that system for the case of the long term by reinstating the role of savings in the macroeconomic landscape, perhaps viewing uncertainty as a transient phenomenon occurring in the short run (Chapter 12).

Orthodox economics was still following the Classical message. Later, harsh reviews from Milton Friedman (1912–2006) (see Appendix 9.2 for a full but hypothetical review) and Paul A. Samuelson (1915–2009) appear, among others. Friedman the monetarist (not monetary) economist stated that the present is a continuation of the past, that policies must be based on rules, that monetary policy only leads to inflationary spirals returning to 'QTM,' and gave relevance to permanent income, which means that he advocates for long-term policies (Chapter 10). Friedman states that the best book written by Keynes is *TMR* (1923), which is scarcely revolutionary. Samuelson (1947) ascertains that *GT* is the disorganized—mutant—work of a genius, ignoring the transitional stage in Keynes's *oeuvre*. None of them incorporate the *Keynes Effect* into their models about the impact of expectations on disequilibrium via the effect of interest rates on investment (Chapter 7). Samuelson contended that deviations are the exception and created the *Keynesian Cross*, which depicts the relationship between output and aggregate demand in an orthodox manner. Samuelson may prove to be wrong. There is nothing more evolutionary and less spontaneous[17] than the making of the heterodox *GT*. Gestation phases are obvious in *GT*, as Keynes's nurturing from several viewpoints leads to the attainment of a different product. The Golden Book deepens the core of economics while jettisoning most of its previous contentions. Unfortunately, Keynes's message on uncertainty will be misunderstood, neglected, or misapplied for a long time.

Keynes's lost prominence in the late 1970s and early 1980s. Late commentators expressed the view that he never envisages the appearance of stagflation, but this is inaccurate since he devised models for unemployment and inflation (seeing them as the poles of a unity, the latter in 1940), and affirmed that both phenomena may cohabitate since unemployment is for him the normal state-of-affairs. The mediate reactions of the 'Keynesian' schools to *GT* experienced their heyday in the 1970s. These schisms are assessed now in Chapter 10 in the form of *SRPs*.

Notes

1. This section relies upon the literature review and the outline of Keynes's general philosophy conducted in Chapter 5 (Sects. 5.2 and 5.3). Both Chapters are similar as they are based on philosophy while also analyzing economic concepts.
2. The basis of this chapter is the author's article published under a similar name in SSRN. It does not require any permission to be published.
3. He also exhibits this prophetic power in 'My Early Beliefs,' among other works (Chapter 11).
4. Freedom from the fetishism of money is his next topic (Chapter 11), but is also addressed in Chapter 8.

5. John Stuart Mill's Victorian calm was torn down by the philosophy of evolution of Darwin.
6. Both 'The economic consequences of Mr. Churchill' and 'The end of the Laissez faire' anticipate this notion (Chapter 8 of this book).
7. Even some Marxists praise Keynes for reinstalling the analysis of society in economics. Recall that the Classical Political Economy was atomic, that is, concentrated upon the individual.
8. This is also related to the dichotomy 'bearishness-bullishness' in *TM* (Chapter 7).
9. See Appendix 11.1.
10. See Chapter 8.
11. Most men tend to become conservative and realist as well as less self-centred in their 40s or 50s since they are normally more involved in real world affairs than in their youth or in their last days.
12. Hume opposed rationalism as the unique form for the sake of truth.
13. This is the apex of the "republic of my imagination" (see Chapter 7 on 'The economics possibilities of our grandchildren').
14. Every Keynesian has his (her) own favourite chapter.
15. Notice that the *leitmotiv* of economics is the provision of knowledge and information for Hayek.
16. John Hicks (1904–1989).
17. Samuelson classifies the Golden Book as a "mutant" ("Lord Keynes and the General Theory", 1946, *Econometrica* 14 (3)) then again losing both the origin and thread of Keynes's reasoning.

References

Sources

Aspromourgos, Anthony. 2004. "'The Functionless Investor': Keynes's Euthanasia of the Rentier Revisited". In *History and Political Economy: Essays in Honour of P. D. Groenewegen*, edited by Tony Aspromourgos and John Lodewijks, 217–35. London: Routledge.

Blaug, Mark. 1980. *The Methodology of Economics: Or How Economists Explain*. Cambridge: Cambridge University Press.

———. 1991. "Second Thoughts on the Keynesian Revolution." *History of Political Economy* 23, no. 2: 171–92.

Chick, Victoria. 1983. *Macroeconomics after Keynes: A Reconsideration of the General Theory*. Boston, MA: MIT Press.

Davidson, Paul. 2002. *Financial Markets, Money and the Real World*. Chentelham, UK: Edward Elgar.

———. 2007. *John Maynard Keynes*. London: Macmillan.

Davis, John B. 1991a. "Keynes's Critiques of Moore: Philosophical Foundations of Keynes's Economics." *Cambridge Journal of Economics* 5, no. 1 (March): 61–77.

———. 1991b. "Keynes's View of Economics as a Moral Science." In *Keynes and Philosophy: Essays on the Origins of Keynes's Thought*, edited by Bradley W. Bateman and John B. Davis, 89–103. Aldershot, England: Edward Elgar.

———. 1994. *Keynes's Philosophical Development*. Cambridge: Cambridge University Press.

Darity Jr., William. 1995. "Keynes' Political Philosophy: The Gesell Connection." *Eastern Economic Journal* 21, no. 1 (Winter): 27–41.

Dostaler, Gilles. 1996. "The Formation of Keynes's Vision." *History of Economics Review* 25, no. 1: 14–31.

Fitzgibbons, Athol J. 1988 [1990]. *Keynes's Vision: A New Political Economy*. Oxford: Clarendon Press.

Harcourt, Geoffrey C., and Peter Riach (eds.). 1997. *A 'Second' Edition of the General Theory, Volume I*. New York: Routledge.

Harrod, Roy F. 1951. *The Life of John Maynard Keynes*. New York: Harcourt.

Hession, Charles H. 1984. *John Maynard Keynes. A Personal Biography of the Man Who Revolutionized Capitalism and the Way We Live Today*. New York: MacMillan.

Keynes, John Maynard. 1905a. "Modern Civilization." In *JMK/UA/22*.

———. 1905b. 'A Theory of Beauty', unpublished manuscript deposited in King's College Library, Cambridge University

———. 1906. "Egoism." In *JMK/UA/26*.

———. 1921 [1973]. *The Collected Writings of John Maynard Keynes (CW)* Vol. 8: *A Treatise on Probability* , edited by Elizabeth Johnson (19–28) and Daniel E. Moggridge (15–18). London: Macmillan, for the Royal Economic Society.

———. 1923. A Tract on Monetary Reform. In *JMK CW Vol. IV A Tract on Monetary Reform*, edited by D. Moggridge. London: Royal Economic Society.

———. 1925. *The Economic Consequences of Mr. Churchill*. London: Hogarth.

———. 1930a. "Economic Possibilities for Our Grandchildren." In *JMK CW Vol. IX Essays in Persuasion*, edited by D. Moggridge. London: Royal Economic Society.

———. 1930b. "A Treatise on Money." In *JMK CW Vols. V and VI A Treatise on Money*. edited by D. Moggridge. London: Royal Economic Society.

———. 1936 [1997]. *The General Theory of Employment, Interest and Money. Reprint edition*. London: Prometheus.

———. 1937a. "The General Theory of Employment." *The Quarterly Journal of Economics* 51, no. 2: 209–23.
———. 1937b. "The Ex-ante Theory of the Rate of Interest." *Economic Journal* 47, no. 188 (December): 663–69.
———. 1939. "Relative Movements of Real Wages and Output." *The Economic Journal* 49, no. 193 (March): 39–51.
———. 1946. "Fluctuations in Net Investment in the United States." *The Economic Journal* 46, no. 183 (September): 540–47.
Lambert, Paul. 1963. "The Social Philosophy of John Maynard Keynes." *Annals of Public and Cooperative Economics* 34, no. 4 (October): 483–515.
Moggridge, Daniel E. 1992. *Maynard Keynes: An Economist's Biography*. London: Routledge.
Pasinetti, Luigi L. 2007. *Keynes and the Cambridge Keynesians: A 'Revolution in Economics' to be Accomplished*. Cambridge: Cambridge University Press.
Patinkin, Don. 1987. "Keynes, John Maynard." In *The New Palgrave: A Dictionary of Economics*, Volume 3, edited by John Eatwell et al. (K to P): 19–41. New York: Macmillan.
Robinson, Joan. 1932. "Economics Is a Serious Subject: The Apologies of an Economist to the Mathematician, the Scientist and the Plain Man." *The Papers of Professor Joan Violet Robinson. Correspondence between Joan Robinson and Her Mother, Lady Margaret Helen Maurice*, JVR77/284, Maurice, Lady (Margaret) Helen (nee Marsh), 1932–1938. https://janus.lib.cam.ac.uk/db/node.xsp?id=EAD%2FGBR%2F0272%2FPP%2FJVR_%2F7%2F284. Accessed 7 July 2012.
———. 1983. "Has Keynes Failed?" In *John Maynard Keynes. Critical Assessments*, Volume IV, edited by John. C. Wood, Chapter 136. New York: Routledge.
Samuelson, Paul A. 1946. "Lord Keynes and the General Theory." *Econometrica* XIV, no. 3: 187–200.
Skidelsky, Robert. 1992. *John Maynard Keynes. Volume II: The Economist as Saviour 1920–1937*. London: Macmillan.
———. 1996. *Keynes. Past Masters*. Oxford: Oxford University Press.
———. 1997. "Chapter 24 Keynes's Concluding Notes. Robert Skidelsky Writing as John Maynard Keynes." In *A 'Second' Edition of the General Theory*, Volume I, edited by Geoffrey C. Harcourt and Peter Riach, Chapter 24, 430–9. New York: Routledge.
———. 2000. *John Maynard Keynes. Volume III: Fighting for Britain 1937–1946*. London: Macmillan.
Streeten, Paul. 1954. "Keynes and the Classical Tradition." In *Post Keynesian Economics*, edited by Kenneth K. Kurihara, Chapter 13, 345–64. New York: Rutgers.

Viner, Jacob. 1936. "Mr. Keynes on the Causes of Unemployment." *The Quarterly Journal of Economics* 51, no. 1 (November).
Wood, John Cunningham. 1982. *John Maynard Keynes: Critical Assessments. Critical Assessments of Leading Economists*. London and New York. Routledge.
Wray, R. 2007. "The Continuing Legacy of John Maynard Keynes." The Levy Economics Institute of Bard College WP No. 514.

CHAPTER 10

Confirming Robinson's Statement on Keynes's Rejection of the Classical Economy and His Immediate Orthodoxy

Discussions and criticism after *GT* in the late 1930s and throughout the 1940s ultimately led to the creation of the orthodox Post-keynesian schools in the 1950s. This chapter about the internal history of macroeconomics between 1950 and 1990—perhaps through 2008, see Appendix 13.1—investigates whether Keynes's message was betrayed by his followers during the late twentieth century. For this purpose, this chapter contrasts the *SRPs* of Keynes, mainly from *GT*, with those of its immediate orthodox schools: Monetarism (*MS*), Neoclassical Synthesis (*NS*), New Classical Macroeconomics (Rational Expectations or *RE*), and General Disequilibrium (*GD*). This is a theme on the reception of Keynes's evolution following the controversy firstly enunciated by Axel Leijonhuvfud in 1968 about the difference between Keynes's and Keynesian economics (Appendix 9.2). Even though many economists would differ, it is hereby hypothesized that in both economic and philosophical terms the *MS*, *NS*, *RE*, and *GD SRPs* are variants of

The basis for this Chapter is the author's own article published under a similar name in SSRN.

J. Muñoz-Bandala, *Keynes's Evolutionary Spirit*,
Palgrave Insights into Apocalypse Economics,
https://doi.org/10.1007/978-3-030-90150-9_10

Keynes's *SRP* but not in terms of its core. The rationale for this ascertainment is that Keynes's reasoning chain (a non-self-regulated system, non-neutral money, organicism, ergodicity,[1] historical time, and uncertainty) is misapplied by these deviant schools, or even transformed into 'Bastard Keynesianism,' to quote Joan Robinson (1974[1973], p. 125). This is a case of modification of heuristics or the return to basic Classical principles.

This chapter thus explains why Keynes's core has not been sufficiently or validly challenged. Section 10.1 offers a brief analysis of Keynes's core under the guidelines of both Chapters 2 and 5, including an initial note on Classical economics. Section 10.2 describes the initially faithful Post Keynesianism. Sections 10.3–10.6 outline the respective hard cores of *MS*, *NS*, *RE,* and *GD*, with a note on *New Classical Macroeconomics* and *Heterodox Post-Keynesian Economics*. Section 10.7 concludes with the commonalities and differences among these theories and offers a contention regarding what all these economic conceptions mean in terms of Keynes's evolution. Appendix 10.1 is written as a fictional dialogue between Keynes and Friedman (the latter being a leading monetarist) exhibiting the difference in their respective cores and perhaps memorable moments in both the history of macroeconomics and economics philosophy.

10.1 Keynes's Core Revisited[2]

The Classical *SRP* assumes the existence of a closed heuristic system comprised of microeconomic foundations, especially the belief in wage flexibility for alleviating unemployment and the identification of savings with real investment. Furthermore, methodological individualism[3] underlies the micro-theory of demand supply. Individual choice is conducted under the framework of a self-regulating, timeless, and ubiquitous market assuming that rationality is universal; that is, not socially differentiated. The Classical message is conservative, ignoring social facts.

For Verdon (1996), scientific revolutions are mostly cosmological. Cosmology affects the definition of concepts and is revealed in the form of analogies. In the case of Classical economics, universal harmony denies the possibility for human or social action in favor of or against the market. The Classical *SRP* thus presents analogies with proto-energetics, reflecting the certainty prevailing in physics, the market system being the mobile. For some, there is medieval theology in Classical Economics. For others, the Classical individual acquires the same status as in the Bible and money is an illusion. The consequence is that the Classical *SRP* is equated with self-regulating atomistic (Newtonian) markets, wherein perfect rationality leads to free competition. Here time is only a logical category, and uncertainty is aberrant as the system is almost always in equilibrium and money is a veil, that is only a means of exchange.

Outstanding Classical economists, most of them irrationally putting faith in the *Laissez-faire* and rationality, are: Adam Smith, the initiator of microeconomics (1723–1790); and his successors David Ricardo (1772–1823), a straw man for Keynes; Robert Malthus (1766–1834), the favorite political economist for Keynes with interest in aggregate demand deficiencies; and Jean-Baptiste Say (1767–1832), the creator of Say's Law; all of whom believe in a sacred double-sided system which would lead to a supply and demand scheme. This system like most conventionalisms never wears out. The most important late Neoclassical economists (in Keynes's view) are John Stuart Mill, with an interest in stationary states and social improvement; the Frenchman Leon Walras (1834–1910), the creator of the notion of General Equilibrium; William S. Jevons (1835–1882), with an emphasis on mathematical methods and a primitive interest in uncertainty (like Hume); and Keynes's half-contemporary Alfred Marshall (1842–1924), an outstanding microeconomist and the creator of the term economics. The latter microeconomist had a huge lively influence on Keynes, though in the ambivalent forms of adherence and rejection. Interestingly, Keynes accepted Marshall's method of comparative statics (the use of *ceteris paribus*) but rejected Marshall's contentions about guaranteed equilibrium and the passive role of money. In other words, Keynes accepted Marshall's heuristics but rejected Marshall's core.

10.1.1 The Classical (and Neoclassical) Versus Keynes's Core

Keynes rejected the Classical (Smithian) core about the *Laissez-Faire*, the invisible hand, the atomistic and the certain view of the economy, a natural Cartesian order,[4] physicalism, a self-regulating system (including stable financial markets), and especially the 'old' perception of full employment (*FE*) as a transient microeconomic phenomenon related to wage levels. The Neoclassical core also includes perfect knowledge, perfect expectations, and certainty. Entrepreneurs and investors are homogeneous, symmetrical, atomistic, and rational, and hence equilibrium exists, and its deviations are exceptional. The Neoclassical economists depart from order to arrive at the notion of self-regulation like Classical economists. Classical economics (wherein macroeconomics is superfluous) is based on rationalism, atomism, and the notion of *Homo Economicus*, which are concepts taken from the natural sciences. This is an example of the so-called inferiority complex of the social sciences (see Machlup 1978). The Classical economists simply follow a Newtonian atomicist concept of the world coupled with mathematical formalism.

Then Keynes stepped into the scene with his three economics books (1923, 1930, and 1936). Keynes's evolutive research on involuntary unemployment is his central concern (Chapter 9) and aggregate demand (*AD*) determines national income (*Υ*). He views money as a store of value linking the real and the monetary sectors (Klein 1947). Other concepts he researches are: the ineffectiveness of price flexibility for curing unemployment, the irrelevance of wages as an equilibrating factor (Chapter 18 of *GT*), uncertainty (Skidelsky 2001, 2009; O'Donnell 1991), the instability of investment (*I*) due to asymmetric expectations, and the disparity between savings and investment (Heilbroner 1951). Under this reasoning for the selection of variables (and the heuristics for them represents a core), the Classical and the Neo-classical economists are living behind the times, at least for true Keynes's followers (see Chapter 2). How true is this statement? The next section is an outline of how orthodox *Post Keynesianism* arose after Keynes's death, precisely in the 1950s as well as an account of the respective implications.

10.2 The Initial Orthodox *Post Keynesianism* Revisited

The initial representatives of orthodox Keynesianism are the faithful members of the *Keynes Circus* in the early 1930s (see Chapter 4), followed by the Neoclassical Keynesians who are also faithful to Keynes's legacy and core. They are followed by the heretics Orthodox Keynesian *SRPs*, who allegedly surpass his core, which is the subject matter of this chapter. To put matters into context, see Box 10.1.

Box 10.1: Keynes's Revolution and the Keynesian Orthodoxy

1) Keynes → The Keynes Circus (UK)
   2) Neo Keynesianism or Neoclassical Cambridge Keynesians (UK)

3) Orthodox Post-Keynesian Revolution (mainly US)

The Neoclassical Synthesis (Samuelson, Hicks, Modigliani 1960s, 1970s)
Monetarists (Friedman 1970s, 1980s)
New Classical Macroeconomics or Rational Expectations (Lucas, Sargen, 1970s, 1980s)
General Disequilibrium (Clower, Patinkin, Leijonhuvfud 1970s, 1980s, 1990s)
↓

4) Heterodox Post-Keynesian Revolution

Post-Keynesians (mainly US, UK) and Neo Ricardians (mainly Italy, UK)

Source Based on HET Website, "J. M. Keynes and The Neokeynesian World", 2016

The Orthodox Post-Keynesian revolution (a contradictory term) in the 1950s is involved in subjective readings of *GT*. For Snowdon et al. (1994, 1999, 2005), the schools of modern macroeconomics are (1) Orthodox Keynesianism (the Neoclassical Synthesis), (2) Monetarism, (3) New Classical Macroeconomics, (4) Real Business Cycle Theory, (5) New Keynesian Economics, (6) Austrian, and (7) Post-Keynesian Economics.

This chapter examines the first three *SRPs* as they notoriously break Keynes's core by maintaining that shocks to equilibrium generate exceptional deviations with certainty as a rule. Both the Neoclassical Synthesis (the symbol of Orthodox Keynesianism) and Monetarism treat Keynes's theory as a set of equations,[5] while Keynes advocated the simultaneous use of several types of discourse also relying on qualitative statements. The New Classical Macroeconomics School exhibits extreme deviations from the original Keynes system. The General Disequilibrium (omitted in Snowdon et al.) is apparently faithful to Keynes's message. But this is an observational hypothesis. The Lakatosian analyses of these *SRPs*, focused on the study of *AD* (aggregate demand), are now conducted. By illuminating these distinctions in *SRP*s, we capture the gist of Keynes' evolutionary thinking in economics.

10.3 The Core of the Monetarist School

Outstanding members of the Monetarist School (*MS*) are Milton Friedman, whose individual message is outlined in Appendix 10.1; Friedrich Hayek, though he also pertains to the Austrian school; Harry G. Johnson (1880–1951), and Philip D. Cagan (1927–2012). *MS* is initiated during the 1960s, but its heyday takes hold in the early 1980s, falling out of favor in terms of use as a whole system around 1984. But it is still influential today, especially regarding both method and isolated—heuristic—insights on monetary policy, for example, its attention to lags on the part of effects (see texts by Friedman himself, where mentions to money supply are ubiquitous especially his speech for the acceptance of the Nobel Prize in 1976).

10.3.1 Definitions and Objectives

Nature and society possess a self-regulating Cartesian-Newtonian-Kantian-type mechanism, a real transnational—though North American and European-tilted—paradigm. Hence, the free-market system achieves the objectives—delivers the goods, an insight which is related to an atomistic vision of agents. The objective is also the analysis of cycles coupled with that of inflation; but severe fluctuations are exceptional and always, allegedly, caused by unusual monetary disturbances (for example, the Great Recession was provoked by the Federal Reserve System), thereby maintaining that money is neutral in the long term. Followers of the *MS* believe in the existence of a unique long-term natural equilibrium and a natural rate of interest. In parallel terms, the price system (for Hayek) or the market system signal information about activities enhancing certainty and efficiency. The money supply (M^S) is the instrumental variable in the determination of *AD* and inflation (π), unemployment being—in microeconomic terms—voluntary. This is almost a repetition or a reincarnation—not even a new version—of the Classical core.

10.3.2 Methodology

MS in the person of Friedman famously disentangles positive from normative economics—a contention firstly found in John Neville Keynes but going back to Hume, providing a new methodological basis: the system is comprised of empirical relations founded on historical data. Thus, *MS* describes the functioning rather than explaining the essence of variables. Another epistemological stance is instrumentalism (an operational variety of pragmatism). Knowledge is based on the concept of logical time and events are relatively uncertain as they are either ergodic or rooted in the past-tradition?—corresponding to a closed system. *MS* is also eclectic, but its departure point is that disequilibria are simple and identifiable. *MS* proposes solutions founded on extreme realism, wherein generalizations must predict change (Friedman 1953), and protective-belt assumptions are irrelevant. The steps for the elaboration of hypotheses are construction and validation, wherein a continuous test of hypotheses against experience is necessary. Thus, its logic for valuing theories is naïve Falsificationism (Chapter 2). Finally, this *SRP* blends micro and macroeconomics due to its atomistic (Classical) interpretation.[6]

10.3.3 Institutions

Astonishingly *MS* is based on the *Laissez-Faire*, perhaps because the history of US Capitalism is relatively new—as compared to that of Britain. Both entrepreneurs and consumers are rational whereas the State has a poor record on problem resolution (Friedman 1980). Therefore, the State must limit surveillance, as *MS* considers that private actions should be unrestrained and motivated. Property rights and institutions must be respected. *MS* advocates an egalitarian market economy in terms of the provision of opportunities.

In this Leibnizian-type harmony (Gottfried Leibniz 1646–1716), monetary variables impact real variables only under specific circumstances. This reasonable system is cyclically but softly unstable. Money must arise from activity rather than being created by the State (Hayek even contends that money must be privately produced, like the BitCoin but by competitive enterprises). Like in Keynes, money links the present with the future, but in a predictable manner as it only plays a transactional role. In a word, money is neutral unless the money supply (M^S) is mismanaged by following discretionary measures. The central bank is credible only if it follows long-term rules. The anti-Keynes tone is visible.

10.3.4 Behavior of Agents

MS returns to the concept of *Homo Economicus*. This means that there is homogeneity in individual behaviors and criteria. Adaptive expectations predominate (the future is a continuation of the present), grounded on perfect information for private agents,[7] who choose the best option given their knowledge and means. Risk is calculable randomness replacing uncertainty. Private units act in coordination, so that no market dichotomies, asymmetries, typologies, or dichotomist behaviors prevail. Variables are symmetric and flexible (market-responsive) since rational agents take real, sequential, and independent decisions. Many variables exhibit lagged or (ergodic) inter-temporary characteristics but always (yes, always) under an equilibrium setback. Accordingly, interrelations are unidirectional and continuous. Keynes's dismissal circa 1978 is heralded by this school (Appendix 10.1). Now a softer stance is outlined.

10.4 The Core of the Neoclassical Synthesis

The Neoclassical Synthesis (*NS*) was initiated by John Hicks (1937), Paul Samuelson (1946), and Alvin Hansen (1887–1975) (1953). It was fortified by the contributions of Seymour Harris (1897–1975), Franco Modigliani (1918–2003), James Tobin (1918–2002), James Duesenberry (1918–2009), Lawrence Klein (1920–2013), Robert Eisner (1922–1998), Robert Solow (1924–), and Robert Mundell (1932–). It ruled during the 1950s and the 1960s but was superseded thereafter, since for the *NS*, among other issues, money has a secondary relevance. Production and consumption are the protagonists along with certain investment (see Jorgenson 1967).

10.4.1 Definitions and Objectives

The system possesses the ability to self-regulate, except whenever proper actions are required in a relatively disorganized universe. Thus, this *SRP* combines planned, welfare, and free-market positions. Free markets and state intervention interact, and hence micro- and macroeconomics cohabitate. Social and individual objectives are simultaneously achieved. The role of macroeconomics is thus the stabilization of activity as well as the management of prices by means of the determination of the levels of Y (national income or output) and r (interest rate). The means is the analysis of the constituents of both *AD* (Aggregate Demand) and *AS* (Aggregate Supply), which intersection permits equilibrium. *NS* thus frames Keynes's analysis into the Classical tradition, implying that the former only contributes innovative but occasional—perhaps heuristics—insights. The crucial advances for *NS* are the seminal heuristic notions *IS-LM* representation of Keynes's system by Hicks (1937) and the *Keynesian Cross* (circa 1947) by Samuelson for explaining the dynamics of the income-expenditure model. The former had a deep impact on policy management, but each analysis is now considered a pedagogical device.

10.4.2 Methodology

NS also disentangles positive from normative economics. *NS* recognizes that social and exact sciences differ since the former is determined by historical events and possesses different formulation and interpretation processes. Still, the *NS* framework is encapsulated into Hicks's *IS-LM* model, using the concepts of 'logical time' and 'certainty.' Thus, this model or paradigm considers equilibrium as the normal state-of-affairs. For the *NS*, theories must provide answers to real problems. The process is eclectic as conclusions are drawn by means of contrasting observed facts. The use of assumptions is a matter of degree. Standpoints are pattern modeling through formalism, identification of facts, apriorism mixed with empiricism, and verificationism (the other side of the coin with respect to falsificationism). The question is: how are activities coordinated? By the mechanism of the market, which is sometimes out of the picture but for a short time as opposed to the *MS* belief in the long period.

10.4.3 Institutions

Both the private and the public sectors stabilize activity in coordination, although fear of crowding out (when the public sector displaces the private sector) is pervasive. Like in *MS*, investors follow the principle of maximization with adaptive expectations ($\Upsilon_T = \alpha + \Sigma \Upsilon_{T\text{-}n}$). Likewise, *NS* respects social and political institutions not launching questionings in the broad fields of political or social philosophy. Monetary variables possess a neutral conventional role as in the Classical Theory (except in turbulent periods), leaving room for fiscal policy implemented by means of the use of the expenditure-tax adjustment mechanism. On the other hand, money rarely acts as an asset of value and hence it does not have influence on macroeconomic activity, like for the Classical economists and the followers of *MS*. Financial assets only experience calculated risk. One may wonder then, what is the use for the stock market?

10.4.4 Behavior of Agents

This category is the same as that in *MS*, especially about the role of expectations and inter-temporary decisions. The analysis possesses a certain and atomistic vision of agents but supposedly accepts the organicist view in the study of aggregate variables. Adaptive expectations lead to the implementation of lagged models,[8] based on the 'insight' that events are symmetrical and continuous (no unexpected changes exist, at least consistently), with Newtonian-type homogenous unidirectional movements. The example is Modigliani's theory of consumption, the counterpart of Friedman's theory of consumption. The idea of autonomous consumption in them is the same, the brand differs.

10.5 The Core of New Classical Macroeconomics

Members of *New Classical Macroeconomics* are Robert Lucas (1937–), Thomas Sargent (1943–) and Robert Barro (1944–), prevailing in the 1980s. This *SRP* is based on the operating principle of 'Rational Expectations' (*RE*), a refinement of the concept proposed by John F. Muth (1930–2005) in 1953. They conclude that the implementation of anticipated policies is futile in a self-regulating system unless they are surprising. At any rate, policies must be implemented in a non-systematic manner. *RE* thus contends that deviations from the average offset each other, where rational expectations refer to foresight on macroeconomic variables or in financial assets. *RE* has been influential in econometric prediction in the very short term as policy (mainly in the US) was apparently only followed in the face of extraordinary events. Rationality, certainty, organicism, equilibrium, and stable money go hand in hand in this elegant variant of Monetarism, which must wait for times when all agents possess perfect information and are able to process—and interpret—it efficiently (it might be so in the future). The Homus Eonomcus is similar to a robot.

10.5.1 Definitions and Objectives

This *SRP* assumes away the existence of individual freedom and the use and processing of perfect and symmetrical information. The relevant role pertains to the private sector, assuming perfect corporate and financial systems, which contribute efficient information to economic policies. *RE* conducts research about the role of policies, thereby reviving Keynes's message that expectations are the shaping factor but neglecting the existence of either 'animal spirits' or irrationality (here rationality is simply obtaining benefits out of costs). Expectations are based on both historical and future ergodic facts. The present is basically a continuation of the past.

Due to aggregate demand (*AD*), deviations from equilibria are exceptional, markets are free and quick in terms of adjustment, and information is included in prices. Thus, stabilization policies are here pointless as only the non-systematic parts of policies (σ^2, according to this author) affect variables. The goal is the stabilization of both activity and the price level by systematically using money supply management (such variables as the money supply (M^S) only respond to unanticipated policies), along with extraordinary shocks in the aggregate supply (*AS*). Therefore, the theory applies Classical economics to macroeconomics bringing consistency to micro-optimization (involuntary unemployment is non-existent), superseding *MS* message in the sense that the future is highly predictable. An implicit goal is the achievement of individual welfare, which automatically brings about social welfare.

10.5.2 *Methodology*

RE bridges the inconsistency between empirical and theoretical macroeconomics. Its methodology is atomistic and pragmatic. However, it is aprioristic (unlike for the *MS*) since rationality is axiomatically stated (as in Benthamism). This *SRP* is thus a mental construction, the results of its implementation not being necessarily confirmed by reality. Otherwise, this analysis is identical to that in *MS* leaving no room for macroeconomics or fiscal policy, leaving them wondering what economists are needed for. Nonetheless, the principle of rationality possesses operationality for tracking agents' activities. Surprisingly, *RE* contends that it relies on observation of facts, contrasting them vis-a-vis reality. It improves models through continuous research but always within the same core.

10.5.3 *Institutions*

RE, as a school of thought, does not break with the orthodox (non-Keynesian) system because those who follow it accept current institutions, a thought which normally precludes anomalous theoretical paths in the economy. As in the contentions of *MS*, the State must limit surveillance activities for *RE*. Money is neutral (unless mismanaged) since it is not an asset of value but a medium of exchange, reflecting their idea that expectations are rational so that financial markets are stable. However, one may contend that the mere essence of financial markets is uncertainty, and beyond that organicism brings about uncertainty.

10.5.4 Behavior of Agents

Individual actions in this *SRP* are homogeneous (approaching μ) so that average democratic behaviors are stabilizing. Individuals possess perfect information about events and process it in an efficient and generalized manner. They do not make decisions based on historical processes or under the assumption that times change. Hence the future is predictable being a result of pervasive certainty; what may be unpredictable is the path toward equilibrium, but only under extraordinary circumstances. Aggregate variables are relatively stable due to rationality; for instance, unemployment only has a small—occasional—variance. The notion of Lucas's surprise supply function is relevant, meaning that only irrational agents may be fooled, and only for short spans of time (Lucas 1972). The system is represented by a model of continuous equilibria due to market homogeneity as well as a relative standard speed of adjustment. The time is right for introducing a more 'Keynesian' but then a contemporary variant of *SRP*s.

10.6 The Core of General Disequilibrium

Walrasian or General Equilibrium economics depicts the attainment of equilibrium in a microeconomic system comprised of 'n' markets where the money and the labor markets are the last markets, but the very last one does not play a special role, and information on both prices and quantities is provided by an auctioneer, an insight making disequilibria the exception since even paths are always predictable. This is the neoclassical—rational—model *par excellence*, being according to historians of economic thought an extension of Classical Say's Law: supply generates its own demand, but in this elegant version there are no excesses of supplies or demands. This is atomism at its best yielding a model of simultaneous equations (and originally) with no restrictions. This model is useful as a heuristic benchmark, but Keynes did not believe in this message because of both his philosophy (see 'The end of the Laissez-faire', 1925) and his life experience. For some Keynes is a Walras without an auctioneer.

Under this framework, the General Disequilibrium School (GD) based on Keynesian dynamism is also known as the Walrasian-Keynesian Synthesis (a real misnomer) or Post-Walrasianism (or general disequilibrium [*GD*]). The *GD* approach to Keynesian theory is associated with the research of Robert Clower in 1965 (1926–2011), Axel Leijonhufvud in 1967, 1968 (1933–), Robert J. Barro between 1971–1976 (1944–), Herschel Grossman (1939–2004) until 1976, Edmond Malinvaud (1923–2015) and Jean-Pascal Benassy (1948–). The core of *GD* is that involuntary unemployment may exist due to coordination problems between buyers and sellers in a system associated with stock-flows analyses for the purpose of providing micro-foundations to monetary macroeconomics. The center of the critiques of *GD* is the Walrasian Law. Like Keynes, *GD* states that the sum of exceeding demands and supplies is not immediately equal to zero, unlike in Walras (the economist of the economists as well as the apotheosis of Neoclassicism). Therefore, the labor (n–1) and money markets (n), especially the former, must receive more attention as potential destabilizing factors according to *GD*, unlike in Walras for whom all markets were homogeneous and predictable.

According to this author, Keynes's implicit philosophy was that the labor market is distinct because of being comprised of human beings, and according to consensus, the money market is also different as money embodies uncertainty in both itself and the system. This is the hidden setting for the notions of *GD*. At the microeconomic level, there exists for the *GD* the *dual-decision hypothesis* as the—heuristic mobile of the system, which is referred to the case when transaction quantities—especially in the labor market—like in Keynes—not prices—affect adjustments in output at other than the full-employment level. *GD* states: Keynes was right: the labor market is heterogeneous regarding decision-making. This is what modern orthodox economists now simplistically call downward sticky wages.

10.6.1 Definition and Objectives

One may infer this *SRP* only contributes heuristic—operational—notions. The system is complex as its interrelations are non-linear (unlike in the Neo Classic Walras). *GD* operates in an economic system that is normally unable to self-regulate, meaning that transitions are winding. For that purpose, *GD* uses the concepts of logical time (as opposed to historical time like in Keynes) and 'path-dependence'[9] a variant of ergodicity. The goal is to deepen Keynes's insights in terms of the continuous trajectory to equilibrium on the part of the system, which for Keynes is static and discrete. *GD*'s assumption is that agents' exchanges occur at moments of disequilibrium. Hence adjustments must be fast and traceable. But permanent disequilibrium is due to the slowness in its 'automatic' adjustment mechanisms, which depends on the behaviors of both relative prices and the aggregate quantity of goods (for Keynes disequilibrium is inherent to the economic uncertain universe). Hence for *GD* market disequilibria occur at any moment, diverting the system from full employment. The objective, then, is to explain the evolution of cycles, capturing the transition phases in variables.

A secondary objective of *GD* is the examination of the difference between their analysis and those of Keynes and the Neo Walrasians. Therefore, this *SRP* is a theory of 'accidental' but continuous—involuntary—unemployment in the context of a constrained effective demand. A non-Walrasian Keynesian and hence more complete explanation was required, recalling that the Walrasian model is linear, homogeneous, and unidirectional. The *GD* approach uses instrumental variables; goal variables such as national income (Υ); and then again the tool of the 'Dual Hypothesis' in the labor market, which arises from individuals making subsequent and constrained decisions about prices and quantities. The elements of planned consumption, savings, and labor supply in the current period comprise for Clower the theoretical demand and supply. The concept of theoretical demand is related to the Walrasian idea of planned demand,[10] but here involuntary unemployment arises whenever theoretical demands and supplies are not realized. Consequently, effective demand faces an additional labor constraint, like in Keynes but for different motives.

10.6.2 Methodology

Unlike the pre-Keynesian Walrasian models of General Equilibrium *GE* and the orthodox post-Keynesian *MS*, although these two have distinct reasons, *GD* advocates the permanent implementation of active policies. It synthesizes several methods to display and test its hypotheses related to the improbable existence of an equilibrium. It is not concerned with ends so that its question is: how does the system function? Keynes would also have replied that the system is inherently inefficient, although his own policies would also be frequent (less than in *GD* but more than in orthodoxy) and set to achieve full employment. For *GD*, failures in the self-regulation ability of the system must also be neutralized, but here the dynamics of the system explain its essence: the concern is with the means. This is a heuristics school.

10.6.3 Institutions

GD does not break with economic, political, or social institutions. The State plays the same role as Keynes: it corrects structural problems. *GD* uses the concept of 'logical time'—unlike Keynes's historical time—within an organicist perspective, implying that the system is path-dependent. Money is a key institution for system adjustments, but it is the labor market that requires that—dual—choices be made. Thus, money and labor markets are more than exceptionally unstable, they are the mobile of the system.

10.6.4 Behavior of Agents

GD assumes both heterogeneous expectations and asymmetrical speed in the functioning of markets (in terms of time rather than space like in Keynes), especially in the labor market. It somehow supposes uncertainty as both mixed expectations and irrational behaviors are ubiquitous. *GD* specializes in the analysis of the path of disequilibria. Disequilibria would persist even under rational expectations since decisions are made at different moments and under dissimilar scenarios. No auctioneer (screaming the equilibrium between prices and quantities, the two dimensions of economics) exists. Hence *GD* validates the existence of macroeconomics. Individuals base their opinions on the experience. Beliefs, traditions, and technology are taken as given in this thermodynamic version of Keynesianism (the IS-Lm model is the hydraulic version).

10.6.5 A note on New Orthodox Keynesian Economics and Heterodox Post-Keynesian Economics

The *New Orthodox SRP* is championed by *N*. Gregory Mankiw (1958–) among others and arises from *RE*, or shares insights with Monetarism.

Its analysis, developed mainly in the 1980s, 1990s, and 2000s, is built on a Neoclassical setting, emphasizing the relevance of rational expectations but under imperfect competition and shyly mentioning downward sticky wages. Welcome back to pure microeconomics! For them, Keynes's message is not relevant, so it disappears from the main textbooks. Their objective is to clarify macroeconomics, not the insights of a particular man. They use some Keynesian ideas but propose the heuristics—exceptionally used—ideas of efficient wage, menu contracts and coordination failures for explaining fluctuations in the economic cycle and temporary—voluntary—unemployment, which simply means that low wages are not attractive.

On the other side of the spectrum, the *Heterodox Post Keynesians* are Keynes's fundamentalists who are—apparently?—outside the mainstream, since the 1940s. Their fields are both Post-Keynesian Economics and Modern Monetary Theory. Some of their preeminent affiliates are Alfred S. Eichner (1937–1988), Frederick S. Lee (1949–2014), Paul Davidson (1930–) and Jan Kregel (1944–), descending in one way or another from Joan Robinson, Michal Kalecki, and Piero Sraffa, among others. Most of them put their faith in 'The General Theory of Employment.' They fight macroeconomic instability by means of income policy, addressing the problems of uncertainty and involuntary unemployment, frequently using stock-flow models and econometrics. They have an interdisciplinary and historical focus.

10.7 Conclusions on the Former Scientific Research Programs

Where is Keynes's message in the period from 1950 to 1990? The adoption of theories without a revision of their cores is misleading. *MS* labels Keynesianism as a theory about money illusion, contending that disequilibria arising from uncertainty will be solved in the long run. Wishful thinking. *NS* has understood Keynes's message under the light of microeconomic insights, labeling disequilibria as an exception. For *RE*, the idea of involuntary unemployment is superfluous. *GD* interprets the absence of auctioneering (equilibrating) processes in the economy as the main Keynes message in a thermodynamic reading. These orthodox *SRPs* may be dubbed as an erratic kind of Keynesianism, in terms of their consideration of unemployment, policy management, and ultimately the ability of the system to self-regulate. They also consider degrees of flexibility rather than systemic uncertainty in the making of policies. Further, these *SRPs* seem to be involved in theoretical inconsistencies, such as *NS* about the consideration of organicism and atomism at the same time. Amazingly, *NS* does not explain current events either, as it neglects the impact of unstable financial systems.

Since the basic Keynes objectives and analytical tools are the same as those of the Orthodox Post-Keynesian *SRPs*, Keynes's core has not been superseded. In other words, these *SRPs* do not bring about theoretical or empirical progress, except by isolated heuristic insights. Both *MS* and *RE* support the existence of a self-regulating system representing a case of scientific regression. Furthermore, Keynes's *SRP*—represented by the emergence of *GT*—is only modified in external terms on the part of both *NS* and *MS*, since their cores return to the *Laissez-Faire*. According to the Lakatosian methodology, *MS* is a Sub-SRP and *NS* is a Progressive Scientific Movement of Keynes's *SRP*. This type of statement is based on the conduction of the Internal History of Keynes's *SRP*.

The progress contributed on the road to full employment by these four *SRPs* is debatable since *MS* and *NS* are characterized by the acceptance of the *IS-LM* diagrams; and *MS*, *NS*, and *RE* are characterized by a reliance on the efficiency of wages and prices to regulate the system. *GD* attacks the General Equilibrium Theory discarding the method of comparative statics. But this refers to positive heuristics innovations and changes to the Protective Belt of Keynes's *SRP*. *NS* even considers Keynes's theories as a special case, supplying macroeconomics with micro-foundations, ignoring the contention of organicism. It modifies the mechanics of both investment and money demand, adding up theoretical and empirical heuristics, such as the Consumption Function of Modigliani and support for the use of the fiscal policy. Thus, *NS* is similar in some heuristic positions to Keynes's 'Classical contemporaries,' for example Pigou.

MS's core is distinct from that of Keynes in its vision about individual freedom and non-animal behavior. Moreover, *MS* is strongly opposed to Keynes's core and this opposition is manifested through its return to the Classical perfect world. *MS* contributes a new positivist methodology, epitomized by an emphasis on prediction (Friedman 1953), but this is not sufficient to initiate a new *SRP*. Additionally, its instrumentalist methodology clashes against some parts of Keynes's heuristics. In terms of protective belts, they revive the 'QTM,' considering money as neutral in the long term. *MS*, however, seems rigid and only suitable for developed economies.

The *RE SRP* is a more dynamic and flexible version of Monetarism. *RE* includes in its core the concept of '*Aprioristic* Rationality,' but its methodology is instrumentalist. It assumes homogeneity in behaviors and its objectives are akin to those of the *MS*: the reduction of inflation. For these reasons and its presupposition of a self-regulated system, *RE* is a Scientific Movement or a Subprogram of Monetarism. Yet *RE* contributes empirical content by contending that only a surprising monetary policy might impact activity. No new methodology, objectives, or behavior are provided as descriptions. *GD*, however, partly modifies Keynes's message by reverting to the original question about the functioning of the system. *GD* is hence a sub-Scientific Program of Keynes's *SRP*.

10.7.1 Final Remarks on Scientific Betraying

Keynes's original message was to some extent either betrayed or misunderstood by the schools discussed here, with their unfulfilled promises, and the Lakatosian-type implication that Keynes had not been appropriately interpreted. Keynes's methodological chain (the non-self-regulated system, the non-neutrality of money, organicism, discretionary, and uncertainty) is misunderstood by these so-called 'Bastard' schools. The weakness in their core contributions is found in deviations from Keynes's thoughts on uncertainty and hence on the role of money, with some of the schools returning to the Classical way of thinking in economics. For Lakatosian standings, the return to pre-Keynesian theory might be a special case of the General Theory. The analysis conducted in this Chapter is scarcely original to this author (except by the Lakatosian approach). Mann (2019) discusses innovations by followers of Keynes with chapters centered on Kalecki, on the neoclassical synthesis, the New Keynesians, and Piketty. Systemic transformation brought about by *SRPs* must begin with the suggestion of new epistemological considerations (internal history of *SRPs*) and the prediction of novel facts (external history), but Keynes's discernments are here—in 'Bastard Keynesianism—only mathematically formalized for the purpose of prediction which is a soothsayer's task. Likewise, attempts to develop Keynes's model in the long run may be due to a misunderstanding of his gist rather than an extension of his core contentions (see the outline of Harrod's theory in Chapter 12). For distinct views on the reception of Keynes's legacy by modern economists, see Snowdon and Vane (1999) and Blaug (1990), who undertook interviews with leading economists about many issues, including Keynes's legacy.

The conclusion is that the four studied orthodox Post-Keynesian *SRPs* believe to varying extents in the train of thought that runs from the *Laissez-faire* to rationality, to approachable equilibrium, to voluntary unemployment, to atomism, to the frequency theory and, finally, to certainty; in actuality, going nowhere toward a deeper understanding of Keynes's significance. But that did not matter between the 1970s and the late 1980s when they set the standards in the discipline of macroeconomics when inflation was the main macroeconomic problem. However, Keynes's legacy on uncertainty, money and disequilibria resurges after the crisis of 2007 (Appendix 13.1), a trend initiated with the reappraisal of his philosophical writings in the 1990s. What have economists supposed so far? How original are their accepted wisdom and heuristics? Leijonhuvfud's breakthrough distinction between Keynesian economics and the economics of Keynes (Leijonhufvud 1968) may close this chapter. Yet the economic personality of Friedman is described in the appendix.

But where are we now in the philosophical outline of Keynes's message? Not everything is macroeconomics. Chapter 11 describes the anti-Moorean stance of the mature Keynes in terms of ethics in 1938, before the occurrence of the Second World War.

Appendix 10.1 'To Milton Friedman: A Rebuttal on the Significance of Macroeconomics' (*A Fictional Confrontation, Written By the Author Using the Imagined Pen of John Maynard Keynes*)

Innovations leave an imprint on progress, but history is cyclical, and eventually reactions arise. The main reaction to GT was the 'bastardization' conducted by the 'Keynesian' SRPs, particularly the insights propounded by the leading monetarist Friedman (1967–1991). In this hypothetical 'rebuttal,' Keynes clarifies his stance on such relevant themes as economic philosophy, money, equilibrium, organicism, uncertainty, epistemology, political philosophy, and ethics, all of them linked to the foundations of macroeconomics. His imagined purpose is to avoid misleading conceptions for future generations by 'responding' to Friedman's contentions. Keynes died in 1946 whereas Friedman experienced his heyday in the 1970s and early 1980s.

'Many years have elapsed since my death.' At the time I was advocating for the creation of a free international financial system based on cooperation. It finally took the form that Americans gave to it. However, my legacy, related to the creation of macroeconomics, became the scientific basis for the Golden Age of Capitalism, taking place between 1941 and 1973. My main contribution was *The General Theory of Employment, Interest and Money*. At its core there was both my discovery of a new role for money and the rejection of an existent automatic equilibrium, a point which was however irrationally defended by orthodox theory, not to mention organicism.

You never accepted my major book, which is based on the notion of uncertainty. You said that my best book was *A Tract on Monetary Reform* (1923). But what about my *Treatise on Money* (1930)? I will admit, my ideas were preliminary at that stage. *The Tract* fits the slump that occurred in 1920–1921. I imagine your advocacy for a free-market economy with its heyday in the early 1980s as an explanation for your choice, which is part of an early thinking derived from our British classics. Indeed, you never agreed with me on many points but somehow you took my heuristics. Certainly, macroeconomics is more relevant than microeconomics. Since my Bloomsbury years, I have advocated for organicism. Instead, you stated that the proof of the link between macro and microeconomics is an empirical matter. I am a realist, so I am always going to deeply explore causal mechanisms. According to recent research, the falsification of scientific findings goes beyond empirical points.

No factual guarantee exists that the macro-system may return to equilibrium after any disturbance. Agents are irrational, and no Walrasian auctioneer exists (except in some stock markets).[11] Hence there may be multiple sub-equilibria below the level of full employment, and this is not what conventional economics preaches. That is why I advocate for State interventionism for the management of instability, which for you is a signal of both inefficacy and corruption. You believe that markets must be set free of impediments and that the system will be in equilibrium except by transitory shocks, although you had the merit of accepting the existence of lags in policy implementation. You even contended that speculation—for example in foreign exchange markets—is stabilizing (Friedman 1953), expecting a fair (natural?) value. But financial uncertainty produces inherently unstable economies. This explains my interest in behavioral economics. Instead, you think that investors are rational on average.

We may have some commonalities though. Some Austrians would claim that both Keynesians and Monetarists accept the same high level of aggregation. Then again dissension emerges. According to Garrison (1974 [1992]), your model suggests that no cycles exist to be explained, even though I created macroeconomics to explain cyclical instability. You believe in natural laws and their accurate application to social events. I will comment more on this in the methodological part of this reply. You demonstrated the fallacy assumed in a permanent trade-off between inflation and unemployment. But this is not a permanently falsifiable issue since as I once said the objective depends on the circumstances. Some commentators even stated that the existence of stagflation marked the end of my theories. Perhaps the point is a misperception of my view about wage functioning. But considerations of labor markets are not all-encompassing since real and financial markets are intertwined.

I applaud your activism for free exchange rates. They were nonetheless inviable in the aftermath of war due to turbulence and political motives. My experience both as a civil servant and as a speculator taught me that excessive uncertainty in financial markets may lead to chaos and is not self-regulating. Also, uncertainty in this sense explains the necessity of money in its liquid form. My other point, unlike yours, is that investment leads whereas saving follows. This insight has implications for output, as investment is the most unstable component. Moderns would call it the motivator of the system. Instead, you were more interested in the workings of individual prices and inflation, thereby neglecting the Fallacy of Composition. You also returned to the Quantity Theory of Money, the reach of which I hoped to extend during my early years. I improved this theory with my notion of liquidity preference, which captures the developments of modern monetary variables. As for me, proving the primacy of monetary factors in macroeconomics meant that I linked the real and the monetary sectors, please notice, via the interest rate. I hence provided the monetary side of macroeconomics.

I have no taste for incomplete or non-general theories. Fortunately, Kalecki provided the distributional side of macroeconomics, whereas Sraffa provided its real side. Both are labeled as heterodox Post Keynesians. Monetarists affirm that money has no influence on real variables. Is this true in developed financial systems? Further, your notion of permanent income was an avoidable return to classical economics and to an ergodic system. In your formulation, there is no room for my assumption of discontinuous behavior. You also discredited my consumption function on microeconomic grounds.

In the late 1970s some observers—perhaps due to your influence—dubbed me as a 'fiscalist,' possibly implying that monetary policy was irrelevant for me. I never said that, and my perspective is dynamic not believing in zero-sum games. I was aware that fiscal policy could be effective especially when the economy is depressed, and its capacity low. I preferred to create employment by digging ditches. The ultimate relevance of monetary policy depends on the level of interest rates. In fact, policymakers now prefer targeting interest rates rather than money supply. Moreover, as I was focused on the effects of money in the short term, I dismissed your 'helicopter' analogy. I never advocated inflationary measures except in my book in 1940, but my recommendations were contingent on circumstances. You also ignored the issue of money illusion as well as the notion that flexible wages are destabilizing. I would add that theories of equilibrium are suitable for perfectionists.

For you, fine-tuning—another name for induced macroeconomic adjustments—was not feasible. You were constructing your piece-meal scheme insisting that the inclusion of the interest rate—my key mobile—in the money demand function was a small detail. I consider that consumption, investment, and public expenditure—as the elements of aggregate demand—must be expedient—and why not? discretionarily—managed. Instead, you advocated fixed rules in monetary policy. But is there a rule for moving a complex system? You stated that the money supply affects the price level in the long run and output in the short run. Your secret lies in that all depends on the behavior of the Federal Reserve System, which must pay allegiance to rigid procedures. But how instructive are your historical findings in this and other senses? Do they simply confirm your opinions?

You discussed the method of social sciences and implicitly classified it as equal to the universal physical method, therefore continuing a line of thought related to the Newtonian paradigm but neglecting the distinction between natural and human-determined events. For you only results rather than assumptions were relevant. In 1953 you wrote an article championing the irrelevance of assumptions. This is exactly the opposite of what I recommended between 1936 and 1946. Samuelson and you agreed on many points, thereby he inaugurated the school that would be called the Neoclassical Synthesis (*NS*). Both of you ignored my core:

uncertainty. Instead, *NS* was interested in developing heuristic points in macroeconomics, though I was interested in the whole structure of the *SRP* of macroeconomics. The *IS-LM* model designed by Hicks and the Keynesian Cross devised by Samuelson did not capture the gist of my creation. On the other hand, my objective was to find the right method for making people happier. Happiness is not relevant in conventional economic theory but only profits and utility. Knowledge must be an instrument for finding the truth. I was a realist and therefore a relativist, who presented an open-ended theory, as certain researchers in my philosophy would comment in the early 1990s.

You even had a specific response to my insights on scientific validation. According to your words: '[i]ndirect evidence from related hypotheses explains in large measure the difference in the confidence attached to a particular hypothesis by people with different backgrounds' (Friedman 1953, p. 17). I am an inductivist like Malthus. Deductivism is rarely used in science and is hostile to organicism. I think that you agree on the crucial importance of that aggregate factor called effective demand, and in that sense our thoughts are similar. Thus, we mainly differ in terms of political thought. You were an analyst of Capitalism, but made no comment on Chapter 24 of my *GT*. For you, full employment automatically brings about a fair income distribution. No one believes this to be true anymore.

The *Laissez-faire* was heaven for you, just as it was for Adam Smith. Has there been any progress in science? I was also a conservative, but I was not blind. Hence, I addressed some issues that could be improved in Capitalism, after full employment had been attained. Most people were astonished at my advocacy for 'socialized' investment, which for me is only the complement of a policy aimed at reducing interest rates. Perhaps the label 'socialized' is misleading, though long-term interest rates must be reduced to activate economies. What would you say on equality? I was involved in the issue of the 'euthanasia of the rentier.' I also preached results-oriented policies, I would call them expedient policies, but my ethics are related to motives rather than to outcomes. Mine is an ethics of virtue, just as it was championed by most of the thinkers in Classical Greece.

We have differences in terms of social philosophy too. For you, private interests are aligned with the public—atomic—*good*. Nonetheless, Capitalism does not ensure either goodness or freedom. Values must come from both self-awareness and social action rather than from the adoption of bourgeois aims. For you, even ethical problems are resolved by means of market practices. Capitalism is not a panacea, but I agree with you: it leads to efficiency. I also believe in the Platonic message: aristocracy is superior to democracy. In your view the democratic State must preserve the free-market system, but can it be done at any cost? Democracy is suitable for rules, and aristocracy for discretionary interventions. Finally, we share a dislike for totalitarian systems. I am eclectic in my beliefs because circumstances can be unpredictable. You consider that monetary freedom is a precondition for market liberty, joining forces with Hayek in Mount Pellerin Society. Further, the consideration of money as an end is detestable.

But people labeling me as a socialist would require a course in psychology. I was born with an orientation toward free markets, but I am more sophisticated than that now, and consequently more moderate. I link money to uncertainty. My notion of uncertainty is rooted in the Humean skeptical tradition on induction. Many of my claims are thus founded on short-term aims. Small things may produce larger effects but a change in the rate of interest has a huge effect on aggregate investment—'my' effect. No Wicksellian natural rate exists just like there is neither a *deux machine* nor a permanent state-of-affairs—in scarcity. By the way, your core is that scarcity is paradoxical and certainly pervasive, but then why do crises arise?

Marshall and you discussed the existence of atomistic firms engaged in perfect competition. I lacked concern with discussing the nature of competition. This might be due to my practice of focusing on the correspondence between ideal and real entities in concrete issues. For example, the relationship between wages and unemployment—or the case of savings—does not function at the aggregate level. This signifies interrelations and their generating mechanisms are important. I employ—and thus plan for—fuzziness in my interpretation of both events and models. I recognize you contributed rigor to research in economic science, but, did you want to put an end to my core? You co-wrote an empirical counterhistory of the United States (1867–1960) in 1963, aiding to dig the rift between the real and the monetary sectors. Your associated discussion was about the effectiveness of an autonomous monetary policy. I prefer autonomous spending as a cause for solving aggregate demand fluctuations since its impact may be larger in some cases. But, were you right in the 1980s in thinking that inflation is more relevant than unemployment? You almost persuaded me, but your pre-ordered Smithian entrepreneurial world was difficult for me to accept.

My legacy is that uncertainty is inherent to human nature, rather than government-provoked, and it has a bearing on money and unemployment. Nevertheless, I applaud your contention that empirical content and policy relevance are more applicable than theoretical notions. But at the same time, I am concerned about the use of the right method: 'organicism.'

Notes

1. A stochastic system is ergodic if it tends toward a limiting form that is independent of the initial conditions. Breakdown of ergodicity gives rise to path dependence.
2. For the complete outline of Keynes's core, see Chapter 2.
3. The core of Classical probability arises from methodological individualism (Verdon 1996).
4. Keynes is, however, an admirer of Newton's atomistic work on physics (Appendix 3.1).
5. Hicks revises his notion of certainty in his *IS-LM* model in an article in the *Journal of Post Keynesian Economics* (1980).
6. However, Friedman states that the test of the influence of microeconomics on macroeconomics must be subjected to empirical tests (Snowden et al. 2005).
7. Unlike Keynes, Friedman states that the realism of assumptions is irrelevant (Friedman 1953).
8. Such as the Jorgenson model (1963, 1967), where investment is also a function of time.
9. Path dependence explains how current decisions are limited by previous choices.
10. Effective demand is the basic heuristic idea in Keynes.
11. But the problem is not only about information, but about uncertainty.

References

Bateman, Bradley. W., and John B. Davis. 1993. "Introduction". In *Keynes and Philosophy: An Essay on the Origins of Keynes's Thought* , edited by Bradley W. Bateman and John B. Davis: 1–5, Marquette University Faculty 141.https://epublications.marquette.edu/marq_fac-book/141.

Blaug, Mark. 1990. *John Maynard Keynes: Life, Legacy, Ideas*. London: Palgrave.

Clower, Robert. 1965. "The Keynesian Counter-Revolution: A Theoretical Appraisal." In *The Theory of Interest Rates*, edited by F.H. Hahn and F.P.R. Brechling, 34–58. London: Macmillan (reprinted in Clower, 1987)

Friedman, Milton, and Rose Friedman. 1980. *Free to Choose. A Personal Statement*. London and New York: Harcourt.

Friedman, Milton. 1953. "The Methodology of Positive Economics." In *Essays in Positive Economics*, edited by Milton Friedmanm, 15–57. Chicago: University of Chicago Press.

Garrison, Roger W. 1974 [1992]. Is Milton Friedman a Keynesian? In *Dissent on Keynes: A Critical Appraisal of Keynesian Economics*, edited by Mark Skousen, 131–147. New York: Praeger.

Hansen, Alvin. 1953. *A Guide of Keynes*. New York: McGraw Hill.

Heilbroner, Robert. 1951. *The Worldly Philosophers: The Lives, Times and Ideas of the Great Economic Thinkers*. New York: Simon & Schuster.

Hicks, John R. 1937. "Mr. Keynes and the "Classics", A Suggested Interpretation." *Econometrica* 5: 147–59.

———. 1980. "IS-LM: An Explanation." *Journal of Post Keynesian Economics* 3, no. 2 (Winter): 139–54.

Jorgenson, Dale W. 1967. 'The theory of investment behavior.' University of California, Berkeley. https://www.nber.org/system/files/chapters/c1235/c1235.pdf.

Keynes, John Maynard. 1923 [1924]. *A Tract on Monetary Reform*. London: MacMillan. https://delong.typepad.com/keynes-1923-a-tract-on-monetary-reform.pdf.

———. 1930. "The Economic Possibilities for Our Grandchildren." http://www.econ.yale.edu/smith/econ116a/keynes1.pdf. Accessed 1 January 2019

———. 1936 [1997]. *The General Theory of Employment, Interest, and Money*. London: Prometheus.

Klein, Lawrence R. 1947. *The Keynesian Revolution*. New York: Macmillan.

Leijonhufvud, Axel. 1968. *On Keynesian Economics and the Economics of Keynes: A Study in Monetary Theory*. New York: Oxford University Press.

Lucas, Robert E. 1972. "Expectations and the Neutrality of Money." *Journal of Economic Theory* 4, no. 2: 103–124.

Machlup, Fritz. 1978. *Methodology of Economics and Other Social Sciences*. New York: Academic Press.

Mann, Geoff. 2019. *In the Long Run We Are All Dead: Keynesianism, Political Economy, and Revolution*. London: Verso.

O'Donnell, Roderick M. 1991. *Keynes as Philosopher-Economist*. Proceedings of The Ninth Keynes Seminar held at the University of Kent. London: Macmillan.

Robinson, Joan. 1973. "What has become of the Keynesian revolution?" In *After Keynes*, edited by Joan Robinson, 1–11. Oxford: Basil Blackwell.

———. 1974. "History Versus Equilibrium." *Thames Papers in Political Economy* 48–58.

Samuelson, Paul A. 1946. "Lord Keynes and the General Theory." *Econometrica* XIV, no. 3: 187–200.

Skidelsky, Robert. 2001. *John Maynard Keynes. Volume III: Fighting for Britain 1937–1946.* London: Macmillan.

———. 2009. Keynes. *The Return of the Master.* New York: Public Affairs.

Snowdon, Brian, Howard R. Vane, and Peter Wynarczyk. 1994. *A Modern Guide to Macroeconomics: An Introduction to Competing Schools of Thought.* Aldershot, UK: Edward Elgar.

Snowdon, Brian, and Howard R. Vane (eds.). 1999. *Conversations with Leading Economists: Interpreting Modern Macroeconomics. From Tobin to Romer.* Chentelham, UK: Edward Elgar.

Snowdon, Brian, and Howard R. Vane. 2005. *Modern Macroeconomics. Its Origins, Developments and Current State.* Chentelham, UK and Northampton, MA, USA.

Verdon, Michael. 1996. *Keynes and the 'Classics': A Study in Language, Epistemology, and Mistaken Identities.* New York: Routledge.

PART IV

Keynes's Later Activities: 1938–1946

Keynes at this stage was more involved with worldly and world affairs, unlike in his previous phase (1913–1937)[1] when he was only interested in Britain, and prior to that (1902–1912) when he was more occupied with philosophy, his own personal life, and his family and a small circle of friends and colleagues. However, the mature Keynes still found time to make a digression on his past philosophical life after he wrote *GT*.

Chapter 11 is an evaluation of Keynes's mature reflections related to the insight that main shocks, in this case moral, are internal (see Chapter 7). In 1936 he took advantage of being at the pinnacle of his energy. Once *GT* was finished, Keynes entered a more relaxed phase in his life leaving aside—albeit temporarily—the making of economic theory. Although he devoted two years to defending *GT*, he wrote 'My Early Beliefs' (or 'MEB') in 1938 which is an ethically oriented pamphlet. Chapter 11 even contains an Appendix comparing the elitism of Keynes with that of Nietzsche, mainly devoted to ethics. Nietzsche's oeuvre is a *tour de force*. An appendix on Appendix 11.1 deepens on Nietzsche's contentions.

Chapter 12 is an outline of Keynes's later—once again extroverted—activities. In the 1940s, during the Second World War and its aftermath, he was occupied with writing simpler economic treatises or conducting

[1] Although in 1921, he published TP (Chapter 6), an evidence of a break from worldliness and a re-switch of focus to philosophy.

heuristic reviews of his theories, but especially with innovating international economics and finance through purposeful practice. At this stage Keynes became an advocate for European regional governance. The Appendices outline how he set the foundation for development economics, found time to provide a healthy criticism of econometrics, and contributed his own esthetical sense and financial experience to the artistic life of Britain. Appendices relate his parallel contributions to science (development, econometrics) and culture (arts). Conclusions on his encompassing legacy are outlined in the final chapter.

CHAPTER 11

A Philosophical Autobiography: 'My Early Beliefs' in *Two Memoirs* (1938, 1949)

This chapter deals with Keynes longing his life away, extending the contents of his early papers and widening the topics dealt with in *ECP* (Chapter 5), EPG (Chapter 8) and *GT* (Chapter 9), leading to what is perhaps his most remarkable philosophical contribution: a new ethical envisagement in the form of self-reconsideration. This marvel was delivered by way of his discussion of Moore's contentions on *good* and states of mind from a stance of independence, even from himself. Keynes became more conventional at this stage but also less naïve and more realistic because of his reflections on war and human nature. His contentions embed a trans-generational message about the path that should be followed by civilization. Let's see how this great insight is accomplished.

'MEB,' written and read in 1938 to the 'Memoir Club' but published in 1949, is a treatise on the evolution of Keynes's philosophical—mainly ethical—beliefs as well as a new vision of intuition. It reveals his stance against such connected themes as non pensive attitudes, overstated moralism, Benthamism, certainty, homogeneous movements, living in the past,[1] extreme individualism, severe rationalism, money as an end, reliance on unguaranteed assumptions, continuous progress, and idealist metaphysics. The multifaceted innovative vision exhibited in 'MEB' cannot be fully appreciated in his former works—namely *ECP*, *EPG*, *TMR*, *TM*, and *GT*—and is rooted in both open systems and organicism in 'MEB.'

J. Muñoz-Bandala, *Keynes's Evolutionary Spirit*,
Palgrave Insights into Apocalypse Economics,
https://doi.org/10.1007/978-3-030-90150-9_11

According to O'Donnell (1995), Keynes's topics in 'MEB' are beauty in nature and culture, arguments, states of mind, purposes, experiences, taste, criticism, ethical judgment, progress, metaphysical properties, as well as the crucial concepts of *good*, rationality, and organicism. The next step is to ground and tie all these notions.

Moore's ethics and Burke's political notions are the principal philosophical influences on Keynes in terms of reflection and prudence, respectively. In social sciences *good* is the final objective. Hence, welfare and happiness must be understood in organic terms as in Moore. Moore's insights on *good* are both consistent and flawless for the middle-aged Keynes. But there was still rebellion in him in 1938 (before 'MEB'). Moore's contentions seemed to him now too complex or unworldly in terms of real-life application. Consequently, he became a pluralist about the *fitness* of *good*, also realizing that ideal states of consciousness are not everything. Moore's teachings—perhaps too abstract for explaining facts, and especially for acting in the light of them—explained Keynes's now reflected aversion for rules, since they may lend themselves to an attitude of contemplation and inaction. Since action is the adequate attitude, Keynes championed the ethics of discretion, but this awareness requires aristocratic power.

Keynes began to distance himself from the traditional Cambridge philosophers (Chapters 3 and 4) at this stage, as he now rejected errors in individual judgment, even his own. For example, he was a member of the Liberal Party but was always desiring its betterment. Nevertheless, ethical reflections may arise from personal changes and projections. Perhaps at the beginning of 'MEB' he felt guilty when he condemned greed. For Zhang (n.d.), Keynes generated moral questions on the money motives of individuals, probably due to the idea that the ethical assertions on money set by the Neoclassical purists were unreal. Keynes's discernments on money evolved (Chapter 7) perhaps because he realized that transitions and crises prevail in economics rather than either ideal states of mind or natural developments.

In 1921, Keynes investigated the essence of degrees of belief, the weight of the argument, uncertainty, and conventions, all of them as related to probability (our Chapter 6). In 1930 he served as a policy-adviser and wrote his trilogy on economics. Each of these attainments led him to investigate the qualitative nature of human beliefs and propositions in 'MEB.' The skeptic bedrock for this research is Hume's conception of causation as imaginary, making both intuition and induction at least partially unreliable, and leaving probability as the only road for investigating the truth of propositions. This crucial discovery had a bearing on Keynes's ethics. Induction and common sense—the tenets of Moore's philosophy—are intertwined. On the other hand—though *good* is universal—there were paradoxes in Keynes's thinking on individualism. But Keynes advocated uncertainty and irrationality—or at least another type of rationality, which go hand in hand (Chapter 6).

Keynes was more than a revolutionary; actually, a radical thinker. His contentions in *GT* are that saving differs from investment and that nominal wages differ from real wages. The background for that economic contention is that he also was a moral critique recognizing that the behaviors and perceptions of dissimilar individuals have a bearing on economic variables, leading to the rise of uncertainty. Moore was involved in objectivity in love, beauty, and truth. But Keynes, as an individualistic Bloomsbury captive, examined irrationality in civil society. He was aware that individuals use rational judgment but also that reliance on rationality is excessive (this was the authentic end of the nineteenth century), all of which formed the basis of ethics. This is just the preliminary road. Subsequently, Keynes examined in 'MEB' the ontology and the usefulness of convention.

According to Shionoya (1991), O'Donnell (1991), and Skidelsky (1983, 1992, 2001), ethics was for Keynes above economics. Philosophy 'provide[s] the foundations of Keynes's life' (Skidelsky 1983, p. 133). In other words, Keynes's vision of a *good* life requires resolute self-governance.[2] In summary, Keynes's 'MEB' rejects—or evolves from—most of what he learned in his Bloomsbury and 'Apostles' years. Enough as an introduction. The next section examines traditional morality more thoroughly.

11.1 Being *Good* and Doing *Good* Revisited

In *ECP* (Chapter 5), Keynes still maintained his early beliefs, especially regarding rationality. But Keynes evolves not only because of the war but because he became an active participant in economic policy and theory creation, and he was living a rewarding life in an interesting epoch. For Skidelsky (2016), in 'MEB' Keynes has outgrown the Apostles' ethical ideas. But in what respects? What is *good* (theoretical ethics)? And what must be done (duty and practical ethics)? More specifically, what is the difference between being *good* and doing *good*? This question, launched by Moore, is dealt with by Keynes in his unpublished manuscripts but chiefly in this famous 1938 adult rebellion via a remarkable pensive essay (perhaps as great as *GT*), which is partly a self-criticism and partly a treatise on smart elitism.

Here Keynes follows to some extent Moore's route to the ideal departing from ideal consciousness (see Chapter 4). But he rejects intuitionism, not only as an epistemological starting place but also because it is less *fitting* than his notion of social awareness in the realm of his philosophy of action. Keynes rejects Moore's trust in reasonableness and decency, predominantly in terms of expediency, but also considering those two virtues as representative of decadent Victorian values. Keynes refutes Moore's teachings about the preponderance of our internal lives in terms of decision-making, though he took these teachings literally during his younger days. For the late Keynes external objects, more than internal objects, generate our states of mind. Here in 'MEB' Keynes talks about complex states of mind in the line of his early unpublished papers but as said before more externally oriented, where aesthetic appreciation is also embedded. As he evolved after *GT*, Keynes wondered about his former Moore-inspired 'unworldliness' in conduct. Transitions are invisible for most human beings, but one may notice that the evolutionary change in thinking represented by Keynes's path from the Bloomsbury Group (1920s) to 'MEB' (1938) may parallel his trajectory followed from *TM* (1930) to *GT* (1936) in the sense that he consequently delivered a deeper and original intellectual product.

Echoing Burke's teachings, Keynes rejected doing *good* for the sake of happiness in an immediate but undefined future. Keynes did not rely upon a frequentist—mechanicist—view but rather upon intuition and human judgment (see Chapter 6) and hence on expediency. In 'MEB' he uses this philosophical perspective to question Moore's conclusions on general rule following using the idea of liberty in action as the appropriate manner for decision-making. Hence, the elements for generating proposals about a phenomenon are intuition, induction, probability judgments, and convention; the last being useful when there is no room for resorting to individual judgment. Alternatively, the notion of direct judgment as the supreme manifestation of individualism is extensively developed in *TP* (Chapter 6), coming from 'Ethics in relation to conduct' (1906). The implication is that ethics is connected to probability but also to mathematics, logic, epistemology, social philosophy, and political philosophy. The inference is that judgments of probability and on *good* ought to be undertaken jointly. Thus, Keynes rejected Moore's views on custom and habit which may be based upon Hume's writings (Chapter 3) but contributed the idea that people can undertake rational judgments even in the face of convention always in a framework of uncertainty.

According to Lawson (1993), Keynes's personal ethical standards evolved over time which can be explained in terms of a progressive Lakatosian Scientific Research Program. Ultimately in the 1940s Keynes changed the object of his pursuit, leaving behind individualism and rationality in favor of the analysis of issues related to the British society and, subsequently, to the theme of the welfare of the world. In the new ideals of Keynes, especially in the late 1930s, there was no tension between *being good* and *doing good* because his conceptions of human nature were biased toward judgmental conventions for undertaking action in practice. During the process, he rejected Moore's assumptions of decency and rationality in human nature as vestiges of Victorian times. How was it done?

11.2 Civilization

For Bateman and Lawson (1993), Keynes rejects the viability (and the marvelous essence) of free markets in both 'The end of the Laissez-faire' and 'MEB.' Markets normally function in irrational terms and do not tend to equilibrium because the world is an organic entity in which agents (and time) are heterogeneous and information is asymmetrical. As a case in point, irrationality makes money an asset of value. But fear of irrationality generates convention,[3] which allows for the existence of civilization. However irrational conduct is fleeting so the choice for irrationality is a matter of elitism; additionally, irrationality may be overcome with the use of probability (Chapter 6). In other words, according to Keynes, even though rules must be obeyed in normal circumstances, each case must be judged on its own merits, that is discretionarily. There is a short leap from irrationality to uncertainty, or vice versa, at least in the initial stages of the development of an event. These are the moral and epistemological motivators in Keynes's reasoning at this epoch (circa 1938). At this point, Keynes rejects Moore's reliance upon utilitarianism since he has finally left egotism behind.

On the other hand, 'windfall' profits in *TM* (examined in our Chapter 7) are the result of conventional wisdom, as the response to uncertainty and irrationality. For Lawson (2003) uncertainty disconnects long-term motives from action. Since intrinsic values are lost in times of extreme uncertainty, 'animal spirits' emerge, and the solution lies in following habit, at least for the time being. Keynes's ethical stance regarding choice has an element of 'educated' irrationality, but this does not come as a surprise since ethics—unlike logic but like epistemology—ought to be realistic in the face of uncertainty, although values never must be lost. These insights connect the economic contentions penned in both *TM* and *GT* with those expounded upon in the more philosophically oriented *EPG* and 'MEB.' In both *TM* and *GT* choices (either for macro policy or for micro-consumption or investment) are contingent upon the weight of the argument like in *TP*, but in *GT* they are also contingent upon convention and human judgment, especially the latter. Good judgment in data collection and data utilization is necessary to cope with uncertainty since the present is not merely a continuation of the past producing internal disequilibrium, and even less so in the presence of external fluctuations. These facts demonstrate the effect of ignorance on civilized societies. However, the ultimate question in terms of choice is the pursuit of *good*.

In this sense, Keynes now adhered to convention for maintaining the possibility of civilization. For Bateman and Davis (1993), convention provides continuity to the species and its institutions. Keynes believes this when writing the metaphor of the 'beauty pageant' related to the decision of choice, under different degrees of uncertainty in Chapter 13 of *GT*. Judges are tilted to conventional beauty—that is, toward what other considered as beauty. Nevertheless, the Keynes of 1938 takes a step forward by treating convention—being a series of norms—in a different manner than physical laws, giving space to discretion in behavior, including that of either policy designers, investors or private agents, or even individuals. Once again paraphrasing Lawson (1993), convention only provides context. Hence, convention must not be followed literally since it varies from society to society, from generation to generation, and from moment to moment. This is the mistake committed in the intertwined doctrines of the invisible hand, in Benthamism and Walrasian economics. These doctrines assume stone-written convention along with perfect rationality, intentionality, and atomism, and hence comprehend the essence of the behavior of agents in the form of the application of such universal eternal rules as the creed of a self-regulating system and the monolithic *Homo Economicus.* Keynes rejects 'rational' Benthamism as mechanical atomistic calculus lacking profound considerations about ethics. Keynes also exhibits an ethical attitude with respect to the uncertain future, epitomized in his description of the value of money as a means in our lives. This has been mentioned but must now be seen as the core of 'MEB.'

The future is uncertain. Nonetheless, Keynes prophesies in qualitative terms about the arrival of new times when writing 'MEB.' According to Shackle, [b]'y 1939 an economic slump without parallel, allied to the re-emergence of military ambition in Europe, had brought economic theorists face to face with reality' (Shackle 1967 [2010], p. 78). Keynes's contentions on economics were on their way to transform the orthodoxy but he was also leaving room for the consideration of realism in 'MEB' about the fate of humankind. To place Keynes's prophesies in context, other European philosophies shake out as a logical upshot of the aftermath of the First World War and the emergence of the Second World War. Examples are Freud's 'Civilization and its Discontents' (1930) and 'Why war?' (1933). Freud realizes at the end that it is civilization rather than self-awareness—as he had taught in his psychoanalytic period—that is the precondition for *good* states of mind.

For Kirshner (2015), 'MEB' is written under the shadow of an especially disheartening war, and this contributes to Keynes's view of human nature as rather thin. Keynes realizes that his former (pre-MEB) narrow concept of rationality was naïve. But this is new only to him, since rationality is absent in most of human conduct, for example, in Nietzsche (Appendix 11.1) and a subjective part of human mind prevails, as Keynes himself learns from Ramsey in 1931 (Appendix 7.1). The implication is that social relationships are hardly stable in the early 1940s, but hyperrationality returns as the mandate in subsequent years, when the Second World War is over. This war confirms that probability analysis is not useful in subjective times and uncertainty reigns, though in *ECP* Keynes nearly predicted this upcoming catastrophe.

11.3 Additional Considerations

Good states of mind and personal affections go hand in hand with aesthetic contemplation for Keynes in 1938, in part leading to a reversal of his former orthodox convictions, perhaps for seeing ethics and esthetics from a novel angle in a new age. No intrinsic *good* or self-regulating system exists; people must control their own destiny. There are no ideal or simple measures or choices but only a changing reality. This may lay the foundation for Keynes's aesthetic ideals. Hendry (1993) appeals to the use of Lakatosian ideas in science (Chapters 2, 5, 9, and 10) and this dynamic and encompassing framework may be applied to Keynes's evolving ethics and esthetics. These discernments obviously entertain practical implications, most noteworthily for the appeal of 'MEB,' a writing that offers a new conceptual nexus, a novel language, a fresh way of thinking, and an innovative framework in both ethics and economics. Keynes confirms here thus his characterization of economics as a moral science.

Moore is partly based or even anchored in Benthamism, but it is widely known he considers it as a simplistic appraisal of agents, believing instead in intrinsic values. It is well-known Moore ascribes to Neo-platonism—as expressed in the quest for universal *good*, which the mature Keynes extended by linking doing *good* and being *good* (Moore), predicating the existence of a fixed cosmos or a closed system. Perhaps for this reason, Moore stayed in the academic sphere; unlike Keynes, whose concrete insight is that a disorganized economic cosmos imposes a barrier to prosperity and this dictum leaves room for practice. For Skidelsky (2016), there is a link in Keynes between induction, intuition, and Neo-platonism as well as between convention, expediency, and facts. According to this view, Keynes appropriately linked these philosophical categories in 1938, defining his mature moral strand. It is true that in his younger days Keynes advocated for a subjective Neo-platonic world. But his attitude changes in 'MEB' wherein he begins to advocate for convention instead of intuition, and for organicism along with discreetness and discontinuity in the face of unusual events. Near the end of his career Keynes advocated for convention which is related to both common applicable knowledge and systems organization, wherein the latter cannot be taken for granted. It is noticeable that Keynes's philosophy evolved from the time that he distances himself from the 'Locke connection' and a comfortable intellectual environment (Chapter 3). New insights necessarily imply a neglect of some of our former beliefs.

'MEB' was also a reaction to D. H. Lawrence's (1885–1930) remarks on Bloomsbury's superficiality. Nevertheless, Keynes's issues in ethics—such as *good* and conduct—and in epistemology—such as reality and language—are non-trivial in philosophical terms. Indeed, he refines them in 'MEB' where transitions, and not merely goals or ideal states, are relevant. Indeed Keynes resolves a great ethical quandary in there: to detect what is *good*, one must know what kinds of things ought to exist for their own sake and what actions we must perform. Thus Keynes not only innovates probability and economics but ethics. 'MEB' assesses the implications of the love of money, contending that if money acquires more relevance than both production and consumption then injustice stems and people's nature becomes alienated (see Appendix 13.1). Human destiny also acquires more relevance in his *oeuvre*, following his ideas in Chapter 24 of *GT*. Keynes believes at this point more in generational change than in immutable rules. Moore's influence on Keynes's original remarks on both *good* and individualism had set the bases for the latter's subsequent intellectual hallmark. They were a bridge for surpassing a former personal—but humane—abyss.

Thus, Keynes's ultimate rebellion against Moore is about the latter's method for defining *good*. Since being *good* and doing *good* are interconnected after conducting a philosophical investigation, Keynes provides epistemic and ethical but rational (in the sense of presenting his arguments) grounds for valuing the responsibility of the government and dismissing the *Laissez-faire*. The inference of these refinements is that Capitalism must be a morally (not only an economically) progressive system. For the middle-aged Keynes, Moore had a lucid influential mind, as he revealed the truth and launched questions that were not considered before or after. However, Moore—the founder of modern ethics and one of the founders of analytical philosophy in Britain—represented for Keynes in 1938 idealism and conservatism as well as certain stolidity of mind. Conversely, he affirmed that *good* may be pluralistic rather than monolithically abstract in terms of *fitness*.

On the other hand, economics lacks ethical foundations.[4] Keynes in 'MEB' criticizes the values of the Victorian society and his early groups. But Moore is not the only straw man in this *oeuvre*. In the process he thoughtfully examines his own juvenilia. When Keynes returns in 'MEB' to the conflict between being *good* and doing *good*, he discards his previously held a priori ideas on human nature as a rational entity. In 'MEB' as has been said he even rejects Moore's method for philosophical argumentation which he had initially adopted without reserve. However for O'Donnell (1995), Keynes knew since the publication of Moore's *Principia Ethica* (1903) that admiring beauty is *good*, but that virtue is not identical to beauty and is certainly different from usefulness or pleasure. Keynes always aimed to develop a whole vision in the issues of beauty and virtue. He stated, echoing Moore, that only *good* is an intrinsic value. However, Keynes no longer considered *good* as a state of consciousness, but rather as a state-of-affairs. Finally, Keynes partially rejected Moorean idealism when defending freedom. 'MEB' is then full of philosophical understandings, arguments, and observations. For instance, he affirms that Utilitarianism is a 'worm destroying civilization' (p. 14). On the other hand, there is existentialism in *GT* and 'MEB' since decisions made under uncertainty may lead to a situational problem as agents are caught in a changing world, hastily deciding between idealism and rationalism, and between reason and the truth.

This self-biographical writing is also about the enquiry related to knowing whether *good* or duty are both objective and subjective and whether *good* will outlast special moments. Keynes's assumption is that instantaneous utility is a harsh measure, in accordance with Mill. Keynes also criticized Moore's individualism and utopianism. Additionally, Keynes appreciated intrinsic merits under the influence of Moore, who is a consequentialist, but Keynes did not appreciate consequentialism in ethics (Chapter 8), unlike in political philosophy (Chapters 7 and 9). But Keynes's emancipation is not only from Moore. The Bloomsbury Group believed in pleasure being consequentialist in ethical terms. Although they appreciated states of mind, they did not necessarily believe in virtue, as Keynes did. The Bloomsbury group enchantment began to die in the 1930s exactly when Keynes modified his goals in favor of a participative agenda in public sector issues.

Perhaps the most important words in this proverbial memoir[5] are: 'The appropriate subjects of passionate contemplation and communion were a beloved person, beauty and truth ... Of these love came a long way first (p. 436).' This Keynes statement is about the *fittest* objects of *good* for Moore that Keynes then diversifies. As an aside, 'MEB' blames the Benthamite tradition for overvaluing the economic criterion, out of which both vulgar passions and Marxism emerge, according to Keynes. A second revealing paragraph is: 'We repudiated...customary morals, conventions and traditional wisdom. We were ... in the strict sense of the term, immoralists (p. 446).' It is well-known that religion is here about behavior toward ourselves and morality about behaviors toward others. This rebellion is the hallmark of Keynes's evolutionary—he would never be a revolutionary—stance at this stage. Both the affiliates of the 'Apostles' and Bloomsbury were engaged in politics, religion, social activities, international relations, and arts (painting and literature) (see Chapter 4), but Keynes distinguished himself from them due to his interdisciplinarity and public exposure, as it was somehow expected by the members of these groups.

Keynes acknowledges here that they are 'immoralists' in their over-estimation of a peculiar kind of *good* (pleasure of mind) and advocacy of rationality, while neglecting conventions and irrationality itself.[6] In this sense another crucial Keynes contribution in 'MEB' is encapsulated in the acknowledgment that: 'Civilization is a thin and precarious crust, elected by the personality and will of a very few, and only maintained by rules and conventions (p. 447).' The middle part of this phrase may be associated with both Keynes's opinions on aristocracy and Nietzsche's thought (see Appendix 11.1). The third part of the phrase can be interpreted to mean that rules of conduct are now explained by convention (at any rate in Keynes's mind), but occasionally leaving room for mending errors. In other words, social propositions may also be defied, perhaps by analyzing the logical validity of probability. This consideration is born from Keynes's realization[7] that sometimes social norms and values may be misleading. Thus, in 'MEB' he unifies all his philosophical contentions in different fields, outstanding among them his envisagement that *good* may be categorized as both a concept and a form of action. Putting it differently, Keynes writes an ethical note by melting tradition with rebellion, as it is normally done by a middle-aged person, but of course with remarkable depth.

11.4 'Dr. Melchior. A Defeated Enemy,' and a BBC Broadcasting

This leads us to the second memoir. 'MEB' is part of *Two Memoirs* (1938) [1949] and the other memoir is 'Dr. Melchior. A Defeated Enemy' (written in the early 1930s). Carl Melchior (1871–1933) was a German banker who traveled with Keynes for a while through some parts of the Continent with the purpose of settling German debt reparations and who was an adviser to the German government on reparations (1919–1932), exhibiting a moderate and reasonable attitude. The memoir is an analysis of the characters of the men responsible for continuing the food blockade of Germany in 1919, when this nation was defenseless. Keynes the future self-labeled immoralist criticized inexpedient social actions conducted by the European establishment. This memoir reaffirms Keynes's stance on *ECP* (1919) when he criticized the irrationality of the French, British, and American leaders but particularly their political and financial claims. In those times, he still sustained his early beliefs in the rationality of human beings. As it is argued in *ECP* (Chapter 5), for Keynes blind alleys in knowledge or in action are both unjust and inefficient, not to mention that the proposers of blockades implicitly advocate that the philosophy of atomism must be applied to the solution of social problems. Keynes also demonstrates in this memoir that he is not a Cambridge-type or Kantian-type ivory-tower theorist, but a European human being witnessing suffering.

Finally, in 1939 Keynes broadcasted a *BBC* radio speech called 'When the day of peace comes.' Recall that the Bloomsberrians were peace lovers. He was still an optimist though he was now aware of human propensity toward evil and greed. In other words, the new war had modified both his thinking and his assessment of the moral standards on human conduct. Soon he would be involved in international affairs related to moral and economic standards but also to war. Mini (1991) analyzes Keynes's intellectual creativity and its impact on his evolution, by means of an existentialist and psychological scope. In this vein, Mini refers to tensions between Keynes's spiritual and practical lives (otherworldliness *versus* persuasion and influence) which defined his reach. The interrelated points of reference are values, outlook, experiences, and ideas, all of which are the foundations of his *oeuvre* as well as the reconstruction of established concepts on the part of a man who was the owner of a deep sensitiveness. This chapter deals with the critical thinking exposed in 'MEB' where Keynes takes advantage of all his theoretical and lively experience to set the foundations of ontological, epistemological, and ethical matters, contending that conventions are the ultimate guide for struggling against uncertainty, thus reinforcing his contentions in *GT*. The philosophy of Keynes as exposed here offers a more cohesive system reflecting his integral attitude to life. After this chapter, the outlook about his philosophy becomes even clearer though not necessarily less complex. What is next? This chapter complements the examination of Keynes's later life by describing how he uses all his philosophical armor coupled with his experience in economics to delineate the configuration of the international financial system and generate a boom in the North-Western hemisphere which would last from 1945 to 1975. How did he accomplish this gigantic task? Between 1939 and 1945, the Second World War re-attracted him to work as a government adviser and a superb writer.

Appendix 11.1 The World in Their Hands: Keynes and Nietzsche on Elitism

Then again one can compare any pair of visions. But this story is somewhat distinctive. Keynes is considered as a major philosophical author with a predictive gift. Nietzsche is selected not only because of the reach of his *oeuvre* but also because his philosophical insights are elitist and aristocratic as well as futuristic, and hence they illuminate the legacy of Europe for the twentieth century. This double but hopefully unifying appraisal may widen the interpretation of Keynes's vision against a Continental European scenario. Nietzsche is obviously more than an elitist (see Appendix 11.1.1 on Appendix 11.1). Indeed this is an old-fashioned view of his legacy. But this is a humane account of visions of a man fighting against the intellectual establishment. Altogether, ethics is the basis of the comparison between Keynes and Friedrich Nietzsche (1844–1900) since it is the realm in which both men transpire their disillusionments along with their *grandeur*.

Keynes leaves idealism after the First World War but he states in 'MEB': 'I remain, and will always remain, an immoralist' (*CW JMK X*, p. 446), we would say an amoralist. Nietzsche pens in his intellectual autobiography: 'all of them still believe in the ideal ... I am the first immoralist' (Nietzsche 1888a [2005], p. 80). No mention is made of Nietzsche as an influence in 'MEB.' Nevertheless, they coincide in that there is nothing more vulgar and decadent than the moral for the masses.

Keynes and Friedrich Nietzsche contribute a vision of human evolution centered on the growth of human intelligence besides on a new moral outlook. Keynes is an intuitionist, Nietzsche a counter-intuitionist in morals, and one can add that rationality is a conceptual role for Nietzsche, but a practical one for Keynes. Their lives exhibit individualistic, authoritarian, and aristocratic manners (the renunciation of common sense for the sake of progress). Keynes behaves as an elitist throughout his life (Fitzgibbons 1988), just like Nietzsche. Elitism is linked in Keynes to beauty, love; attitude to the herd; style; convention, the truth, and knowledge; and progress. Elitism in both thinkers may be an attitude associated with either the return to an imperial age or a lineage regarding power and ideals. However, it must be controlled and control brings about success, especially self-control.

Both philosophers are selective in terms of social class scrutiny and taste. Keynes lives in the real world; both preach the supremacy of irrationality. Keynes's values are creativity and liberalism, against Victorian codes, realizing persuasion gives power. Nietzsche feels Christian morality inhibits life's energy in a universe wherein power is virtue. Power and hence vitality stem from them. If the Apollonian and the Dionysian virtues are related to the moderation of impulses, they—Keynes and Nietzsche—exhibit a Dionysian orientation in their youths, although both are plagued with ills and aches, dying relatively young.

Nietzsche's vision of progress is symbolized by the perennial movement around a semi-circle. This is the notion of eternal recurrence. Both Keynes and Nietzsche are emphatic in their criticisms of the truth, maintaining that superior persons must sweep aside religiously inspired values. The availability of time for the individual is crucial for a good life. For Nietzsche labor must occupy no more than 20% of the day, for Keynes only three hours per day once unemployment is conquered ('EPG').

Keynes believes equality might result from proper institutional arrangements perhaps confining his perspective to convention. In the meantime, he is interested in eugenics, probably due to macroeconomic reasons. Nietzsche contends that nature abhors equality, and his vision overcomes convention, being biased in favor of perspectivism, especially his own. Their works are prone to overstatement, and subject to misappropriation. Both require reader's involvement, being embellished writings hiding deep insights with a foot in post-modernism.

Nietzsche is silent on money, and enigmatic about social philosophy and the role of public power, whereas Keynes loses—at some stages—faith in politicians. Nietzsche buries those old conventional or orthodox values starting with Socrates, and the 'European' Keynes with Bentham. Both are trans-generational thinkers (even the short-term oriented Keynes), but Nietzsche possesses a long-term (timelessness?) perspective heralding the death of God and the will to power.

They share an interest in art as an enhancer of life and modernism. Friends instruct them on the best of European culture. Nietzsche has liquidity of opinion through space. Yet Keynes has liquidity of mind through time (Skidelsky). Nietzsche defends natural rights, thinking utilitarianism is appropriate for the masses. For Keynes humankind is a part of an organic universe, but for Nietzsche humans are part of the Earth in the present, meaning that he lets go of otherworldly illusions. For both, the post-modern person must exhibit an energetic soul, like Napoleon who was never physically tired. Nietzsche is proud of his eccentric humanism in the search for perfectionism. For Keynes individualism is a value especially in the event it is supported by charisma and intentionality.

For Keynes, human beings possess distinct motivations, advocating for expedient and discretionary measures. Both possess uniqueness in method and are interested in psychology. Nietzsche writes about strife but states that humankind is goalless. Keynes understands the pace of life, and that direction is about the accomplishment of freedom. Nietzsche is the critique of bourgeois—not of aristocratic—morality. Keynes preaches wealth as a precondition for achieving happiness. They enhance subjective knowledge, their ideologies reflecting outstanding perspectives about deep issues. WWI is a prophecy for Nietzsche but a social reality for the young Keynes. The Bloomsbury Group may be representative of Nietzsche's *Overman* exhibiting no fear whatsoever of social morals.

'My Early Beliefs' and *Thus Spoke Zarathustra* (incidentally written in 1883) are both gospel and about judgment. Keynes practices introspective elitism (Fitzgibbons 1991), but eventually mutes to extroverted elitism. His peculiar conception of paradise is full-employment (1925). Nietzsche's ethics are beyond good and evil, advocating risk, and his paradise is human overcoming. If elitism is related to the ego, Descartes re-discovers this psychological instance, but Keynes and Nietzsche have much to say on both selfishness and egotism, especially Nietzsche who perceives himself as the *Übermensch*. However, their reflections are generous. Both have faith in geniuses and preach the transmutation of values, always preparing us for liberty. Consider their dichotomies *good-doing good* and *good-bad*. Nietzsche, however, deserves a deeper outline.

An Appendix on Appendix ii.i.i Opinions on Nietzsche Himself

The re-evaluation of all values is Nietzsche's *leitmotiv*. He was not tyrannized by logic, instead being underpinned by ethics. Nietzsche discusses language and shakes old faiths, especially those approaches to matters of value and morality. He does not believe things are eternal, recognizing the becoming; possessing a passion for a new future. Hence he is a philosopher of evolution. However it is the theme of elitism which delineates the gist and charm of their personalities. Nietzsche is an elitist for Bertrand Russell or John Rawls (whereas Keynes is for Fitzgibbons). The point at this stage is outlining why Nietzsche is an encompassing cultural critic as well as a multifaceted philosopher with a holistic message.

Nietzsche is the advocator of perspectivism, nihilism, the slave revolt against morals, the will to power, the superman, the eternal recurrence, and the death of God. He is a life improver, invoking a return to the Earth. He is a writer displaying unworldly imagination; and the last of the metaphysicians (in Heidegger's reading). Nietzsche ironically experienced the overwhelming sense of the past, translating it into some of his notions. According to Sánchez-Meca (2000), Deleuze sees Nietzsche opposing the tradition which considers that thought loves the truth, supposing that alien forces detach us from it. Deleuze remarks that the extent to which pleasure- and pain-related sensations—and the effect of a random encounter with images—may ignite reflection in us (a fuzzy monster in the back of our heads, in Keynes's wording). For Nietzsche thought does not think by itself nor does it find the truth. It is limited by forces emerging from our bodies. The consequence is that for Nietzsche philosophy is a realm belonging to valuation and interpretation via judgment, validating his critical thought as affirmative. This ascertainment matches Keynes's practice of economics.

For Lefebvre (2016 [1975]), Nietzsche captures modernity when reflecting on both civilization and values. This triple determination of the contemporary world (Hegel and Marx being the remaining philosophers in Lefebvre's account) takes account of multiple perhaps perennial conflicts which are embedded in our reality. This statement makes a perfect fit with Keynes's practice of international relations.

Foucault (1926–1984) inherits from Nietzsche a constructivist notion of knowledge and the truth as related to power. Foucault also sees an ethical-esthetic subject able to gain freedom. The relationship between these two thinkers is relevant to the nature of modern life. The Nietzschean topics—disunity of the subject, power, historical discontinuity, experimentation—define Foucault's philosophical orientation, especially the conceptualization of epistemic relations as constitutionally dependent on social relations. Foucault and Nietzsche rely on a notion of truth in connection with the task of self-overcoming; that is, we must break with habits of knowing and perceiving. Finally, Foucault, when writing about Nietzsche, talks about morals, epistemology, the non-reason, and both cultural and aristocratic elitism. Nietzsche contends that a dichotomy exists between a concern for the truth and esthetics of existence residing at the heart of Western culture (see Patton 2019). This account is acceptable for the Bloomsberrian Keynes.

Schacht (1983) presents an account of Nietzsche's view on the nature of truth and knowledge, theism, the will to power, morality, art, metaphysical errors, life, man's destiny, and values. Notice atomism is an ontic error. Nietzsche provides a construction with cognitive content (Schacht, Introduction 1983) but interpretation is indispensable for describing his nucleus. In the last respect, Nietzsche's idea is also akin to Keynes's.

Notes

1. As opposed to both Burke and Moore, who recommend living in the present.
2. The human mind is not self-sufficient, closed, or static, so that neither individuals nor societies govern in a vacuum. Ethical actions, social policies or scientific advances are the factors leading to self-government.
3. When everyone is irrational, it is rational to be irrational.
4. Economic crises are also moral crises.
5. *Essays in Biography, CW*, Vol. X, pp. 433–450.
6. Swings in mood emerge when conventions are overlooked for practical purposes.
7. This is so, especially after writing *GT*.

References

Bateman, Bradley. W., and John B. Davis. 1993. "Introduction". In *Keynes and Philosophy: An Essay on the Origins of Keynes's Thought* , edited by Bradley W. Bateman and John B. Davis: 1–5, Marquette University Faculty 141.https://epublications.marquette.edu/marq_fac-book/141.

Fitzgibbons, Athol J. 1988 [1990]. *Keynes's Vision: A New Political Economy*. Oxford: Clarendon Press.

———. 1991. "The Significance of Keynes's Idealism." In *Keynes and Philosophy: Essays on the Origins of Keynes's Thought*, edited by Bradley W. Bateman and John B. Davis, Chapter 8. Aldershot, UK: Edward Elgar.

Freud, Sigmund. 1930 [1953–74]. "Civilization and Its Discontents." In *The Standard Edition of the Complete Psychological Works of Sigmund Freud* 21, translated by James Strachey, 57–145. London: Hogarth.

———. 1933. "Why War?" In *The Standard Edition of the Complete Psychological Works of Sigmund Freud* 22, translated by James Strachey, 195–215. London: Hogarth.

Hendry, David F. 1993. "Econometric Methodology: A Personal Perspective." In *Advances in Econometrics: Fifth World Congress*, Volume II, edited by T. F. Bewley, Chapter 10. Cambridge: Cambridge University Press.

Keynes, John M. 1938. "My Early Beliefs." In *JMK CW Vol. X. Essays in Biography*, edited by D. Moggridge. London Royal Economic Society.

———. 1930. "A Treatise on Money." In *JMK CW Vols. V and VI A Treatise on Money*. edited by D. Moggridge. London: Royal Economic Society.

———. 1936. "The General Theory of Employment, Interest and Money." In *JMK CW Vol. VII The General Theory of Employment, Interest and Money*, edited by D. Moggridge. London: Royal Economic Society.

———. 1939. BBC Radio Speech. "When the day of peace comes." https://archiveshub.jisc.ac.uk/data/gb272-jmk. Archive Search. Archive Centre, King's College, Cambridge. https://archivesearch.lib.cam.ac.uk/repositories/7/archival_objects/285279.

Kirshner, Jonathan. 2015. "Keynes's Early Beliefs and Why They Still Matter." *Challenge* 58, no. 5: 398–412.

Lawson, Tony. 1993. "Keynes and Convention." *Review of Social Economics* 5, no. 2 (June): 174–200.

———. 2003. "Keynes's Realist Orientation." In *The Philosophy of Keynes's Economics: Probability, Uncertainty and Convention*, edited by Jochen Runde and Sohei Mizuhara, Chapter 12, 159–69. New York: Routledge.

Lefebvre, Henri. 2016 [1975]. *Hegel, Marx, Nietzsche (o el reino de las sombras).* Madrid: Siglo XVI, translated from *Hegel, Marx, Nietzsche (ou la ryaume des ombres).* Casterman: Tournai.

Moore, George E. 1903. *Principia Ethica*. Reprinted in Prometheus Books' Great Books in Philosophy Series. http://fair-use.org/g-e-moore/principia-ethica/. Accessed 8 January 2015.

Mini, Piero V. 1991. *Keynes, Bloomsbury and the General Theory*. Basingstoke: Palgrave.

Nietzsche, Friedrich. 1888a [2005]. *Ecce Homo. How One Become What One Is. 2. Thoughts out of Season 2.* London: Penguin.

———. 1888b [1990]. *The Twilight of the Idols: or How to Philosophize with a Hammer*. London: Penguin.

———. 1883 [1978]. *Thus Spoke Zarathustra. A Book for All and None*. London: Penguin.

O'Donnell, Roderick M. 1991. *Keynes as Philosopher-Economist*. Proceedings of The Ninth Keynes Seminar held at the University of Kent. London: Macmillan.

———. 1995. "Keynes on Aesthetics." *History of Political Economy* 27, suplement: 93–121.

Patton, Paul. 2019. "Foucault, Nietzsche and the History of Truth." In *Foucault and Nietzsche: A Critical Encounter*, edited by Alan Rosenberg and Joseph Westfall, Chapter 1. Bloomsbury: Bloomsbury Studies in Continental Philosophy.

Sánchez-Meca, Diego. 2000. *Nietzsche En Deleuze: Hacia Una Genealogía Del Pensamiento Crítico*. Madrid: Éndoxa: Series Filosóficas, n. 12: 167–86.

Schacht, Richard. 1983. *Nietzsche (Arguments of the Philosophers)*, 1st ed. London and New York: Routledge.

Shackle, George L. S. 1967 [2010]. *The Years of High Theory: Invention and Tradition in Economic Thought 1926–1939*. Cambridge: Cambridge University Press.

Shionoya, Yuichi. 1991. "Sidgwick, Moore and Keynes: A Philosophical Analysis of Keynes's 'My Early Beliefs.'" In *Keynes and Philosophy: Essays on the Origin of Keynes's Thought*, edited by B. W. Bateman and J. B. Davis, 6–29. Aldershot: Edward Elgar.

Skidelsky, Robert. 1983. *John Maynard Keynes. Volume I: Hopes Betrayed 1883–1920*. London: Papermac.

———. 1992. *John Maynard Keynes. Volume II: The Economist as Saviour 1920–1937*. London: Macmillan.

———. 2001. *John Maynard Keynes. Volume III: Fighting for Britain, 1937–1946*. London: Macmillan.

———. 2016. *The Essential Keynes*. London: Penguin.

Zhang, Ivy. n.d. "A Review of Keynes' 'The End of Laissez-Faire'." https://zmy26.wordpress.com/2011/01/26/a-review-on-keynes%E2%80%99-%E2%80%9Cthe-end-of-laissez-faire%E2%80%9D/. Accessed 18 April 2019.

CHAPTER 12

'How to Pay for the War' and the World Economy

This chapter deals with the evolution of Keynes's interests from internal stability in Britain in the 1930s (and from ethical disquisitions at the end of that same decade) to external concerns in the 1940s. He implemented innovative policy research designed for improving the conditions prevailing during and in the aftermath of the Second World War. His focus at this epoch was the coordination of international policies for accomplishing international stability with growth. Through this he found modern international macroeconomics and finance, always employing the concept of organicism. His means is persuasion grounded in authority. But Keynes's belief that governments could alleviate unemployment (his main long-standing concern) by manipulating the overall level of activity always remained at the center of the debate. Due in great part to his efforts, selected nations would undertake international actions—reinforced by cooperation and coordination—under the assumption that nationalist myths may be debunked. This stage, though occurring in the 1940s, echoes Keynes's guidance of 1919 (Chapter 4), demonstrating evolution does not clash with conviction. His views were refined but his convictions related to both universal and individual *good* remained.

Section 12.1 is about Keynes's suggested treatment of post-war inflation in 'How to Pay for the War: A Radical Plan for the Chancellor of the

J. Muñoz-Bandala, *Keynes's Evolutionary Spirit*, Palgrave Insights into Apocalypse Economics,
https://doi.org/10.1007/978-3-030-90150-9_12

Exchequer' (1940) or 'HPW', which includes Keynes's somehow ignored treatment of inflation (the opposite to depression) demonstrating that his economic theory deserves to be labeled 'general,' as it corresponds to an open system; one with multiple perspectives, solutions, and interests. Section 12.2 is about the philosophy and practice of international lending and loans. Section 12.3 deals with his proposed measures for stabilizing the world economy with financial concerns at the heart: the rod *Bancor* and international institutions. Section 12.4 focuses on such related topics as commodity buffers as a form of stabilization. Section 12.5 offers a conclusion. Then, apparently new and multidisciplinary Keynes's topics ensue. Appendix 12.1 about Keynes's activities also includes the setting of guidelines for the field of development, which is a topic with a view on long term stabilization. Appendix 12.2 deals with his view on econometrics, that is, his critical reflection on orthodox empirical procedures and practices, in the fields of both mathematics and statistics with special reference to assumptions. Appendix 12.3 is on his role as a sponsor and disseminator of the arts, dealing at last with Keynes's aesthetics.

12.1 Flipping the Coin: Inflation

Skidelsky (2001) confirms that the theoretical and practical interrelated topics dealt with by Keynes between 1940 and 1946 are linked to themes of international economics and development (see also Appendix 12.1). The issues that Keynes addresses, according to Skidelsky (2001), are British war finance; theoretical advancements on debt management; and the Post-war economic order. The latter includes the creation of the Bretton Woods System: a fixed but adjustable exchange system, and two international institutions aimed at providing international financial assistance: the International Monetary Fund and the World Bank. A related theme is the creation of an International Clearing Union (ICU) known as the *Bancor Plan* in 1943. Keynes was also interested in the principles of domestic banking, international relations, international trade, basic needs strategy, food security, and as in 1919 the reconstruction of national economies.

Keynes returned to the British civil service as an adviser to the Treasury in the 1940s, barely emulating his activities of 1918–1919 and the early 1930s. Therefore, he wrote 'How to Pay for the War' (1940) while serving as an adviser to the Chancellor of the Exchequer. What are his economic themes after his accomplishment of *GT*? *GT* (1936) is centered upon the triumphant struggle against unemployment and recession and is a product of his skepticism of the notion of the primacy of savings against the relevance of investment. But the Golden Book may also be considered as a theoretical anticipation of 'How to Pay for the War', which is devoted to the management of inflation rather than to unemployment (at the other side of the spectrum of economic evils), based on the notion of forced savings. The forced savings mechanism (or tax increases or self-generated scarcity for that matter as opposed to expenditure increases) is a remedy against inflation as well as an explanation for how monetary expansion results in wage redistribution and reductions in production—and in inflation—outside the Classical world. 'HPW' is then about how to reduce the inflationary gap by means of compulsory savings (leakages must replace injections within the circular flow of national income or output). This manuscript is then the mirror image of *GT* as the times changed radically in just a few years since the problem between 1940 and 1945 became price increases.[1]

Times change, hypotheses, and theories require new devices but based on innovative approaches. Policies require flexibility—discretionary measures—and a willingness to equilibrate both income and expenditures in the issue of aggregate demand but in the context of controlling price increases as well. If saving—considered as the opposite variable to consumption—is increased, then the circular flow of income will register more leakages than injections, thereby exerting diminishing pressure on inflation in the context of an exhausted—vertical—aggregate supply (as in the Classical or the Monetarist models). Keynes hence acted on issues related to inflation and debt management between wars, leaving behind 'normal' aggregate demand management in the time of an unlimited aggregate supply as in 1936, thereafter remedying the war's financial aftermath. He also created international mechanisms and institutions to accomplish or strengthen stabilization. The relationship between inflation and development in the long term was also analyzed by Keynes at this stage (see Appendix 12.1).

Next came the heuristic issue of enlarging the mere concept of aggregate demand: consumption, investment, and public expenditure must be targeted with attention to the international sector (thus adding up exports and imports, see appendix of 'HTP') during and after the Second World War. One may safely suppose all these international topics are interlinked. Consequently, a return to the topic of domestic inflation is imperative.

The primary goal of Keynes's plan on inflation—which could be a matter of contagion—is the attainment of a stable international economic order. This was unlike his plans in the 1930s, which were addressed to resolve recessive problems in Britain; or in 1936 when he offered remedies for minimizing fluctuations in effective demand. For Thirlwall (2007), after 1940 Keynes recommended compulsory saving (which would raise interest rates, r) or even a tax effort in inflationary settings but was adamant on rationing. Keynes wrote about both forced savings and the inflationary tax as early as 1923 in *TMR*, but now those themes became more relevant. The problem was that savings would eventually have to be refunded and this would affect entire countries. Contrarywise, *ECP*, *TM*, and *GT* are about depression and underemployment equilibria, all dealing with the consequences of not reaching the full-employment level. Based on these conceptions, the 'new' Keynes (1940 [1980]) stated that full employment would depend on keeping total expenditure at the optimum figure and on ensuring that investment is equal to savings when incomes are at the desired level. Otherwise, a tendency toward inflation would set in. His conception of external policies was still (but rapidly diminishingly) subordinated to his principal objective: full employment.

Alas, there was a place for ethics at this practical stage dominated by his political philosophy. Keynes sought to achieve, in practice by means of politics, the ideal well-being of the public. For that purpose, he attempted to balance the evils generated by the practical means of rationing (an alternative to forced savings or rising taxes for reducing aggregate demand) with those that come from combatting inflation. Both unlimited (ordinary, not in capital, as Keynes recommended) public expenditure and its consequence post-war inflation were reasonable apprehensions of his teachings in the early 1940s. Inflation makes people suffer and as a tax it affects income distribution.

12.2 International Credits: Britain in the Middle of the Road

Remedying inflation was only the first step for accomplishing international stability during the Second World War. In the meantime, Keynes also had an eye on the quantitative and qualitative practicalities related to lend-lease agreements[2] (Sect. 12.2; see Chapter 4), especially the loan granted to Great Britain, but it must be understood that this loan was related to other loans and the conditions dictated by the lenders. Keynes was critical enough of austerity (Appendix 13.1), which in hard times arises from impediments for obtaining loans. Having authority on policy-making—as the consequence of his presence in meetings and committees, his public relations, and his works—he realized like in 1919 and 1931 that financial wisdom, economic theory, and statesmanship are needed especially in times of crises, extreme uncertainty or even recovery. Teams were dealing with the financial side of the Second World War consequences, with Keynes as their active spokesperson. Just like he served as an adviser to the Chancellor of Exchequer, he became the chief negotiator—a special *envoy*, in the words of Skidelsky—of the United States loans to Britain between 1944 and 1946.

Keynes went back to the Treasury in 1940 with the purpose of applying economics to the problems of war finance. His role helped to preserve the international order in the subsequent years. This was his main activity after years of producing high theory[3] in the 1930s. In fact, he produced a scheme in the 1940s with the purpose of settling payments between creditor and debtor countries in terms of external deficits (including both trade and finance). He also established the international clearing union (ICU) by means of his currency unit *Bancor*. Everything is interrelated in the macro-world. The implementation of practicalities concerning war loans in the aftermath of the Second World War was also associated with his contributions to the theory of development (see Appendix 12.1). Returning to the underlying philosophy of the *ICU*, it is associated to the provision of credits coming from an organic (yes, organic) international financial system based on cooperation wherein loans would provide the stimulus for growth. Since the economic game never ends, transitions must be enhanced by credit provision. Otherwise, austerity will provoke recessions due to a drain in credits to private investment (recall the relevance of this variable in *GT*), especially after turbulences from difficult times have been resolved.

12.3 Reinventing the Post-War International Financial System: Settlement Systems (*Bancor* and *ICU*) and Institutions

One of the consequences of the Second World War was that the United States consolidated its leadership in the financial system of the world with the rising of the Dollar Standard (akin to the Gold Standard). The Dollar

Standard endured until 1973, though the US Dollar is still the leading currency as an asset of value (Appendix 13.1). The United States became the country to grant loans to Great Britain, rescuing her from the debts it contracted during the war. Keynes moved on to a conciliatory philosophy of action. He became the leading negotiator of the Anglo-Saxon Lend-lease project, which brought him to visit the United States several times to conduct negotiations that culminated in the accords of Bretton Woods (BW) in 1944. The International Monetary Fund (*IMF*) and the World Bank (*WB*) were created as an outcome of the accords of BW.

Keynes designed the Post-war International System. He devised routes to world development by creating institutions for providing international lending buffers. He had previously written on this issue in 'Can Lloyd George do it?' (1925), but now he proposed his *Bancor* plan (1940) addressed at the international level. The International Clearing Union (ICU) would be a worldwide central bank, issuing paper currency for international payments and maintaining exchange stability with *Bancor* as the accepted currency. This plan for preserving the benefits of international financial flows was grounded on persuaded rationality, cooperative individualism, and ethics. Keynes envisaged the role of *Bancor* as a common global unit of currency, assuming in practice that all countries would work in coordination and would be ruled by a global central bank. He was interested in achieving financial stability throughout the world and not only for the British Empire as he was at the time of writing *Indian Currency and Finance* in 1913 (Appendix 5.1). The purpose of *Bancor* was for the supply of money to be equated with physical movements in goods and services. He believed that the *ICU* should be built as a mutually beneficial partnership of nation-states by taxing persistent surpluses on current accounts.

In this epoch, Keynes was also devoted to such practical interrelated 'international' themes as Post-war finance in many countries and reparations in Germany. Another interest was a remedy for British financial ruin after the Second World War, leading to active efforts to manage debt. He also developed plans for managing fiscal spending and sustaining debt forgiveness (like in *ECP*). He would undertake these endeavors because of his influence on international politics, as the anti-utilitarian (non-Benthamist) aiming to create an organic welfare state. Keynes's plan offered greater freedom than that implemented by the United States which was called the *Stabilization Fund*. In the end, his original proposals did not prevail due to differing priorities (and levels of influence) on the part of the top economic policymakers. *ICU* (the international clearing union) and *Bancor* were devised by Keynes, but the specifications of the American-led 'White Plan' were followed. Keynes gave a speech in 1944 in the House of Lords on the International Monetary Fund and the perils of mismanaging the world economy in this transition of power from Britain to the United States. His speech mixed ethics, economics, and political philosophy, but in his own nationalistic way.

For Keynes economic policies, international finance measures, and international trade negotiations should be supervised by either local governments or international institutions, by means of an aristocratic and disinterested 'organic' management along the lines of Chapter 24 of *GT* (see our Chapter 9). In the 1940s he became preoccupied with international disequilibria. He visualized disequilibria in the balance of payments as a hindrance to full-employment policies. Hence, he developed proposals for achieving symmetry in the international financial system as it relates to treatment of all countries. His attitude in all periods but especially in the late 1940s was defined by his consciousness of inexpediency and injustice as a part of both his liberal ideology and ethics. In fact, his international adjustment mechanism was about the even placement of burden on both the creditor and the debtor countries precisely by means of *ICU*.

12.4 Related Topics

Keynes now envisaged uncertainty as having—objective—international causes. He was always aware that both speculators and policymakers overstate or understate, respectively, the normal economic cycles and volatility, sometimes due to greed or even to ignorance. But the important issue is that sources of instability could arise from either misalignments in exchange rates or qualitative changes in trade conditions or in the prices of commodities, that is from imbalances in any balance of payments. He was thus involved in the implementation of a system of fixed but adjustable exchange rates (the Bretton Woods System or BW) with autonomous coordinated monetary policies in the foreground set to reduce interest rates. Assuming international cooperation especially in terms of trade, attempts were made to rebuild pre-war sub-regional agreements around exchange rates in 1943. However, Germany's opposition to the policies of both the United States and Great Britain in the aftermath of the Second World War came as an unpleasant surprise. Further, the need to defend domestic exchange rates by rising interest rates or to fund local public expenditure complicated the reduction of interest rates.

Simultaneously during and after the Second World War Keynes conceived proposals for the expansion of multilateral international trade. In the early 1940s, he was interested in implementing a buffer stock for the prices of commodities and reducing speculation in real and financial markets; this was part of his stabilization plan and a means for accomplishing long-term development (Appendix 12.1). Keynes was also involved in analyzing the problem of the balance of payments of the United States in 1946. The problem was that Post-war governments did not enjoy the freedom to manage their own economies; specifically, rising trade deficits restricted the freedom to expand through tax cuts or public spending, which is the typical Keynes policy. Further, the Sterling Pound was pegged to the US Dollar under the Bretton Woods system, and monetary policy in Britain was therefore constrained. Up until this point, Keynes had been interested in the fostering of aggregate demand to achieve full employment in the international arena. But at this stage, the theoretical and practical concerns of Keynes were moving toward supply-side policies after full employment and welfare are addressed. His inspirational insights on these topics were not widely understood. The next sub-section is a return to his traditional concerns.

12.4.1 The White Paper

Keynes also supervised the design of the 'White Paper on Employment Policy'[4] in 1944 in Great Britain on the matter of the responsibility of the government to maintain a high and stable level of employment. For Harcourt and Riach (1997), Keynes 'White Paper on Employment Policy' summarizes his economic philosophy. According to Peden (1988), the 'White Paper' is a policy document about national accounts, especially details about public expenditure and taxation. The document incorporates compromises between traditional ideas and the theories of Keynes and his followers.

The 'White Paper' outlines a threefold approach. The first measure is to expand exports in collaboration with other countries. The second is to prevent (micro) unemployment that might arise from a maldistribution of industry and labor in the transition from a war economy. The third is to establish macroeconomic measures to maintain aggregate demand (Chote 1994). The 'White Paper' described five methods by which the level of spending could be kept high, including the Keynes-inspired recipe for lowering interest rates and increasing public spending to counter the effects of low temporary investment. The budget, however, would have to be balanced in the medium term to prevent exacerbations of the cycle. According to Chote (1994), the 'White Paper' also suggests fiscal moderation to restrain inflation, being designed as a flexible scheme. Keynes was not alone in his thinking; he was never a lone philosopher. Innovatively enough, Beveridge (1944) writes that full employment must be the responsibility of the state, arguing that pre-war unemployment is due to ineffective demand and (in microeconomic terms) a disorganized labor market.

12.5 Conclusions on Keynes the Internationalist

If Keynes had a devotion to the public interest, then he was not an elitist. Indeed, the implementation of one's vision can be complex due to unforeseen events. For Skidelsky (2016), Keynes in the 1940s offered an escape from a closed fixed system in both the domestic arena and the international setting. For Temin and Vines (2016), Keynes conducted research on international affairs throughout his working life. Examples of them are his arguments in *ECP* in 1919, his testimony before the MacMillan Committee in 1931, and his role in the negotiations at Bretton Woods during and after the Second World War.

For Keynes, the motivator in Capitalism must be a domestic choice but at the same time, a country must consider the place of other nations in the world. Great. To him the world now seemed more suitable for designing interrelated schemes because he understood the dynamic—and interrelated—structure behind global monetary orders. Perhaps economics is less deep than philosophy but more applicable, especially in the short term. But circumstance matters. The time was right for praxis. Keynes writes that '[t]heoretical economic analysis has reached a point where it is fit to be applied' (CW *Vol. XXVII*, p. 371). Even though the 'White Plan' triumphed, Keynes had set the foundation for the golden age with his awareness that effective demand management at the global level could solve the problem of employment. Under this framework growth and distribution became the remaining problems to be solved. In the aftermath of the Second World War Britain entered into a crisis: individualism, patriotism, and inequality (motivated by greedy strands) temporarily re-emerged; as a result almost everyone was questioning the foundations of

Capitalism (see Appendix 13.1). But the stage was set for the golden age of this mode of production, which took hold between 1950 and 1973. Keynes's ideas on the world economy became relevant.

This chapter deals with the expansion of Keynes's thinking in the 1940s, since now he is able to recognize that international problems are center-stage in economics. He thus devised theoretical measures and practicalities to create a new order with international resonance. Hence he went beyond his 1930s interest in the British realm, and even further beyond his personal but worthwhile disquisitions of the early 1920s and 1938. How can these apparently heterogeneous chapters conform a unity or even a circle? This question is relevant if only because unity is the mere objective of philosophy, apart from practice. Last chapter (13) is a unifying reflection on the philosophical legacy of Keynes with the purpose of a demonstration by means of falsification, the hypothesis that his thinking is evolutionary. Since the aftermath of Keynes's theory (1950–1990) is dealt with in Chapter 10, the last chapter includes after producing conclusions an interesting Appendix (13.1) dealing with the relation between Keynes and the 'future'—the end of the twentieth century and the beginning of the twenty-first century. It has financial crises as its glowing object of study.

Appendix 12.1: Keynes, Harrod, and Sen on Development

Thirlwall (2007) writes that today's orthodoxy—before the 2007 financial crises—considers inflation reduction to be a pre-condition for growth based on long-term capital accumulation. Yet seen from another angle, stability must generate growth and growth must automatically result in development (roughly defined as growth coupled with equality). Development is also related to ethics, but there are differences in interpretation. For us, development might be the future of Keynes's *SRP* in the sense that it becomes his main concern after the short or medium-period problems of full employment and inflation are resolved. On the other hand, long-term models are useful for setting the foundations of long-term growth, wealth, and stability, not to mention that development also brings about an egalitarian income distribution (at least in the eyes of Classical economists). Keynes was not a classical economist, but his philosophy at this stage might be reconciled with orthodox thinking. Moreover, development may be the final goal of international macroeconomic cooperation, though some thinkers conceive that development must be firstly established at the microeconomic level. As a matter of fact, development can work at both levels and Keynes acknowledged the value of the slow invisible hand and the *Laissez-faire* a few weeks before his death.[5] He likely would have developed these models had he lived longer, widening his *SRP* (Chapter 2)—especially in heuristic terms—since many of his preoccupations in the 1940s were related to the future of humankind.

Keynes's influence on the formative years of development economics is visible through his disciples, mainly the expert on growth Roy F. Harrod (1900–1978). The story goes as follows: Keynes had set the foundations for the theory of modern economic development, departing from his theory of income determination for arriving at full employment. But his models are purposefully static and oriented to the short term, unlike those of Harrod who brings dynamism to them by reconsidering the decisive role of savings (to be explained in the next paragraphs) at the cost of neglecting the role of injections to the circular income flow and forgetting uncertainty. According to Thirlwall (2007), Keynes connects his former theories on income determination with his insights related to development by considering unemployment as the main development problem. Notice that for Keynes the government plays a preparatory role in the attainment of development by means of the management of aggregate demand. Development economics for him was thus the study of how economies progress from stagnation to growth and from low-income to high-income status. The passthrough is hence from income determination to growth to development. But the Keynes's model is concentrated in the short period so that there should be more unexplored issues related to development and as said before this gap is covered by Harrod.

Roy F. Harrod

Harrod was the first official biographer of Keynes in 1951. In Harrod's dynamic model (1939)[6] savings (the strawman for Keynes) is the engine of long-term growth. This new Harrod's construct based on Keynes's contentions is about new permanent investments (capital accumulation) and has frequently been applied in developing countries. Growth is the ratio between gross savings (s^G/c) and the rate of capital depreciation (d). Labor growth and technological progress are the motivators, captured in productivity. The good news is that if capital is not accumulated or investment falls short, then foreign aid, private foreign investment, or loans might guarantee the return to growth. The required capital/output ratio (not fixed as in Keynes's models) can evolve in response to developments in financial markets or the policy environment. This is supposedly the dynamic version of the Keynes remedy for stagnation. For Thirlwall (2007), the Keynes-Harrod structure selects the policy options suitable for all economies. However, Harrod's model neglects the role of uncertainty (which also reigns in the long period). The received view is that growth can only commence when full employment is attained (Chapter 9).

Amartya Sen

Sen does not descend from the Keynes heritage, but he aims at social welfare as a result of development. This is a different conception of development than that propounded by Keynes in terms of the role of the State and hence of public policies for development since Sen's yardstick for the analysis of these insights is microeconomic in spirit. Nonetheless, Amartya Sen (1933–) begins where Keynes and Harrod end. Sen is concerned with overcoming the problem of absolute poverty and has been working on his approach of capabilities, which allows classifying his conception of individual development by means of the concept of *functionings*. *Functionings* refer to what people do or can do with the commodities of given characteristics that they may come to control. Here income and wealth are not an end in themselves, but instruments for other purposes. This perception goes back at least as far as Aristotle. In this view what matters is not what a person has, but what a person is, or can be, and does, or can do. Keynes would share this view due to his ethical milieu. This view of poverty is also distinct from the Neoclassical utility view because Sen's approach deals with what the consumer makes of commodities. Other values that are meaningful for Sen are self-respect and community life.

The difference between real income and actual advantages are personal heterogeneities; environmental diversities; variations in social climate; and distribution within the family (the basic unit of consumption). In contrast, the reference unit in Keynes is either the individual or the country, the second in macroeconomics. For Sen, differences in relational perspectives such as conventions impact both knowledge and ethics. There are different personal and social contexts. If development is accelerated it enhances capital accumulation, but the obstacle to development is structural unemployment; unlike for Keynes, where the obstacle is demand-deficient (involuntary) unemployment. For Sen underdevelopment is related to excessive public intervention and the regulation of economies, which has nothing to do with Keynes's vision. However, in the view of Thirlwall (2007), Keynes prepared the groundwork for the flourishment of development economics. He offered the starting point for understanding income stability by considering that unemployment detains development. This concept of Keynes's perhaps serves as the core for Sen. In modern times development is considered to be determined not only by growth in income—income determination being the first object of analysis, but also by income distribution, health, education, leisure, management, governance, and values as reflected in attitudes and institutions—and Keynes's notion is still valid as his is an ethics of virtue. In other words, development is full of human sense and this statement justifies Sen's inclusion here.

Appendix 12.2 Keynes's Empiricism: National Accounts and His Reasonable View of Econometrics

Some heuristic constructs of the Classical Economy are criticized by many authors for being too abstract and hence difficult to operationalize, especially those related to micro-demand theory, wherein the result is "anything goes." Conversely, part of Keynes's reputation rests on the operationality of his models. He constructs innovative theoretical models, but also provides procedures for testing the validity of his system. There are two related instances: one notion and one field which are particularly suitable for conducting this type of assessment of empirical[7] investigation: national accounts and econometrics. In an Appendix to 'HPW' (1940 [1980]), Keynes proves the validity of his model of income determination by undertaking a numerical account of its elements: consumption, investment, public expenditure, exports, and imports as well as savings. His accounting models set in this manner still dominate income determination and development policies in empirical macro-econometrics. According to Tily (2009), in terms of national accounts, Keynes was a "theoretician, compiler, supporter and user" (Tily 2009, Abstract).

The development of national accounts—a superb heuristics issue—was further advanced by Colin Clarke (1905–1989), Simon Kuznets (1901–1988), James Meade (1907–1995), and Richard Stone (1913–1991), mainly in the late 1920s and the 1930s. Keynes collaborated with Clarke in the early 1930s, whereas the first system of national accounts functioned in the United States in 1947. The national accounts not only measure levels in the components of output (Υ) but also its growth and development. Keynes also left his imprint on the design of public budget statements. National accounts stimulate the compilation of data on financial and socio-economic variables, a task which is typically carried out by national central banks. Uncertainty does not appear as an item in national accounts, but perhaps it may be measured in future interest rates, stock market indices, or exchange rates. The point is to interpret it.

Realism and Econometrics

With respect to econometrics, Keynes first criticized the pioneering models of Jan Tinbergen (1903–1994) in 1939[8]—as a purely formal orthodox branch. Keynes was methodologically opposed to econometrics mainly because he believed in organic or interdependent unities and was skeptical about the indiscriminate use of normal probabilities functions. Keynes's critique of econometrics in 1939 was also about the stability of the representative equations throughout both time and space, an issue associated to both uncertainty and ergodicity (Chapter 2). Other problems were those related to the selection of variables or their manipulation for purposes of verifying the truth. He contended that a previous analysis of circumstances must be conducted before doing econometrics, but he partly changed his attitude when he realized that this branch would be useful for testing his models. Henceforth, he welcomed the use of econometrics for treating variables included in national accounts. This is especially true from 1943 on, when he moved from philosophy to expediency. This type of research emerges from the theoretical scheme offered in *GT* about the components of aggregate demand or output ($\Upsilon = C + I + G + X - IM$).

Returning to Keynes's epistemic stance on econometrics, Keynes maintained that induction is always an extremely difficult procedure (Chapter 6) and this position justifies his aversion to the plain use of econometrics. That is, not only econometric specifications are difficult to be selected, econometric results are also difficult to be interpreted. This critique is equivalent to saying that the behavior of variables is neither uniform nor homogeneous[9] across subperiods. For him, human and social behaviors are mostly discontinuous and asymmetrical, and reality changes from time to time (see Chapter 2). At the end, he suggested caution in interpretation rather than ruling out econometrics (use it!, but consider there are also other methods for verifying statements or measuring change) (Chapter 2). Yet his initial views are correct as many modern researchers avoid the pitfalls of using simple representations of the past.

Keynes thus rejects the unexamined or indiscriminate use of mathematics and statistics for explaining economic phenomena. Prediction can also be undertaken by using qualitative methods and this lends itself to the consideration of uncertainty. George L. S. Shackle (1903–1992), a later explainer of uncertainty, backs Keynes by stating that ignorance of the true probability distribution (Gaussian, normal or standard) must prevent economists from gaining 'absolute' knowledge since the environment is dynamic. Then again the economic topics in Keynes are related to behavioral research under uncertainty. The implication is that unexamined econometrics rests on shaky foundations. Notice the Bayesian statistical models, an alternative to standard models, are consistent with certainty.

An additional explanation for Keynes's core incredulity with respect to econometrics, though at the end he allowed for the advance of empirical macroeconomics as a heuristic resource, is that he abhorred the excessive use of mathematical formalism for explaining economic events, explanations becoming concoctions (see *GT*). This is because formalism is related not only to the Classical conception of probability but also to the notion of economics as a set of atomistic mathematical formulas with no room for modifications except in turbulent periods, which in themselves are only considered as exceptions from equilibria (see Chapter 10). Keynes also conducted at this stage a methodological critique against the use of simplistic econometric methods, denying that neither atomic nor closed systems exist in economies (Chapters 6 and 9) and that accurate predictions cannot be the outcome of models based on Classical probabilities (Chapter 6), certainty (Chapter 9), or ergodicity (see Davidson 2002; see Chapter 10).

The retrograde position of simplistic econometricians is also related to the exclusive choice of logical contextual analyses in detriment of contextual narratives for interpreting economic phenomena, wherein Keynes favors the latter. Orthodox econometrics is the science apt for measuring the extent of dependence between explanatory and explained variables assuming that certainty is itself a presupposition that is useful for both explanation and prediction! However, even uncertainty is uncertain. Hence Keynes at this stage became the anti-priori econometrician in terms of regressions; that is, he opposed the automatic assumption that Υ is a function of X ($\Upsilon = f(X)$) without previously resorting to economic theory, not to mention that causality may be doubly induced and erratic and that the Gaussian Bell (Normal Curve of Probabilities) is a 'physicalist' construction (see Chapter 6).

Mr. Tinbergen and Followers

The Keynes–Tinbergen debate occurred between 1938 and 1940. Keynes contended that unexamined results have little value since methods must be tested beforehand. Tinbergen answered in a Friedmanite[10] manner that results are the 'definitive' proof. Keynes also conducted a critique of econometrics not only in terms of the assumption of independence between two variables but also wondering why the relationship between X and Υ must be linear. Keynes evaluated the twin assumptions of homogeneity in variables (X and Υ are always comparable in conventional wisdom) and their movements (ΔX is comparable to $\Delta\Upsilon$; Δ meaning increase in). This was also a critique to Walras's economics, for whom systems of linear equations about *n* markets explained by *n* variables interact and provide results without considering uncertainty (or the role of money in general equilibrium) or questioning the static dependence among those *n* variables. Moreover, it was necessary according to Keynes to know before doing a regression what the causes for choosing variables and parameters are, and to identify whether they are measurable or tractable. In other words, the exogenous and endogenous variables (X and Υ, respectively) must be identified by way of economic analysis instead of through mathematical procedures. Another critique was that econometrics measures equations by means of either path dependence or lags (explaining X_t as function of X_{t-1}, X_{t-2}), but it is obvious that a variable's behavior is influenced by its past behavior.

The most important philosophical critique of econometrics was that Tinbergen conducts inductive generalizations (from the independent X to dependent Υ) when regressing those variables for obtaining causal explanations of behavior, but Keynes's view—partly derived from Hume's skepticism (Chapters 4 and 6)—was that the intermediate steps must not be taken for granted in this empirical methodology. Keynes also rejected both apriorism and induction, based on his own insights in *TP*, considering them as raw methods that pale in the face of realism (Chapter 6). In some Neoclassical models, econometrics relies on axioms and certainty. But no axioms exist in social science since phenomena are organic and unpredictable, according to Keynes. Furthermore, for Garrone et al. (2004), Keynes ascertains observations must be scattered through different periods, thus mixing stable with unstable moments. Notice that the number of observations must be large. Tinbergen wanted to mathematize the *Fundamental Equations* in *TM* (see Chapter 7), which is the prototype—reduced—model of output determination ($Y = C + I + G + X - IM$) assumed in *GT* (Chapter 2) and exposed in the appendix of 'HPW' (this chapter). Keynes had conceived his psychological consumption function ($C = Ca + bY$; where Y is output or income, and Ca is autonomous consumption) in mathematical terms. At the end—after 1940—the model of output determination was operationalized and tested in econometric terms but assuming methodological caution. For deepeening matters, please see Tinbergen (1942, 1947), and Muñoz 2020 on the debates between Keynes and Tinbergen.

According to Garrone et al. (2004), Tjallin Koopmans (1903–1985) provides a more systematic logic of the methods employed in 1942, perhaps recognizing the role of the expectations and the state of confidence in macroeconomics (Koopmans 1942). Trygve Haavelmo (1911–1999) eschews many of these methodological problems in 1943, despite their continued relevance (Haavelmo 1943). Thus, Keynes's summarizing critique of econometrics in his communication with Harrod (Keynes 1938), in both essence and method, contends that generalizations are difficult to believe whereas prediction is an uncertain task. Uncertainty is ignored in conventional econometrics since it is not identical to the classical variance, σ^2 with respect to the mean, μ (by means of which orthodox econometricians capture risk, not uncertainty) unless the heterogeneity of variances across observations (or errors, σ^2) is admitted, which is not the case in standard econometrics. They immediately correct them making them appear as noise and eschewing reality. Hence uncertainty is normally neglected as it would break the Classical Gaussian statistical core.[11] Conversely, for Keynes errors are not unsystematic and possess a qualitative dimension, waiting for specific remedies.

Keynes outlined in a letter to Harrod (Keynes 1938) an apparently contradictory definition of economics. He contends there that economics is both a branch of logic and moral science. This means that he is grounded in his epistemological and ethical assumptions to find the essence of the economic method. He conducts along the way a critical assessment of Edgeworth's work, since the latter attempts to mathematize economics in the way that physics is mathematized. For Keynes prose and mathematics must cohabitate. He also defines economic science as a mode of thought, which means that it is more than either the analysis of a fixed mathematical set of equations or a manual comprised of rigid rules (Keynes 1938). According to Garrone et al. (2004), Keynes required methods and assumptions in the practice of econometrics to be both interlinked and precise, respectively. This vision arose from his attempts to unify theoretical and empirical approaches in terms of the struggle against unemployment and extreme polarized cycles, aiming to leave a message of moderation on the epistemological ground. Like all interesting things, econometrics must be handled and interpreted with care. The time is right for dealing with another of his interests in the 1940s: aesthetics.

Appendix 12.3: The Arts and *CEMA*

This Appendix does focus on the application of Keynes's aesthetic insights as championed in Chapters 8 and 11. If ethics deals with the moral principles governing an individual's behavior, aesthetics is concerned with the nature and appreciation of art, beauty, and good taste in the forms of representation, expression, and shape. Ethics and aesthetics are thus connected because they are related to values and intuition even though the former is about actions whereas the latter is about sensorial applied qualities. Art, like nature, expresses what words cannot. Both affect us at the emotional and cognitive levels and are associated with states of the mind or soul. Both entail critical judgments, may take 'irrational' forms, and require creativity and originality to do *good*. The arts also exhibit both beauty and sublimity. At the individual level, the arts are related to freedom but are also a form of capturing (or fleeing from) the uncertainty pervasive in the world. Whereas ethics may be private, aesthetics is a form of communication of cosmological, existential, ethical, or political stances.

In addition to their aesthetic value, the arts must be financially viable to survive in the real world. Keynes understands that every market is chaotic as it may experience non-exceptional shocks, even the arts market.

However, every market has regularities as well. In this view convention is a guideline for succeeding in market exchange even in troubled times. Keynes, in the mid-1940s, opined that the arts market is structured in many ways as a lottery. This is a microeconomic application of his concept of uncertainty being in this case due to the lack of public information, which generates unstable markets. In other words, successful investment in the arts market is a game for the capitalist agents who take advantage of asymmetries in information between buyers and sellers (Moggridge 2005). As a case in point, Keynes possessed a concentrated portfolio of artistic works as a by-product of the power of his public relations. Keynes took advantage in 1918 of depressed prices in works of art, perhaps due to the imminence of the First World War, by purchasing continental paintings made by the French painters Paul Cézanne, Eugène Delacroix, Dominique Ingres, and Edgar Degas, reportedly holding two pieces by the Spanish-born Picasso (one in 1937). Paintings may be the least liquid assets, but not in the presence of extreme uncertainty. While he personally appreciated ballet and collected paintings and rare books, he also desired for the arts to be disseminated to the masses. In this way Keynes, harkening back to the 'Locke Connection', honored the insights of John Stuart Mill on the dissemination of public education.

'But Money Is the Means...'

Keynes participated in the foundation of the London Artist's Association (1925). Even more importantly he became the chairman of the Council for the Encouragement of Music and the Arts (CEMA) in 1940. His mission was to ensure the patronage of the arts in Britain. His purpose was to raise spirits through music, drama, and pictures. In June 1945 he launched the Arts Council. In a sort of homecoming to his juvenilia, Keynes became president of CEMA and was involved in the Covent Garden renaissance. As president, he intended to protect culture from superficiality in the new age. According to the *Arts Policy Special* (2017), his early priority was to protect the creative liberty of artists. He wanted the principle of silence (privacy?) to be respected and aimed to rescue companies from bankruptcy while rebuilding theatres, concert halls, and galleries. Since his time in the Arts Council Keynes wanted to promote the arts on the political agenda without being subjected to political control. CEMA supported only second-class amateur production; the idea was to offer opportunities to both young and lesser-known people. From the time that he backed The Arts Cambridge Theatre, he conveyed a trans-generational message taking advantage that demand had grown. According to Arts Professional (2017), the demand for the arts soon flourished due to increasing social mobility post-war, the growth of the mass media, and the gradual shift from the heavy industries to the creative industries.

In *CEMA* he designed a model for the patronage of the arts in early 1946, addressed to support private individuals and privately operated arts institutions. His model consisted of grants coming from public funds obtained through semi-autonomous government bodies (see *GT*) but conceded to private individuals and privately owned enterprises. Keynes thus became an arts entrepreneur. Keynes was also behind the Temporary Arts Society. With this new frame of mind, Keynes gave a speech in 1945 on his purpose of enhancing the practice of the arts in Britain. His idea was to investigate how cooperation with government departments might work.[13] In contrast to his former elitism, in 1944 he favored democracy over aristocracy in the arts (Appendix 11.1).

Keynes had evolved with respect to his 1938 views if for no other reason than being able to synthesize all his theoretical and practical knowledge from a wider angle (see Chapter 11). His philosophy of practice gave him the opportunity to appreciate the arts but always with an eye on the difficult issues arising from their enhancement. He wanted to financially support the arts without sacrificing their excellence. He realized the arts go beyond understanding, ignited by inspiration and unconscious processes. He was able to see that the artistic nature of impulses is what distinguishes us from simple souls. In summary, the arts in Keynes's view are closely connected to education, ethics, elitism, social concerns, and altruism but also to both financial and logistic expediency. Keynes's interest in the arts, partly inspired by his mates in Bloomsbury, demonstrates that he was involved in many facets of knowledge. This interest was not new: he is following the spirit of his early writing 'A theory of beauty' (1905). He was surrounded by artists—especially Roger Fry, Vanessa Bell, and Duncan Grant—all of whom loved expressions of beauty that were full of social, emotional, and intellectual but especially aesthetic meaning. At last Keynes fulfilled his interest in love, friendship, and beauty in the 1940s as enunciated in 'MEB' by means of aesthetics. What ensues is a recapitulation of Keynes's philosophy in Chapter 13, also outlining its current interest (the force of new interpretations) in Appendix 13.1.

Notes

1. The dynamism of the times exacerbates Keynes's flexibility of mind.
2. Europe was a debtor to Britain, and Britain to the US.
3. An expression coined by George L. Shackle (1967 [2010]).
4. The White Paper is related to the 'Churchill White Paper' (1922), meant to present policy preferences before introducing legislation in Britain. It is not related to the *White Plan*, devised by Harry Dexter White (1892–1948) in the United States.
5. He thereby validated the continuous message of the 'Locke Connection.'
6. Co-authored by Evsey Domar (1914–1997) in 1946.
7. For most members of the 'Locke Connection', only what can be measured is useful for undertaking decisions.
8. Lawrence Klein (1920–2013) would claim that this empirical type of exercises aided to validate the Keynesian Revolution.
9. Locke believed like Newton in the existence of uniform and homogeneous movements (Chapter 3).
10. Friedman was not concerned about assumptions but about results, although he was also against excessive formalism in economics (Appendix 10.1).
11. This mistake is committed by conventional financers who do not distinguish between risk and uncertainty.
12. Conversely, political philosophy is the ethical expression of a whole society. However for Keynes, the difference between political philosophy and ethics is that morals refers to our form of conduct unto others whereas religion is a form of conduct unto ourselves ('MEB').
13. This is another real example of the 'socialisation of investment' in *GT*: collecting funds with efficiency.

References

Sources

Arts Professional. 2017. "Arts Policy Special—Is Keynes Dream Still Alive?" https://www.artsprofessional.co.uk/magazine/article/arts-policy-special-keynes%19s-dream-still-alive. Accessed 17 July 2017.

Beveridge, William H. 1944. *Full Employment in a Free Society*. London: Allen & Unwin.

Chote, Robert. 1994. "Economics: A Missing Link in the White Paper." *Independent*, Saturday, 28 May 1994. https://www.independent.co.uk/news/business/economics-a-missing-link-in-the-white-paper-1439232.html. Accessed 17 August 2019.

Davidson, Paul. 2002. *Financial Markets, Money and the Real World*. Chentelham, UK: Edward Elgar.

De Ugarte, David. 2011. "Lord Keynes especulador post-impresionista." Retrieved from https://www.mundoclásico.com.

Garrone Giovanna, Roberto Marchionatti, and Ricardo Bellofiore. 2004. "Keynes on econometric method. A reassessment of his debate with Tinbergen and econometricians, 1938–1943." CESMEP Working Papers 200401, University of Turin.

Harcourt, Geoffrey C., and Peter Riach (eds.). 1997. *A 'Second' Edition of the General Theory, Volume I*. New York: Routledge.

Harrod, Roy. 1939. "An Essay in Dynamic Theory." *The Economic Journal* 49, no. 93 (March): 14–33.

Haavelmo, T. 1943. "The statistical implications of a system of simultaneous equations". Econometrica. Reprinted in *The Foundations of Econometric Analysis*, edited by D.F. Hendry and M.S. Morgan, 440–453. Cambridge: Cambridge University Press, 1995. 11, No. 1: 1–43.

Keynes, John Maynard. 1925. *The Economic Consequences of Mr. Churchill*. London: Hogarth.

———. 1936 [1973]. *The Collected Writings of John Maynard Keynes (CW) Vol. 7: The General Theory of Employment, Interest and Money*, edited by Elizabeth Johnson (19–28) and Daniel E. Moggridge (15–18). London: Macmillan, for the Royal Economic Society.

———. 1938. "J. M. Keynes's Letter to Harrod." 4 July 1938. In *CW, Vol. 14 The General Theory and After: Part II. Defence and Development*, 295–97. London: Basingstoke.

———. 1940 [1980]. "How to Pay for the War: A Radical Plan for the Chancellor of the Exchequer." In *CW, Vol. 9: Essays in Persuasion*, 367–439. London: Basingstoke. https://archive.org/details/in.ernet.dli.2015.499597.

———. 1944. "White Paper, Economy: 1944 Employment White Paper [MT's annotated copy]." Margaret Thatcher Foundation, 1944 May 1 Mo, Archive (Thatcher MSS). https://www.margaretthatcher.org/document/110368.

Koopmans, Tjalling C. 1942. "Serial correlation and quadratic forms in normal variables". *Annals of Mathematical Statistics. Institute of Mathematical Statistics* 13, no. 1: 14–33,

Moggridge, Daniel E. 2005. "Keynes, the Arts, and the State." *History of Political Economy* 37 (3): 535–55.

Muñoz-Bandala, Jesús. 2020. "A complex but interesting relation: Keynes, mathematics, and statistics." In *How Economists Explain with Mathemathics or Should They?*, REEM IV, no. 1: 104–30.

Peden, George C. 1944 [1988]. "The 1944 White Paper on Employment Policy." In *Keynes, the Treasury and British Economic Policy: Studies in Economic and Social History*. London: Palgrave. https://link.springer.com/chapter/10.1007%2F978-1-349-07019-0_6. Accessed 13 May 2020.

Shackle, George L. S. 1967 [2010]. *The Years of High Theory: Invention and Tradition in Economic Thought 1926–1939*. Cambridge: Cambridge University Press.

Skidelsky, Robert. 2001. John Maynard Keynes: Fighting for Britain, 1937: 1946. London: Macmillan.

Skidelsky, Robert. 2016. "How Keynes Came to Britain." *Review of Keynesian Economics* 4, no. 1 (Spring): 4–19.

Temin, Peter, and David Vines. 2016. "Keynes and the European Economy." *Review of Keynesian Economics* 4, no. 1 (Spring): 36–49.

Thirlwall, Anthony P. 2007. "Keynes and economic development." *Economía Aplicada (Brazilian Journal of Applied Economics)* 11, no. 3: 447–57.

Tinberger, Jan. 1942. "Critical remarks on some business cycle theories." *Econometrica* 10, no. 2: 129–46.

———. 1947. "The use of correlation analysis in economic research." EkonomiskTidskrift XLIX: 173–92.

Tily, Geoffrey. 2009. "John Maynard Keynes and the Development of National Accounts in Britain, 1895–1941." *Review of Income and Wealth* 55, no. 2 (June): 331–59.

CHAPTER 13

Conclusions on Keynes's Legacy

Is reality a construction? According to Keynes, the peculiarity of Newton was that he remained immersed in the solution of a quandary up until the phenomenon revealed its permanent secret to him, but this happened in the physical world, in the universe. The social world is ruled by ideas according to Keynes's celebrated Chapter 24, but ideas come unsuspected sources, are in permanent flux, and must be dangerous (according to Oscar Wilde). Some of Keynes's ideas are brilliant such as uncertainty and the emphasis on the short period, some are arguably realistic such as casino economies, and some are amoral such as eugenics. All his ideas are articulated and disgorge into ethics. If Keynes ever taught us something it is that economics has a huge potential as a science, and this is not an economic contention but a philosophical one. The story goes as follows. After the mercantilists in the sixteenth century, political economy starts to distinguish itself from philosophy, with the exception of John Stuart Mill, leaving a gap that would be filed by Keynes. Keynes teaches us to apprehend the essence of such concepts as time, good, beauty, knowledge, probability, happiness, and measurement. He also teaches that *good* must be intuited. Keynes demonstrates that stability is transitory but most importantly that it is something to be gained. He demonstrates that politics is related to expediency. Keynes is another philosopher teaching us that the process of scientific discovery does not necessarily belong to the

J. Muñoz-Bandala, *Keynes's Evolutionary Spirit*, Palgrave Insights into Apocalypse Economics, https://doi.org/10.1007/978-3-030-90150-9_13

realms of either realism or rationalism. In any event he transited from the use of pure logic in the *Treatise on Probability* to employing intuitive and observational insights in *GT*. What kind of remarks does Keynes produce? We avoid casting the doubts that arise from a subjective interpretation by using Lakatosian methodology. But if the interpretation of this author does discern a direction, it is Keynes's creation of categories and preaching of an evolutionary moral progress by means of virtue. Definitively Keynes is a non-conventional philosopher, but what is one going to do to conclude about this complex information?

The aim of this book is to delineate how Keynes's interests and contributions purposefully change throughout time. The analytical tools used here for describing Keynes's philosophical career are both dynamic and interrelated accordingly with the postulate that his philosophical path is full of life. Complexity, evolution, and uncertainty (and surprise) which were placed by him at his core, require a real understanding of life. There are three stages in Keynes's philosophical and psychological progress: Individualistic, nationalist, and internationalist. He was also always in a transition since his work comprised a harmonic arrangement of themes. His spirit was evolutionary but also unitary, a contention that is illustrated in the ensuing paragraphs. The philosophical themes he studied, and which left an indelible imprint on the world, are how humans should behave; the essence of things; genuine knowledge; the principles of reasoning; societies mode of living; and the art of life and the culture encompassing human activities. After this recapitulation, we turn to the rounded examination of his work and activities which is a fascinating exercise. Appendix 13.1 is an interlude about the relation between Keynes and the economists of the twentieth-century. Modernity resonates in this brief essay.

13.1 The Conclusion Is an Integration of Insights

Any book must be written out of a passionate conviction for the relevance of a comprehensive subject. The motivations for writing a new book on Keynes are the outlines of the strength of his ethical legacy, the magnet of his personality, and his triumph over both a transitional society and an immature science. He generated policies and new theories. Since the beginning Keynes applied Moore's unworldly philosophy to events in real life, especially Moore's ultimate idea of organic unities (as can be seen in the former 12 Chapters). Like Smith he synthesized the knowledge of many thinkers, but possibly in a more critical and dialectical manner. Keynes highlighted typically unnoticed differences. This ability arose perhaps from his perception of the dual nature of movements: quantitative and qualitative. The point is that when undertaking the task of distinguishing, he conducted a redefinition of social concepts which is contingent upon interpretation. However, and this is only superficially contradictory, he proposed a single and evolving interrelated cosmology. For that purpose, he moved from individual consciousness to an interest in social quandaries and a concern for international problems. His perception of time and transition normally underscored the relevance of his ideas.

Deepening matters, Keynes moved from an intuitionist atomic cosmic vision to the envisagement of an organic system outside of a vacuum. His focus shifted from an internal to an external state of mind by defining the main steps in knowledge. Thus, his work is as holistic as that of anyone else, but Keynes has many types of influences and touched many social, logical, and mathematical fields. This book integrates his accounts in philosophy to prove that Keynes's thought possesses structure and dynamic—shifting—continuity, and therefore is evolutionary. A spirit is only captured by tracing its evolution and hence its essence. Keynes himself moved beyond his own experiences, creating an *SRP* that is universally applicable to many fields of knowledge. He submitted a new paradigm wherein rationalism is an imperfect guide for understanding life. His *SRP* thus rejects conventional wisdom (Chapter 2),[1] and his economics was the engine for attaining his ethical ideals (Skidelsky 2016). While rebuilding economics Keynes suffered a spiritual transformation propelled by his philosophical disquietudes.

Then again, his *leitmotiv* was alleviating human suffering embodied by the scourge of unemployment as an evil produced by the financial capitalistic society (see Appendix 13.1), for which he found the origins, repercussions, and cures. He affirmed that '[t]he cause of unemployment is ... high interest rates' (*CW XII*, pp. 37–43). He exhibited an evolutionary unity of thought and action while being at the service of values, knowledge, and human freedom (Chapter 11). He faced knowledge gaps, re-shaping his relationship with his beliefs many times, and continuously modifying his starting point (Chapters 7 and 9). He then took advantage of lost opportunities, wrong turns, and blind alleys, almost always supporting his stances, prospects, historical interpretations (Chapter 5), and ideas (Chapter 9). Hopefully, this book may add a grain of sand to the aim of reinstating the value of Keynes's legacy.

13.2 A Personal Interpretation

This is also an active interpretation. Keynes had been in imaginative places where no one has been before or since, permitting him to herald new conceptions of human wealth, dignity, and identity. This conclusion is drawn from the process of visualizing his work as a unity. Since Keynes was the initial piece in the making of macroeconomics with the provision of a new core, his work must be restored to macroeconomics books just as the history of economic thought is gaining preeminence since 2007.[2] He obtains some superficial mentions in those books. Why reinstating Keynes's in common knowledge? Among the issues analyzed in this book in this respect are intentionality, foundations, legacy, reception, and acceptance. He went through the essence of intuition and induction by studying probabilities of action under uncertainty in the face of moral choices, concluding that convention reduces uncertainty, the topic which he then left to the world. His final word was that uncertainty is qualitative.

In worldly terms, Keynes's economics returned to the center of the international arena in the aftermath to the crisis of 2007 (see Appendix 13.1) due to both its common sense and its ability to predict several facets associated with the reality of economics. This re-emergence permitted the profession to classify his legacy as progressive according to the methodological criteria proposed by Lakatos (see Backhouse 1994; Hendry 1993; Blaug 1991; Hands 1996). Going in retrospect, Keynes's career in economics experienced many turning points. But he had an impact on policymaking especially in the *Treatise in Money* (1930), wherein he studied a mundane question: the dynamic structure of modern monetary economies. Another turning point of his is the *Principle of Effective Demand* in *GT* (1936) as the cornerstone for his theoretical revolution in economics (Chapter 9). But his legacy even in terms of principles is interdisciplinary. One of Keynes's principles is the *Principle of Limited Independent Variety* (TE) or of *Indifference*, which is strategically assumed throughout *A Treatise on Probability* (Chapter 6). Yet another is the *Principle of Organic Uniformity* in human beings as exposed in his early articles, for example, in 'Miscellanea Ethica' (Chapters 4 and 11), which somehow contradicts his notions of heterogeneity and asymmetries in social processes.

The connecting thread is that Keynes addressed the foundations of economic philosophy, knowing that science must be oriented toward the resolution of problems. The social evils in his schemes were uncertainty, ignorance, irrationality, and thoughtless and unexamined traditionalism. For solving these defies, he created a complex philosophical encompassing system offering contentions on such subfields as finance, psychology, the arts, and international relations. For Keynes methodological thinking was the application of Moore's doctrine of organic unities to day-to-day issues, taking into consideration the Burkean ascertainment that the long term does not yield predictable patterns in social events. For O'Donnell (1991), the distinctive theory of rationality found at the heart of Keynes's philosophy molded his discretionary notion of policymaking, his down-to-earth scientific method, and his expedient politics. Other authors contend that Keynes's methodology was empiricist but this author instead contends that Keynes leaves room for the consideration of irrational forces at play. Despite the heterogeneity of these interpretations, the interconnectedness of Keynes's core ideas—uncertainty and organicism—explains the survival of his *SRP*. All his insights place the ethics of virtue at the center of the stage. The dominant intellectual influences on Keynes in this aspect are Hume, Moore, and Ramsey. Still this study makes visible the path in British 'intelligentsia' running from Locke's empiricism to Lakatos's Falsificationism (Chapters 3 and 4).

Concerns on the ethical value of money, the ignorance about the characteristics of human nature, and the visualization of international coordination in terms of policymaking in the emergence of crises have returned Keynes's work to the center of the stage for explaining the consequences of instability in economic systems (see Appendix 13.1). His prominence also had political implications. Moreover, the two facets of knowledge, namely diagnosis and cure, were amalgamated for him (only in some occasions had political economists been practical). Perhaps his most relevant appraisal in this sense was that of both the recollection and processing of knowledge as encompassed in his interpretation of Hume's problem of induction. This critique gave birth to *TP* which permitted him to obtain a clear vision of knowledge in logic, and which paved the road for such nuclear concepts as uncertainty, denying that knowledge is bi-polar but stating that it is fuzzy.

Reflection gives unity to the inferential understanding of both ideas and facts, and then the transit to practice is ensured. Contrariwise, moral beliefs do not require classification because they vary across space and through time (except in the sense that they emerge from virtue according to Keynes), which signifies they are not inferential. The implication is that a cosmovision mixes philosophy, ideology, science, morals, and life experiences, and this is especially true in the case of Keynes. But what sparked Keynes's intuitive creativity? Was it due to his origins, his environment, his legacy, or the challenges of his age? Method and creativity go hand in hand, but also inner forces matter (see Mini 1994). He is the first monetary economist to be based on a philosophical vision, evolving from an egotistic position to a concern for cooperation in world affairs. These characterizations may demonstrate that Keynes's spirit is interconnected; rich in sources, interpretations, perspectives, and focus (at the individual, societal, and international levels). His body of work is more than a worn collection of papers because he is constantly revising the foundations of his theories which eventually become the backbone of the orthodoxy. In this sense Keynes was a trend setter. As can be read in 'Obituary,' *The Economist* (November 26, 2013), when he was accused of being orthodox, he replied 'Orthodox has caught up with me.'

13.3 Probable Opposing Views

Probability is an epistemic devise. The question on whether his legacy is either evolutionary or revolutionary may be arduous to answer except if one realizes his path to knowledge passed through contradictory phases which together formed a long-term upward trend. But with a high probability an evolution involves some regression. All evolutions are indirect and more than discontinuous. For example, Keynes abandoned most of his formerly deep-rooted convictions in 'My Early Beliefs.' For Ward (1972), Keynesianism is a formalist revolution, widely considered as an integrated Lakatosian *SRP* rather than a spontaneous and isolated Kuhnian paradigm (Chapter 2). For Backhouse (1993, 2007), Keynes's innovative modified *SRP* is useful for assessing the relevance of modern macroeconomics due to its conceptual solidity.

Throughout his career, Keynes filed many explanatory vacuums in certain fields. In this sense he was continuous. The common perception is that Keynes only produced unique and innovative insights on his operational concepts (positive heuristics), which were the means for transforming economics. These include aggregate demand, government expenditure, interest rates, the *Keynes Effect*, financial variables, and discretionary policies, to name a few. However, Keynes anticipates many 'modern' (core) philosophical issues, according to Hausmann (2007, 2008, 2016). He contributed perceptiveness to the epistemology of economics, to the dichotomy between the values of reasoning versus automatic acceptance of cause, to social scientific nonnaturalism, and to abstraction and *ceteris paribus*. But he had great bases. The specific legacies of the men that Keynes admires are those of Moore and Burke, their imprint on Keynes is noticeable and is outlined throughout this book. In this sense, the intellectual image of Keynes offered in this book is a balanced view of his contributions and borrowed insights in the realms of science and philosophy.

The apparently small discrete (but resonant) changes in Keynes's thinking are most evident in *ECP* (Chapter 5), *GT* (Chapter 9), and MEB (1938), his breakthrough works, but they are ubiquitous throughout his *oeuvre*. Perhaps from those outstanding examples, some writers conclude that Keynes's trajectory is discontinuous (*GT* is a mutant in Samuelson's words, Samuelson 1946). Small changes undertaken throughout the way, for example, in 1933, however, can they add up to an affirmation of his uneven evolutionary stance, especially in ethics as Keynes is above all a human being.

Reflecting on this book, some chapters are more difficult to read, some others are shorter than the rest. But life in organicism is discontinuous and asymmetric, and this is one of the teachings of Keynes. In this vein, this book is written in many styles as a scientific report, in prose, and as an economic treatise reflecting the evolutionary trait of Keynes's *oeuvre*. Keynes's *aficionados* can go to any chapter of this book to find their preferred version of Keynes's bequeath. The writings of Keynes shed light on the complex aspects of Capitalism, which can now be more widely examined thanks to his contributions, perhaps confined to the industrialized world. Keynes's insights on these discussions were curiously cutting-edge because he reinforced economics with human considerations, though he never meditated on some relevant social issues, for example, the authenticity of the foundations of the legal system. Nonetheless, his apparently mundane conclusions, as proven here to be based on philosophical considerations, have far-reaching extra-economic implications in terms of social application. In economics we have Smith, Mill, Marshall, Walras, Marx, Schumpeter, and Hayek along with such modern authors as Samuelson, Friedman, Krugman and Stiglitz, but due to the journey traveled through these pages which leads to a unique modern philosophy, Keynes remains the only one (with the exception of the highly interdisciplinary and individualistic Mill) whom this author would call a genius.

13.4 Probable New Avenues for Research

Keynes examined consciousness in society and the world as proof of his belief in organic unities. But other fields of knowledge can help to clarify Keynes's concepts; sociology and physics, for example; the latter with respect to the essence of non-self-regulating systems. A second contribution would be as follows: Keynes, as most adults, moved from focusing on himself to concern for others and social systems. This ascertainment is partly built on the insights about Keynes's intellectual development by Bateman and Davis (eds.) (1991). Davis focuses on Keynes's philosophical conversion from the belief in the intuition-induction dichotomy to the reliance on convention as the explanation for human behavior. In this view, Keynes progressed from the study of a closed world to an understanding of an open system wherein uncertainty prevails, and this had an impact in his personal life. This theme deserves further research.

For Keynes, no fixed policy prescriptions, universal ethical mandates, or epistemological rules are valid since his thought moves freely in both time and space even to the point of being considered inconsistent—yet never devoid of sense or innovativeness. In other words, his emphasis on demolishing theory for the sake of evaluating scientific evolution produced more dynamic methodologies. The understanding of Keynes's dynamic system, for example, as applied to policymaking, may prove to be a useful theme. Another epistemological problem that can be further examined is that many scientists, including economists, recognize the complexity of their subjects but still retain the framework of rationality, according to Hausman (2008). Hausman (2012) also affirms that orthodox theories typically have not been falsified. Instead, oftentimes theories have been 'superseded' by inferior theories. Is this the case of the Keynes's *SRP*? A further investigation may be addressed to find out whether Keynes's theories and concomitant empirical predictions lend themselves more to observation than others and hence are fundamentally operational.

Keynes traced his own evolutionary path as he did not share the same mindset as the *state-of-the-arts* in the anthropology and ethics which are implicit in modern economic orthodoxy. For instance, the *Homus Economicus* conception underpinning the orthodox view of the world can be widened by acknowledging Keynes's notion of labor as a moral and spiritual activity since humans are a part of nature. Finally, the intellectual context of a thinker reflects the history of philosophy and is akin to the history of ideas. The aim of an intellectual biographer or a cultural historian is to seek to place concepts, texts, and activities of the past into multiple contexts, including the present. This interpretation of Keynes's work resignifies his ideas by contrasting them with those of other thinkers. This speculative field (undertaken in Appendices 10.1 and 11.1), leaves room for a further understanding of Keynes. The large Appendix 13.1 portrays a bridge to modernity in terms of the rescue of Keynes's contention. It speaks by itself and leaves room for further investigations.

Appendix 13.1: Uncertainty Revisited and the Force of New Interpretations: Keynes's Relevance in an Epoch Characterized by Recurrent (Financial) Crises

Keynes disseminated the formula for combating the impact of the Great Depression (see Davidson 2007, 2009): the enhancement of investment via interest rate reductions. But is this formula useful for solving our current problems? The ensuing paragraphs deal with the relationship between Keynes's predictions and contemporary financial crises, which define modernity while reviving Keynesian problems. Crises retard growth generating unemployment, and give rise to world uncertainty, increasing nationalism. In addition, modern financial crises—especially that of 2008, which is in need of rethinking—are not only about bad economics (as Keynes says about the Classical approach) but are related to political, epistemological, ethical, and ecological concerns. It is time to conduct an anatomy of Keynes's gift for prophecy. According to Mann (2019), the resurrection of Keynes and Keynesianism in the wake of the recent financial crisis indexes the similarities between the present conjuncture and the Great Depression. Let's leave now the remote past.

Preamble: From Keynes to the Modern World (1990–2008)

The background to the crises that occurred in the 1980s and the 1990s is comprised of private capital accumulation fostered by public policies, inexpedient macroeconomic policies, and irrational financial deregulation, leading to uncontrolled or uncontrollable (but somehow invisible) financialization. This is to some extent a prediction of Keynes (1936, Chapter 12). Consider for example, the power of the concept of liquidity preference.

A consequence of the dissemination of the Keynes's message is the exaltation of the power of money, which ended up as financialization, meaning that financial developments will affect the real system in casino-type economies (Keynes 1936, Chapter 12). The challenge is defining financialization for our times. We seek 'to distinguish between two broad perspectives on financialization. The first takes the view that financialization relates to the growth of the financial sector in its operations, power, etc. ... The second perspective views financialization (financialized capitalism) as a stage or epoch of capitalism dating from circa 1980' (Sawyer 2013). Financialization is defined as 'a recognition that finance has come to play a key role on the modern capitalist economy ... The main themes in the literature on financialization ... [may] ... lack a coherent account of financial processes that goes beyond the evidence of financial activity' (Michell and Toporowski 2017, Abstract).

Financialization leads to financial crises in the 1990s when the system enters firstly into a confusing turbulent phase and then into a corrective stage. If the mechanics of financial crises lies in investigating why speculation dominates, policies are based on discretion, and the use of money is misleading, then it can be said that these topics were dealt with before Keynes, but no one covered them in such a unitary manner since. The changeover from Keynes to Friedman and the New classical authors (see Chapter 10) in the times of a new consideration of stagflation in the late 1970s produced a penchant for self-regulation in the financial sector propitiating a divorce between the real and financial sectors. But the self-regulatory influences of such authors as Friedman and the Neoclassical prevailing in the 1980s were beyond academic scenarios since they permeated the world of policies in a non-Keynesian manner, though they did not follow rules either. Keynes suggested that interest rates must be consistently lowered (Keynes 1936 [1973], Chapter 24) and stable, but at this stage (late 1970s) rates were either high (set for inflation mitigation) or fluctuating along with the prices of other financial assets. These factors generated incentives for globalized speculators and this would become a trend which imploded in the early 1990s producing recurring economic meltdowns. But what were the characteristics of the transition from Keynes to deregulated scenarios, ultimately leading to financialization?

Kregel (2008) states: [T]'he evolution of housing finance in the United States from the deregulation of the financial system in the 1970s to the breakdown of the savings and loan industry and the development of ... government-sponsored enterprise securitization and the private financial system ... is a background to the forces that have produced the present system of residential housing finance.' Continuing with Kregel (2008), 'the dramatic fall in prices ... led to requests for the banks and the ... insurers to meet their commitments to credit default ... [T]his led to the fall in prices ... and the rapid rise in interest rate spreads ..., to calm markets, major ... banks were led to borrow equity capital from sovereign wealth funds and foreign investors at above-market rates.' At this stage, uncertainty was only affecting the financial system, but organicist confidence loss would suddenly appear. In Keynes's time, the spatial sequence is industry, politics, and policy. In our time that sequence is propelled by artificial and unreliable finance. A chronicle of crises ensues to clarify this point.

The Crises of the 1990s and 2000s and the Generation Models

The 2008 subprime lending crisis was anticipated in a minor scale by the financial crisis of Mexico 1994 (although its effects were very severe in Latin America) along with subsequent crises in the developing world. In the Mexican episode, the speculative vehicle—false money and credit as mobiles that lent themselves to speculative purposes—was the exchange rate. Overvaluation of the currency and bad assessment triggered the massacre revealing weaknesses in policies and in the performance of enterprises. When growth as seen in the stability of the Mexican currency was perceived as spurious the crisis ignited, showing macroeconomic underperformance and bringing about instability in 1995, namely a severe fall in output and employment coupled with inflation. The first 'modern' financial crisis was followed by other crises in the developing world, namely East Asia in 1997, Brazil 1998, Russia 1999, Turkey 2000, Argentina 2001, all of them with epicenter in the financial sector (Krugman 1999; Dornbusch 2002). The term 'modern' means in this context that perceptions are key, like in say, the paintings of Picasso. The difficulties in these economies were overstated by 'animal spirits,' and after the gold rush (the speculators did not follow the game, they started and controlled the game) the effects were once again spread onto the real sectors, revealing inefficiency and obsolescence. Moreover, a lot of them generated contagion. At the time it was thought that the crises would not be replicated in the developed world.

The Keynes point is that saving might not be channeled into productive investment and the concomitant disequilibrium may be aggravated by spurious hoarding in the form of unreliable financial instruments. This is exactly the case of the more general crisis that took place in 2007 in the North-Western world, and beyond. Its epicenter was a problem of Lehman Brothers in the financial system (with the housing sector as the mobile), being translated onto crises in the real sector and in weak economies, bringing about lack of confidence and of course uncertainty and contagion, fueled by adjusting perceptions. This crisis demonstrated that a self-regulation system was a myth but paradoxically verified organicism exists in the economic world. This macro-financial episode was propelled by 'animal spirits' (Krugman 2009). However, in ideological terms it was caused by the abandonment of the *laissez-faire* and the frenzy for self-regulating—a fact acknowledged even by orthodox economists (Krugman 2009). The process took impulse when Keynes was dismissed but a dismissal deserves practical reconsideration. Uncertainty took the form of a pervasive feeling of economic angst, organicism was translated into regional contagion, and the lack of a self-regulating system was perceived in both economies and the international financial system. This is the 'croaking of Cassandra' at its best. Notice that all financial crises have the same sequence: origin, interrelations, mobile, consequences, and enhancement (see Muñoz 2011, 2017) but the emergency of a particular crisis is a matter of degree and timing. Knowledge was dormant.

There exist, however, four generations of—orthodox—models of financial crises, which were initially labeled as currency crises (see Muñoz 2011). The first is associated with exogenous balance of payment problems (Krugman 1979). The second is related to endogenous balance of payments or public expenditure problems (Obstfeld 1994). The third is referred to simultaneous real and banking crises (Kaminsky and Reinhart 1999). The fourth has to do with the resulting balance sheet problems in enterprises (Krugman 1999; Dornbusch 2002). But this type of orthodox—Keynesian?—view on financial crises resembles the neoclassical spirit for considering crises to be exceptional (temporary) or specifically provoked (neglecting that overstated saving is at the heart of the problem), or even shyly hinting at corporate governance as a micro-culprit (see Blundell-Wignall et al. 2008). In this reading, Keynes is a dissenter by preaching that money is a measure of disquietude. Enter Minsky.

Current Policy Dilemmas I: The Minsky Moment

Orthodox Post-Keynesians only contribute heuristic points to macroeconomics (see preceding paragraphs, Chapter 9) which make them unable to explain the endogenous genesis of financial crises. Essentiality is crucial in philosophy. In contrast, heterodox Post-Keynesians follow Keynes's message of uncertainty and may predict the crises, especially Hyman Minsky (1919–1996) who admittedly departs from Keynes, overstating the role of money as the endogenous agent (Minsky 1986). Minsky considered financial crises as an endemic and permanent but also internal result in any capitalist system. For him, the crisis of 2008 is a natural response of financial markets to a period of relative stability (or even boom) enhanced by saving in the form of (yes) debt and instruments, wherein innovations in risk management flourish. With these insights, Minsky addressed the problem of the inherent instability of financial markets in the late 1950s.

His idea was to understand 'today's' capitalism in the context of a global macroeconomic framework affected by crises. The role of financial instruments and debt, and the preeminence of uncertainty in the world economy, led to confidence loss and ultimately to recessions. This is the pass-through from uncertainty to instability. Minsky's idea (absolutely deducted from Keynes's *SRP* and actions as an investor) is that booms generate busts. Or, alternatively, concentration on euphoria and endogeneity makes stability destabilizing. The roots of the explanation of crises are visible at this stage: policies must be addressed in order for saving (debt) not to exceed productive investment. For Minsky the effects of crisis pass through stages. At first debtors are able to pay capital, then they only pay interests, at the end they are not able to pay anything, but they have already speculated or incurred in misleading investments (Ponzi finance), leaving the problem to financial agencies and ultimately to the government which at the end may socialize debts.

In the 2000s, saving in the form of speculation rather than in physical investment produced financial turmoil and ultimately recessions, so that this shift from saving to private debt is the essence of Minsky's contribution related to the Financial Instability Hypothesis (FIH). For

Caverzasi, 'the combination of banks, radical uncertainty, unregulated financial markets (just as described by Minsky) makes the system endogenously unstable and the FIH still up-to date' (Caverzasi 2014, p. 1). For Venero (2018), there is in Minsky an account of the tradition of endogenous financial market instability, that is, an inner propensity for markets to embark on disequilibrium paths. According to Venero (2018), Schumpeter, Fisher, Keynes, and Minsky continue the monetary tradition. But Keynes and Minsky analyzed financial integration and liquidity in the face of uncertainty. Keynes's spirit is present: Equilibrium is the exception and money the reason for the existence of divergences.

Current Policy Dilemmas II: Modern Views on the Financial Crisis of 2008. Revisiting Keynes

The distinction between saving and investment set forth by Keynes is at the core of the way of functioning of Capitalism (see Gnoss and Rochon 2011), which is directed by big businesses (including financial firms) and even worse by speculators. In modern views, high, fluctuating, or spurious interest rates neglect the message of Chapter 24 of *GT* or, stated in a deductive form, fluctuating asset prices ignite modern crises. However, a Keynes type of remedy may be needed for activating economies after a recession, which means philosophy is necessary to avoid and manage crises. There are diverging opinions about what is the issue to be gleaned from Keynes. Leijonhuvfud (2009) states that [w]'e should learn from Keynes to focus on the macroproblems of our day ... [such as] ... the financial crisis and the resulting great recession. Neither the standard Keynesian policies of decades past nor the monetary policy doctrine of recent years provides useful solutions ... A balance sheet recession requires that policy addresses the problems in the private sector's capital.' Leijonhuvfud, yes the former Keynesian, now supports the fourth-generation models.

Another relevant modern issue (Gnoss and Rochon 2011) is the intensity of the developments in a finance-dominated Capitalism. The Keynes connection lies in that in financialized economies firms evolve from commodity producers to financial managers (e.g., General Motors or Chrysler), as this is more profitable and less regulated. The combination of profitability-seeking banks, radical uncertainty, irregulated markets, and endogenous money triggers crises. Moreover, central banks mysteriously changed their procedures. For Gnoss and Rochon (2011) the US

Federal Reserve System, the US monetary system, and its federal funds rate are the main sources of mismanagement in monetary economies, as according to this author they have contradicted Keynes's heuristics. The type of management in central banks is also a matter of political economy, impacting the directions of policies. The patterns of financial risk were generated according to some sources after the Second World War, but we contend they were accelerated after Keynes's dismissal in 1979. Moreover, public expenditure supported capital accumulation (Aquanno 2021), and the public and the private sectors were colluded, at least in Mexico 1994 and Greece 2007. Additionally, the institutional basis of global debt markets (see Minsky's contentions) and the role of the US Treasury debt in the international financial system were relevant in the unfolding of the crisis. On the other hand, according to Gnoss and Rochon (2011) the mixing of fast-moving risks permitted the contagion of crises displaying a new but lethal chemistry. Practicalities associated with financial regulation require advice at a higher philosophical level. Risk must not be invoked. Put it simply, the financial crises and misleading fine-tuning were caused by the mismanagement of interest rates; that is, by endogenous forces.

According to Rochon and Bougraine (Introduction 2020), two issues are of utmost importance in the analysis of causes, interactions, and remedies of the financial—subprime lending—crisis of 2008: the importance of credit and money and the impact of austerity measures. The obvious answer is that Keynes is the monetary economist *par excellence* as well as an advocator for spending rather than for austerity. A second question is whether expenditure was made in the key areas, for which it is necessary to dissect the stimulus packages in the US and Europe, as Keynes did in some of his writings.

For Gnoss and Rochon (Introduction, 2011), fundamental problems triggered the 'Minsky moment,' a conclusion they reach after analyzing the causes, severities, and damages of crises. In other words, the root in terms of the real sector was bad fiscal and monetary policies. In Keynes's time, finance was regulated in an industrial Capitalism with non-overstated market friendly policies. Around 2008 (ibid.) new banks were more fragile and unsustainable. There also were effective demand constraints and finance was subserving production, the so-called financialization. According to Gnos and Rochon (Introduction, 2011) inaccurate risk calculations based on poor information proliferated in a general context of high economic growth and low-interest rates, but uncertain.

This explains, for this author, the renewed interest in Keynes's posthumous career. The 'euthanasia of the rentier (financer?)' did not occur and 'the paradox of thrift' did not work, which left imprints on the policy processes. The Minsky Moment and the aftermath of the crisis emerged as an upshot of qualitative fails in the system exacerbated by uncertainty. This was a finance-led accumulation regime and as such ephemeral with lasting consequences, like any short-term pleasure.

To avoid recurrent crises, monetary policy needs discretion and the reconsideration of a lack of a self-regulating system. Monetary policy must be more transparent (Rochon and Rossi 2010, Chapter 6). There is not of course the *trade-off* between unemployment and inflation which started Keynes's dismissal in the late 1970s. But Keynes also intuited some key relationships in the financial world such as risk and return *trade-offs* and overall (and this is very relevant in terms of solutions) that no natural anchor exists but also that interest rate reduction has limits at the international level. In the evolution of banking, a more densely structured and transparent set of rules must prevail, enhancing stability and a more efficient capital and wages allocation. According to Rochon and Bougrine (2020), the non-existing basis in macroeconomic policies for equating saving and investment broke down the interrelation between the real and the financial sectors (not to mention the labor sector according to this author), which led to a deficient assessment of risk, which was the mobile of the system. It was rational to be irrational between the 1990s (especially after the internet bubble in 1995) and 2007, provided that the timing was right for speculative purposes. [W]'e moved away from a Keynesian production economy to a 'predatory' type of financial capitalism...the bank-firm relationship...was replaced with a bank-financial market relationship' (Rochon and Rossi 2010, Abstract).

From a historic angle, Bibow (2020) revisits Keynes's writings from *Indian Currency and Finance* (1913) to *The General Theory* (1936) with a focus on financial instability. His (Bibow's) analysis reveals Keynes's concerns about the fragility of the banking system, especially under deflationary conditions. Keynes's writings during the Great Depression uncover insights into how the Great Depression may have informed his *General Theory*. Keynes assumes in his Golden Book a constant money stock as central. This has not been the case and has led to new theoretical strands such as the circuitist Post-Keynesian approaches.

Bibow (2020) also cites Bernanke: 'As a scholar of the Great Depression and Federal Reserve Chairman at the time of the modern crisis ...

Bernanke provides an important intellectual bridge between the historical crisis of the 1930s and the modern crisis of 2007–9.' Bernanke concludes that 'while policy practice has changed, the "classical" theory Keynes attacked in 1936 remains hegemonic today.' For him, 'the common (mis-)interpretation of The General Theory as depression economics continues to describe the mainstream's failure to engage in relevant monetary economics' (quoted in Bibow 2020, Abstract), perhaps with unpredicted financialization as an upshot. And this is an orthodox but refreshing—real—Keynesian view. So is the Stiglitz's view.

According to Stiglitz (2010), the explanation of the crisis of 2008 lies in 'a poor job in allocating capital and in managing risk ... a considerable part of ... [the blame] ... lies in the economic profession... [with] ... the notion economists pushed—that markets are efficient and self-adjusting ... they provided the basis of financial stability in the decades after the great depression.' In this view, the issue of how financial agents and authorities obtain, process, and interpret information must not be taken for granted. The efficient markets doctrines—which became fashionable before the crisis—can be contrasted against imperfect and asymmetric information.

Continuing with Stiglitz (2010), if markets would have been efficient or rational no gains would have existed, and this author contends that no economists would have been necessary. Contrarywise, part of the confusion is the affirmation that causes of the crises are not advanced. But impulses, manias, panic, and crashes are described in the writings of many authors. The mobiles and speculative vehicles include free currency, securities, and mortgage markets, derivatives, unregulated banking, and free agents and rating agencies. Other factors apart from irrationality are predatory lending, leverage, incentives, and excessive risk-taking, like in the Mexican crisis of 1994. Risks were grasped and discerned in 2008 through 'physicalist' models. But the point is to discern the sequence among factors. Stiglitz (2010) states 'only the period of strong financial markets was free of crises,' that is between 1946 and 1978: Keynes's heyday. According to Stiglitz (2010), aggregate demand was lowered by high saving ratios and investment dearth.

Enter Keynes

According to Mann (2019), the resurrection of Keynes and Keynesianism in the wake of the recent financial crisis indexes the similarities between the present conjuncture and the Great Depression. For Stiglitz (2010), Skidelsky sustains that the arising of crises—and their management—cannot be addressed by means of Keynes's recipes. Nonetheless, this author contends that the characterization of the crisis can be deducted from Keynes's vision, namely as an event arising from low expectations (eventually agents realize that the boom is fictitious). Moreover uncertainty also affects labor markets and inflation (further reducing aggregate demand). Keynes would have resorted to public expenditure to remedy unemployment but as mentioned before it was also attributed to speculation in the form of debt in the money market. Before Keynes, downturns were addressed by means of austerity as were the crises of 1997, but not that of 2008 (at least in the US). This is also a crisis impacting aggregate supply. In other parts of the North-western hemisphere market failures were compounded with policy failures. Stiglitz (2010) ascertains that Keynes's insufficiency of monetary policy was recognized in favor of fiscal policy, but the problem was that the latter produced unsustainable deficits (see the models of first generation). It does not matter that the speculative vehicle was credit default swaps. According to Skidelsky, economics did not take uncertainty seriously but there also was the problem of the lack of transparency. Recall that after the Great Depression regulation and reforms worked: 'Thatcher and Reagan ushered in a new era of regulation' (Stiglitz 2010). The effects of this second episode are at the time of writing still being experienced in fragile economies, namely Greece (Muñoz 2017). Capitalism must be saved again.

The heterodox Keynesian Davidson (2012), in his rebuttal to Stiglitz (2010), restates that saving differed from investment and uncertainty was confused with risk (the latter being an epistemological problem due to the reliance on exact mathematics, see Appendix 12.2). But Davidson makes clear that Stiglitz does not mention that the future is always uncertain and ergodic (non-repetitive and unpredictable). Stiglitz thinks that everything is related to inefficient information. For Davidson (2012), Stiglitz is an orthodox economist accepting all contracts are conducted in real terms (ignoring inflation), which converts the economy into a barter (pre-Keynes's) economy. Beyond that, for Keynes the system may face a drying up of liquidity. But money is not a veil, and uncertainty calls for specific provisions. For this author, if all topics dealt with in *TM* belong to the orthodox tradition, since uncertainty only appears in *GT* though it was intuited by Keynes as the missing link (Chapter 7), the economists managing crises only read the Silver Book. There also other interpretations of the crisis of 2008, but the understanding of macroeconomic nexuses may safely be dated back to Keynes's oeuvre.

Epilog: Keynes's Generosity Demands Faithfulness Based on Understanding

For Keynes there is a macroeconomic nexus among bank credit, money, and production which entails the rejection of Say's Law (see Chapter 2) which discards crises. First of all Keynes gives importance to central banks: 'Keynes based the rationale of a central bank not only in its regulatory functions … but even more on its developmental role as an agency to promote financial development' (Chandavarkar 1985, p. 1). On their part, commercial—in modern parlance—banks foster economic activity as banks are special (Keynes 1931 [1963]). In the age of small investors, bad lending propitiated the crisis; but perhaps more importantly, it led to a fluctuating aggregate demand as well as inequality and distributional problems in many countries. In sum, the banking system is a determinant of the level of economic activity[1] with the central banks as the lender of last resort. While this is obvious, the government (via non autonomous central banks) has helped reinforce this network effect by facilitating banks in the course of regulations and central clearing during the crises. In this sense, Keynes was right in contending that the rate of interest is the distributive variable affecting the cost of both lending and borrowing as well as income (via investment). The point is mentioned now as—in terms of a reading of *GT* (Chapter 9)—'rentiers' were not eliminated; instead, barriers were, and some central banks became accomplices rather than managers.

This author believes Keynes's relevance also lies in his clarity and his language, both of them underpinning his economics. Beyond these innovations, organicism is related to the treatment of economic material, uncertainty to timing and the interrelation with others, and the lack of a self-regulating system to intervention and secretion and ultimately to *the laissez-faire*. To put it differently, at the beginning of the twenty-first century uncertainty is enhanced by information technology, organicism linked to contagion, and self-regulation defined by its absence in the

[1] Even more in a system of imperfect competition.

financial system. Finally, atomism in the form of saving is referred to as a useful austerity. Back in 1931, Keynes enhanced the virtues of spending, contending that saving is an anachronism (see Chapters 2, 7, and 9).

At any rate, Keynes's reception throughout the world evolved in the form of a shift in 2007 (Davidson 2007; Skidelsky 2016). Following Keynes's recipes properly, translated into developed financial systems, could have led to an avoidance or a mitigation of the financial crises in the twenty-first century. Keynes's predictions and pioneering (but encrypted) recognition of financialization provide the ground for avoiding future financial crises, and even more so considering that his heuristics provides clues for finding relevant connections, such as that between political philosophy and policies. According to Lakatos, a progressive theory explains novel facts (see Chapter 2). There are of course, other relevant contributions to the understanding to financial crises. Keynes was just a leader.

This reconstruction of the Keynes's *SRP*, aimed at investigating its modern application, departs from economics, having interdisciplinarity as a destination, just the opposite of Keynes's construction in terms of sequences. Organic units are at the root of the effects of crises but also fortunately of its remedies. In political terms, Keynes's conservatism is in favor of a middle-way stance still resilient against the inexpediency of the *Laissez-faire*, which would require the presence of agents' homogeneity, asymmetry in the occurrence of events, and perfect information about probabilities (see Chapter 6). Still the trans-generational Keynes—for whom money bridges lapses—would question the fate of capitalism and globalization, though he was one of the pioneers in this last respect (see Chapters 5, 8, and 12). In the field of ethics, Keynes's conceptions of value and duty would make him reject the love of money and the lack of regulation (see Chapter 8), especially if rationalism (especially on the part of 'animal spirits') casts doubts (see Chapter 11). In epistemic terms, it is necessary to side against some core parts of orthodoxy to combat the recurrent character of the crises, specifically warranted equilibrium and atomism (see Chapters 2 and 10).

In the ecological terrain regarding the results of crises, scientific speculation is non-viable as this theme was not formerly or systematically addressed by Keynes (only some insights can be inferred from some of his premises, for example about the topic of the place of economics) not even when he deals with the topic of development after the Second World War (see Chapter 12). Keynes believed in an elastic aggregate supply; that is, in an economy possessing unlimited resources. Fortunately, many authors are responding to this challenge (see Berr 2008, 2009).

Notes

1. As manifested in deduction, *ceteris paribus* and the excessive reliance on axioms, crass materialism, abstractionism, physicalism and Euclidean Geometry, the Enlightenment rationalism, equilibria, homogeneity and convergence, unlimited logical abilities, certainty, atomism, apriorism, universal and eternal truths, innate ideas, and Descartes's mechanicism.
2. Before 2005 many heterodox programs and courses on the history of economic thought in the developed nations were dismantled in favour of a positivistic stance centred on 'facts.'

References

Sources

Aquanno, Scott M. 2021. *The Crisis of Risk: Subprime Debt and US Financial Power from 1944 to Present*. Chentelham, UK and Northampton, MA: Edward Elgar.

Backhouse, Roger E. (ed.). 1993. "The Lakatosian Legacy in Economic Methodology." Discussion Papers 93–14, Department of Economics, University of Birmingham. https://ideas.repec.org/p/bir/birmec/93-14.html. Accessed 28 January 2017.

———. 1994. New Directions in Economic Methodology. London: Routledge.

——— (ed.). 2007. *Explorations in Economic Methodology: From Lakatos to Empirical Philosophy of Science*. New York: Routledge.

Backhouse, Roger E., and Bradley W. Bateman. 2009. "Keynes and Capitalism." *History of Political Economy* 41, no. 4: 645–71.

Bateman, Bradley W., and John B. Davis (eds.). 1991. *Keynes and Philosophy: Essays on the Origins of Keyne's Thought*. Aldershot, UK: Edward Elgar.

Berr, Eric. 2008. "Keynes and the Post Keynesians on Sustainable Development." *Cahiers du GREThA* no. 2008–1. https://www.researchgate.net/publication/5081677_Keynes_and_the_Post_Keynesians_on_Sustainable_Development. Accessed 17 July 2016.

———. 2009. "Keynes and Sustainable Development." *International Journal of Political Economy* 38, no. 3: 22–38.

Bibow, Joerg. 2020. "The General Theory as 'Depression Economics'? Financial Instability and Crises in Keynes's Monetary Thought." *Levy Economics Institute WP 920*, October.

Blaug, Mark. 1991. "Second Thoughts on the Keynesian Revolution." *History of Political Economy* 23, no. 2: 171–92.

Blundell-Wignall, Adrian, Paul Atkinson, and Se Hoon Lee. 2008. "The Current Financial Crisis: Causes and Policy Issues." *Financial Markets Trends*. OECD.

Caverzasi, Eugenio. 2014. "Minksy and the mortgage subprime crisis." The Levy Economics Institute Working Paper 796.

Chandavarkar, Anand G. 1985. "Keynes and Central Banks." *Indian Economic Review* XX, no. 2: 283–97.

Davidson, Paul. 2007. *John Maynard Keynes*. London: Macmillan.

———. 2009. *The Keynes Solution: The Path to Global Economic Prosperity*. London and New York: Palgrave.

———. 2012. Letters 32, no. 10, May. https://Lrb.co.uk/the-pper/v32/no8/Joseph-Stiglitz/the-non-existent-hand. Accessed 21 February 2020.

Dornbusch, Rudiger. 2002. "A primer on emerging-market crises." NBER. https://www.nber.org/system/files/chapters/c10648/c10648.pdf.

Gnoss, Claude and Louis Philippe Rochon (eds.). 2011. "Introduction". In *Credit, Money and Macroeconomic Policy: A Postkeynesian Approach*. Chentelham, UK and Northampton, MA: Edward Elgar.

Hausmann, Daniel M. 2007. *Philosophy of Economics: A Contemporary Introduction*. Cambridge: Cambridge University Press.

———. 2008. *Essays on Philosophy and Economic Methodology*. Cambridge: Cambridge University Press.

———. 2012. *The Inexact and Separate Science of Economics*. Cambridge: Cambridge University Press.

———. 2016. "On the Econ within." *Journal of Economic Methodology* 23, no. 1: 26–31.

Hendry, David F. 1993. "Econometric Methodology: A Personal Perspective." In *Advances in Econometrics: Fifth World Congress, Volume II*, edited by T. F. Bewley, Chapter 10. Cambridge: Cambridge University Press.

Hands, Wade, D. 1996. "Book Reviews." *Journal of Economic Methodology* 3, no. 2: 317–22.

Keynes, John Maynard. 1931. "Keynes Rejoinder to Mr. D. H. Robertson." *Economic Journal XLI* 163 (September). In *JMK/EJ/6/7*. Cambridge: Cambridge University Press. https://discovery.nationalarchives.gov.uk/details/r/afc22cbd-5472-49c8-8ba4-a585275185c2. Accessed 15 November 2019.

———. 1913 [1971]. *The Collected Writings of John Maynard Keynes (CW)* Vol. 1: *Indian Currency and Finance*, edited by Elizabeth Johnson (19–28) and

Daniel E. Moggridge (15–18). London: Macmillan, for the Royal Economic Society.
———. 1936 [1973]. *The Collected Writings of John Maynard Keynes (CW)* Vol. 7: *The General Theory of Employment, Interest and Money*, edited by Elizabeth Johnson (19–28) and Daniel E. Moggridge (15–18). London: Macmillan, for the Royal Economic Society.
Kaminsky, Graciela and Carmen Reinhart. 1999. "The twin crises: The causes of balance-of-payments problems." *American Economic Review* 89, no. 3: 473–500.
Keynes, John M. 1930. *Treatise on Money. Vol. 1–2.* London: Macmillan, 1930.
———. 1931 [1963]. "The Consequences to the Banks of the Collapse of Money Values." In *Essays in Persuasion*. New York: Norton.
———. 1936. *The General Theory of Employment, Interest and Money*. London: Macmillan
Kregel, Jan. 2008. "Changes in the U.S. Financial System and the Subprime Crisis." Levy Economics Institute of Bard College WP 530, April.
Krugman, Paul. 1979. "A model of balance of payments crises." *Journal of Money, Credit and Banking* 11: 311–25.
———. 1999. "Analytical afterthoughts on the Asian Crises." Mimeo, Massachussets Institute of Technology.
———. 2009. "Why Aren't We All Keynesians Now?" *Krugman's Website*. http://web.mit.edu/krugman/www/#fortune. Accessed 31 December 2018.
Leijonhufvud, Axel. 2009. "'Out of the Corridor' Keynes and the Crisis." *Cambridge Journal of Economics* 33, no. 4: 741–57.
Mann, Geoff. 2019. *In the Long Run We Are All Dead: Keynesianism, Political Economy, and Revolution*. London: Verso.
Michell, Jo and Jan Toporowski. 2017. "Financialization and the financial process." *Cambridge Journal of Economics* 41, no. 1: 105–25.
Mini, Piero V. 1994. *A Study of the Psychology of Original Work*. New York: Saint Martin's.
Minsky, Hyman. 1986. *Stabilizing an Unstable Economy*. New Haven, CO: Yale University Press.
Muñoz, B. Jesús. 2011. "Orthodox versus Heterodox (Minskyan) Perspectives of Financial Crises: Explosion in the 1990s Versus Implosion in the 2000s." Levy Economics Institute of Bard College WP 695.
———. 2017. "Commonalities between the 'Bookends' Financial Crises of Mexico 1994 and Greece 2007." In *The Internal Impact and External Influence of the Greek Financial Crisis*, edited by J. Marangos, Chapter 11. CH: Palgrave Macmillan.
Obstfeld, Maurice. 1994. "The Logic of Currency Crises." *Cahiers Economiques et Etudes Monetaires. Banque de France* 43: 189–213.

O'Donnell, Roderick M. 1991. *Keynes as Philosopher-Economist*. Proceedings of *The Ninth Keynes Seminar* held at the University of Kent. London: MacMillan.

Rochon, Louis Philippe, and Hassan Bougrine. 2020. *Credit, Money, and Crises in Postkeynesian Economics, Introduction*. Chentelham, UK and Northampton, MA, US: Edward Elgar.

Rochon, Louis Philippe, and Sergio Rossi. 2010. "Has 'it' happened again?" *International Journal of political Economy* 39, no. 2: 5–9.

Samuelson, Paul A. 1946. "Lord Keynes and the General Theory." *Econometrica* XIV, no. 3: 187–200.

Sawyer, Malcolm. 2013. "What Is Financialization?" *The International Journal of Political Economy* 42 (4): 5–18.

Skidelsky, Robert. 2016. *The Essential Keynes*. London: Penguin.

Stiglitz, Joseph. 2010. "The Non-existent Hand." *Review of Keynes: The Return of the Master by Robert Skidelsky*, Allen Lane, September 2009, *London Review of Books* 32, no. 8, 22 April, including Davidson Paul. 2012. *Letters* 32, no. 10, May. https://Lrb.co.uk/the-pper/v32/no8/Joseph-Stiglitz/the-non-existent-hand. Accessed 21 February 2020.

Venero, Frank. 2018. "The Economics of Instability: An Abstract of an Excerpt." Levy Economics Institute WP 903, April.

Ward, Benjamin, 1972. *What's Wrong with Economics?* London: Palgrave MacMillan.

References

Main Sources

CW = The Collected Writings of John Maynard Keynes. 1971–1989. 30 volumes. London: Macmillan, for the Royal Economic Society, United Kingdom.

JMK/UA. 1902–1921 [1988]. Keynes unpublished articles or papers or manuscripts at King's College Library, Cambridge University, United Kingdom. *The John Maynard Keynes Papers in King's College, Cambridge, The Unpublished Writings of John Maynard Keynes* (KUP). https://www.proquest.com/products-services/Keynes.html. Accessed 27 February 2016.

JMK/PP (or *TP*). Keynes published papers.

Sources

Ahiakpor, James C. W. (ed.). 1998. *Keynes and the Classics Reconsidered*. Boston: Kluwers.

Amadeo, Edward J. 1989. *Keynes's Principle of Effective Demand*. Aldershot, UK: Edward Elgar.

Andrews, David R. 1999. "Continuity and Change in Keynes's Thought: The Importance of David Hume." *The European History of Economics Thought Journal* 6, no. 9: 1–21.

———. 2010. *Keynes and the British Tradition, the Moral Purpose of the Market*. New York: Routledge.

J. Muñoz-Bandala, *Keynes's Evolutionary Spirit*, Palgrave Insights into Apocalypse Economics, https://doi.org/10.1007/978-3-030-90150-9

Annals of the Fondazione Luigi Einaudi. An Interdisciplinary Journal of Economics, History and Political Science. 2017. "Special Issue: 'Keynes Relevance to the Contemporary World. Eighty Years Since the General Theory'" 51, no. 1. https://econpapers.repec.org/article/flejournl/. Accessed 11 December 2017.

Aquanno, Scott M. 2021. *The Crisis of Risk: Subprime Debt and US Financial Power from 1944 to Present*. Chentelham, UK and Northampton, MA: Edward Elgar.

Arts Professional. 2017. "Arts Policy Special—Is Keynes Dream Still Alive?" https://www.artsprofessional.co.uk/magazine/article/arts-policy-special-keynes%19s-dream-still-alive. Accessed 17 July 2017.

Aspromourgos, Anthony. 2004. "'The Functionless Investor': Keynes's Euthanasia of the Rentier Revisited." In *History and Political Economy: Essays in Honour of P. D. Groenewegen*, edited by Tony Aspromourgos and John Lodewijks, 217–35. London: Routledge.

———. 2009. "John Maynard Keynes and the Preservation of Liberal Capitalism." *Australian Quarterly* 81, no. 4: 17–24.

Baccini, Alberto. 2007. "Edgeworth on the Foundations of Ethics and Probability." *The European Journal of the History of Economic Thought* 14, no. 10 (March): 79–96.

Backhouse, Roger E. 1993. "The Lakatosian Legacy in Economic Methodology." Discussion Papers 93–14, Department of Economics, University of Birmingham. https://ideas.repec.org/p/bir/birmec/93-14.html. Accessed 28 January 2017.

——— (ed.). 2007. *Explorations in Economic Methodology: From Lakatos to Empirical Philosophy of Science*. New York: Routledge.

Backhouse, Roger E., and Bradley W. Bateman. 2010. "Whose Keynes." In *Keynes's General Theory after Seventy Years*, edited by Robert W. Dimand, Robert A. Mundell, and Alessandro Vercelli, Chapter 1, 8–27. Basingstoke: Palgrave.

———. 2011. *Capitalist Revolutionary: John Maynard Keynes*, November. Cambridge, MA: Harvard University Press.

Baldwin, Thomas. 1990. *G. E. Moore: The Arguments of the Philosophers*. New York: Routledge.

Bateman, Bradley W. 1987. "Keynes's Changing Conception of Probability." *Economics and Philosophy* 3, no. 1: 97–119.

———. 1988. "G. E. Moore and J. M. Keynes: A Missing Chapter in the History of the Expected Utility Model." *American Economic Review* 78 (December), no. 5: 1098–1106.

———. (1996). *Keynes's Uncertain Revolution*. Detroit: University of Michigan Press.

Bateman, Bradley W., and John B. Davis. 1991. "Introduction." In *Keynes and Philosophy: An Essay on the Origins of Keynes's Thought*, edited by Bradley W. Bateman and John B. Davis, 1–5. Marquette University Faculty 141. https://epublications.marquette.edu/marq_fac-book/141. Accessed 17 August 2017.

Bell, Daniel, and Irving Kristol (eds.). 1971. *The Crisis in Economic Theory*. New York: Basic Books.

Bellofiore, Ricardo, and Joseph Halevi. 2011. "A Minsky Moment? The Subprime Crisis and the 'New' Capitalism." In *Credit, Money and Macroeconomic Policy: A Postkeynesian Approach*, edited by Claude Gnoss and Louis Philipe Rochon, Chapter 1. Chentelham, UK and Northampton, MA: Edward Elgar.

Bentham, Jeremy. 1789 [2017]. *An Introduction to the Principles of Morals and Legislation*. Copyright © Jonathan Bennett 2017. https://www.earlymoderntexts.com/assets/pdfs/bentham1780.pdf. Accessed 17 June 2016.

Berman, Nathaniel. 1995. "Economic Consequences, Nationalist Passions: Keynes, Crisis, Culture, and Policy." *American University Law Review* 10, no. 2: 619–70.

Berr, Eric. 2008. "Keynes and the Post Keynesians on Sustainable Development." *Cahiers du GREThA* no. 2008–1. https://www.researchgate.net/publication/5081677_Keynes_and_the_Post_Keynesians_on_Sustainable_Development. Accessed 17 July 2016.

———. 2009. "Keynes and Sustainable Development." *International Journal of Political Economy* 38, no. 3: 22–38.

———. 2014. "The Socio-Economic Philosophy of Keynes: Lessons for the 21th Century." The Third Nordic Post-Keynesian Conference, Aalborg-Denmark, May. https://www.pkconference.aau.dk/digitalAssets/104/104679_berr--eric---the-socio-economic-philosophy-of-keynes-lessons-for-the-21st-century.pdf. Accessed 9 July 2019.

Beveridge, William H. 1944. *Full Employment in a Free Society*. London: Allen & Unwin.

Bibow, Joerg. 2020. "The General Theory as 'Depression Economics'? Financial Instability and Crises in Keynes's Monetary Thought." Levy Economics Institute WP 920, October.

Blanco, Andrés. 2017. "Reflections on Neoclassical Theory and the Philosophy of Science." *Journal of Australian Political Economy* 80: 43–64.

Blaug, Mark. 1990a. *John Maynard Keynes: Life, Legacy, Ideas*. London: Palgrave.

———. 1990b. *John Maynard Keynes: Talking to Leading Economists About Keynes*. New York: St. Martin's.

———. 1991. "Second Thoughts on the Keynesian Revolution." *History of Political Economy* 23, no. 2: 171–92.

———. 2002. "Paradigms Versus Research Programmes in the History of Economics." In *The Philosophy of Economics: An Anthology*, edited by Daniel Hausman, 348–75. Cambridge: Cambridge University Press.

Blundell-Wignall, Adrian, Paul Atkinson, and Se Hoon Lee. 2008. "The Current Financial Crisis: Causes and Policy Issues." *Financial Markets Trends*. OECD.

Boland, Lawrence A. 1985. "The Foundations of Keynes' Methodology: The General Theory." In *Keynes' Economics: Methodological Issues*, edited by Tony Lawson and Hashem Pesaran, 181–94. New York: Croom Helm. http://www.sfu.ca/~boland/keynes85.pdf. Accessed 16 June 2018.

Brady, Michael E. 2012. "Keynes, Mathematics and Probability: A Reappraisal." *International Journal of Applied Economics and Econometrics* 20, no. 2 (April–June): 324–57.

———. 2017. "From Keynes Back to Smith and Aristotle: Liquidity Preference, Hoarding, and Speculation," December 23. https://ssrn.com/abstract=3092485.

Brady, Michael E., and Rogerio Arthmar. 2012. "Keynes, Boole and the Interval Approach to Probability." *History of Economic Ideas* 20, no. 3: 65–84.

Braithwaite, Richard B. 1980. "Keynes as a Philosopher." In *Essays on John Maynard Keynes*, edited by Milo Keynes, Chapter 22. Cambridge: Cambridge University Press.

Braman, Chuck. 1996. "The Political Philosophy of John Locke and Its Influence on the Founding Fathers and the Political Documents They Created." In *My General Views on Philosophy, Politics and Economics*, blog Chuck Braman. https://www.chuckbraman.com/political-philosophy-of-john-locke.html. Accessed 15 June 2015.

Brown-Collier, Elba K. 1985. "Keynes' View of an Organic Universe: The Implications." *Review of Social Economy* 43, no. 1 (April): 14–23.

Brown-Collier, Elba K., and Randall Bausor. 1988. "The Epistemological Foundations of The General Theory." *Scottish Journal of Political Economy* 35, no. 3: 227–41.

Butler, Eamon. 2011. *Milton Friedman: A Concise Guide to the Ideas and Influence of the Free-market Economist*. Hampshire, UK: Harriman.

Carabelli, Anna. 1986. On Keynes's Method. PhD Dissertation, University of Cambridge.

———. 1988. *On Keynes's Method*. Basingstoke: Macmillan.

———. 1992. "The Method of the Critique of Classical Theory: Keynes on Organic Interdependence." In *John Maynard Keynes, Language and Method*, edited by Alessandra Marzola and Francesco Silva, 128–52. Chentelham, UK: Edward Elgar.

———. 1998. "Keynes on Probability, Uncertainty and Tragic Choices." *Cahiers d'économie politique* no. 30/31, 187–226. Keynes: Économie et philosophie.

———. 2003. "Economics as a Branch of Probable Logic." In *The philosophy of Keynes's Economics: Probability, Uncertainty and Convention*, edited by Jochen Runde and Sohei Mizuhara, 216–26. New York: Routledge.

———. 2019. "Keynes's Aristotelian 'Eudaimonic' Conception of Happiness and the Requirement of Material and Institutional Preconceptions: The Scope for Economics and Economic Policy." *Anualli della Fundazione Luigi Einaudi* LIII, 213–26.

Carabelli, Anna M., and Mario A. Cedrini. 2010. "Keynes and the Complexity of International Economic Relations in the Aftermath of World War I." *Journal of Economic Issues* 44, no. 4: 1009–27.

———. 2010–11. "Indian Currency and Beyond: The Legacy of the Early Economics of Keynes in the Times of Bretton Woods II." *Journal of Post Keynesian Economics* 33, no. 2: 55–80.

———. 2014. "Keynes's 'General Theory', 'Treatise on Money' and 'Tract on Monetary Reform': Different Theories, Same Methodological Approach?" *The European Journal of the History of Economic Thought* 21, no. 6.

———. 2016. "Great Expectations and Final Delusion. Keynes and the Ultimate Values of Capitalism." Conference: 40 Years of the Cambridge Journal of Economics, 12–13 July. https://www.cpes.org.uk/dev/wp-content/uploads/2016/06/Carabelli_Cedrini_Great_Expectations_and_Final_Delusion.pdf. Accessed 14 December 2019.

Cardim de Carvalho, Fernando. 2012. "Keynes and the Endogeneity of Money." The 16th Conference of the Research Network Macroeconomics and Macroeconomic Policies (FMM) on The State of Economics after the Crisis, Berlin, October. http://www.boeckler.de/pdf/v_2012_10_25_cardim_de_carvalho.pdf. Accessed 16 May 2015.

Caverzasi, Eugenio. 2014. "Minsky and the Subprime Mortgage Crisis." Levy Economics Institute WP 796, April.

Chambers, David, Elroy Dimson, and Justin Foo. 2015. "Keynes the Stock Market Investor: A Quantitative Analysis." *Journal of Financial and Quantitative Analysis* 50, no. 4: 843–68.

Chandavarkar, Anand G. 1985. "Keynes and Central Banks." *Indian Economic Review* XX, no. 2: 283–97.

———. 1989. *Keynes and India: A Study in Economics and Biography*. London: Palgrave.

Chase, Richard X. 1991. "Keynes's Dichotomy: A Methodological Escape for a Theoretical Revolution." *Methods* 3, no. 2 (December): 79–85.

Chew, A. P. (recorder). 1936. "Abstract of Conversation with John Maynard Keynes." In *The New Deal Documents*. Washington, DC: Department of Agriculture. https://newdeal.feri.org/misc/keynes1.htm. Accessed 14 September 2018.

Chick, Victoria. 1992. "On Money, Method and Keynes." In *Selected Essays of Victoria Chick*, edited by Philip Arestis and Sheila Dow. Basingstoke: Macmillan.

———. 2003. "Theory, Method and Mode of Thought in Keynes's General Theory." *Journal of Economic Methodology* 10, no. 3: 307–27.

———. 2011. *Macroeconomics after Keynes: A Reconsideration of the General Theory*. Cambridge, MA: MIT Press.

———. 2018. "On the Relevance of the General Theory at 80: Economic Change and Economic Theory." In *The General Theory and Keynes for the 21st Century*, edited by Sheila Dow, Jesper Jespersen, and Geoffrey Tilly, Chapter 1. Chentelham, UK and Northampton, MA: Edward Elgar.

Chick, Victoria, and Sheila C. Dow. 2001. "Formalism, Logic and Reality: A Keynesian Analysis." *Cambridge Journal of Economics* 25, no. 6: 705–22.

Chote, Robert. 1994. "Economics: A Missing Link in the White Paper." *Independent*, Saturday, 28 May 1994. https://www.independent.co.uk/news/business/economics-a-missing-link-in-the-white-paper-1439232.html. Accessed 17 August 2019.

Clarke, Peter. 1998. "John Maynard Keynes, 1883–1946: The Best of Both Worlds." In *The Keynesian Revolution and Its Consequences, P. Clarke's Selected Essays*, 38–51. Chentelham, UK: Edward Elgar.

———. 2009. *Keynes: The Rise, Fall, and Return of the 20th Century's Most Influential Economist*. London: Bloomsbury.

Clerc, Pierrik, and Rodolphe Dos Santos Ferreira. 2020. "On Keynesian Economics and the Economics of Keynes after 50 Years." *The European Journal of the History of Economic Thought* 27, no. 6: 919–37.

Clower, Robert. 1965. "The Keynesian Counter-Revolution: A Theoretical Appraisal." In *The Theory of Interest Rates*, edited by F.H. Hahn and F.P.R. Brechling, 34–58. London: Macmillan (reprinted in Clower, 1987)

Coleman, William. 1992. "Lydia and Maynard: The Letters of Lydia Lopokova and John Maynard Keynes." *History of Political Economy—HIST POLIT ECON* 24: 540–42. https://doi.org/10.1215/00182702-24-2-540.

Commons, John. 1893. *The Distribution of Wealth*. New York: Macmillan.

Congdon, Tim. 2007. *Keynes, the Keynesians, and Monetarists*. New York: Edward Elgar.

Conway, Edward. 2015. *The Summit: Bretton Woods, 1944: J. M. Keynes and the Reshaping of the Global Economy*. London: Penguin.

Copleston, Frederick. 1967 [1994]. *A History of Philosophy. Volume VIII: Modern Philosophy: Empiricism, Idealism, and Pragmatism in Britain and America*. New York: Image.

Cristiano, Carlo. 2007. "Keynes and India: 1904–1913: A Study on Foreign Investment Policy." *The European Journal for the History of Economic Thought* 16, no. 2: 301–24.

Cross, Rodney. 1992. "The Duhem-Quine Thesis, Lakatos and the Appraisal of Theories in Macroeconomics." *Economic Journal* 92, no. 366 (June): 320–40.
Darity Jr., William. 1995. "Keynes' Political Philosophy: The Gesell Connection." *Eastern Economic Journal* 21, no. 1 (Winter): 27–41.
Davidson, Paul. 1987. "Sensible Expectations and the Long-Run Non-neutrality of Money." *Journal of Post Keynesian Economics* 10: 146–53.
———. 2002. *Financial Markets, Money and the Real World*. Chentelham, UK: Edward Elgar.
———. 2007. *John Maynard Keynes*. London: Macmillan.
———. 2009. *The Keynes Solution: The Path to Global Economic Prosperity*. London and New York: Palgrave.
Davis, John B. 1989. "Keynes on Atomism and Organicism." *Economic Journal* 99, no. 398 (December): 1159–72.
———. 1991a. "Keynes's Critiques of Moore: Philosophical Foundations of Keynes's Economics." *Cambridge Journal of Economics* 5, no. 1 (March): 61–77.
———. 1991b. "Keynes's View of Economics as a Moral Science." In *Keynes and Philosophy: Essays on the Origins of Keynes's Thought*, edited by Bradley W. Bateman and John B. Davis, 89–103. Aldershot, England: Edward Elgar.
———. 1994. *Keynes's Philosophical Development*. Cambridge: Cambridge University Press.
———. 1995. "Keynes's Later Philosophy." *History of Political Economy* 27, no. 2: 237–56.
———. 1998. "Sraffa and Keynes: Differences and Shared Preconceptions." *Il Pensiero Economico Italiano* 6, no 1: 57–78.
De Long, Bradford. 1996. *Review of John Maynard Keynes: A Tract on Monetary Reform*. London: Macmillan. http://www.j-bradford-delong.net/Econ_Articles/Reviews/monetaryreform.html.
———. 2006. "Friedman Completed Keynes." *The Economic Times*, December 2, 8.
De Marchi, Neil. 1991. "Introduction: Rethinking Lakatos." In *Appraising Economic Theories? Studies in the Methodology of Research Programs*, edited by Neil De Marchi and Mark Blaug. Aldershot, UK: Edward Elgar.
De Vroey, Michel, and Pierre Malgrange. 2011. "The History of Macroeconomics from Keynes's General Theory to the Present." Discussion Papers 2011–28. IRES: University College of London. https://sites.uclouvain.be/econ/DP/IRES/2011028.pdf.
Dimand, Robert W. 1986. "The Macroeconomics of the Treatise on Money." *Eastern Economic Journal* 12, no. 1 (October–December): 431–41.
———. 2010. "What Keynesian Revolution?" In *Keynes's General Theory after Seventy Years*, edited by Robert W. Dimand, Robert. A. Mundell, and Alessandro Vercelli, 287–311. London and New York: Palgrave.

Dimand, Robert, and Harald Hageman (eds). 2019. *The Elgar Companion to John Maynard Keynes.* Chentelham, UK and Northampton, MA: Edward Elgar.

Donini Maccio, Daniela. 2013. "On Economics and Philosophy: G. E. Moore's Imprints on the Cambridge Apostles from Principia Ethica to My Early Beliefs." Unpublished PhD thesis. https://www.academia.edu/17475513/PhD_Thesis_On_economics_and_philosophy_G._E._Moore_s_imprint_on_the_Cambridge_Apostles_ca._1903_-_ca._1936. Accessed 17 February 2018.

Dostaler, Gilles. 1996. "The Formation of Keynes's Vision." *History of Economics Review* 25, no. 1: 14–31.

———. 2007. *Keynes and His Battles.* Chentelham, UK: Edward Elgar.

Dow, Sheila C. 1991. "Keynes's Epistemology and Economic Method." In *Keynes as Philosopher-Economist*, edited by Roderick O'Donnell, 144–67. London: Macmillan.

———. 2001. "Hume: A Re-assessment". In *Knowledge, Social Institutions and the Division of Labour*, edited by Pier L. Porta, Roberto Scazzieri and Andrew Skinner, 75–92. Aldershot, UK: Edward Elgar.

———. 2002. *Economic Methodology: An Inquiry.* Oxford: Oxford University Press.

———. 2010. "Was There a (Methodological) Keynesian Revolution?" In *Keynes's General Theory after Seventy Years*, edited by Robert Dimand, Robert Mundell, and Alessandro Vercelli, 268–86. Basingstoke: Palgrave.

———. 2013. "David Hume and Modern Economics." *Capitalism and Society* 4, no. 1.

———. 2017. "Cambridge's Contribution to Methodology in Economics." In *The Palgrave Companion to Cambridge Economics*, edited by Robert A. Cord, 27–49. London: Palgrave.

Dow, Alistair, and Sheila C. Dow. 2011. "Animal Spirits Revisited." *Capitalism and Society* 6, no. 2.

Dow, Sheila, Jesper Jespersen, and Geoff Tily. 2018. *The General Theory and Keynes for the 21st Century. New Directions in Modern Economics Series.* Chentelham, UK: Edward Elgar.

Drakopoulos, Stavros A., and Anastassios Karayiannis. 2005. "A Review of Kuhnian and Lakatosian Explanations in Economics." *History of Economics Ideas* 13.

Durant, Will. 1926 [1930]. *The Story of Philosophy: The Lives and Opinions of the World's Greatest Philosophers from Plato to John Dewey.* New York: Garden City.

Emre, Merve. n.d. "John Maynard Keynes and Artistic Conventions." *EDITING MODERNISM in Canada.* https://modernistcommons.ca/islandora/object/yale%3A647. Accessed 13 January 2019.

Erturk, Korkut A. 2008. "Why Keynes' A Treatise on Money Might Have Greater Relevance Today Than His General Theory?" *Middle East Technical University Studies in Development* 35, no. 1 (August): 101–20. https://www2.feas.metu.edu.tr/metusd/ojs/index.php/metusd/article/view/216. Accessed 15 September 2018.

Esty, Joshua. 2000. "National Objects: Keynesian Economics and Modernist Culture in England." *Modernism/Modernity* 7: 1–24. https://www.researchgate.net/publication/236802204_National_Objects_Keynesian_Economics_and_Modernist_Culture_in_England. Accessed 14 May 2016.

Felix, David. 1999. *Keynes: A Critical Life*. Westport, CT: Greenwood.

Fioretti, Guido. 2001. "Von Kries and the Other 'German Logicians': Non-numerical Probabilities before Keynes." *Economics and Philosophy* 17, no. 2: 245–73.

Fischer, Stanley. 1990. "Rules Versus Discretion in Monetary Policy." In *Handbook of Monetary Economics*, edited by Benjamin M. Friedman and Frank H. Hahn, 1155–84. North Holland: Elsevier.

Fitzgibbons, Athol J. 1988 [1990]. *Keynes's Vision: A New Political Economy*. Oxford: Clarendon Press.

———. 1991. "The Significance of Keynes's Idealism." In *Keynes and Philosophy: Essays on the Origins of Keynes's Thought*, edited by Bradley W. Bateman and John B. Davis, Chapter 8. Aldershot, UK: Edward Elgar.

———. 1992. "From Keynes's Vision to Keynesian Economics." In *Recent Developments in Post Keynesian Economics*, edited by Philip Arestis and Victoria Chick, 17–26. Chentelham, UK: Edward Elgar.

———. 2003. "Keynes's Epistemology." In *The Philosophy of Keynes's Economics: Probability, Uncertainty and Convention*, edited by Jochen Runde and Sohei Mizuhara, Chapter 5. London and New York: Routledge.

Fontana, Giuseppe. 2003. "Keynes's Treatise on Money." In *The Elgar Companion to Post Keynesian Economics*, edited by John E. King, 237–41. Chentelham, UK: Edward Elgar.

———. 2005. "Mr. Keynes and the 'Classics' Again: A Methodological Enquiry." *Atlantic Economic Journal* 34: 161–74.

Forstater, Mathew. 2010. "Keynes and the Social Sciences: Contributions Outside of Economics, with Applications to Economic Anthropology and Comparative Systems." In *Keynes's General Theory after Seventy Years*, edited by Robert Dimand, Robert Mundell, and Alessandro Vercelli, Chapter 7. Basingstoke: Palgrave.

Foucault, Michel. 1970. *The History of Sexuality: An Introduction*, Volume 1. London: Vintage.

———. 1988. "The Culture of the Self." Conference UC-Berkeley.

Freud, Sigmund. 1930 [1953–74]. "Civilization and Its Discontents." In *The Standard Edition of the Complete Psychological Works of Sigmund Freud* 21, translated by James Strachey, 57–145. London: Hogarth.

———. 1933 [1953–74]. "Why War?" In *The Standard Edition of the Complete Psychological Works of Sigmund Freud* 22, translated by James Strachey, 195–215. London: Hogarth.

Friedman, Milton. 1953. "The Methodology of Positive Economics." In *Essays in Positive Economics*, edited by Milton Friedmanm, 15–57. Chicago: University of Chicago Press.

———. 1956. "The Quantity Theory of Money: A Restatement." In *Studies in the Quantity Theory of Money*, edited by Milton Friedman. Chicago: University of Chicago Press. http://www.luk-korbmacher.de/Schule/VWL/milton.htm.

———. 1957. *A Theory of the Consumption Function: National Bureau of Economic Research*. Princeton: Princeton University Press.

———. 1958. "Capitalism and Freedom." In *Essays on Individuality*, edited by Felix Morley, 168–82. Philadelphia: University of Pennsylvania.

———. 1965. *The Great Contraction 1929–1933*. Princeton: Princeton University Press.

———. 1968. "The Role of Monetary Policy." *American Economic Review* 58: 1–17.

———. 1970. "A Theoretical Framework for Monetary Analysis." *Journal of Political Economy* 78, no. 2: 193–238.

———. 1976. "Inflation and Unemployment." Paper presented at the Nobel Memorial Lecture, December. Stockholm, Sweden.

———. 1991. "Old Wine in New Bottles." *The Economic Journal* 101: 33–40.

———. 1997. "John Maynard Keynes." *Federal Reserve Bank of Richmond Economic Quarterly* 83, no. 2: 1–23.

———. 1999. "John Maynard Keynes." *The Laissez Faire City Times* 3, no. 10 (March). www.geocities.com/ecocorner/iintelarea/mf1.html?20085. Accessed 8 March 2019.

Friedman, Milton, and Anna Schwartz. 1963. *A Monetary History of the United States, 1867–1960*. Princeton: Princeton University Press.

García Duarte, Pedro. 2007 [2009]. "Frank P. Ramsey: A Cambridge Economist." *History of Political Economy* 41, no. 3 (July): 445–70.

Garner, Alan, C. 1982. "Uncertainty, Human Judgment, and Economic Decisions." *Journal of Post Keynesian Economics* 4, no. 3 (Spring): 413–24.

Garrison, Roger, W. 1992. "Is Milton Friedman as Keynesian?" In *Dissent on Keynes: A Critical Appraisal of Keynesian Economics*, edited by Mark Skousen, 131–47. New York: Praeger.

Garrone, Giovanna, and Alberto Marchionatti. 2004. "Keynes on Econometric Method: A Reassessment of His Debate with Tinbergen and Other Econometricians, 1938–1946." Working Paper No. 01/2004. CESMEP: Università di Torino.

Gerrard, Bill. 1991. "Keynes's General Theory: Interpreting the Interpretations." *Economic Journal* 101: 272–87.

Gerrard, Bill, and John Hillard (eds.). 1992. *The Philosophy and Economics of J. M. Keynes*. Aldershot, UK: Edward Elgar.

Gillies, Donald. 2016. *Probability and Uncertainty in Keynes's General Theory*. London: University College of London. http://discovery.ucl.ac.uk/16387/1/16387.pdf. Accessed 15 December 2019.

Gnoss, Claude, and Louis Phillipe Rochon (eds.). (2011). "Introduction." In *Credit, Money and Macroeconomic Policy: A Postkeynesian Approach*. Chentelham, UK and Northampton, MA: Edward Elgar.

Gómez Betancourt, Rebeca. 2013. "One Hundred Years from Today: John Maynard Keynes' *Indian Currency and Finance*." *History of Economics Review* 58, no. 1: 83–95.

Gotti, Maurizio. 1994. "The 'General Theory' as an Open-Ended Work". In *John Maynard Keynes: Language and Method*, edited by Alessandra Marzola and Francesco Silva, 155–91. Aldershot, UK: Edward Elgar.

———. 2009. "Aspects of Individuality in J. M. Keynes's General Theory." In *Commonality and Individuality in Academic Discourse*, edited by Maurizio Gotti, 279–302. Bern: Peter Lang.

Graziani, Augusto. 2003. *The Monetary Theory of Production*. Cambridge: Cambridge University Press.

Grieve, Roy H. 2012. "Keynes, Sraffa and the Emergence of the General Theory". *Review of Political Economy* 24, no. 1 (January): 51–67.

Guizzo, Danielle. 2014. "Ethics Beyond Morality in Economic Thought: Some Lessons from J. M. Keynes." https://www.ineteconomics.org/uploads/papers/Feb-Guizzo_Ethics-and-Morality-in-Keynes.pdf. Accessed 17 November 2020.

Von Haberler, Gottfried. 1946. "The Place of the General Theory of Employment, Interest and Money in the History of Economic Thought." *Review of Economics and Statistics* 28: 187–94.

Hands, Wade. 1985. "Second Thoughts on Lakatos." *History of Political Economy* 17, no. 1: 1–16.

Hansen, Alvin. 1953. *A Guide of Keynes*. New York: McGraw Hill.

Harcourt, Geoffrey C. 1994. "Kahn and Keynes and the Making of The General Theory." *Cambridge Journal of Economics* 18: 11–23. https://citeseerx.ist.psu.edu/viewdoc/download?doi=10.1.1.1011.8690&rep=rep1&type=pdf. Accessed 21 March 2019.

———. 2001. "Is Keynes Dead?" In *50 Years a Keynesian and Other Essays*, edited by Geffrey C. Harcourt, Part I, Chapter 2. Basingstoke, UK: Palgrave.

———. 2016. "Reflections on Keynes's Essays in Biography." Discussion Papers 2016–2019. School of Economics, The University of New South Wales.

Harcourt, Geoffrey C., Peter Kriesler, and John Neville. 2014. "The Attacks on the General Theory: How Keyens's Theory Was Lost." Discussion papers 2016–19, School of Foreign Studies, The University of New South Wales.

Harcourt, Geoffrey C., and Peter Riach (eds.). 1997. *A 'Second' Edition of the General Theory*, Volume I. New York: Routledge.

Harris, Laurence. 1985. *Monetary Theory*. New York: Macmillan.

Harrod, Roy. 1939. "An Essay in Dynamic Theory." *The Economic Journal* 49, no. 93 (March): 14–33.

Hausmann, Daniel M. 2007. *Philosophy of Economics: A Contemporary Introduction*. Cambridge: Cambridge University Press.

———. 2012. "Philosophy of Economics." In *Stanford Encyclopedia of Philosophy*, edited by Edward N. Zalta (Winter), 376–89. https://plato.stanford.edu/entries/economics/. Accessed 9 March 2018.

Hayek, Friedrich A. 1931 [2017]. "Reflections on the Pure Theory of Money of Mr. Keynes." *Economica* 12-Part II: 22–44, in *Mises Daily Articles*. https://mises.org/library/reflections-pure-theory-money-mr-jm-keynes. Accessed 17 February 2017.

———. 1998. *Los Fundamentos de la Libertad*. México: Unión Editorial.

Heilbroner, Robert. 1951. *The Worldly Philosophers: The Lives, Times and Ideas of the Great Economic Thinkers*. New York: Simon & Schuster.

Heilbrun, James. 1984. "Keynes and the Economics of the Arts." *Journal of Cultural Economics* 8, no. 2 (December): 37–49.

Helburn, Suzanne. 1991. "Keynes and Burke." In *Keynes and Philosophy: An Introduction*, edited by Bradley W. Bateman and John B. Davis, Chapter 2. Aldershot, UK: Edward Elgar.

Hendry, David F. 1993. "Econometric Methodology: A Personal Perspective." In *Advances in Econometrics: Fifth World Congress*, Volume II, edited by T. F. Bewley, Chapter 10. Cambridge: Cambridge University Press.

Hicks, John R. 1937. "Mr. Keynes and the "Classics", A Suggested Interpretation." *Econometrica* 5: 147–59.

———. 1974. *The Crisis in Keynesian Economics*. Oxford: Blackwell.

Hill, Greg. 1996. "The Moral Economy: Keynes's Critique of Capitalist Justice." *Critical Review* 10, no. 1: 33–61.

Hoover, Kevin D. 2006. "Doctor Keynes: Economic Theory in a Diagnostic Science." In *The Cambridge Companion to Keynes*, edited by Roger E. Backhouse and Bradley W. Bateman, 78–97. Cambridge: Cambridge University Press.

Hume, David. 1739 [2012]. *Treatise of Human Nature: Being an Attempt to Introduce the Experimental Method Reasoning Into Moral Subjects*. London: John Noon. The Project Gutenberg EBook. http://www.gutenberg.org/files/4705/4705-h/4705-h.htm. Accessed 13 June 2018.

———. 1748 [2003]. *An Enquiry Concerning Human Understanding*. The Project Gutenberg EBook. http://www.gutenberg.org/files/9662/9662-h/9662-h.htm. Accessed 13 September 2014.

Hurka, Thomas. 2015. "Moore's Moral Philosophy." In *The Stanford Encyclopedia of Philosophy*, edited by Edward N. Zalta (Fall Edition). https://plato.stanford.edu/archives/fall2015/entriesmoral/. Accessed 9 March 2018.

Hutchison, Terence W. 1984. "On Verification in Economics." In *The Philosophy of Economics: An Anthology*, edited by Daniel E. Hausman, 158–67. Cambridge: Cambridge University Press.

Jensen, Hans. E. 1988. "Marx and Keynes: Alternative Views of Capitalism?" *Atlantic Economic Journal* 17: 29–38.

Johnson, Elizabeth S., and Harry G. Johnson. 1977. *The Shadow of Keynes*. Chicago: Chicago University Press.

Kahn, Richard F. 1931. "The Relation of Home Investment to Unemployment." *The Economic Journal* 41, no. 162 (June).

———. 1950. "The European Payments Union." *Economica New Series* 16, no. 64: 293–304.

———. 1984 [2011]. *The Making of Keynes' General Theory*. Cambridge: Cambridge University Press.

Kalecki, M. 1936. "Some Remarks on Keynes's *General Theory*." *Ekonomista* 3: 18–26.

Kania, Witold. 2006. "Principia Ethica de G. E. Moore y los comienzos de la ética analítica." Śląskie Studia Historyczno-Teologiczne, t. 39, z. 2, s.: 347–59. http://www.wtl.us.edu.pl/ssht/39,2/SSHT_39,2(2006)347-359.pdf. Accessed 16 October 2019.

Kemmerer, Edwin W. 1914. "Reviewed Work(s): Indian Currency and Finance by John Maynard Keynes." *The Quarterly Journal of Economics* 28, no. 2 (February): 373–77.

Kent, Richard J. 2016. "A Third Fundamental Equation for Keynes's Treatise on Money." *Journal of the History of Economic Thought* 38, no. 2 (May): 175–88.

Keynes, John Maynard. n.d. "Have we a Panacea?" In *JMK/UA/37*.

———. n.d. *Keynes's Page at the Newton Project*. Newton-Related Papers of John Maynard Keynes. In *CW/67/*: 60, *CW/67/*: 61. https://www.newtonproject.sussex.ac.uk/prism.php?id=19. Accessed 10 May 2019.

———. n.d. "Letter to Professor A. V. Hill." *Correspondence Concerning Keynes' Donations of Newton Material to Trinity College, Cambridge and the Soviet Academy of Science*, King's College, Cambridge, UK.

———. n.d. *JMK CW XII. Economic Activities and Correspondence. Investment and Editorial*, edited by D. Moggridge and E. Johnson. London: Royal Economic Society.

———. 1902. "Essays on Bernard de Mortaix of Clunny." In *JMK/PP/33*.

———. 1902–1903. "Essay on Peter Abelard." In *JMK/UA/16*.

———. 1902–1910 [1921]. Keynes's Unpublished Eton Papers, JMK/UP 1902–1910, 1921. https://archiveshub.jisc.ac.uk/data/gb272-jmk. Archive Search. Archive Centre, King's College, Cambridge. https://archivesearch.lib.cam.ac.uk/repositories/7/archival_objects/285279.

———. 1902–1921 [1988]. *Keynes Papers*, King's College. Keynes unpublished articles or papers or manuscripts at King's College Library, Cambridge University, United Kingdom., *The John Maynard Keynes Papers in King's College, Cambridge*, *The Unpublished Writings of John Maynard Keynes* (JMK/UA). https://janus.lib.cam.ac.uk/db/node.xsp?id=EAD%2FGBR%2F0272%2FPP%2FJMK%2FUA, or https://www.proquest.com/products-services/Keynes.html. Accessed 27 February 2019.

———. 1903a. "Essay on Time." In *JMK/UA/17*.

———. 1903b. "Ethics in Relation to Conduct." In *JMK/UA/19/2*.

———. 1903c. "Modern Ethics." In *JMK/UA/1/1*.

———. 1904a. "Beauty." In *JMK/UA/19/3*.

———. 1904b. "The Political Doctrines of Edmund Burke." In *JMK/UA/20/3*.

———. 1904c. "Truth." In *JMK/UA/18/1*.

———. 1905a. "Miscellanea ethica." In *JMK/UA/21*.

———. 1905b. "Modern Civilization." In *JMK/UA/22*.

———. 1905c. 'A Theory of Beauty', unpublished manuscript deposited in King's College Library, Cambridge University

———. 1905d. 'Miscellanea Ethica', unpublished manuscript deposited in King's College Library, Cambridge University.

———. 1905–1906. "Posterior Analytics." In *JMK/UA/28*.

———. 1906a. "Egoism." In *JMK/UA/26*.

———. 1906b. "Shall We Write Melodramas?" In *JMK/UA/25*.

———. 1906–several dates. *Keynes Letters to Lytton Strachey*. In *JMK/PP/45/316/2*.

———. 1908a. "Paradise." In *JMK/UA/31*.

———. 1908b. "Prince Henry or Prince Rupert?" In *JMK/UA/30*.

———. 1908c. "The Principles of Probability." In *TP/A/12*.

———. 1909 [1983]. "Recent Economic Events in India." *Economic Journal*, March: 1–22. In *CW Vol. 11 Economic Articles and Correspondence: Academic*. London: Basingstoke.

———. 1909a. "Can We Consume Our Surplus or the Influence of Furniture on Love." In *JMK/UA/34*.

———. 1909b. "Science and Art." In *JMK/UA/32*.

———. 1909c. "The Present Position of Metaphysics in Our Society." In *JMK/UA/33*.

———. 1909–1946. *Research on Newton*. In *JMK/PP/60*.

———. 1910. "8 Lectures on Company Finance and Stock Exchange, Lent Term (Notebook)." In *JMK/UA/6/3*.

———. 1910 [1921]. "On the Principle of Organic Unity." In *JMK/UA/35*.

———. 1913a [1971]. Indian Currency and Finance. In *JMK CW Vol. I Indian Currency and Finance*, edited by D. Moggridge. London: Royal Economic Society.

———. 1913b [1971]. Vol. 1: *Indian Currency and Finance*.

———. 1916a. "John Maynard Keynes as a Conscientious Objector." In *JMK/PP/7*.

———. 1916b. "Statement from Keynes to the Holborn Tribune." Manuscript Letter 28, no. 2. King's College, Cambridge. https://en.wikisource.org/wiki/File:Keynes_conscentious_objection_1916.jpg. Accessed 15 July 2019.

———. 1919 [1971]. Vol. 2: *The Economic Consequences of the Peace*.

———. 1921 [1973]. Vol. 8: *A Treatise on Probability*.

———. 1922. "Editorial Forward." *CW JMK XVII*, *The Genoa Conference*, 420–25.

———. 1922a [1971]. Vol. 3: *A Revision of the Treaty*.

———. 1922b [1971]. A Revision of the Treaty. A Sequel. In *JMK CW Vol. III A Revision of the Treaty*, edited by A Sequel. D. Moggridge. London: Royal Economic Society.

———. 1923a [1971]. Vol. 4: *A Tract on Monetary Reform*.

———. 1923b [1971]. A Tract on Monetary Reform. In *JMK CW Vol. IV A Tract on Monetary Reform*, edited by D. Moggridge. London: Royal Economic Society.

———. 1925a. *The Economic Consequences of Mr. Churchill*. London: Hogarth.

———. 1925b. *'Am I a Liberal?' The Nation & Athenaeum*, (Part I: 563–4, and Part II: 587–8).

———. 1925c. 'Am I a liberal'. In *JMK CW Vol. IX Essays in Persuasion*.

———. 1926a. "The End of Laissez-faire." Based on the Sidney Ball Lecture at Oxford in November 1924 and on a lecture at the University of Berlin in June 1926. *Panarchy*. London: Hogarth. https://www.panarchy.org/keynes/laissezfaire.1926.html. Accessed 17 June 2020.

———. 1926b. 'The end of the Laissez-faire.' In *JMK CW Vol. IX Essays in Persuasion*, edited by D. Moggridge. London: Royal Economic Society.

———. 1926 [2004]. '*The end of Laissez-faire*.' Washington DC: Rowman.

———. 1927 [1931] [1972]. 'Clissold.' In *JMK CW Vol. IX. Essays in Persuasion*, edited by D. Moggridge. London Royal Economic Society.

———. 1928. "Unpublished letter to F. L. Lucas." February, King's College, Cambridge University, UK.

———. 1930a. "The Economic Possibilities for Our Grandchildren." http://www.econ.yale.edu/smith/econ116a/keynes1.pdf. Accessed 1 January 2019.
———. 1930b. "Auri Sacra Fames." In *JMK CW Vol. IX Essays in Persuasion*, edited by D. Moggridge. London: Royal Economic Society.
———. 1930c. "Economic Possibilities for Our Grandchildren." In *JMK CW Vol. IX Essays in Persuasion*, edited by D. Moggridge. London: Royal Economic Society.
———. 1930a [1971]. Vol. 5: *A Treatise on Money. The Pure Theory of Money.*
———. 1930b [1971]. Vol. 6: *A Treatise on Money. The Applied Theory of Money.*
———. 1930c [1971]. A Treatise on Money. In *JMK CW Vols. V and VI A Treatise on Money*. edited by D. Moggridge. London: Royal Economic Society.
———. 1930 [1932]. "Economic Possibilities for Our Grandchildren." In *Essays in Persuasion*, 358–73. New York: Harcourt. https://assets.aspeninstitute.org/content/uploads/files/content/upload/Intro_and_Section_I.pdf. Accessed 21 March 2019.
———. 1931a. *The Internal Mechanics of the Trade Slump*. London: The Royal Institution of Great Britain. https://www.baumanrarebooks.com/rare-books/keynes-john-maynard/internal-mechanics-of-the-trade-slump/81459.aspx. Accessed 31 May 2018.
———. 1931b. "Keynes Rejoinder to Mr. D. H. Robertson." *Economic Journal XLI* 163 (September). In *JMK/EJ/6/7*. Cambridge: Cambridge University Press. https://discovery.nationalarchives.gov.uk/details/r/afc22cbd-5472-49c8-8ba4-a585275185c2. Accessed 15 November 2019.
———. 1931c. "Mr. Keynes' Theory of Money: A Rejoinder." *The Economic Journal* 41, no. 163: 412–23.
———. 1931d. "Review of Foundations of Mathematics by Frank P. Ramsey." *The New Stateman and the Nation* 21: 407.
———. 1931e. "The Pure Theory of Money: A Reply to Dr. Hayek." *Economica* 34: 387–97.
———. 1931f. "The Means to Prosperity." In *JMK CW Vol. IX. Essays in Persuasion*, edited by D. Moggridge. London Royal Economic Society.
———. 1931g. "An Open Letter to President to Roosevelt." New York Times, December 31, 1931. In *JMK CW Vol. IX Essays in Persuasion*, edited by D. Moggridge. London: Royal Economic Society.https://la.utexas.edu/users/hcleaver/368/368KeynesOpenLetFDRtable.pdf.
———. 1931 [1963]. "III The Return to the Gold Standard 1: Auri Sacra Fames." In *Essays in Persuasion*. New York: Norton.
———. 1931 [1972]. Vol. 9: *Essays in Persuasion.*
———. 1931 [1980]. "Ramsey as a Philosopher." In *CW Vol. 10*, 336–39. London: Basingstoke.

———. 1933a. "A Monetary Theory of Production." *Festschrift for Arthur Spietoff.* https://web.archive.org/web/2010121813158/http://homepage.newschool.edu/hot/profiles/Keynes.htm. Accessed 21 February 2017.
———. 1933b. "An Open Letter to President Roosevelt." *New Deal Documents.* https://newdeal.feri.org/misc/keynes2.htm.
———. 1933c. *Articles and Correspondence: To R. F. Kahn*, 3 May, CW, Vol. 12, 100–1. London: Basingstoke.
———. 1933d. *The Means to Prosperity.* London: Macmillan. https://archive.org/details/in.ernet.dli.2015.227329. Accessed 17 June 2017.
———. 1933e. "The Monetary Theory of Production." *Der Stand und die nächste Zukunft der Konjunkturforschung: Festschrift für Arthur Spiethoff*. Munich: Duncker & Humboldt: 123–25.
———. 1933 [1946]. "Newton the Man." *The Royal Society of London.* https://www-history.mcs.st-andrews.ac.uk/Extras/Keynes_Newton.html.
———. 1933a [1972]. "Thomas Robert Malthus." In *JMK CW Vol. X. Essays in Biography*, edited by D. Moggridge. London Royal Economic Society.
———. 1933b [1972]. "Frank Ramsey." In *JMK CW Vol. X. Essays in Biography*, edited by D. Moggridge. London: Royal Economic Society.
———. 1933c [1972]. Vol. 10: *Essays in Biography.*
———. 1933 [1978]. "Clissold". In CW, Vol. 12, 315–20. In *Essays in Persuasion*. London: Macmillan.
———. 1936 [1964]. *The General Theory of Employment, Interest and Money.* New York: Harcourt.
———. 1936 [1973]. The General Theory of Employment, Interest and Money. In *JMK CW Vol. VII The General Theory of Employment, Interest and Money*, edited by D. Moggridge. London: Royal Economic Society.
———. 1937a. "Alternative Theories of the Rate of Interest." *Economic Journal* 47, no. 186 (June): 241–52.
———. 1937b. "The General Theory of Employment." *The Quarterly Journal of Economics* 51, no. 2: 209–23.
———. 1937c. "The Ex-ante Theory of the Rate of Interest." *Economic Journal* 47, no. 188 (December): 663–69.
———. 1937d. "Some Economic Consequences of a Declining Population." *Eugenics Review* (April).
———. 1938 [1949]. *Two Memoirs: "Dr. Melchior, a Defeated Enemy?", and "My Early Beliefs."* New York: Kelley.
———. 1938a. "The Policy of Government-Storage of Foodstuffs and Raw Materials." *Economic Journal* 48 (September): 49–60.
———. 1938b. "J. M. Keynes's Letter to R. F. Kahn." 5 May 1938, In *CW, Vol. 12 Investment and Editorial*. London: Basingstoke.

———. 1938c. Articles and Correspondence. *Memorandum for the Estates Committee*, King's College, Cambridge: 8 May 1938. Post Mortem on Investment Policy, CW, Volume 12, 102–9. London: Basingstoke.

———. 1938d. "J. M. Keynes's Letter to Harrod." 4 July 1938. In *CW*, *Vol. 14 The General Theory and After: Part II. Defence and Development*, 295–97. London: Basingstoke.

———. 1938e. *Miscellaneous Reviews*. A Review of Volume VII of The Cambridge Modern History from the Cambridge Review, 5 November 1903. In CW, *XI*, 502–7. London: Basingstoke.

———. 1938f. "My early beliefs." In *JMK CW Vol. IX Essays in Persuasion*, edited by D. Moggridge. London: Royal Economic Society.

———. 1938 [1933] [1972]. "My Early Beliefs." In *JMK CW Vol. X. Essays in Biography*, edited by D. Moggridge. London Royal Economic Society.

———. 1939a. "Professor Tinbergen's Method." *Economic Journal* 49: 558–68.

———. 1939b. "Relative Movements of Real Wages and Output." *The Economic Journal* 49, no. 193 (March): 39–51.

———. 1939c. BBC Radio Speech. "When the day of peace comes." https://archiveshub.jisc.ac.uk/data/gb272-jmk. Archive Search. Archive Centre, King's College, Cambridge. https://archivesearch.lib.cam.ac.uk/repositories/7/archival_objects/285279.

———. 1940a. *How to Pay for the War: A Radical Plan for the Chancellor of the Exchequer*. In *CW , Vol. 9 : Essays in Persuasion*, 367–439. London: Basingstoke.

———. 1940b. How to Pay for the War. In *JMK CW Vol. VIII How to Pay for the War*, edited by D. Moggridge and E. Johnson. London: Royal Economic Society.

———. 1940c. "The Concept of National Income: A Supplementary Note." *Economic Journal* 50, no. 197: 60–5.

———. 1941–1946. "*Correspondence Concerning J. M. Keynes Work as the Trustee of the National Gallery*." In *JMK/PP/77*.

———. 1943 [1987]. *Appendix: The Keynes Plan. Proposals for an International Clearing Union (Cmd 6437) April*, reprinted in *Keynes and Development*, edited by Anthony. P. Thirlwall, 147–78. New York: Springer.

———. 1943. "Memorandum: The Long-Term Problem of Full Employment." In *CW Vol. 27*: 320–5. London: Basingstoke.

———. 1944a. "White Paper, Economy: 1944 Employment White Paper *[MT's annotated copy]*." *Margaret Thatcher Foundation*, 1944 May 1 Mo, Archive (Thatcher MSS). https://www.margaretthatcher.org/document/110368. Accessed 17 October 2016.

———. 1944b. "Post-war Employment: Note on the Report of the Steering Committee." 14 February–1944. In *CW Vol 27*. London: Basingstoke.

———. 1946. "Fluctuations in Net Investment in the United States." *The Economic Journal* 46, no. 183 (September): 540–47.
———. 1971–1989. *The Collected Writings of John Maynard Keynes (CW)* 30 vols, edited by Elizabeth Johnson (19–28) and Daniel E. Moggridge (15–18). London: Macmillan, for the Royal Economic Society. Volumes are:
———. 1973a. Vol. 12: *Economic Articles and Correspondence: Investment and Editorial.*
———. 1973b. Vol. 13: *The General Theory and After: Part I: Preparation.*
———. 1973c. Vol. 14: *The General Theory and After: Part II: Defence and Development.*
———. 1977. Vol. 17: *Activities 1920–22: Treaty Revision and Reconstruction.*
———. 1978. Vol. 22: *Activities 1939–1945: Internal War Finance.*
———. 1979a. Vol. 29: *The General Theory and After: A Supplement (to Vols. 13 and 14).*
———. 1979b. Vol. 24: *Activities 1944–1946. The Transition to Peace.*
———. 1980a. Vol. 25: *Activities 1940–1944: Shaping the Post-War World: The Clearing Union.*
———. 1980b. Vol. 26: *Activities 1940–1944: Shaping the Post-War World: The Bretton Woods and Reparations.*
———. 1980c. Vol. 27: *Activities 1940–46: Shaping the Post-War World: Employment and Commodities.*
———. 1981. Vol. 19: *Activities 1922–29: The Return to Gold and Industrial Policy*, 2 vols, 1981.
———. 1982a. Vol. 21: *Activities 1931–1939: World Crises and Policies in Britain and America.*
———. 1982b. Vol. 28: *Social, Political and Literary Writings.*
———. 2012. *JMK CW Vol. XXVII Activities 1940–1946: Shaping the Post-War World: Employment and Commodities*, edited by D. Moggridge and E. Johnson. London: Royal Economic Society.
Keynes, John Maynard and Hubert David Henderson. 1931. "Can Lloyd George do it? An Examination of the Liberal Pledge." Florida Atlantic University Library. file:///C:/Users/kaka/AppData/Local/Microsoft/Windows/INetCache/IE/8G760D2D/1925505_Can%20%20Lloyd%20George%20Do%20it.pdf. Accessed 17 July 2018.
Keynes, John Maynard, and Piero Sraffa. 1938. *An Abstract of a Treatise on Human Nature.* Cambridge: Cambridge University Press.
Keynes, Milo (ed.). 1975. *Essays on John Maynard Keynes.* Cambridge: Cambridge University Press.
Kirshner, Jonathan. 2015. "Keynes's Early Beliefs and Why They Still Matter." *Challenge* 58, no. 5: 398–412.
Klein, Lawrence R. 1947. *The Keynesian Revolution.* New York: Macmillan.

Knight, Frank. 1921. *Risk, Uncertainty and Profit*. Boston: Hart, in *The Library of Economics and Liberty*. https://www.econlib.org/library/Knight/knRUP.html. Accessed 27 December 2019.

Kregel, Jan. 2008. "Changes in the U.S. Financial System and the Subprime Crisis." Levy Economics Institute of Bard College WP 530, April.

———. 2012. "Was Keynes's Monetary Policy, à outrance in the Treatise, a Forerunner of the Model of ZIRP and QE?" *Ensayos Económicos* 1, no. 12 (September): 7–22.

———. 2017. "A Two-tier Eurozone or a Euro of Regions? A Radical Proposal Based on Keynes's Clearing Union?" Policy Brief 144, The Levy Economics Institute, September. https://www.levyinstitute.org/publications/a-two-tier-eurozone-or-a-euro-of-regions-a-radical-proposal-based-on-keyness-clearing-union. Accessed 23 September 2019.

Krugman, Paul. 2007. "Who Was Milton Friedman? *The New York Review of Books*, March 29. http://www.nybooks.com/articles/archives/2007/feb/15/who-was-Milton-Friedman? Accessed July 24, 2018.

———. 2009. "Why Aren't We All Keynesians Now?" *Krugman's Website*. http://web.mit.edu/krugman/www/#fortune. Accessed 31 December 2018.

Kuehn, Daniel. 2013. "Keynes, Newton and The Royal Society: The Events of 1942 and 1943." *The Royal Society*. https://rsnr.royalsocietypublishing.org/content/early/2012/12/12/rsnr.2012.0053.article-info. Accessed 10 July 2017.

Kuhn, Thomas S. 1970a. *The Structure of Scientific Revolutions*. Chicago: Chicago University Press.

———. 1970b. "Reflections on My Critics." In *Criticisms and the Growth of Knowledge*, edited by Imre Lakatos and Alan Musgrave. Cambridge: Cambridge University Press.

Laidler, David. 1999. *Fabricating the Keynesian Revolution: Studies of the Inter-war Literature on Money, the Cycle, and Unemployment*. Cambridge, MA: Cambridge University Press.

Lakatos, Imre. 1971. "History of Science and Its Rational Reconstructions." In *Boston Studies in the Philosophy of Science* 8, edited by R. Buck and Richard S. Cohen, 91–136.

———. 1978a. *The Methodology of Scientific Research Programmes*. Cambridge: Cambridge University Press.

———. 1978b. *Philosophical Papers*, 2 vols. Cambridge: Cambridge University Press.

Lakatos, Imre, and Alan Musgrave (eds.). 1970. *Criticism and the Growth of Knowledge*. Cambridge: Cambridge University Press.

Lambert, Paul. 1963. "The Social Philosophy of John Maynard Keynes." *Annals of Public and Cooperative Economics* 34, no. 4 (October): 483–515.

———. 1968. "The Evolution of Keynes's Thought for the Treatise on Money to the General Theory." *Annals of Public and Cooperative Economy* 40, no. 3 (July): 243–63.

Lawlor, Michael S. 2006. *The Economics of Keynes in Historical Context: An Intellectual History of the General Theory*. New York: Palgrave.

Lawson, Tony. 1993. "Keynes and Convention." *Review of Social Economics* 5, no. 2 (June): 174–200.

———. 1997. *Economics and Reality*. London: Routledge.

———. 2003. "Keynes's Realist Orientation." In *The Philosophy of Keynes's Economics: Probability, Uncertainty and Convention*, edited by Jochen Runde and Sohei Mizuhara, Chapter 12, 159–69. New York: Routledge.

Lawson, Tony and Hashem Pesaram. 1985 [2010]. *Keynes' Economics: Methodological Issues*. London: Croom Helm.

Lefebvre, Henri. 2016 [1975]. *Hegel, Marx, Nietzsche (o el reino de las sombras)*. Madrid: Siglo XVI, translated from *Hegel, Marx, Nietzsche (ou la ryaume des ombres)*. Casterman: Tournai.

Leijonhufvud, Axel. 1968. *On Keynesian Economics and the Economics of Keynes: A Study in Monetary Theory*. New York: Oxford University Press.

———. 1999. "Mr. Keynes and the Moderns." In *The Impact of Keynes on Economics in the 20th Century*, edited by Luigi Pasinetti and Bernard Schefold, 16–35. Cheltenham, UK: Edward Elgar.

———. 2009. "'Out of the Corridor' Keynes and the Crisis." *Cambridge Journal of Economics* 33, no. 4: 741–57.

LeRoy, Stephen F. 1983. "Keynes's Theory of Investment." *History of Political Economy* 15, no. 3: 397–421.

Levy, Paul. 1980. *Moore and the Cambridge Apostles*. New York: Holt.

Littleboy, Bruce, and Ghanshyam Metha. 1983. "The Scientific Method of Keynes." *Journal of Economic Studies* 10, no. 4: 3–14.

Lubenow, William C. 1998. *The Cambridge Apostles, 1820–1914: Liberalism, Imagination, and Friendship in British Intellectual and Professional Life*. Cambridge: Cambridge University Press.

Machlup, Fritz. 1978. *Methodology of Economics and Other Social Sciences*. New York: Academic Press.

MacIntyre, Alisdair. 1981 [2007]. *After Virtue: A Study in Moral Theory*. Notre Dame: University of Notre Dame Press. https://epistemh.pbworks.com/f/4.+Macintyre.pdf. Accessed 14 May 2020.

Maddock, Rodney. 1984. "Rational Expectations Macrotheory: A Lakatosian Case Study in Program Adjustment." *History of Political Economy* 16, no. 2: 291–309.

Magee, Bryan. 2000. *Popper*. México: Colofón.

Maher, Patrick. 2010. "Keynes Concept of Probability." *Scientific Thought II* (Spring).

Makasheva, Natal'ja. 2013. "Uncertainty, Probability, Ethics: J. M. Keynes, L. Mises, F. Knight." Voprosi Economiki, N.P. Redaktsiya zhumala.

Mankiw, N. Gregory. 2010. *Macroeconomics*. 7th ed. New York: Worth.

———. 2015. *Macroeconomics*, 9th ed. New York: Worth.

Mann, Geoff. 2019. *In the Long Run We Are All Dead: Keynesianism, Political Economy, and Revolution*. London: Verso.

Mann, Geoff. 2016. "Keynes Resurrected? Saving Civilization, Again and Again." *Dialogues in Human Geography* 6, no. 2: 119–34.

Mantoux, Étienne. 1946. *The Carthaginian Peace: The Economic Consequences of Mr. Keynes*. Oxford: Oxford University Press.

Marchionatti, Roberto. 2010. "J. M. Keynes, Thinker of Economic Complexity." *Journal of Economic Ideas* 18, no. 2: 115–46.

Marcuzzo, M. Cristina. 2002. "The Collaboration Between J. M. Keynes and R. F. Kahn from the Treatise on Money to the General Theory." *History of Political Economy* 34, no. 2: 421–8.

———. 2008. "Sraffa and Cambridge Economics, 1928–1931." In *Piero Sraffa's Political Economy: A Centenary Estimate*, edited by Terenzio Cozzi and Roberto Marchionatti, 81–99. London and New York: Routledge.

Markwell, Don. 2006. *John Maynard Keynes and International Relations: Economic Paths to War and Peace*. New York: Oxford University Press.

———. 2009. "Keynes and International Economics and Political Relations." *A Seminar on the Contemporary Relevance of John Maynard Keynes*, April. The University of Western Australia. https://www.trinity.unimelb.edu. Accessed 19 March 2019.

Marzola, Alessandra. 1994. "Rhetoric and Imagination in the Economic and Political Writings of J. M. Keynes." In *John Maynard Keynes: Language and Method*, edited by Alessandra Marzola and Francesco Silva, 192–223. Aldershot, UK: Edward Elgar.

Marzola, Alessandra, and Francesco Silva. 1994. *John Maynard Keynes: Language and Method*. Brookfield, VT: Edward Elgar.

Mellor, D. Hugh. 1995. "F. P. Ramsey." *Philosophy* 70, no. 2: 243–62.

Meltzer, Alan H. 1981. "Keynes's General Theory: A Different Perspective." *Journal of Economic Literature* 19, no. 1: 34–64.

———. 1983. "Interpreting Keynes." *Journal of Economic Literature* 21 no. 1: 66–78.

Michell, Jo, and Jan Toporowski. 2013. "Critical Observations on Financialization and the Financial Process." *International Journal of Political Economy* 42, no. 4: 67–82.

Mini, Piero V. 1991a. *Keynes, Bloomsbury and the General Theory*. Basingstoke: Palgrave.

———. 1991b. "The Anti-Benthamism of J. M. Keynes. Implications for The General Theory." *The American Journal of Economics and Sociology* 50, no. 4: 453–68.

———. 1994. *John Maynard Keynes: A Study in the Psychology of Original Work.* Basingstoke: Palgrave.

Minsky, Hyman. P. 1975. *John Maynard Keynes*. New York: Columbia University Press.

———. 1986. *Stabilizing an Unstable Economy*. New Haven, CT: Yale University Press.

Mizuhara, Sohei, and Jochen Runde (eds.). 2003. *The Philosophy of Keynes' Economics: Probability, Uncertainty and Convention*. London: Routledge.

Moggridge, Daniel E. 1986. "Keynes and His Revolution in Historical Perspective." *Eastern Economic Journal* 12, no. 4: 357–69.

———. 1992. *Maynard Keynes: An Economist's Biography*. London: Routledge.

———. 2005. "Keynes, the Arts, and the State." *History of Political Economy* 37, no. 3: 535–55.

——— (ed.). 2010. "Keynes on the Wireless," September. New York: Macmillan. https://g.co/Kgs/XeWord. Accessed 16 August 2019.

Moore, George E. 1903a. *Principia Ethica*. Reprinted in Prometheus Books' Great Books in Philosophy Series. http://fair-use.org/g-e-moore/principia-ethica/. Accessed 8 January 2015.

———. 1903b. "Refutation of Idealism." *Mind New Series* 12, no. 48 (October): 433–53. https://es.scribd.com/document/163302582/Moore-G-E-The-Refutation-of-Idealism-1903. Accessed 20 January 2015.

Muchlinsky, Elke. 1998. "The Philosophy of John Maynard Keynes (A Reconsideration)." *Cahiers D'economie Politique* 30, no. 1: 227–53.

Muñoz, B. Jesús. 2011. "Orthodox Versus Heterodox (Minskyan) Perspectives of Financial Crises: Explosion in the 1990s versus Implosion in the 2000s." Levy Economics Institute of Bard College WP 695.

———. 2017. "Commonalities between the 'Bookends' Financial Crises of Mexico 1994 and Greece 2007." In *The Internal Impact and External Influence of the Greek Financial Crisis*, edited by J. Marangos, Chapter 11. CH: Palgrave Macmillan.

Muñoz, B. Jesús, and Joel Bonales. 2008. "Keynes the Keynesian: A Lakatosian Insight into Keynes's 'Probable' Theoretical Contributions to Macroeconomics after 1937." In *Keynes and Macroeconomics after 70 Years: Critical Assessments of the General Theory*, edited by L. Randall Wray and Matthew Forstater, 20–33. Chentelham: Edward Elgar.

Nelson, Stephen C. 2015. "Paper Entanglements: Why (and How) Keynes's Ideas about Debt Still Matter." *Challenge* 58, no. 6: 492–528.

Nevile, John W. 2000. "What Would Keynes Have Thought of the Development of IS–LM." In *IS–LM and Modern Macroeconomics*, edited by Warren Young and B. Zilberfarb. Boston, MA: Kluwer.

Nietzsche, Friedrich. 1883 [1978]. *Thus Spoke Zarathustra*. London: Penguin.

———. 1886 [2013]. *Beyond Good and Evil*. The Project Gutenberg EBook. https://www.gutenberg.org/files/4363/4363-h/4363-h.htm. Accessed 16 February 2019.

Nolan, Mark C. 2013. *Keynes in Dublin: Exploring the 1933 Finlay Lecture*. Cork: Sweeney.

O'Connell, Joan. 1996. "Uncertainty in 'A Treatise on Probability' and the 'General Theory'." WP 9, Department of Economics, National University of Ireland, Galway. https://hdl.handle.net/10379/1369. Accessed 18 April 2017.

O'Donnell, Roderick M. 1989. *Keynes: Philosophy, Economics and Politics: The Philosophical Foundations of Keynes's Thought and their Influence on his Economics and Politics*. London: Macmillan.

———. 1991a. *Keynes as Philosopher-Economist*. Proceedings of The Ninth Keynes Seminar held at the University of Kent. London: Macmillan.

———. 1991b. "The Epistemology of John Maynard Keynes." *The British Journal for the Philosophy of Science* 41, no. 3: 333–50.

———. 1992a. "The Unwritten Books and Papers of John Maynard Keynes." *History of Political Economy* 24, no. 4: 767–817.

———. 1992b. "Keynes's Weight of the Argument and Popper's Paradox of Ideal Evidence." *Philosophy of Science* 59, no. 1: 44–52.

———. 1994. *A Supplementary Edition of J. M. Keynes Writings, Rationale, Nature and Significance*. Sydney: Macquarie University School of Economic and Financial Studies. https://trove.nla.gov.au/version/37682075. Accessed 17 March 2018.

———. 1995. "Keynes on Aesthetics." *History of Political Economy* 27, suplement: 93–121.

———. 2006. "Keynes's Principles of Writing (Innovative) Economics." *Economic Record* 82, no. 259: 396–407.

———. 2011. "Two Post-Keynesian Approaches to Uncertainty and Irreducible Uncertainty." In *The Oxford Handbook of Post-Keynesian Economics. Volume 2: Critiques and Methodology*, edited by Geoffrey C. Harcourt and Peter Kriesler, 124–42. New York: Oxford University Press.

———. 2016. "Third Contribution to the Ergodic/Nonergodic Critique: Reply to Davidson, Part 2." *Journal of Post Keynesian Economics* 39, no. 2 (April): 145–71.

———. 2021. "Keynes's Treatise on Probability: The First Century." *Review of Post Keynesian Economics* 33, no. 4: 585–610.

O'Rourke, Kevin H. 2015. "Economic Impossibilities for Our Grand-Children?" Discussion Papers in Economic and Social History 139, December. University of Oxford.

Padayachee, Vishnu et al. 2013. "Barbaric Gold and Civilized Banking: Keynes's Indian Currency and Finance: A View from the South after 100 Years." *International Review of Applied Economics* 2, no. 6 (October): 822–33.

Parsons, Stephen D. 1996. "Post Keynesian Realism and Keynes' General Theory." *Journal of Post Keynesian Economics* 18, no. 3: 419–41.

Pasinetti, Luigi L. 1997. "J. M. Keynes's 'Revolution' the Major Event of Twentieth-Century Economics?" In *The Impact of Keynes on Economics in the 20th Century*, edited by Luigi L. Pasinetti and Bernard Schefold, Chapter 1, 3–15. Edward Elgar: Chentelham, UK.

———. 2007. *Keynes and the Cambridge Keynesians: A 'Revolution in Economics' to be Accomplished.* Cambridge: Cambridge University Press.

Patinkin, Don. 1975. "The Collected Writings of John Maynard Keynes: From the Tract to the General Theory." *Economic Journal* 85, no. 338: 249–71.

———. 1987. "Keynes, John Maynard." In *The New Palgrave: A Dictionary of Economics*, Volume 3, edited by John Eatwell et al. (K to P): 19–41. New York: Macmillan.

Patton, Paul. 2019. "Foucault, Nietzsche and the History of Truth." In *Foucault and Nietzsche: A Critical Encounter*, edited by Alan Rosenberg and Joseph Westfall, Chapter 1. Bloomsbury: Bloomsbury Studies in Continental Philosophy.

Pecchi, Lorenzo, and Gustavo Piga (eds.). 2008. *Revisiting Keynes Economic Possibilities for Our Grandchildren.* Cambridge, MA: The MIT Press.

Peden, George C. 1944 [1988]. "The 1944 White Paper on Employment Policy." In *Keynes, the Treasury and British Economic Policy: Studies in Economic and Social History.* London: Palgrave. https://link.springer.com/chapter/10.1007%2F978-1-349-07019-0_6. Accessed 13 May 2020.

Pernecky, Mark. 1992. "The Keynesian Revolution from a Philosophy of Science Perspective: Revolutionary or Evolutionary?" *Methodus* 4: 126–34.

———. 2011. "Keynes' Preface to the German Edition of the General Theory: Nazi Sympathies or Methodological Empathies?" *Forum for Social Economics* 40, no. 2 (October): 253–64.

Pettifor, Ann, and Geoffrey Tilly. 2015. "What are the Economic Consequences for Our Grandchildren." *The King's Politics Society at King's College Chapel*, November. Cambridge: Cambridge University. https://static1.squarespace.com/static/541ff5f5e4b02b7c37f31ed6/t/564a1bc0e4b06fd62eb2453a/1447697344068/Keynes.pdf. Accessed 17 May 2018.

Pheby, John. 1985 [2009]. "Are Popperian Criticisms of Keynes Justified." In *Keynes' Economics: Methodological Issues*, edited by Tony Lawson and Hashem Pesaran, Chapter 6. Armonk, NY: Sharpe.

Phelps, Edmund S. 2006. "Capitalism and Keynes: From the Treatise on Probability to The General Theory." Conference Commemorating Keynes 1883–1946, July. http://www.columbia.edu/~esp2/CapitalismAndKeynes2007June22.pdf. Accessed 20 December 2016.

Popper, Karl. 1973. *Conjectural Knowledge: My Solution to the Problem of Induction*. Oxford: Oxford University Press. https://www.kcvs.ca/martin/phil334/papers/popper.pdf. Accessed 14 March 2018.

———. 1974. *Prediction and Prophecy in the Social Sciences*. London: Routledge.

Quine, Willard Van Oman. 1951. "Two Dogmas of Empiricism." *The Philosophical Review* 60, no. 1: 20–43.

Raffaelli, Tizziano. 2006. "Keynes's Interaction with Cambridge Philosophers." In *The Cambridge Companion to Keynes*, edited by Roger E. Backhouse and Bradley W. Bateman, Chapter 6. Basingstoke: Palgrave.

Ramsey, Frank P. 1922 [1989]. "Mr. Keynes on Probability." *The British Journal for the Philosophy of Science* 40, no. 2 (June): 219–22.

———. 1925. "Letter to John Maynard Keynes." In *John Maynard Keynes Papers*, PP/45/262/1-9.

———. 1926. "Truth and Probability." In *The Foundations of Mathematics and other Logical Essays*, edited by Richard B. Braithwaite, Chapter VII. London: Kegan. https://core.ac.uk/download/pdf/7048428.pdf. Accessed 17 November 2019.

Regan, Donald H. 2003, "How to be a Moorean." *Ethics* 113: 651–77.

Regan, Tom. 1986 [2012]. *Bloomsbury's Prophet: G. E. Moore and the Development of his Moral Theory, Eugene*. Oregon: Wipf & Stock.

Robert, Christian P. 2011. "Reading Keynes' 'Treatise on Probability'." *International Statistics Review* 79, no. 1 (April): 1–15.

Robert, Veronica, Gabriel Yoguel, and Octavio Lerena. 2017. "The Ontology of Complexity and the Neo-Schumpeterian Evolutionary Theory for Economic Change." *Journal of Evolutionary Economics* 27, no. 4 (September): 761–93.

Robertson, H. M. 1987. "J. M. Keynes and Cambridge in the 1920s." *South African Journal of Economics* 51, no. 3.

Robinson, Austin. 1947. "John Maynard Keynes 1883–1946." *Economic Journal* 57 (March): 1–68.

Robinson, Joan. 1932. "Economics Is a Serious Subject: The Apologies of an Economist to the Mathematician, the Scientist and the Plain Man." *The Papers of Professor Joan Violet Robinson. Correspondence between Joan Robinson and her mother, Lady Margaret Helen Maurice*, JVR77/284, Maurice, Lady (Margaret) Helen (nee Marsh), 1932–1938. https://janus.lib.cam.ac.uk/db/node.xsp?id=EAD%2FGBR%2F0272%2FPP%2FJVR_%2F7%2F284. Accessed 7 July 2012.

———. 1962 [2006]. *Economic Philosophy*. UK: Aldine Transaction. https://digamo.free.fr/ecophilo.pdf. Accessed 17 February 2017.

———. 1973. "What Has Become of the Keynesian Revolution?" In *After Keynes*, edited by Joan Robinson, 1–11. Oxford: Basil Blackwell.

———. 1974. "History versus Equilibrium." In *Thames Papers in Political Economy*, 48–58.

———. 1978. *Contributions to Modern Economics*. Oxford: Blackwell.

———. 1979. *Collected Economic Papers, II*. Oxford: Blackwell.

———. 1983. "Has Keynes Failed?" In *John Maynard Keynes: Critical Assessments*, Volume IV, edited by John. C. Wood, Chapter 136. New York: Routledge.

Rochon, Louis Phillipe and Hassan Bougrine. 2020. *Credit, Money, and Crises in Postkeynesian Economics, Introduction*. Chentelham, UK and Northampton, MA: Edward Elgar.

Rochon, Louis Phillipe and Sergio Rossi. 2010. "Has 'It' Happened Again?" *International Journal of Political Economy* 39, no. 2: 5–9.

Roncaglia, Alessandro. 2009. "Keynes and Probability: An Assessment." *The European Journal of the History of Economic Thought* 16, no. 3: 489–510.

———. 2012. "Keynesian Uncertainty and the Shaky Foundations of Statistical Risk Assessment Models." *PSL Quarterly Review* 65, no. 263: 437–54.

———. 2014. "Keynes Is Alive and Well: A Survey Article." *PSL Quarterly Review* 67, no. 268 (March): 105–24.

Rothbard, Murray N. 1992. "Keynes, the Man." In *Dissent on Keynes: A Critical Appraisal of Keynesian Economics*, edited by Mark Skousen, Chapter 11. New York: Praeger.

Rowe, Nicholas. 2016. "Keynesian Parables on Thrift and Hoarding." *Review of Keynesian Economics* 4, no. 1: 50–5.

Runden, Jochen. 1994. "Keynes after Ramsey: In Defence of a Treatise on Probability." *Studies in History and Philosophy of Science* 5: 197–221.

Russell, Bertrand. 1922. "Review of A Treatise on Probability by John Maynard Keynes." *Math Gazzette* 11: 119–25.

Rymes, Thomas K. 1989. *Keynes's Lectures, 1932–35, Notes of a Representative Student*. Ann Arbor: The University of Michigan Press.

———. 1998. "Keynes and Anchorless Banking." *Journal of the History of Economic Thought* 20, no. 1: 71–82.

Samuelson, Paul A. 1946. "Lord Keynes and the General Theory." *Econometrica* XIV, no. 3: 187–200.

———. 1985. "Succumbing to Keynesianism." *Challenge* 27, no. 6 (January/February): 4–11.

Sánchez-Meca, Diego. 2000. *Nietzsche En Deleuze: Hacia Una Genealogía Del Pensamiento Crítico*. Madrid: Éndoxa: Series Filosóficas, n. 12: 167–86.

Sanfey, Michael. 2006. "Understanding Nietzsche." *Studies: An Irish Quarterly Review* 95, no. 378 (Summer): 205–11.

Sawyer, Malcolm. 2013. "What Is Financialization?" *The International Journal of Political Economy* 42, no. 4: 5–18.

Schacht, Richard. 1983. *Nietzsche (Arguments of the Philosophers)*, 1st ed. London and New York: Routledge.

Schultz, Burton. 2015. "Henry Sidgwick." In *The Stanford Encyclopedia of Philosophy*, Summer 2015, edited by Edward N. Zalta. https://plato.stanford.edu/sum2015/entries/sidgwick/. Accessed 13 July 2019.

Schumpeter, Joseph A. 1933. "Review of Keynes' 'Essays in Biography'." *Economic Journal* 43, no. 172: 652–57.

———. 1954 [1981]. *History of Economic Analysis*, 12th re-impression. London: Routledge.

Seccareccia, Mario. 2002. "Aspects of a New Conceptual Integration of Keynes's Treatise on Money and The General Theory: Logical Time Units and Macroeconomic Price Formation," April, Department of Economics, University of Ottawa. https://aix1.uottawa.ca/~robinson/english/wp/keynestreatise.pdf. Accessed 16 February 2018.

Sen, Amartya. 1983. "Development: Which Way Now?" *Economic Journal* 43, no. 372 (December): 745–62.

———. 2000. *Development as Freedom*. New York: Anchor Books.

Shackle, George L. S. 1967 [2010]. *The Years of High Theory: Invention and Tradition in Economic Thought 1926–1939*. Cambridge: Cambridge University Press.

Shinoya, Yuichi. 1991. "Sidgwick, Moore and Keynes: A Philosophical Analysis of Keynes's 'My Early Beliefs'." In *Keynes and Philosophy: Essays on the Origin of Keynes's Thought*, edited by Bradley W. Bateman and John B. Davis, 6–29. Aldershot, UK: Edward Elgar.

Shuker, Stephen A. 2014. "J. M. Keynes and the Personal Politics of Reparations: Part I." *Diplomacy & Statecraft* 25, no. 3 (August): 453–71.

Sicsu, Joao. 2012. "Keynes's State Planning: From Bolshevism to the General Theory." *The European Journal of the History of Economic Thought* 28, no. 3: 352–71.

Sidgwick, Henry. 1877 [1907]. *The Methods of Ethics*, 6th ed. Connecticut: Macmillan.

Skidelsky, Robert. 1977. "La rebelión contra los victorianos." In *El Fin de la Era Victoriana*, edited by Robert Skidelsky, Chapter I. Mexico: Lala.

———. 1983. *John Maynard Keynes. Volume I: Hopes Betrayed 1883–1920*. London: Papermac.

———. 1992. *John Maynard Keynes. Volume II: The Economist as Saviour 1920–1937*. London: Macmillan.

———. 1997a. "Chapter 24 Keynes's Concluding Notes. Robert Skidelsky Writing as John Maynard Keynes." In *A 'Second' Edition of the General*

Theory, vol I, edited by Geoffrey C. Harcourt and Peter Riach, Chapter 24, 430–39. New York: Routledge.

———. 1997b. "The Conditions for the Reinstatement of Keynesian Policy." In *The Impact of Keynes in the Twentieth Century*, edited by Luigi Pasinetti, 36–51. Cheltenham, UK and Lyme: Edward Elgar.

———. 1998. "Keynes and Employment Policy in the Second World War." Warwick Economics Research Paper 508, August Department of Economics. https://www2.warwick.ac.uk/fac/soc/economics/research/workingpapers/1995-1998/twerp508.pdf. Accessed 16 July 2019.

———. 2000. *John Maynard Keynes. Volume III: Fighting for Britain 1937–1946*. London: Macmillan.

———. 2010. "The Crisis of Capitalism: Keynes Versus Marx." *The Indian Journal of Industrial Relations* 45, no. 3 (January): 321–35.

———. 2016a. *The Essential Keynes*. London: Penguin.

———. 2016b. "How Keynes Came to Britain." *Review of Keynesian Economics* 4, no. 1 (Spring): 4–19.

———. 2017. "Keynes and the Ethics of Capitalism." https://www.Oocities.org/monedem.htm. Accessed 10 July 2017.

Sleinis, Edgar. 2003. "Nietzsche." In *The Cambridge History of Philosophy 1870–1945*, Volume I, edited by Thomas Baldwin, Chapter 19, 266–76. Cambridge: Cambridge University Press.

Smithin, John. 2010. "Keynes's Theories of Money and Banking in the Treatise and the General Theory." *Review of Keynesian Economics 1* (April): 242–56.

Snowdon, Brian and Howard R. Vane (eds.). 1999. *Conversations with Leading Economists: Interpreting Modern Macroeconomics. From Tobin to Romer*. Chentelham, UK: Edward Elgar.

Snowdon, Brian, Howard R. Vane, and Peter Wynarczyk. 1994. *A Modern Guide to Macroeconomics: An Introduction to Competing Schools of Thought*. Aldershot, UK: Edward Elgar.

Stamp, Josiah C. 1931. "Mr. Keynes Treatise on Money." *Economic Journal* 41, no. 162 (June): 241–49.

Stiglitz, Joseph. 2010. "The Non-Existent Hand." *Review of Keynes: The Return of the Master by Robert Skidelsky*, Allen Lane, September 2009, *London Review of Books* 32, no. 8 (April 22), including Davidson Paul. 2012. *Letters* 32, no. 10, May. https://www.Lrb.co.uk/the-pper/v32/no8/Joseph-Stiglitz/the-non-existent-hand. Accessed 21 February 2020.

Stohs, Mark. 1980. "Uncertainty in Keynes's General Theory." *History of Political Economy* 12, no. 3: 372–82.

Strachey, Lytton. 1880–1932 [2005]. *The Letters of Lytton Strachey*, edited by Paul Levy. New York: Farrar, Straus and Giroux. https://ia802307.us.archive.org/7/items/lettersoflyttons00lytt/lettersoflyttons00lytt_encrypted.pdf. Accessed 28 November 2019.

Streeten, Paul. 1954. "Keynes and the Classical Tradition." In *Post Keynesian Economics*, edited by Kenneth. K. Kurihara, Chapter 13, 345–64. New York: Rutgers.

Telser, Lester G. 2012. "How Keynes' General Theory Enters Economics." Unpublished Paper, University of Chicago. https://works.bepress.com/lester_telser/38/. Accessed 17 October 2018.

Temin, Peter, and David Vines. 2016. "Keynes and the European Economy." *Review of Keynesian Economics* 4, no. 1 (Spring): 36–49.

The Bloosmbury Group. n.d. https://is.muni.cz/el/1421/jaro2014/AJ04002/e_woolf_and_Bloomsbury_Group.pdf. Accessed 19 November 2018.

Thirlwall, Anthony P. (ed.). 1978. "Keynes and Laissez Faire." 3rd Keynes Seminar, University of Kent at Canterbury.

———. (writing as J.M. Keynes). 1999. "A 'Second Edition' of Keynes' General Theory." *Journal of Post Keynesian Economics* 21: 367–86.

———. 2013. "Keynes and Economic Development." In *The Oxford Handbook of Post-Keynesian Economics. Volume 1: Theory and Origins*, edited by Geoffrey C. Harcourt and Peter Krielser. Oxford: Oxford University Press.

Tinbergen, Jan. 1937. *An Econometric Approach to Business Cycle Problems*. Paris: Herman & Co.

Tily, Geoffrey. 2009. "John Maynard Keynes and the Development of National Accounts in Britain, 1895–1941." *Review of Income and Wealth* 55, no. 2 (June): 331–59.

———. 2012. "Keynes's Monetary Theory of Interest Rates." ONS, BIS Paper no. 65c.

Togati, Dario T. 2006. *The New Economy and Macroeconomic Stability: A Neo-modern Perspective Drawing on the Complexity Approach and Keynesian Economics*. London and New York: Routledge.

Toye, John. 1997. "Keynes on Population and Economic Growth." *Cambridge Journal of Economics* 21, no. 1 (January): 1–26.

Troyer, John. 2003. *The Classical Utilitarians: Bentham and Mill*. Indianapolis: Hackett.

Upchurch, Anne. 2004 [2007]. "John Maynard Keynes, the Bloomsbury Group and the Origins of the Arts Council Movement." *International Journal of Cultural Policy* 10, no. 2. https://www.tandfonline.com/doi/abs/10.1080/1028663042000255817. Accessed 12 February 2018.

Van Den Hauwe, Ludwig. 2011. "John Maynard Keynes and Ludwig von Mises on Probability." *Journal of Libertarian Studies* 22: 471–507.

Veblen, Thorstein. 1920. "Review of John Maynard Keynes, the Economic Consequences of the Peace." *Political Science Quarterly* 35: 467–72.

Venero, Frank. 2018. "The Economics of Instability: An Abstract of an Excerpt." Levy Economics Institute WP 903, April.

Vercelli, Alessandro. 1991. *Methodological Foundations of Macroeconomics*. Cambridge: Cambridge University Press.

Verdon, Michael. 1996. *Keynes and the 'Classics': A Study in Language, Epistemology, and Mistaken Identities*. New York: Routledge.

Viner, Jacob. 1936. "Mr. Keynes on the Causes of Unemployment." *The Quarterly Journal of Economics* 51, no. 1 (November): 147–67.

Vines, David. 2003. "John Maynard Keynes 1937–1946: The Creation of International Macroeconomics." A review article on *John Maynard Keynes 1937–1946. Fighting for Britain* Vol. III by Robert Skidelsky (2002). *Economic Journal* 113, no. 488: 335–61.

Waligorski, Conrad P. 1994, "Keynes and Democracy." *The Social Science Journal* 31, no. 1: 79–91.

Walsh, Justyin. 2008. *Keynes and the Market: How the World's Greatest Economist Overturned Conventional Wisdom and Made a Fortune on the Stock Market*. New York: Wiley.

Walters, Alan. 1987. "Friedman, Milton (Born in 1912)." In *The New Palgrave Dictionary of Economics*, edited by John Eatwell et al., 422–27. New York: Macmillan.

Weatherford, Roy. 1982. *Philosophical Foundations of Probability Theory*. London: Routledge.

Weintraub, Sidney. 1971. "Keynes and the Monetarists." *The Canadian Journal of Economics/Revue Canadienne d'Economique* 4, no. 1: 37–49.

Wells, Herbert G. 1926. *The World of William Clissold*. London: Benn.

Werle, Nicholas. 2011. "More Than the Sum of Its Parts: A Keynesian Epistemology of Statistics." *The Journal of Philosophical Economics* 4, no. 2: 65–92.

Williamson, John. 1987. "Bancor and the Developing Countries: How Much Difference Would It Have Made?" In *Keynes and Development*, edited by Anthony P. Thirlwall, Session 2, 92–106. The Seventh Keynes Seminar held at the University of Kent at Canterbury, 1985. New York: Palgrave.

Winch, Donald. 2010. "J. M. Keynes. Economist as Biographer and Intellectual Historian." *History of Political Thought Seminar*, Sussex Centre for Intellectual History, Sussex, St. Andrews, UK (Michaelmas). https://sussex.ac.uk.broadcast/read/7131. Accessed 19 March 2019.

Winslow, Ted. n.d. "Keynes and Freud." https://yorku.academia.edu/TedWinslow. Accessed 15 May 2020.

———. 1986. "'Human Logic' and Keynes's Economics." *Eastern Economic Journal* 12, no. 4 (October–December): 413–30.

———. 1989. "Organic Interdependence, Uncertainty and Economic Analysis." *Economic Journal* 99, no. 398 (December): 1143–82.

———. 2005. "Keynes's Economics: A Political Economy as Moral Science Approach to Macroeconomics and Macroeconomic Policy." Research

Network Alternative Macroeconomic Policies. Conference: Macroeconomics and Macroeconomic Policies-Alternatives to the Orthodoxy, October, Berlin.
Wittgenstein, Ludwig. 1921 [1922]. *Tractatus Logico-Philosophicus*. New York: Harcourt.
———. 1953 [2009]. *Philosophical Investigations*, 4th ed. New York: Wiley.
———. 1969. *On Certainty*. New York: Basil Blackwell.
Wong, Ho-Po Crystal. 2013. "From 'A Treatise on Money' to the 'General Theory': John Maynard Keynes' Departure from the Doctrine of Forced Savings." CHOPE WP No. 2013–14, September.
Wray, R. 2007. "The Continuing Legacy of John Maynard Keynes." The Levy Economics Institute of Bard College WP No. 514.
Zanini, Adelino. 2003. "Un capitalismo incerto. Incertezza e normazione nel pensiero di J.M. Keynes (1921–1939)." Working Paper 194, Universita' Politecnica delle Marche (I), Dipartimento di Scienze Economiche e Sociali.
———. 2008. *Economic Philosophy: Economic Foundations and Political Categories*. Bern: Peter Lang.
Zappia, Carlo. 2012. "Re-reading Keynes after the Crisis: Probability and Decision." Department of Economics, University of Siena, Quaderni del Dipartamento di Economia Estadistica No. 646. https://ideas.repec.org/p/usi/wpaper/646.html. Accessed 19 October 2017.
Zhang, Ivy. n.d. "A Review of Keynes' 'The End of Laissez-Faire'." https://zmy26.wordpress.com/2011/01/26/a-review-on-keynes%E2%80%99-%E2%80%9Cthe-end-of-laissez-faire%E2%80%9D/. Accessed 18 April 2019.

Index

J. Muñoz-Bandala, *Keynes's Evolutionary Spirit*, Palgrave Insights into Apocalypse Economics,
https://doi.org/10.1007/978-3-030-90150-9

V

The manufacturer's authorised representative in the EU is Springer Nature Customer Service Centre GmbH, Europaplatz 3, 69115 Heidelberg, Germany. If you have any concerns regarding our products, please contact ProductSafety@springernature.com

Printed and bound by CPI Group (UK) Ltd, Croydon, CR0 4YY
30/09/2026
02225502-0012